D1278025

One *to* One

Resources for Conference-Centered Writing

FIFTH EDITION

CHARLES W. DAWE
Orange Coast College

EDWARD A. DORNAN
Orange Coast College

with Foreword by
NEAL LERNER
Massachusetts Institute of Technology

PEARSON
Longman

New York • San Francisco • Boston
London • Toronto • Sydney • Tokyo • Singapore • Madrid
Mexico City • Munich • Paris • Cape Town • Hong Kong • Montreal

Acquisitions Editor: Lauren A. Finn
Senior Marketing Manager: Sandra McGuire
Production Manager: Bob Ginsberg
Project Coordination and Electronic Page Makeup: Tom Conville Publishing
    Services, LLC
Cover Design Manager/Cover Designer: Wendy Ann Fredericks
Cover Photos: Left: Jeffery Titcomb/Stock Connection Blue/Alamy;
    Right: Corbis Royalty Free
Manufacturing Buyer: Roy L. Pickering, Jr.
Printer and Binder: RR Donnelley & Sons Company, Harrisonburg
Cover Printer: Phoenix Color Corporation

For permission to use copyrighted material, grateful acknowledgment is made
to the copyright holders on pp. 481–482, which are hereby made part of this
copyright page.

Visit us at www.ablongman.com

ISBN 0-321-43902-3

1 2 3 4 5 6 7 8 9 10--DOH—09 08 07 06

CONTENTS

22 ADDITIONAL WRITING TASKS 262

FOREWORD

Remarkable is the staying power of Charles Dawe and Edward Dornan's *One to One: Resources for Conference-Centered Writing*, first published in 1981. Appropriately enough, it was Roger Garrison who offered the preface to that first edition, for Garrison had influenced many teachers with his 1974 article, "One-to-One: Tutorial Instruction in Freshman Composition." Garrison could easily turn Dawe and Dornan's title into a slogan of sorts, telling readers that "nearly all of those who have gone 'one to one' refuse to return to traditional instruction patterns. Their own satisfactions, and their students' achievements have been too marked to be ignored" (iii–iv). The longevity of *One to One,* now in its fifth edition, is testament to the power of the text itself, offering teachers and students a way of interacting that could potentially transcend the limits of overcrowded classrooms and required five-paragraph themes. At the same time, the student-friendly text that Dawe and Dornan have offered can be seen as a key part of a long-standing effort to re-configure the teaching of writing at all instructional levels.

Teaching writing one-to-one was not a new concept by 1981. As far back as 1894, Charles Sears Baldwin of Columbia argued for "the value of the office-hour in the teaching of rhetoric" (290). That same year, John Franklin Genung of Amherst College described in *The Dial* that "the best term, perhaps, by which to characterize the way in which the teachers of English at Amherst have met [the] challenges [of teaching composition] is *laboratory work*" (174). What these authors were recognizing was that the teaching of writing needed to transcend the lecture/recitation model that had dominated all classrooms up to this point and be replaced by a system of frequent writing, meaningful feedback, and thoughtful revision (Kitzhaber 219). Teaching writing as *laboratory work* meant that the experimentation and constant feedback that students were familiar with in chemistry or physics labs were applicable to the writing classroom. At the University of Minnesota, General College Writing Laboratory, created in 1932, students would find this scene: "In a quiet skylight room we provide chairs and slanting tables for ease in writing" (MacLean 244).

While one-to-one conferencing became an accepted teaching technique in many classrooms, difficult working conditions—too many students, too many essays, too little time—would always limit the extent of one-to-one teaching (see Lerner). As described in 1939 by W. Alan Grove of Miami University, "The value of conferences cannot be overestimated, but to attempt personal ones would be absurd" (232). One alternative and a precursor for the work described in *One to One* was stand-alone spaces known as writing clinics, writing laboratories, or, more currently, writing centers. Just as Roger Garrison offered *One to One* as a counterpoint to traditional instruction, writing centers have long offered a contrast to the teaching that has persisted in many writing classrooms. Participants at a 1950 Conference on College Composition and Communication Workshop staked out their territory: "The writing laboratory should be what the classroom often is not—natural, realistic, and friendly" ("Organization and Use of a Writing Laboratory" 18). Essential to this *friendly* environment was one-to-one instruction, teacher/tutor and student/writer meeting at the student's point of need.

By the late 1960s, however, a new generation of teachers, instilled with a far more sophisticated knowledge of the composing process than their predecessors, were ready to transform the classroom. Roger Garrison and Donald Murray convinced many that they could take on that task. As Dawe and Dornan wrote in the introduction to their first edition, "Those [students] that do need help will be in a real learning situation because instruction will be based on what the individual writer needs to improve his or her work, not on a theoretical model we carry around in our minds" (3).

The popularity of *laboratory approaches* to the teaching of writing resulted in a flurry of books published in the late 1970s and early 1980s, giving readers a mix of practical strategies and theoretical justifications. Those texts included Thom Hawkins's *Group Inquiry Techniques for Teaching Writing* (1976), Carol Laque and Phyllis Sherwood's *A Laboratory Approach to Writing* (1977), Thom Hawkins and Phyllis Brook's *Improving Writing Skills* (1981), Joyce Steward and Mary Croft's *The Writing Laboratory: Organization, Management, and Methods* (1982), Muriel Harris's collection *Tutoring Writing: A Sourcebook for Writing Labs* (1982), and Marian Arkin and Barbara Shollar's *The Writing Tutor* (1982). Yet of all of those texts, only Dawe and Dornan's One to One remains in print, twenty-five years after its initial publication. The long-standing appeal of what Dawe and Dornan offer their readers is testament to the place of textbooks in writing instruction.

The second part of the title of *One to One—Resources for Conference-Centered Writing*—offers a compelling case for the value of this book. Dawe and Dornan make clear that the heart of the teaching writing is not an instructor lecturing from a textbook (even their textbook!) or a student dutifully filling out supplemental grammar/usage worksheets. Instead, their text augments a kind of teaching and learning that puts student writing at the center. As the authors described in their note to teachers in the first edition, "The conference-centered class puts writing where it belongs—on center stage. . . . [T]he teacher devotes class time to a series of three- to ten-minute conferences with individual students. . . . [I]n this format student writing becomes the hub of the course" (2–3). The role of the textbook in this system is as a true *resource*. Dawe and Dornan offer students multiple writing tasks, student and professional models, and helpful tips all designed to support the writing, responding, and revising that is at the heart of their ideal classroom. The text is extremely flexible, then, suitable for a writing class at multiple developmental levels and for a writing center in which students can practice the techniques Dawe and Dornan describe.

Certainly, one other ingredient that has accounted for the long appeal of *One to One* is its extensive use of student writing and students' commentary on their writing to *show*, not just *tell* its readers how writing is best taught and learned. From underdeveloped first drafts to messy revisions to polished essays, Dawe and Dornan consistently tell their readers the message that *other students have been where you are and have accomplished much—so can you.*

In their preface to the fifth edition of *One to One*, Dawe and Dornan note that they have now included professional essays for reading and response, and added sections on peer review and collaborative writing. While these are welcome updates, at the heart of the book remains the authors inviting their readers to write, to seek feedback, and to revise. It's a warm invitation, one not easily refused or ignored, for the community of writers that *One to One* cultivates is a group well worth joining.

Neal Lerner
Massachusetts Institute of Technology

WORKS CITED

Arkin, Marian, and Barbara Shollar. *The Writing Tutor.* New York: Longman, 1982.

Dawe, Charles W., and Edward A. Dornan. *One to One: Resources for Conference-Centered Writing.* Instructor's Edition. Boston: Little, Brown, 1981.

———. *One to One: Resources for Conference-Centered Writing,* 5th ed. Boston: Longman, 1997.

Garrison, Roger H. "One-to-One: Tutorial Instruction in Freshman Composition." *New Directions for Community Colleges* 5 (1974): 55–84.

Genung, John Franklin. "English at Amherst College." *English in American Universities*. Ed. William Morton Payne. Boston: D.C. Heath, 1895. 110–15.

Grove, W. Alan. "Freshman Composition: It's Great Middle Class." *College English* 1 (1939): 227–36.

Harris, Muriel, ed. *Tutoring Writing: A Sourcebook for Writing Labs*. Glenview, IL: Scott, Foresman, 1982.

Hawkins, Thom. *Group Inquiry Techniques for Teaching Writing*. Urbana, IL: NCTE/ERIC, 1976.

Hawkins, Thom, and Phyllis Brook, eds. *Improving Writing Skills (New Directions for College Learning Assistance, #3)*. San Francisco: Jossey-Bass, 1981.

Kitzhaber, Albert R. *Rhetoric in American Colleges, 1850–1900*. Dallas: Southern Methodist UP, 1990.

Laque, Carol, and Phyllis Sherwood. *A Laboratory Approach to Writing*. Urbana, IL: NCTE, 1977.

Lerner, Neal. "The Student-Teacher Writing Conference and the Desire for Intimacy." *College English* 68.2 (2005): 186–208.

MacLean, Malcolm S. "A College of 1934." *Journal of Higher Education* 5.5 (May 1934): 240–46.

Murray, Donald M. *A Writer Teaches Writing: A Practical Method of Teaching Composition*. Boston: Houghton Mifflin, 1968.

"Organization and Use of a Writing Laboratory: Report of Workshop No. 9." *College Composition and Communication* 2 (1951): 17–18.

Steward, Joyce, and Mary Croft. *The Writing Laboratory: Organization, Management, and Methods*. Glenview, IL: Scott, Foresman, 1982.

PREFACE

One to One was first conceived as a resource for conference-centered instruction. Now it is used in a variety of academic settings, as a rhetoric in lecture-discussion and in collaborative learning classrooms, for example. For this revision, however, we have kept to our original concept by making the explanations, sample papers, and writing task directions thorough enough and clear enough to allow the teacher to devote class time to the instruction of individuals rather than to the explanation of individual assignments.

For this fifth edition of *One to One*, we made some major changes. First, we added fifteen professional essays in a section titled "A Collection of Essays." We have also integrated peer review and collaborative writing opportunities under the title "Group Work" at the end of the writing tasks throughout the first two parts of the text, "Getting Started" and "Writing Tasks." We updated MLA style in the chapter titled the "Research Essay." We moved the discussions of point of view, tone, coherence, introductions, and conclusions from what was formally "A Guide for Revision," which we've deleted, to the Appendix. Finally, we refined the text and added fresh student and professional examples, most notably in Chapters 2 and 14, "Getting Started" and "Deductive Essay."

At the urging of teachers, students, and reviewers who have used *One to One* over several years, we've worked to keep a "user friendly" (love computerese, don't you!) tone and tried to make our explanations of writing concepts as clear as possible.

Throughout the text we continue to have students speak about their own writing—both in introductory comments and in comments positioned alongside their works. We believe these additional voices in *One to One* deepen the lessons that student writers will draw from the examples.

We would like to acknowledge the contribution of those reviewers whose insightful comments helped us improve the work: Joanne James, Pitt Community College; Deanna M. White, University of Texas at San Antonio; Philip L. Zweifel, University of Wisconsin at Waukesha; Sylvia A. Stathakis, Oakton Community College; Joan Tyler Mead, Marshall University; Debra Sprague, North Idaho College; Donna N. Sumanas, College of DuPage; Joanne Gerken, Lehigh County Community College; Richard Profozich, Prince George's Community College; Patricia Barney, Citrus College; and Dorothy Miller, Kentucky State University. We owe a special debt to Executive Editor Anne Elizabeth Smith for her unwavering commitment to see this Fifth Edition of *One to One* in print.

Charles W. Dawe
Edward A. Dornan

TO THE STUDENT

Two activities are important in learning to write well. First is to write, and to write a lot. Second is to get sound advice about your writing from someone who knows how to write. The class you're in will bring these two activities together.

A quick glance at *One to One* will show you it's divided into four main parts, which are subdivided into several sections, each identified by number, essay title, or week. Since the book teaches writing by getting you to write, each subsection ends with an assignment called a "Writing Task" that's designed to help you concentrate on a writing method or on a topic.

In Part One, Getting Started, you'll learn to write for a reader, how to work through a four-step composing process, and how to combine the particulars of an experience with your reactions to it. In Part Two, Writing Tasks, you'll learn different ways to develop paragraphs and several ways to develop essays. In Part Three, Readings for Writers, you'll learn to respond to reading and to use a reading as an entrance into your own work. In Part Four, Daily Writing, you'll go through nine weeks of writing practice that will help you overcome the fears you might have when facing a blank page. By working through daily writing tasks you'll also generate subjects and material for the more formal assignments in the course.

Your instructor has probably selected *One to One* in order to support conference-centered instruction. Although *conference-centered instruction* might sound a little fancy, the concept behind the phrase is quite simple. It involves nothing more than you and your instructor or you and members of your writing group sitting side-by-side and talking about each paper you write. The conference may be short or long, depending on the length of the assignment. But no matter how long a conference lasts, the major activities will be the same—the instructor or your group members will read your work, listen to your comments, and offer advice and directions to help you overcome writing weaknesses and develop your writing strengths. Simple enough, but to make it work takes some effort. We want to give you a few suggestions that will make that effort easier.

INSTRUCTOR CONFERENCES

An instructor conference takes place when you and your writing instructor meet to review an assignment. We suggest you enter each conference with a commitment to gain more information about and insight into the writing process. To achieve that goal we recommend the following:

1. Become an active participant in the conference. Don't just put yourself in the instructor's hands and wait for your fate. Instead, identify and talk about the problems you faced in the assignment. Ask specific questions about solving the problems. Take some brief notes that capture your instructor's responses and recheck them when the conference ends.

2. Try to see your instructor as a writing coach rather than as a judge. Just as a coach wants an athlete to win in competition, your instructor wants you to succeed at writing. If you don't agree with a particular comment about your work, say so and present your view as clearly as you can without arguing or being defensive. Then let your instructor explain the reasons behind the comment. This way the two of you will be building a working relationship that fosters success.

3. Make an effort to treat your papers as works in progress. If you follow the advice of many successful writers who claim that to learn to write well, the beginning writer must learn to rewrite, then you'll have no difficulty improving your writing. But if you come to a conference convinced that you've attained perfection in your writing, you'll have some trouble because a conference will often end with an assignment that requires you either to revise or rewrite a paper. Our best advice is to relax and keep in mind that the purpose of the conference is not just to get your work accepted but to improve your skills. View each assignment as a stage in the process of mastering different kinds of writing. Sometimes that mastery comes faster by rewriting a flawed paper rather than by starting a new one.

4. Help make your conferences work by carefully studying the material your instructor assigns. Read the explanations, analyze the illustrations, review the marginal notes—do all this before you start to write. If you work in this way, you'll save valuable conference time by keeping the focus on your writing and not on explanations of the assignments you didn't read thoroughly.

WRITERS GROUP CONFERENCES

Before a conference, some instructors ask students to submit early drafts to several classmates. Often this is done in established groups whose members work together throughout the semester, but sometimes instructors like to reform writers groups every few weeks. If you are in a class that does not require writers groups, you may wish to form one. Whether your instructor requires group review or whether you and a few classmates meet in informal groups, the primary goal will be the same: to gain several pairs of eyes to help you review your written work.

Often what seems perfectly clear to you may be confusing to a reader who has intellectual and emotional distance from the material. When members of your writers group review an early draft of an essay, for example, they can point out confusing sections and suggest areas for revision before you hold a teacher conference.

You have two responsibilities to meet as a member of a writers group. The easiest of the two is to receive advice about your writing. Read all written responses with care. Although they will often be brief, they may also be valuable. Moreover, you can follow up by asking the reviewer questions to help clarify or amplify any written advice. Listen with care to all oral responses and take notes of the advice that you feel will help improve your draft. If a group member asks you a question, answer, but don't feel you have to justify the decisions you made during the writing process. You may also follow up with questions of your own to help clarify the group's observations. Most importantly, don't become defensive. Your group members will be evaluating the effectiveness of a piece of writing, not your character.

Should you incorporate suggestions from group members? That's your decision. Sometimes the responses will conflict, often reflecting a member's own inexperience or misconceived information. Other times the responses will agree, giving you a clear direction for revision. Remember, only you can decide which responses are appropriate and which are inappropriate. The responsibility for a final draft is yours, not your group's.

A more difficult responsibility is to give your fellow students advice. Always keep in mind that your task is not to rewrite the draft but to respond as a reader and offer advice for improvement. It's up to the writer to write the final draft.

What kind of advice should you offer?

Well, each draft you read will be written in response to a writing task. To respond intelligently, you must be familiar with the concepts presented in the discussion that leads to the writing task and then respond to the draft based on how well the writer reflected those concepts. To help you in this process, we've included some brief directions titled "Group Work" after most writing tasks. These directions will offer some specific suggestions for evaluation.

More generally, there are three guidelines that might help you develop both a written draft or oral response.

OFFER SPECIFIC RESPONSES

Always be as specific in your responses as you can. Identify a draft's strengths and weaknesses. Vague and general observations don't help a writer. For example, the following two responses represent the extremes. One is ineffective and one is effective.

Ineffective Response

> Good work. I like the way it reads, even though it isn't clear. Also good use of words. I like it. Keep it up.

Where's the beef? Clearly, this student is avoiding his group responsibility by scribbling a thoughtless response. Why? Perhaps he fears hurting the writer's feelings. Or perhaps he has not read the writing task the writer is responding to. Perhaps he's just plain lazy. Who knows? Still this fact remains: the student offers only vague, feel-good responses that avoid his single responsibility: to give specific advice to improve the writer's draft.

Effective Response

> Discussion paragraph two is particularly effective. The topic sentence you shaped as a question—"What would happen if a Tyrannosaurus actually should step into our present environment?"—sets the pattern of answers that follow. One problem though is transition. You have nothing that directly connects back to your thesis sentence. Try referring to DNA, such as, "While DNA prepares a creature for the world it was born in, it might not prepare it for a future world." Just a suggestion. Take it or leave it, but you still need a transition. Another strong point is your use of active verbs: "stalk," "maul," "crush," and so on. They all add movement and a sense of visual detail—good.

This student's response fulfills her responsibility. She identifies strengths and weaknesses in specific language. Where she can, she gives advice to help the writer revise. She does all this specifically and clearly.

ASK FIVE MAIN QUESTIONS

When reviewing a group member's draft, don't be distracted by surface errors—that is, do not spend your time correcting grammar, punctuation, and mechanics. Tell the writer that the errors exist, but remember it's the writer's job to proofread carefully and correct surface errors. Instead, concentrate on the larger elements. In order to stay on track, use the following five questions to guide your evaluation:

1. Does the draft reflect the concepts presented in the writing task chapter?
2. What is the dominant purpose and is the organization logical?
3. At what points is the draft confusing?
4. Is the draft adequately developed? Does it need more information or examples?
5. What is the draft's main strength? Weakness?

RESPOND SENSITIVELY

Most beginning writers have no experience submitting their work to a writers group. They may misconstrue genuine advice for criticism. To avoid sounding critical, make objectively descriptive comments instead of subjectively evaluative comments. Keep in mind that your responsibility is to help the participants in your writers group, not to criticize them for their mistakes. When discussing your responses with a writer, keep in mind the following guidelines.

1. A group session should be a dialogue between group members and the writer.
2. Ask questions that might help you develop a clear understanding of the writer's goals.
3. Take notes while reading a draft and use them to discuss the draft's strengths and weaknesses. Emphasize the strengths, but remember the writer needs to know the weaknesses.
4. Relate suggestions for improvement related to the writer's purpose.
5. Close your response by summarizing ways the writer can improve the draft.

In closing we'd like to offer one last thought. Soon after completing Part One, Getting Started, you may discover that you are doing writing tasks that are different from the ones your classmates are doing. Don't be concerned about that. In one-to-one instruction individual students work on what they need at the moment. Our advice is to take advantage of the flexibility in one-to-one instruction and use this text to help you find your own path to the common goal—good writing.

Charles W. Dawe
Edward A. Dornan

Part One
GETTING STARTED

This part will introduce you—in three chapters, with Writing Tasks included in each—to the process of putting your thoughts on paper. You will base the writing you do in this section on your own observation and experience, not on your ability to collect material from other writers' thoughts. In other words, you will not be researching but will be collecting, recording, and organizing your personal experiences.

Besides the primary question that plagues most beginning writers—"What should I write about?"—there is a second question usually linked to it: "How should I get started?" A third question, probably as fundamental as the other two, seldom gets consciously asked yet is important for the success of any written communication: "For whom am I writing?"

As for the first question, for every Writing Task you do in this part of the book we will guide you to something to write about. So for now that problem is solved. Our main goals in this section are to give you a simple way to start writing and to make you aware of your reader.

1

Listing and Writing for a Reader

Getting started on a written project may be the most critical point in the entire enterprise. Perhaps the difficulty has something to do with facing a blank page and knowing that page, and most likely many other blank pages, will have to be filled with words. Moreover, the words must be nudged into sentences. The sentences must link logically together and be fitted into paragraphs. The paragraphs must be assembled into a coherent essay, report, or letter. Besides all the nudging, fitting, and assembling, you must put in the squiggles called punctuation. And then there is spelling—the mind shudders. The part of the brain that sends energy to the arm freezes. Writer's elbow sets in. It's too painful to shape the words with a pen. You're blocked.

There is a way to overcome writer's block. Instead of worrying about all the meticulous arranging you have to do to finish a piece of writing, concentrate on randomly collecting the raw material that will make up the content. One way to do the collecting is to draw up a list.

Listing

Everyone is familiar with grocery lists. Consumer advocates often advise shoppers to make grocery lists before shopping. With a list in hand, the expedition won't turn into a spending spree. Well, the advice is equally valid for a writer.

A list works as a device through which you can quickly gather the material you want to communicate to a reader. By writing a list you can rapidly capture fleeting details. A list can also fire your imagination and guide your direction. No doubt you can see how a piece of writing could easily form around a list of joyful or frightening experiences or around a list of dreams, fears, or memories. Now let's see a simple illustration of how a list works.

Imagine a homemaker who is planning an Italian supper. After surveying the cupboard, she realizes she needs a few items to complete the menu and sees she's also short of juice and coffee. She quickly makes a simple list to remind herself to get what she needs.

juice
tomatoes
coffee
bread
onions

Five simple items. It is about a ten-minute trip with the list in hand to keep her on target. Of course, the plan may change—she may rearrange the list as she goes. For instance, she would probably pick up the tomatoes and onions at the same time because they would be in the produce section, then go to the nearby frozen-food compartment before stopping for coffee located somewhere near the center of the market, and end up at the bread rack near the checkout counter. The simple list makes her shopping a breeze.

Now imagine that our homemaker is going to use this simple list to write a note to someone else who plans to stop at the grocery store for her. She must now communicate with an audience—a reader. Somehow, to make the communication clear, the writer must anticipate the reader's mind.

Audience

Any reader you address will influence choices you make about content and vocabulary when writing. If you were separately to tell a police officer, a parent, and a friend about the events at a party, you would select different details to emphasize for each person and different words to describe what you experienced. In speech you make this adaptation instantly and naturally, but when writing you must actively adjust your thinking to make the adaptation. It is essential, therefore, that before you move too far into planning a piece of writing, you should identify who the reader will be and anticipate what he or she needs to know to understand what you are trying to communicate.

To illustrate the dangers in failing to identify the reader, consider our homemaker's grocery list again:

juice
tomatoes
coffee
bread
onions

Could she give this to her teenage son and expect him to gather what she wants?

If she were naive enough to do so, her teenage son might return with freshly squeezed guava juice when she wanted frozen orange juice. He might buy two green tomatoes when she wanted four ripe ones; instant coffee when she wanted regular grind; wheat bread when she wanted French; white onions when she had purple in mind. The confusion could deepen. Her teenager might even go to the wrong market—you know, the exclusive one where the items cost a nickel or a dime more.

For our homemaker to avoid the confusion, she would have to add specific detail to the list, anticipating her teenager's way of thinking, thus making her own written thought as clear as necessary in order to get what she wanted. The finished list might look something like this:

> I need some items from the market for tonight's dinner and tomorrow's breakfast. Please get them at Safeway.
>
> 1. four ripe tomatoes
> 2. two purple onions
> 3. a six-ounce can of frozen orange juice
> 4. regular grind coffee—whatever brand is on sale
> 5. French bread—the long kind, not the presliced

You can see how composing even a simple grocery list for a particular reader puts demands on the writer. The homemaker needs to include specifics, such as *four ripe* tomatoes, *two purple* onions, a *six-ounce can* of *orange juice,* and so on. Otherwise her teenager will interpret the note according to the characteristics of his own mind.

If the homemaker were writing for someone else, she might need to include more information. If she were writing the note for out-of-town guests or a grandparent or a child, what information would she have to give? Let's see.

Jean Bennett, a composition student, actually began with this simple grocery list as a basis for a note she invented for both her teenage and her ten-year-old sons. Since the note for her teenager did not give enough information for her ten-year-old to follow, Bennett developed more specific information while keeping in mind what she knew about her ten-year-old's way of thinking. Fleshed out with more detail, the list then served as a rough guide for Bennett's final note.

> 1. four ripe tomatoes—deep red, not orange; squeeze them for softness
> 2. two large purple onions, at least as big as a baseball

3. a small can of orange juice, the kind you've helped me make for breakfast
4. a small can of coffee with "regular grind" written at the top—buy the one that costs the least
5. French bread, the kind your brother says looks like a spyglass

For her ten-year-old, Bennett has made the list even more specific than she did for her teenager. Aside from the details, she has made some comparisons: "at least as big as a baseball" and "looks like a spyglass." She also recalls previous experience: "the kind you've helped me make for breakfast." She even gives a brief lesson on how to select a ripe tomato. All this information is necessary because she knows it will help her ten-year-old understand her meaning. There will be less confusion in the communication.

With the list before her, Bennett can begin to write the note. But while writing, she must envision her ten-year-old following the directions and anticipate his responses. For instance, her teenager would have no trouble with money transactions; her ten-year-old might. More than likely, her teenager would easily find his way around the market; her ten-year-old probably would not think in the neat categories in which most market managers arrange their merchandise. And, finally, it is doubtful that her teenager would get sidetracked on the way home; her ten-year-old might stop to play. So you see, even after developing a detailed list, the writer, when arranging the contents in a final draft, must continue to anticipate the reader's mind. In fact, the writer will often pause to assume the role of reader and reread what he or she has written to see if it is clearly expressed.

What follows is Jean Bennett's note to her ten-year-old son, based on the list developed above. Read it and see how she used the list for content and how, as she wrote the note, she added information as she thought of it so that the message would be clear to the child. Also notice how she arranged the information step by step to avoid confusing the communication.

Take this ten-dollar bill and hurry to Safeway to buy some groceries for dinner.

First, go to the vegetable and fruit section on the far side of the market and get four ripe tomatoes. The tomatoes should be deep red—not orange. Be sure to test them with a slight squeeze for softness. Don't buy mushy ones and don't buy hard ones—find some in between hard and mushy. Near the tomatoes, you'll see the onions. I need two purple ones about the size of your baseball or bigger.

Next, while you are on that side of the market, go to the frozen-food section for a small can of orange juice. A small can is the size you've helped me make for breakfast some mornings.

After getting the orange juice, go to the toy section—you should have no trouble finding it—and right behind it you'll find the coffee.

I need one small can, the pound size, that says "regular grind" near the top. Check the prices and take the one that costs the least.

Finally, from the rack near the checkout counter, pick up a loaf of French bread, the kind your brother says looks like a spyglass.

After you've done all that, you may buy a treat. Not candy or ice cream, but some dried fruit or nuts.

When you've finished paying for the groceries and your treat, put the change in your pocket and rush home without stopping at the hobby shop to look at models or at the park to toss the football or at Jack's to watch Star Trek reruns.

"Now scoot!" Bennett might have put at the close, sending her ten-year-old off in a swirl of uncombed hair and baggy clothes. Let's briefly review the process Bennett followed to develop her note. After drawing up the details, she anticipated her child's mind right down to the distractions that might attract him on the way home. She even anticipated how much he would like a treat after facing all the temptations supermarket managers scatter along the aisles to ensnare children, and she guided him to a more healthful choice.

Of course, writing from a list and anticipating your reader will not solve all your writing frustrations, but they do give you a way to start working. Even though this illustration is quite simple, you will discover that the principles behind it will help you write extended papers. Perhaps facing a blank page will be a little easier now.

WRITING TASK—LISTING AND WRITING FOR A READER

Write a 250 to 300 word note to a specific reader that briefly explains how to survive a stressful situation, such as a trip to the dentist, the doctor, the chiropractor, or traffic court. You might tell your reader how to survive a rowdy party, a rock concert, or a dull college course. Or write a note that explains why you did or did not do something, such as why you missed an appointment, abandoned a project, or caught a cold.

Don't take the easy way out of this assignment by choosing a friend as your reader. Instead, choose a reader who will challenge your imagination and writing skills—a younger brother or sister, a grandparent, or perhaps a school official. When this assignment is read, a clear sense of your designated reader should emerge.

Remember:

1. Imagine a reader and anticipate how much information he or she needs to understand what you are saying.
2. Use a list to collect your information.

3. When writing your paper and when rereading it, imagine the reader trying to follow your words.

GROUP WORK

Take turns reading your papers aloud. After each reading, point out where the draft is clear and where it is confusing.

While reading, concentrate on word groups, not individual words, increasing and decreasing the pace for emphasis to set off significant passages. Pause at transition points to help your listeners recognize shifts.

While listening, try to determine the characteristics of the audience. Also ask yourself the following questions: Is the material logically arranged? Are there clear transitions at key points? Is there enough specific detail to make the directions clear?

Suggestion: Relax. Reading aloud before a friendly group will help you concentrate on a draft's organization and descriptive details. Listening with care will help you become aware of what helps clarity. Discussing a draft will help you articulate the information you learned from reading the chapter.

2

The Composing Process

This section is the beginning of four related assignments. We've assembled them to introduce you to a method of working we hope you'll use whenever you begin a writing task. These assignments have been built around the idea that writing is a process best done in drafts. Paragraphs, essays, reports, or entire books do not leap fully formed from the writer's imagination. Instead, works such as these are usually nudged and teased into life, sometimes unfolding in elaborate ways. After all—and you might be either disappointed or reassured by this knowledge—there is no secret formula for creating a successful piece of writing. All writers must develop their own processes to develop their individual works. In fact, one of the secrets of becoming a good writer is to discover your own personal method of nudging and teasing experience and ideas into words.

In this series of tasks, you will first record the details of a brief experience—this will be called the prewriting phase. Second, we'll ask you to write a rough draft by arranging the details of the prewritten material in an orderly form. Once the rough draft is done, you will edit and revise it by tinkering with the arrangement of words, phrases, and sentences so that the entire piece reads smoothly. After editing and revising, the next step in the method will be to integrate the changes by writing a final draft, thus polishing the whole piece.

When you have completed this series of tasks you will have used one observed experience to work through the four main steps of the writing process:

Phase 1: prewriting
Phase 2: rough draft
Phase 3: editing and revising
Phase 4: final draft

Prewriting

If you consider the entire composing process, you'll see that it involves two different kinds of thought: (1) creative thought, which grows from a writer's intuition and allows the mind to connect ideas, events, and images; and; (2) critical thought, which grows from the intellect and allows the mind to organize words into verbal structures, such as sentences, paragraphs, and essays. Creative thought is less self-conscious than critical thought, yet both are important. Prewriting stresses the creative process while restraining the more self-conscious critical process.

When prewriting, you are actually inventing the raw material you'll be working with at other writing stages. You need not be concerned with the nitty-gritty of writing—grammar, syntax, punctuation, and spelling—but you should be concerned with generating an abundance of raw material with which to work in future drafts. Therefore, while you are involved in prewriting activities, open yourself to the creative experience without making critical judgments. The reshaping and organizing—that is, the judging—will come later.

BEGIN WITH A LIST

The method of prewriting we present in this section is an extension of the list described in Chapter 1. Although prewriting works for all kinds of written projects, for learning purposes you'll begin by working with a brief description that captures an experience you set out to record. After we've examined an illustration of prewriting, we'll ask you to stroll around your neighborhood, across campus, through a park, or wherever you wish to go in order to find something to describe.

Once you find something to describe, like a reporter using a notepad and pencil to capture colorful background for an article, you'll record the details of whatever it is that has caught your interest. These details will come to you through your senses—through sight, sound, smell, touch, and taste. The senses are involved to some degree in almost every type of writing. They are particularly important in descriptive writing.

Sight

The trees sway in the wind . . . Their dark silhouettes look like ink blots against the sky . . . Lightning streaks the night.

Sound

Thunder rumbles over the plains . . . Rain beats a steady rhythm on the iron gas drum . . . The kettle whistles in the kitchen.

Smell

The spicy aroma of curry . . . The air, fresh and clean from the rain . . . The dog's wet fur smells woolly.

Touch

The water-smooth stones slip under my feet . . . The cork handle is dry to touch . . . The sun stings my back . . . The feel of fur, soft and silky.

Taste

Sugary-sweet bubble gum . . . The bite of salt spray . . . The rich foam of beer . . . Savoring the meaty taste of spareribs.

Through the use of descriptive language, the task will be to make the reader "see," not to tell the reader what you think. Try to keep in mind that there is a difference between using writing to "think about" or "respond to" an experience and using writing to capture the sensory detail of an experience. Each use has an important place, and the two cannot be cleanly separated. For this assignment, however, we'll be asking you to concentrate on gathering sensory detail.

Here's how student-writer Sarah Lee collected her observations at the campus quad. As you read Lee's observations, keep in mind that she uses a form of listing to collect the details of the events she observes. But before studying Lee's observations, read her comments about beginning the assignment.

The class read the assignment, while my English instructor reviewed it in detail. The task seemed easy enough—merely spend thirty minutes describing something I observed. He emphasized the points the assignment touched on—find a focus, use specific language, remain objective, avoid judgments, and so on. I had an hour between classes, so I decided to complete the task on campus. It was after lunch, but the quad was crowded. I was paying more attention than I usually would. Everyone seemed relaxed, lazily passing away time in the sun.

Now examine Lee's observation list:

The Quad

- Spring. Warm. A slight breeze stirring leaves of the trees circling the quad area.
- Students sitting on the grass. Some sitting alone, reading or lying on their backs sleeping, looking like casualties of academic battles. Some sit in groups, chatting, eating.

- A dog, an Irish setter, walks from group, sniffing. Sunlight glistens off its reddish coat. A handkerchief is tied around its neck, 1960s style. Floppy ears. Someone holds out part of a sandwich and whistles. The dog trots over.
- Four students spread out a blanket. Sit down, laughing and talking. One opens a deck of cards and begins to deal.
- A jet flies overhead. Its engines growing louder from the takeoff. A half mile, maybe a mile away. Its engines—a low rumble, like distant thunder. Becomes a speck as it flies north.
- Two students are tossing a Frisbee in the center of the grass quad.
- They stand about thirty yards apart. The Frisbee soaring, like a flying saucer image from an old SciFi film, between them.
- One is a girl. Blonde, a cheerleader type in khaki shorts and striped tank top. Her hair is long and whips around her face as she swings her body to toss the Frisbee.
- The other, a boy, built like a weight lifter, torn jeans, shirtless, part of a T-shirt dangling from his back pocket. It flops about his legs when he runs to catch the Frisbee.
- The Frisbee floats toward the girl, high, almost out of her reach, she jumps to catch it.
- She gestures to her partner to start running . . . swings back her arm, like she was going to pitch a softball . . . drives her arm forward . . . keeps the Frisbee flat to the ground . . . she releases it from her fingertips as the weight of her body pulls her forward . . . she balances on one foot. Then she lifts her hand to shade her eyes as the Frisbee sails away, climbing higher and higher.
- Her partner has turned and is running to catch the Frisbee he knows will go over his head. He looks back over his shoulder at the disk soaring higher and higher. His face shows surprise.
- The Irish setter barks. Springs into action. It runs after the catcher. Sprinting past his legs.
- The catcher leaps into the air, but the Frisbee passes only inches above his reach and sails on.
- The dog barks again and speeds toward the Frisbee. It is slanting toward the ground. The dog leaps into the air and catches the Frisbee in the air in its jaws. It lands on its feet on the grass and then stands and stares at the boy leaning over and panting. The dog drops the Frisbee. Lifts its head and barks.
- The girl claps and laughs.
- The catcher catches his breath and then walks over and picks up the Frisbee. Then he pats the dog on the head.
- The dog barks again. Chasing around the student's legs.
- Someone whistles and the dog runs across the quad to someone waving.

Before you begin an observation list as the first step in the writing process, we want to give you a few guidelines to follow.

FOCUS YOUR PREWRITING

Notice that Lee concentrates on what she sees in the quad itself, students relaxing, the Irish setter, the Frisbee throwers. She does not spend any time describing the buildings in the distance, the trees, the nearby airport, what she was thinking, the college's history, not even the statue of the founding president. She is intent on the work at hand—that is, describing in specific language the little drama unfolding before her eyes.

RESIST SELF-CRITICISM

Notice that Lee frees herself of critical concerns by paying little if any attention to arranging words into sentences and sentences into paragraphs. She generates an expanded list to gather the raw material of her observation. By relaxing her critical intellect, she sees the external details and connects some of them with images. For instance, to help capture the image of students scattered about on the grass, she compares them to "battle" victims— that is, "casualties of academic battles." She also compares the soaring Frisbee to "a flying saucer image from an old SciFi film." She also compares the girl who tosses the Frisbee with someone "going to pitch a soft ball." Often writers will make comparisons of this sort to establish some common ground with their readers. Carefully selected common images such as these help a reader imagine what the writer experienced. So if you have associations or make connections like these, don't criticize them; record them, and in a later draft you might use them or you might drop them, depending on how appropriate they are.

USE SIMPLE LANGUAGE

Also notice that Lee uses simple words. Simple does not mean simplistic or oversimplified. Simple words are basic, not complicated or complex. You probably know all the words in Lee's draft. Notice too that many of Lee's words, mainly stressing sight and sound, are concrete—words that call up images of what can be seen, heard, touched, smelled, and tasted. Often concrete words are the ones most common in your vocabulary. With them you can build a solid description.

REMAIN OBJECTIVE

Notice how Lee sticks to describing the external detail of the experience in contrast to describing how she "feels" about the experience. In other words, she describes the experience "objectively" instead of "subjectively." Objective description is factual, impersonal, thoroughly scrubbed of direct statements about what the writer is thinking or how a writer feels about a subject. For example, if Lee had included what she was thinking about the Frisbee throwers, she might have written,

> Two students are tossing a Frisbee in the center of the quad. *They don't seem to have any problems or worries. Why else would they have time to play during midterms? I'm already busy, busy, busy—no time to play games.*

Unfocused subjective observations such as these distract from the actual experience. The goal for this task is to exclude subjective observations and concentrate on objective description.

WRITING TASK—PREWRITING

Take a walk around your neighborhood, across campus, or through the library, a market, shopping center, or park and look for something interesting to describe. When that something catches your interest, sit down and record the details. Act like a detached reporter objectively collecting the raw stuff of the experience, the way Sarah did in our example.

A word of caution: Resist the temptation to do this task from memory to avoid writing a "something interesting happened to me last week" piece. We're asking that you set out to record something fresh. If you record a memory, you'll end up writing a narrative—a story—that will lack the specific detail this task requires. So take our best advice: Accept the challenge and take the thirty or forty minutes to do an on-the-spot prewrite.

Remember:

1. Concentrate on an experience you observe.
2. While engaged in prewriting, avoid making critical judgments about grammar, syntax, punctuation, and spelling.
3. Like an objective reporter, capture the external details of the experience, not what you think about the experience.
4. Use simple, concrete language, language of the senses.
5. Select details that will help the reader "see" the experience.
6. When you finish, title your list.

GROUP WORK—PREWRITING

Take turns reading your observation list aloud. Is there enough specific detail? Is it visual? Is the language simple and direct? Offer helpful suggestions after each reading.

Rough Draft

Now that you have completed the prewriting phase, it's time to shape your observation list into a rough draft. While composing a rough draft you'll begin to make more critical judgments about your work—that is, you'll be shifting from a primarily intuitive process to a more intellectual process. To make the shift, you will have to face a whole new set of problems.

The first problem has to do with organizing a rough draft. If your observation list is anything like Sarah Lee's, it is composed of concrete description scribbled in fragments and ragged sentences. A rough draft represents a first attempt to impose some order on this random collection of detail.

ESTABLISH A PURPOSE

We want you to begin shaping your rough draft by setting a limit on its length. Write it in 350 to 400 words. If you have several pages of notes, meeting this limit might be difficult. But it just means that you, like most writers, will have to select the outstanding details to develop in your rough draft. One way to make this selection is to decide what you wish to communicate to your reader about the experience—perhaps a mood, feeling, or event—in other words, decide what your purpose is to be. Once you have a purpose in mind, you can then select and develop the details from your prewritten draft that will help you convey that purpose. This also means that you will abandon other details you have collected because they might not advance your purpose.

CREATE A BEGINNING, MIDDLE, AND END

While writing the rough draft, try to create a sense of roundness: The rough draft should have a beginning, a middle, and an end. Unfortunately, as with most aspects of writing, there is no magic formula for writing a rounded piece. We suggest you start by writing a sentence or two leading readers into the experience without their needing to know anything that came before. The beginning sentence or two will also convey your general purpose, although in a descriptive piece, such as the one you will be writing, you need not make a direct statement of purpose as you would in more expository paragraphs. You can then move into the middle of the piece by developing a sequence of sentences that grow from the lead. The middle will be the bulk of the piece. As you write, you will be constantly referring to the observation list as a source of detail you need to build the sentences. In fact, before you begin your rough draft you might rearrange the observation list material in an informal outline to give you a better sense of the direction the rough draft will take.

There are several common and logical ways to arrange written material so that a reader can follow it. Time arrangement is probably the most common. A writer will often use time arrangement in narration to tell a story or to explain a process—that is, to give directions on how to do something. In time arrangement the writer begins with the first event or step and ends with the last one.

For material that does not fall into a clear time scheme, a writer may use space arrangement, especially in descriptive writing, arranging the visual material from west to east, left to right, high to low, near to far, far to near, or whatever seems appropriate for a particular piece of writing.

A writer can also arrange material in order of climax, selecting the most dramatic part of the piece and holding it back until the end. For this arrangement the writer would begin with the least important details and arrange the rest of the material in order of increasing importance, and then close the piece by showcasing the most dramatic part.

Other arrangements are possible—such as ordering from general to particular or from particular to general—or any combination of them. Remember that no matter how you structure a piece of writing, the arrangement must be clear so readers can follow it.

Finally, you can close the piece where the middle sequence seems to end naturally. And here's where you have to rely on sensitivity. Endings often have a great deal to do with feelings. An ending might create a feeling one has after hearing a box click shut, or an ending might have the effect of a door slamming. One student writer of ours remarked that she often tried to link the end of her descriptive pieces with the lead, like a snake biting its own tail.

SHAPE THE SENTENCES

Besides arranging the detail, developing it, and shaping the overall structure of your descriptive piece, you must also shape the sentences. When you developed an observation list, you recorded your observations on the fly, in phrases or rough sentences. While writing the rough draft, you should shape the phrases into complete sentences. To write in complete sentences at this point does not mean to fret over grammar, syntax (the way sentences are constructed), punctuation, and spelling. It only means that you should be aware of them without getting yourself bogged down. If you remember that in most writing assignments the rough draft will be for your eyes only, you may be able to find the balance between being aware of and getting mired in concerns over writing correctly. Also remember that there are still two more phases in the composing process: (1) editing and revising and (2) polishing a final draft.

Before showing you Sarah Lee's rough draft, we want to remind you of two points from the prewriting discussion. First, when you write your rough draft, try to use simple, concrete language. There's no need to be fancy with words. Second, select part of your prewritten draft to emphasize—that is, to "showcase." Remember, we suggested that you find an experience and concentrate on it for your prewriting. This experience may be the part you wish to showcase, the highlight of your descriptive piece. To display that part, you will build the rest of your description around it, perhaps leading up to it and dramatizing it more than other elements in your description.

WRITING THE ROUGH DRAFT

Let's see how Sarah Lee used her observation list to create a rough draft. First, read what Lee has to say about the process:

> At first I thought this draft would be easy. I believed that I merely had to begin at the beginning and restructure my observations in complete sentences as I recorded them. But this wasn't the case at all. Instead I had to treat my observations seriously. These observations were not merely random details; they were to become the raw material for a serious assignment designed to teach a difficult process. So first I had to create a dominant impression—that is, a "purpose" that would unify the rough draft. Then I had to select and reconstruct the details that reflected that purpose. Of course, the selection process meant that I had to exclude a lot of material. Dropping some of my observations was hard for me. I'm the kind of person who is cursed with the belief that everything I write down should go into the final paper. Well, it shouldn't.
>
> After rereading my observation list several times, I decided to create the impression that this was a relaxed, maybe even lazy, spring day, and at the same time, I wanted to create a picture of the Frisbee throwers. Furthermore, I decided to "showcase" the Irish setter catching the Frisbee.

After I made those decisions, restructuring my observations was not too difficult. They fell pretty much into a simple climactic pattern—that is, a pattern with the most dramatic point coming at the end.

Now study Lee's rough draft. Notice how she dropped some observations recorded on her observation list and reshaped others. Also notice that Lee skipped spaces between lines so she would have plenty of space to complete the third phase of the composing process—that is, space to edit and revise.

```
                The Quad

    Yesterday afternoon I walked across campus to

join students relaxing in the quad. It was spring

and the sun was shining. There I sat alone on the

grass and watched the activity around me.

    Students sat on the grass, reading, chatting,

or napping, like casualties of academic battles.

An Irish setter, with sun reflecting from its red

coat and wearing a handkerchief 60s style around

its neck, walked from student to student, sniffing

for food. In the center of the quad, a girl who

looked like a blonde cheerleader type and a boy

who looked like a weight lifter were tossing a

Frisbee. The blonde girl was in khaki shorts and

striped tank top. The weight lifter was in torn

jeans but was shirtless, his T-shirt dangling from

his back pocket. It flopped whenever he ran to

catch the Frisbee.

    The Frisbee floated toward the blonde and

reminded me of a 50s SciFi flying saucer. It
```

stalled above her head, hovered a moment, and then dropped to her up-stretched hands.

She paused a moment, looked at the weight lifter, and gestured for him to start running. Then she drew back her arm, leaned forward as if she were going to pitch a softball. She flung the Frisbee forward, releasing it from her out-stretched hand. The Frisbee whirled away into the air. She lifted one hand to shade her eyes against the sun as she watched the Frisbee soar away.

The weight lifter turned to run as the Frisbee flew toward him. He looked over his shoulder at the Frisbee soaring higher and higher. A look of surprise crossed his face.

The setter lifted its head toward the soaring Frisbee, barked once and sprang into action. It ran after the weight lifter. It sprinted past his legs.

The weight lifter leaped into the air to catch the Frisbee, but it sailed above his fingertips.

The setter barked again then leaped into the air. Its body stretched toward the Frisbee. Its neck strained to reach it. The Frisbee began to lose speed, stalled in the air, and began to fall as the setter caught the Frisbee in its jaws in the air.

```
The blonde clapped her hands and laughed. The

weight lifter was out of breath. He bent over and

gasped for air. The setter carried the Frisbee and

wagged its tail.
```

Indeed this is a very rough draft with many awkward spots. That's okay. Remember the purpose of a rough draft is to give shape to items on the observation list, not to create a perfect piece of writing.

Now let's examine Lee's selection process. First, Lee had to limit this draft to 350 to 400 words. This limitation forced her to be selective. Notice, for example, that Lee excluded such observations as the jet flying overhead, the four card-playing students, and the Frisbee player patting the dog on the head, taking the Frisbee, and the dog's owner whistling for it.

Why does Lee exclude some observations and not others? Since writers make their own choices—often by using their intuition—the answer may be hard to come by. The reason might have something to do with Lee's general purpose. For example, the image of the jet with engines that "sounded like the low rumble of thunder" does not serve her purpose. Remember she wanted to capture a lazy afternoon in the quad, create a picture of the Frisbee players, and showcase the dog catching a Frisbee. The jet does add some descriptive color, but does very little to develop a sense of a lazy day.

You might wonder why she excludes the four card players. Doesn't their casual attitude reflect a lazy day? Yes, it does, but she probably excludes this observation from the rough draft for another reason. Since she has plenty of material to create a sense of a lazy day, she doesn't need to include the card players. Moreover, if she had included the card players, she would have had less textual space to use to devote to the Frisbee players and the dog, all of which serve as the center of her description.

Finally, you might wonder why she drops the closing dog sequence. Doesn't this sequence offer interesting detail and extend the dog's role in the description? Read how Lee answers this question:

> This was a tough decision. I excluded my observation of the dog being patted on the head and its owner whistling because I wanted to end in a way that kept the focus on the three key elements—that is, the blonde, the weight lifter, and the dog. I also felt that including this sequence at the end would detract from the central image of the dog catching the Frisbee on the fly, which I saw as the passage's climactic moment.

Indeed, catching the Frisbee is the climactic moment, and Lee intensifies it by describing the dog prancing among the spectators.

WRITING TASK—ROUGH DRAFT

Using your observation list as a starting point, write a rough draft in no more than 300–350 words. We suggest you leave plenty of space between the lines—that is, skip lines—so you'll have room to cross out and add words and phrases when you edit and revise your rough draft during the next step in the composing process.

Remember:

1. Review your prewriting and establish a general purpose.
2. Try to discover something in your observation list that would be interesting to showcase and embellish.
3. If necessary, rearrange your observations to create a clear structure for your piece.
4. Write your rough draft in simple language and complete sentences, yet keep in mind that rough drafts are usually "for your eyes only," which should free you from being overly concerned about perfection.

Although we have given you a great deal to consider while writing a rough draft, keep in mind that your goal is not perfection: There are still two more stages in the composing process.

GROUP WORK

Have a copy of your rough draft for each group member and distribute them. Read the rough drafts and write brief comments identifying the strengths and weaknesses in the margins. As you read, ask yourself the following: Is there a clear purpose established in the opening sentences? Is the draft structured effectively—that is, does it have a clear beginning, middle, and end? Is an element showcased?

Return the rough drafts with marginal comments to each writer, who should review the comments before completing the next task.

Suggestion: Keep your responses specific, but brief. Stick to the concepts emphasized in the discussion about writing a rough draft.

Editing and Revising

The time to begin the editing and revising process is when you have a suitable rough draft in hand—a piece drawn from the prewritten draft that you believe adequately covers the experience you are trying to convey. No doubt you have been struggling to make your experience meaningful to yourself, trying to find and get a grip on what you are trying to describe. Mainly, up to this point, you have been writing to please yourself. Now you must begin to consider your audience—that is, to more actively imagine a reader looking over your shoulder. We are not suggesting that you allow the imaginary reader to loom above your work like some insistent taskmaster, but that when you begin to edit and revise, you keep in mind that your descriptive piece will be read by another person. Thinking about the reader will help you decide what to include, what words to select, and how to organize your final paper. More importantly, as a writer you want to be clear and convincing while avoiding the risks of being misunderstood.

While editing and revising, you must muster your intellectual skills to evaluate your work. Under these circumstances, evaluation does not involve deciding whether your work is good or bad. Instead, it involves deciding whether or not your work is as vigorous and concise as you can make it. No sentence should have any unnecessary words; no paragraph, any unnecessary sentences. This is not to suggest that all sentences are to be simple or short, but only that they be as concise as possible.

Although individual writers develop their own approaches to the editing and revising process, we offer the following guidelines and illustrations to get you started.

ESTABLISH A POINT OF VIEW

Decide what point of view will rule your piece. In the task that involved writing a note (Chapter 1), the point of view probably came naturally. Notes are usually written in the first-person singular—"I"—and addressed to the reader in the second person—"you." By using the "I" point of view you wrote as a participant in the process. Whenever writing about first-hand experience, as you will be in these early tasks, the use of first person is appropriate. For some subjects, however, you will need to keep a more impersonal point of view by avoiding the first person altogether. You will sometimes be writing as a detached observer who stands some distance away from the reader and the material. The impersonal point of view is appropriate when the subject needs to be treated in a neutral way—in history, for instance, scientific writing, or news reporting. Whether personal or impersonal, the subject usually determines the point of view. The concept to remember here is that the point of view needs to be consistent. For instance, Lee used the "I" point of view in her rough draft. If she had shifted to "you," her use of point of view would have been inconsistent. So like every writer you too must revise to keep a consistent point of view.

KEEP THE VERB TENSE CONSISTENT

Another conscious choice you must make when editing and revising is selecting the principal verb tense. In practice the choice is simple. Most writing is done in the past tense: "I *sat* on the bench and *watched* the men while they *were jogging* around the track." But some writers decide to record experience in the present tense: "I *am* on the bench *watching* the men while they *jog* around the track."

Since the present tense often sounds awkward when used as the principal tense in a lengthy piece, we suggest you use the past tense. However, the present tense is not necessarily improper. What is improper is to shift from the principal tense to another without having a purpose for the shift: I *sat* on the bench and *watched* the men while they *jog* around the track. Just *watching* them *makes* me *feel* tired." Notice how the writer has shifted the principal tense from past (*sat* and *watched*) to present (*jog, makes, feel*). This mistaken shift is awkward and confusing to the reader. Keep track of your verb tense when you edit and revise to help your reader move easily through your description.

We don't want to give you the impression, however, that it is always awkward to shift verb tenses. In fact, often you must shift tense. Remember, verb tenses show time—past, present, and future. Sometimes you will need to glance backward and forward when writing: "It *had been* four years since I last *visited* my former high school, and after only a few minutes on campus, I *realized* that I *would never be able* to recapture the feeling of my school days." In this sentence the shifts are natural and controlled. The writer is aware of them but keeps the principal tense—in the example the past tense, *visited* and *realized*—consistent.

DELETE EMPTY WORDS

The first words to delete are the empty, meaningless ones: *lovely, pretty, beautiful, good, great, terrific,* and others that lack specific qualities. Also cross out words that you may have added for emphasis: *very, quite, rather, really,* and *so.* Words of this sort carry over into writing from speech habits. When spoken, they add vocal emphasis to intensify a point or feeling. But writing is different from speaking. Writers intensify by being concise and by using concrete detail. Consider, for instance, what the writer actually expresses in the following sentence:

> The very lovely woman with a rather pretty smile walked down the beautiful lane.

Begin by asking yourself what a "very lovely woman" looks like. Or a "rather pretty smile." Or a "beautiful lane." *Very, lovely, pretty,* and *beautiful* fail to give the reader a clear picture of what the writer experienced. These words suggest only a good feeling about seeing the woman; they have no content. Like a child's coloring book, they function as blank spaces for readers to fill in their private perceptions.

For beginning writers, empty words can be deceptive. They can deceive writers into believing they have said something when they haven't. By deleting such words, a writer can get a better look at the content of the sentence.

> The woman with a smile walked down the lane.

Not much content. And when written more concisely,

> Smiling, the woman walked down the lane

the sentence seems to say less.

There is an advantage to this kind of editing. It gives the writer a chance to revise—that is, to return to the prewritten draft or to memory and select more concrete details to add to the work. After revision, the sentence might read like this:

> Smiling, the thin woman with flowing blond hair walked down the lane edged with blooming geraniums.

Now the sentence creates a clearer picture of what the writer experienced. The writer has included details the reader can visualize.

TIGHTEN SENTENCES

There is more to editing and revising than deleting empty words and rebuilding with concrete details. The writer must also tighten the sentences by combining loosely arranged sentences, deleting words that repeat the content of other words, and replacing weak and general verbs with stronger, more accurate ones. As an illustration, let's examine part of a rough draft that sets out to describe an autumn day:

> As soon as I walked outside, I knew fall had come. Clouds came in from the west and filled the afternoon with dark shadows. The wind blew around the leaves. They were dead and dry and made a scraping sound against the pavement. Children walking home from school were bundled in heavy coats, and many of them had scarves wrapped around their necks.

The opening sentence sets up a clear purpose. It also leads the reader into sentences that detail the writer's sudden awareness that fall has arrived. That's good: Setting purposes and leading readers into passages are what opening sentences should do. But notice how the descriptive flow is interrupted by the fourth sentence:

> They [the leaves] were dead and dry and made a scraping sound against the pavement.

As you can see, the details relate to the writer's description of fall, but the piece seems to come to a momentary standstill because the focus shifts to the leaves. The sentence could be cut out, but no writer wants to lose good detail. Rather than cutting it, the writer can combine it with the preceding one. So instead of retaining

> The wind blew around the leaves. They were dead and dry and made a scraping sound against the pavement.

he could revise it to read

> The wind blew around the dead and dry leaves that scraped against the pavement.

The piece is now concise and reads smoothly:

> As soon as I walked outside, I knew fall had come. Clouds came in from the west and filled the afternoon with dark shadows. The wind blew around the dead and dry leaves that scraped against the pavement. Children walking home from school were bundled in heavy coats, and many of them had scarves wrapped around their necks.

This doesn't end the process of editing and revising, though. It only helps the writer see where other changes need to be made. He might continue by working on the part he just rebuilt:

> The wind blew around the dead and dry leaves that scraped against the pavement.

Consider the words *dead* and *dry*. Each has within it the idea of the other—a dead leaf is dry and a dry leaf is dead. There is no reason to use both. Now, consider *wind*, the verb *blew*, and the preposition *around*, which follows *blew*. Also consider the phrase *that scraped against the pavement*: a nice image appealing to the reader's sense of sound, but the wording is sloppy. By pausing to examine these words, the writer will realize that *wind* has the idea of blowing in it. After all, what does wind do if not blow? *Around*, which is used to buttress *blew*, might even be misread. Certainly the wind does blow around leaves, but it also blows around corners, which is not the same thing. A solution to the sloppy wording lies in the phrase *that scraped against the pavement*. From it the writer can lift the verb *scraped* and revise the sentence to read:

> The wind scraped the dead leaves against the pavement.

Keeping in mind the need to delete unnecessary words along with words that repeat the content of other words, combining weak sentences, and substituting accurate verbs for weak or inaccurate ones, a writer might produce an edited and revised version like this:

stepped
As soon as I ~~walked~~ outside I knew fall had
blew
come. Clouds ~~came~~ in from the west and filled
the afternoon with ~~dark~~ shadows. The wind
scraped dead leaves against the pavement.
                                        wore
Children walking home from school ~~were bundled~~
~~in~~ heavy coats, and many ~~of them~~ had scarves
wrapped around their necks.

"Stepped outside" is the usual idiom.

"Blew" is more accurate than "came."

A shadow is dark. No need to say "dark."

The active "wore" easily replaces the wordy, passive "were bundled in."

"Of them" is unnecessary.

The edited and revised passage now reads:

> As soon as I stepped outside, I knew fall had come. Clouds blew in from the west and filled the afternoon with shadows. The wind scraped dead leaves against the pavement. Children walking home from school wore heavy coats, and many had scarves wrapped around their necks.

On rereading the revised draft, the writer might think "scraped against" doesn't convey the movement of the leaves effectively and so change *against* to *along:*

> The wind scraped dead leaves *along* the pavement.

Well, the tinkering has to stop somewhere. Otherwise, papers would never get turned in.

COMPLETING THE REVISION

The way to start editing and revising is with a pencil in hand and the rough draft before you. Begin by reading aloud at a much slower pace than normal to see and hear whether any words or phrases can be deleted without loss of meaning or emphasis. Draw a line through the words and phrases you wish to delete; but don't totally obscure them, for later they may remind you of detail to add when you are working on the final draft. In the margins and the spaces between the lines, write in any additional detail you wish to add.

Now before studying Lee's edited and revised description, read her comments on the editing and revising process.

I thought I would merely be polishing my rough draft, so I was surprised how much I deleted and reworked. I first concentrated on deleting all the needless repetitions and unnecessary language. I then tried to find specific verbs to replace more general ones. Finally, I had to restructure several passages so they would flow logically and smoothly. Overall, I was surprised how much I could delete and in doing so, actually improve my description.

What follows is Lee's edited and revised draft with her comments printed in the margin. First read through her description and then reread it along with the explanations.

LEE'S EDITED AND REVISED ROUGH DRAFT

The Quad

Yesterday afternoon I ~~walked across campus to~~ sat

~~join students relaxing~~ in the quad. ~~It was spring~~

~~and the sun was shinning.~~ ~~There I sat alone on the~~

~~grass~~ and watched the activity around me.

These changes tighten the opening. I had too much unnecessary information.

Students sat on the grass, reading, chatting,

or napping. ~~like casualties of academic battles.~~ *in the sun.*

An Irish setter, with sun ~~reflecting~~ from its red *light*

coat and wearing a handkerchief ~~60s style~~ around

its neck, ~~walked~~ from student to student, sniffing *trotted*

for food. In the center of the quad, a girl who

~~looked like a~~ blonde, ~~cheerleader type~~ and a boy *had long hair,*

who looked like a weight lifter were tossing a *lazily*

Frisbee. The ~~blonde~~ girl was in khaki shorts and

striped tank top. The weight lifter was in torn

jeans but was shirtless, his T-shirt dangling from

his back pocket. ~~It flopped whenever he ran to~~

~~catch the Frisbee.~~

I deleted the "battle" simile because it was too exaggerated. By dropping it, I could then add an unobtrusive reference to the sun.

"Wearing" is unnecessary and "60s style" is a distracting detail. I changed "walked" to "trotted" because "trotted" is more specific.

What is a "cheerleader type?" I don't really know, so I deleted it. I feel "long blonde hair" creates a better picture.

I added "lazily" because I was afraid I hadn't made part of my purpose clear. But maybe I'll take it out in the final draft.

"Dangling" captures what I was describing, so the sentence, "It flopped whenever he ran to catch the Frisbee," is excessive and detracts from the flow of my description.

The Frisbee floated toward the blonde, ~~and~~ ~~reminded me of a 50s SciFi flying saucer.~~, It stalled ~~above her head~~, hovered ~~a moment,~~ and then dropped to her up-stretched hands.

She *studied* ~~paused a moment, looked at~~ the weight lifter and gestured for him to start running.

Then she drew back her arm, leaned ~~forward~~ as if she were going to pitch a softball. *and* ~~She~~ flung the Frisbee *toward him,* ~~forward,~~ releasing it from her out stretched hand. ~~The Frisbee whirled away into the air. She lifted one hand to shade her eyes against the sun as she watched the Frisbee soar away.~~

Surprised ~~The~~ weight lifter turned to run as the Frisbee *soared* ~~flew toward him. He looked over his shoulder at the Frisbee soaring~~ higher and higher. ~~A look of surprise crossed his face.~~

The setter *watched* ~~lifted its head toward~~ the soaring Frisbee, barked ~~once~~ and sprang into action, *sprinting past the weight lifter.* ~~It ran after the weight lifter. It sprinted past his legs.~~

The weight lifter leaped ~~into the air~~ to catch the Frisbee, but it sailed above his fingertips. *Then it lost speed, stalled and began to fall. The setter* ~~The setter barked again then leaped into the~~ *waited, poised, as if it were stalking a bird. Then it jumped.* ~~air. Its body stretched toward the Frisbee. Its~~ *Its body stretched upward. Its neck strained toward the* ~~neck strained to reach it. The Frisbee began to~~ *frisbee. It snapped closed its jaws, catching the frisbee in* ~~lose speed, stalled in the air, and began to fall~~ *its mouth.*

Everyone knows what a Frisbee looks like, so I had no reason to compare it to a 50s SciFi flying saucer. As for the other changes: the word "moment" is suggested by "hovered" and "above her head" is suggested by "dropped to her up-stretched hands," thus I deleted them.

This paragraph needed to be tightened and the verbs sharpened. I decided to concentrate on the main action, that is, the blonde tossing the Frisbee, and delete the language that didn't advance my description. I changed the second "forward" to "toward him" to avoid an unnecessary repetition.

This passage was also overwritten; so I deleted what I felt was unnecessary. I also tightened the description by replacing "A look of surprise crossed his face" with "surprised," I mean, well, other than a face, what body part can look surprised? You understand my point, right?

I wanted to emphasize the action verbs in this passage, so I deleted some language that detracted from the main movement. The setter "watched," "barked," and "sprang." I like the way these action verbs lead to the closing phrase, "sprinting past the weight lifter."

I rewrote this whole passage. The sequence seemed all wrong. I also wanted to dramatize the dog's catching the Frisbee, the action I was showcasing.

~~as the setter caught the Frisbee in its jaws in~~

~~the air.~~

The blonde clapped her hands and laughed. The

weight lifter ~~was out of breath. He~~ bent over and

pranced among the students, holding the Frisbee aloft.

gasped for air. The setter ∧ ~~carried the Frisbee and~~

~~wagged its tail.~~

For the close I tried to create a sense of balance, returning to the Frisbee throwers yet emphasizing the dog.

After completing the editing and revising phase, Lee made the following comments: "To look at my revised draft can be misleading. It may seem that I made these changes all at once—that I did them while working my way through the rough draft the first time. Actually for me editing and revising just doesn't work that way. I need to read and reread. I often try out words and different sentence arrangements on scratch paper before making a change. Sometimes I'll rewrite a passage, integrating the changes, then begin editing again."

WRITING TASK—EDITING AND REVISING

Edit and revise your rough draft. With pencil in hand and rough draft before you, begin to reread and write the changes between the lines and in the margins as illustrated in Lee's example. As you edit and revise your piece, you may notice that it becomes substantially shorter. Don't worry about that. Instead, work toward thoroughly editing and revising this draft.

Remember:

1. Delete empty words and add concrete detail where you find it necessary.
2. Tighten your sentences by combining loose sentences, by deleting words that repeat the meaning of other words, and by replacing weak and general verbs with more accurate ones.
3. Be prepared to reread your description several times aloud, testing new words and phrases to see if they improve your piece.

Suggestion: Although editing and revising can seem tedious, be patient. Concentrate. The effort will pay off in clearer prose.

GROUP WORK

Work in pairs. Take turns reading your last drafts aloud. Is the point of view consistent? Is the appropriate tense maintained? As the two of you read, examine each sentence with care. Delete empty words. Tighten sentences. Rephrase awkward constructions.

Final Draft

When all the editing and revising is done that can be done on the rough draft, one step still remains—the final draft. In many respects the final draft is another revision.

At this point you probably have a piece of writing that looks like a Jackson Pollock painting—you know, the kind with dribbles and streaks across the canvas. A scribbled appearance is typical of edited drafts with revisions penciled between lines and in margins. Professional writers have been known to tape or staple additional strips or sheets of paper to the sides of their rough drafts to accommodate extensive revisions. You may want to try that technique when you are editing and revising future assignments. In the meantime, you are now ready to start your final draft. The final draft continues the revision process. We suggest you begin it by thinking about your readers.

ACT AS A READER

While completing the final draft, you must imagine your reader as a major part of the process. You must remember that whether you are writing for an instructor, your friends and peers, or an audience beyond your campus, your work is going to be read by someone other than yourself. The final stage of the composing process—the final draft—is the time to consider the reader's expectations seriously, which will help you write more clearly.

If you have not identified a specific reader, as you would do for a note to a friend or a report for a college committee, then you must act as your own reader. This is a neat trick that requires you to separate yourself from your work and examine the work as if you had not been its author. You begin by reading your edited and revised manuscript aloud. You include all the revisions—that is, you drop from the reading all that you have crossed out and include all that you have added. While reading, ask yourself some simple questions:

Do the opening sentences guide a reader to what follows?
Do the sentences seem logically connected and flow smoothly from beginning to end?
Does the description end in a satisfying way?

And finally,

> Would a reader unfamiliar with the information or experience understand the description?

To perform like a vigilant reader is tough, demanding that you step from your skin into another's.

Before going on to an illustration of Lee's final draft, we want to mention two concepts that will help you keep a reader on the right track. One is the use of transitions and the other is tone.

USE TRANSITIONS

The use of transitional techniques will help you hold a reader's attention. Although there are many techniques a writer can use to connect sentences, one way to do it is through overt transitions—words and phrases that guide a reader from point to point. Without adequate transitions, papers seem to skip about, letting a reader's attention stray. As a writer, your goal is to keep your readers with you. You must not allow them to stray. Use transitions to smooth their way from beginning to end. (See Coherence in Appendix C.)

CONSIDER THE TONE

Tone is a very complicated part of writing, but if you begin by thinking of it as the voice in which you wish to address a reader, you have started to master its complexity. You might approach a reader in a casual or chatty voice or in a more reserved or formal voice. Either is acceptable. In fact, any tone is acceptable as long as it fits the subject. For instance, to write about the crash of a Boeing 707 in the breezy voice of a sports journalist would be inappropriate. It would also be inappropriate to write about Woody Allen's humor in the deadened tone of a government pamphlet. Those voices just would not fit the subjects. (See Tone in Appendix B.)

WRITING THE FINAL DRAFT

To prepare to write a final draft, you must examine the edited and revised draft to see if there are any further changes you wish to make. As you examine the draft, imagine you are a reader who is unfamiliar with the material. Ask yourself questions as you read: Are there confusing parts? Do the sentences flow together? Can the words be made more concrete and accurate? Is the arrangement easy to follow?

Before examining Lee's final draft, let's reread the edited and revised draft with the penciled notations integrated and the deletions left out. As you reread it, keep in mind what we have just said about asking questions.

LEE'S EDITED AND REVISED DRAFT WITH DELETIONS AND ADDITIONS

                    The Quad

Yesterday afternoon I sat in the quad and
watched the activity around me.

Students sat on the grass reading, chatting,
or napping in the sun. An Irish setter, with sunlight reflecting from its red coat and a handkerchief around its neck, trotted from student to
student, sniffing for food. In the center of the
quad, a girl, who had long blonde hair, and a
boy, who looked like a weight lifter, were lazily
tossing a Frisbee. The blonde was in khaki shorts
and striped top. The weight lifter was in torn
jeans but shirtless, his T-shirt dangling from his
back pocket.

The Frisbee floated toward the blonde, stalled,
hovered, and then dropped to her up-stretched
hands.

She studied the weight lifter and gestured for
him to start running. Then she drew back her arm,

leaned forward, as if she were going to pitch a
softball, and flung the Frisbee toward him, releasing it from her out-stretched hand.

Surprised, the weight lifter turned to run as
the Frisbee soared higher and higher.

The setter watched the soaring Frisbee,
barked, and sprang into action, sprinting past the
weight lifter.

The weight lifter leaped to catch the Frisbee,
but it sailed above his fingertips.

Then it lost speed and began to fall. The setter waited, poised, as if it were stalking a bird.
Then it jumped. Its body stretched upward. Its
neck strained toward the Frisbee. It snapped
closed its jaws, catching the Frisbee in its
mouth.

The blonde clapped her hands and laughed. The
weight lifter bent over and gasped for air. The
setter pranced among the students, holding the
Frisbee aloft.

It doesn't take much reader vigilance to see some of the flaws in Lee's description. Cutting out unnecessary words and description through editing
and revising will help you see the flaws in your work also.

Keep in mind, too, that writing a final draft doesn't merely involve copying the edited and revised draft with the changes integrated and transitions
added. Often you will need to rework your sentences so that they flow more
smoothly together and you might sharpen your language in order to make
your description more dramatic. The completed final draft should also be

completely polished—that is, it should be free of errors in punctuation, grammar, and syntax.

Finally, even though the final revision is mainly an intellectual process, the act of doing it often stirs the creative part of a writer's mind. Forgotten details or new comparisons may appear in your awareness. They shouldn't be shut out. If they fit and add to the description, you may work them into your manuscript.

Before reviewing Lee's revision for the final draft, read what she has to say about the process.

At this point I realized I wasn't describing a scene as I had thought. I was describing action within a scene. Yes, the Quad is my focus, but the action of throwing, chasing, and catching the Frisbee is at its center. As a consequence, I decided to concentrate on capturing movement. I would try to subordinate most of the descriptive details to movement. I also felt my description was too choppy, so I decided to add some overt transition and combine short paragraphs.

Here's a way to study Lee's final draft. First reread the edited and revised draft above. Then read the final draft with changes penciled in. Finally, read the "clean" final draft with the changes integrated. Be sure to study the comments in the margin to understand why Lee made some changes.

LEE'S FINAL DRAFT WITH HANDWRITTEN CHANGES AND COMMENTS

The Quad

Yesterday ~~afternoon~~ I sat in the quad and
It was a hot spring afternoon, and everyone
watched the activity around me.

seemed to enjoy a relief from studies.

¶ To my left four students sat on a blanket and played cards. Others circled the grassy quad,

~~Students sat on the grass~~ reading, chatting, or

napping ~~in the sun~~. An Irish setter, with sun-

light reflecting from its red coat and a ~~handker-~~

bandanna
~~chief~~ around its neck, trotted from student to

student, sniffing for food. In the center of the

I added information—that is, the day was hot; it was spring; a welcome break from studying—because I didn't feel I had my purpose clear in the last draft. I also moved "afternoon" to the second sentence because I didn't want to repeat it or use "day."

Here I set up a direction and added the card players from my observation list as a minor detail, which I feel adds to the image of students relaxing.

I added "circled" to create the sense of movement around the quad and prepare the reader for the Frisbee players who are in the quad's center.

quad, a girl, who had long blonde hair, and a boy,

was shirtless and

who ^looked like a weight lifter, were ~~lazily~~

using a frisbee to play catch.

~~tossing a Frisbee. The blonde was in khaki shorts~~

~~and striped top. The weight lifter was in torn~~

~~jeans but shirtless, his T-shirt dangling from~~

~~his back pocket.~~

I watched the

~~The~~ Frisbee floated toward the blonde, stalled,

hovered, and then dropped to her up-stretched

hands.

Narrowing her eyes against the sun,

^She studied the weight lifter, ~~and gestures for~~

~~him to start running.~~ Then ~~she~~ drew back her arm,

leaned forward, as if she were going to pitch a

softball, and flung the Frisbee toward him, releas-

ing it from her out-stretched hand.

turning to run, *chased*

Surprised, the weight lifter ~~turned to run as~~

as it

the Frisbee ^soared higher and higher.

Nearby t *stopped prowling for food, glanced at*

The setter ~~watched~~ the soaring Frisbee, ~~barked,~~

Then

and ^sprang into action, sprinting past the weight

lifter.

The weight lifter leaped to catch the Frisbee,

but it sailed above his fingertips,

before

~~Then~~ it lost speed and began to fall. The set-

ter waited, poised, as if it were stalking a bird,

t *i* *ing* *i i*
Then it jumped, its body stretched upward, its

ing *until i*
neck strained toward the Frisbee, it snapped

I changed the close of this sentence to avoid ending with "Frisbee" and to emphasize that the couple was playing catch. I deleted "lazily"; the descriptive details seem to speak for themselves.

I dropped much of the description of the Frisbee players because I wanted to concentrate on describing the action. I kept "shirtless" because I felt it would help the reader imagine a bare-chested weight lifter.

I added "I watched" to reestablish the point of view and to serve as a subtle transition. Because of this change, I had to revise the tense of four verbs.

Here I added detail to set up the Frisbee toss. I deleted "and gestured for him to start running" because the blonde's actions reveal that this is going to be a powerful toss.

I wanted to make the weight lifter's actions more distinct. First, he looks surprised; second, he turns to run; then he gives chase while the Frisbee soars higher and higher.

Because the two passages are short, I brought them together with the transition "Nearby."

I combined these sentences to generate more action. The trick here is to avoid writing a comma splice.

it /

closed its jaws, catching, ~~the Frisbee~~ in its

mouth.

The blonde clapped her hands and laughed. The

weight lifter bent over and gasped for air. The

setter pranced among the students, holding the

Frisbee aloft.

I kept the ending. I liked the way it dealt with each figure—the blonde, the weight lifter, and the dog—separately. It seemed to be a natural close.

Lee still had one final step to complete before this task was done. Once additions and deletions are made for the final draft, it must be retyped, integrating the new changes, to be submitted. This draft should be highly "polished"—that is, all the punctuation, mechanical, and sentence errors you find should be corrected. Below, you'll find Lee's carefully polished manuscript. Notice how she combined paragraphs for better effect.

The Quad

Yesterday, I sat in the quad and watched the

activity around me. It was a hot spring afternoon,

and everyone seemed to enjoy a relief from stud-

ies.

To my left four students sat on a blanket and

played cards. Others circled the grassy quad,

reading, chatting, or napping. An Irish setter,

with sunlight reflecting from its red coat and a

bandanna around its neck, trotted from student to

student, sniffing for food. In the center of the

quad, a girl, who had long blonde hair, and a boy,

who was shirtless and looked like a weight lifter,

used a Frisbee to play catch.

I watched the Frisbee float toward the blonde,

stall, hover, and then drop to her up-stretched

hands. Narrowing her eyes against the sun, she studied the weight lifter, then drew back her arm, leaned forward, as if she were going to pitch a softball, and flung the Frisbee toward him, releasing it from her out-stretched hand. Surprised, turning to run, the weight lifter chased the Frisbee as it soared higher and higher. Nearby, the setter stopped prowling for food, glanced at the soaring Frisbee, then sprang into action, sprinting past the weight lifter.

The weight lifter leaped to catch the Frisbee, but it sailed above his fingertips before it lost speed and began to fall. The setter waited, poised, as if it were stalking a bird, then it jumped, its body stretching upward, its neck straining toward the Frisbee until it snapped closed its jaws, catching the Frisbee in its mouth.

The blonde clapped her hands and laughed. The weight lifter bent over and gasped for air. The setter pranced among the students, holding the Frisbee aloft.

At some point explanation fails—the act of writing cannot be defined, but it can be illustrated. We hope that tracing the development of Lee's description has clearly shown you that the composing process is complicated. We can give you guidelines: Use concrete language. Write in complete sentences. Punctuate properly. Arrange your observations in logical order. Create a consistent point of view, verb tense, and tone, but you must do the actual writing. Following the composing process to a final draft takes concentration and patience—neither comes easily to beginning writers, but both can be developed over time.

WRITING TASK—FINAL DRAFT

After examining your edited and revised draft while acting as your own vigilant reader, write the final draft.

Remember:

1. Arrange your description logically.
2. Add transitions to guide the reader's attention.
3. Add and drop details when appropriate to do so.

Suggestion: You're near the end of the composing process. Review the steps that brought you here. Review your early drafts to see the progress you've made.

POLISHING YOUR WORK

Often the final draft is the last version you will have to write before turning in your work. But sometimes you will need to write a polished draft. Preparing the polished draft involves rereading to check for sentence and punctuation errors. Also check that the principal verb tense, point of view, and tone are consistent. Finally, use a dictionary to check your spelling. If you spot any errors, correct them and recopy your paper, integrating your corrections. A polished draft is just what the term *polished* suggests—a piece that represents your best effort at communicating a point while using correct writing conventions.

GROUP WORK

Distribute copies to each group member. Each writer should read the final draft aloud while other group members follow along. Pause to clarify any confusion. Once through the entire draft, discuss its effect. Is it clear? Does it need any more revision? Or does the group recommend polishing the work?

3

Responding to Experience

In the last series of tasks, you worked with description. You stuck closely to what you observed and avoided writing about what you thought or felt. The next writing task will ask you to narrate an experience and to integrate what you think or feel about the experience, not merely to describe it objectively. In other words, we want you to respond to an experience.

Support Generalizations with Specific Detail

Successful writing is a mixture of generalization and specific detail, but beginning writers tend to overgeneralize by offering their judgments or feelings—their responses—without including enough detail to show a reader why they respond as they do.

The tendency to write in general language is a habit carried over into writing from speaking. In our typical conversations there is little need to specifically describe the details behind our judgments. A listener who wants to hear them will ask. For instance, consider a general statement a friend of yours might make: "It was great at the beach yesterday." You might nod your head and agree, saying, "Wish I'd been there." End of conversation. On the other hand, your curiosity might be aroused enough to start asking questions.

"What do you mean by great?" you ask, a frown crossing your brow.

"Hot. The sun was out and there was a lot of action," he answers, his face lighting up with the memory.

"Action? What kind of action?"

"Well," he says, rubbing his chin, "there was a grueling volleyball match between the Daytona Beach and Miami champs. The surf was up—about four feet. And the water was in the sixties."

Depending on the extent of your interest, the questioning might go on. But somewhere you would probably stop and agree that the day was great. The flat assertion might not have convinced you, but the specifics would. Whenever you write, remember nothing so exhausts readers as being led through a bog of general assertions that go unsupported by specifics—like this:

> It was beautiful at the beach yesterday. The weather was terrific. The shore was filled with plenty of action. The waves were great, and the water was the best it's been in months.

On the other hand, if you keep in mind that readers, unlike listeners, lack the right of cross-examination, and if you mix your responses—your thoughts, feelings, judgments, conclusions, assertions, whatever you wish to call them—with the specific details they're based on, readers will move through your work with ease. To write meaningfully, then, you must give readers specific details behind your general responses so that they can make up their own minds about the experience. If the beach conversation had been put in written form, a final draft fleshed out with more detail might have looked like this:

> Yesterday I went to the beach. By eight the sun, like a huge arc light, had burned through the morning haze. The water, which had been choppy for three days, stayed smooth as glass, and the swells reached four feet before breaking in even lines. The water was in the sixties, so warm I didn't need a wet suit. That afternoon about three, two championship volleyball teams held a playoff. Miami had a six-foot-four giant with a spike that hit the sand like a Nike missile. But one scruffy Daytona player kept digging it out. The game lasted for over an hour until Daytona finally caved in. The day was great.

Except for the first and last lines, which carry the writer's responses, the entire piece is made up of specific details. In writing it's never enough just to state your response to an experience; you must also include the specifics behind it.

Use Listing or Clustering to Gather Material from Memory

As your writing assignments become more complex, you'll find that you need to collect more and more material in prewritten form. Either creating an expanded list or clustering your ideas will help you generate enough material to develop a solid rough draft by activating dormant memories. As you compile a memory list, for instance, one notation will lead to another in a series of associations you didn't know existed in your mind.

One way to begin a memory list is to focus your thinking on a subject by writing it at the top of a page. Sit quietly and let your mind drift back to the experience, recording everything that comes to you—descriptive details, names, dates, bits of dialogue, feelings, and such. As you develop the list, try to keep the flow going. Don't reject any items; even a weak idea may lead to better material. Later you can decide which ideas to exclude and which to expand and include in your rough draft. But if you edit your list too soon, you may inhibit the flow of ideas.

The following memory list was written by a student who wanted to recapture a childhood visit to a convalescent home where her grandmother was a patient. As she composed the list, she included as much specific detail as she could recall while noting her inner responses—that is, her thoughts and feelings.

Visit to The Palms

- 10 years old. I was mystified. Didn't know what one was—a convalescent home, that is. But I left with a childhood fear of being old.
- Two shabby palm trees out front. The buildings were pink stucco, though I didn't know what stucco was then.
- Old people everywhere. In wheelchairs sitting around the foyer. They seemed strange to my ten-year-old mind. Some babbled to themselves. Some slept, their heads bobbing forward and back. One woman stared at the stained ceiling and tapped her foot as if she were keeping time to music. Maybe the music was in her head, maybe in her soul.
- Smells: Urine. Disinfectant—Lysol? Everything was stuffy, no air. Felt I was suffocating.
- Walking down the hall. More people mumbling. One man who looked out of place, dressed in shirt and slacks, a full head of gray hair, seemed to be comfortable but kept yelling "Help! Help!" Attendants in white walked by him, paying no attention.
- Confused. Why do people come here? Who wants to live like this? I didn't think of them as "people."
- My grandmother. Withered, shrunken, crippled—she had a stroke. Seeing her made me realize they were all people because I remembered her as a younger, a different person.
- I remember seeing a photograph of her holding my mother and standing next to my grandfather. Then I didn't understand, but now I realize their smiles said how much in love they were.

- I have a snapshot of her much older—my grandfather had died by then—standing with my mother who was pregnant with me. How odd.
- Another photograph of the three of us when I was about seven. All of us squinting into the sun as if straining to see into the future. Her future took her to The Palms—where is mine taking me?

Composing a memory list, such as the one above, is an effective prewriting activity, but many writers prefer to arrange their memories in clusters because they find that clustering makes finding relations between ideas and details easier. To compile material through clustering, place the topic in the center of a page and circle it. Then as you recall your memories, arrange them around the central topic or in secondary clusters of similar ideas or details.

Sometimes clustering takes place in stages. You might begin by developing a general cluster of the dominant memories that come to you. Then you can return to the cluster and add details and other thoughts to refine the experience.

One writer used clustering to recapture the experience of a trip to Safari Land, an open-space animal park. Initially he clustered the experience as shown below.

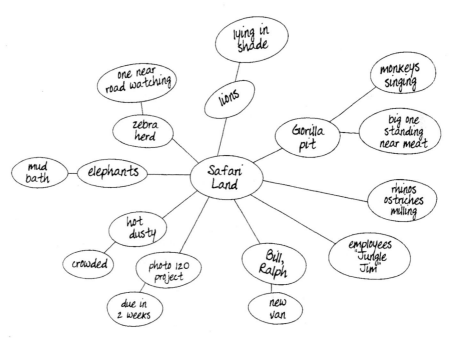

Once he had recaptured the dominant memories, he reviewed the cluster, probed his memory, and added more details and thoughts. A portion of his expanded cluster looked like this:

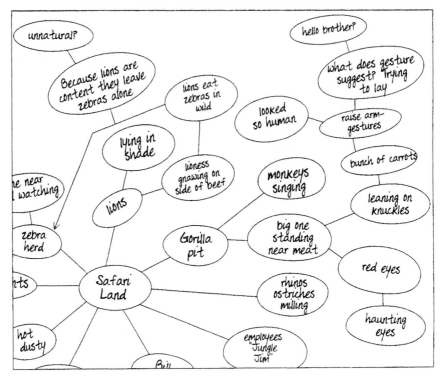

By creating a list or a cluster you will often discover a meaning in an experience that you hadn't realized was there. For instance, while composing a cluster of memories related to his trip to Safari Land, the writer made the ironic discovery that he is much like the wild animals that have been tamed because all their desires are taken care of. He planned to organize his paper around that response.

Use a Response to Organize Experience

Use your response to the experience to organize your narration. Your narration will be composed mainly of specific detail, but the response will let readers know how you feel or what you think about the experience. The abundance of details will help them see why you respond as you do.

A key tactic for this task is to select details that lead the reader to the same response you had. For instance, in the brief piece above, the writer included only the details that supported his response "It was a great day." He didn't describe the frustration he might have felt while searching for a parking place or standing in line for a hamburger. Instead, he selected details that supported his purpose: the heat, surf, warm water, and volleyball match.

There is a specific reason for including these details: to reflect his own response and so to trigger the same kind of response in the reader.

A writer can use specific details to suggest a deep personal meaning in an experience that could never be captured by direct statement. Writing of this kind is rich in implication and requires a great deal of concentration on the part of the reader. This is why it is all the more important for the writer to pay close attention to the narrative arrangement.

When writers relate an experience to readers, they usually arrange the narration in three parts: the orientation, complication, and resolution.

1. The *orientation* is often composed of a few opening sentences. These sentences orient the reader by suggesting the meaning of the experience and identifying the people involved, the place where the experience happened, when it happened, and the activity or situation. An effective orientation entices the reader to read on.

2. The *complication*, the body of the narration, is composed of scenes that dramatize the experience without explaining it. In the complication writers use such devices as description, dialogue, conflict, and suspense. The complication usually ends with a climax, the most dramatic moment of the experience. An effective complication should increase in tension, each scene becoming more dramatic than the last.

3. The *resolution* closes the narration and may be no longer than a sentence or two. In the resolution the writer makes the purpose clear, even though it might not be overtly stated. An effective resolution creates the impression that no other events that might have followed were important to the purpose.

For example, read the following passage to see narrative structure at work:

It Names Me Brother

Last week while touring Safari Land, I had the thought that many of us live like contented beasts. While we were driving through the gate decorated with jungle trimmings, a friend tapped me on the shoulder and pointed to a sign: "Keep your windows rolled up. Don't feed the animals."

The orientation is several sentences long. The writer suggests the meaning of the experience he will narrate. Notice how he also establishes that he is with friends; indicates what the activity is and where it takes place; and gives a sense of the time (last week). Notice, too, that he uses plenty of specific detail.

He laughed and said, "Wait till a lion eats your new van," before passing an open box of chicken to another friend sitting in the back seat.

I joined the procession of cars that twisted along the narrow road toward the hills. Soon we came to a herd of elephants prancing and rolling in a muddy pond. Nearby a man in a tattered safari costume stood by a jeep, filling the pond from a hose attached to a hydrant. Some fifty yards beyond, a pride of lions sprawled under a tree, one swishing its tail, others sleeping. Not far from them a lioness gnawed the remains of a side of beef. Within the lioness's easy spring, a herd of zebras grazed on hay as if blind to the age-old knowledge that lions live on zebra flesh. A strange world it seemed, where creatures that once filled my exotic dreams are tamed by having their needs met with water hoses, hunks of meat, and bales of hay. Then I heard someone mumble through a mouthful of chicken, "Look!"

The complication begins here. The writer develops a series of scenes that show that the animals are unnaturally contented.

Here the writer responds to what he has seen to guide the reader toward his conclusion.

Ahead, circled by a moat, was an island full of apes. Gibbons and chimps swung from rings. Gorillas leaned forward on their knuckles, watching the passing cars. Maneuvering around a Ford, I pulled to one side and stopped. One bull gorilla caught my eye. He lumbered forward, held back by

The bull gorilla moving forward and gesturing is the most dramatic moment of the experience—the climax. This event triggers the writer's insight.

the moat's edge. I raised my camera, my lens tapping against the window glass. My shutter clicked. As if he heard, the gorilla lifted a hairy arm and held out a fist filled with bunches of carrots. I clicked again, while he drew the fist back to his chest. Was he gesturing at me to join him? Did he believe all that separated us was the moat and glass? He continued to stare, the red eyes conveying a message that cannot be spoken.

After a long moment, I glanced away from the gorilla's eyes and surveyed the van that now seemed like a cage: the plush carpet, the expensive stereo system, and my two friends who munched away at chicken wings and legs. Finally, I glanced back at the staring creature and understood his gesture: It named me brother with desires as small as any beast's.

The resolution successfully completes the narration. The writer ends with a response to the experience, thus bringing the narration to a close.

You may have noticed that this piece is thick with specific detail. But did you see that the writer carefully selected those specifics to support the general response that suggests that he, like the creatures in Safari Land, is a captive of his own desires?

After the orientation that gets the piece under way, the writer describes the elephants, lions, zebras, and apes as contented creatures that have given up their natural urges in this "strange world, where creatures . . . are tamed by having their needs met." His response deepens and grows into personal insight when he encounters the gesturing bull gorilla with the massive fist filled with carrots. Of course, the beast isn't attempting to communicate what the writer feels; the writer simply responds to its gesture in this way. He interprets it.

Did you also notice that even the details that might seem unnecessary at first glance serve a purpose? The new van, for instance, functions as a desire that makes the writer captive. His chicken-eating friends may be looked at as contented animals, his companions in captivity. The point is that this writer has selected specific details in an attempt to trigger in the reader a response similar to his own.

Before going on to the next example, we want to mention something about the arrangement of the Safari Land piece. It's constructed in a climactic sequence. The word *climactic* comes from the word *climax*—the point of greatest intensity that ends a series or progression of events. To arrange a piece in climactic order is to put the most significant part last. Climactic order is an effective way to arrange a paper that deals with personal insights.

Take a look at the next example. Notice how the student blends his inner responses with the specific details he has associated with them. Since he's dealing with personal insight, he arranges the piece so that the climactic point comes at the end. First read the selection through without studying the marginal comments. Then reread it along with the commentary for a more thorough understanding.

Lost Children

While walking through the supermarket last night, I became uneasy about my life. I had just come from home where I had seen the evening news. There had been a report of earthquake destruction in Central America. The report featured a film of a city that had collapsed. It showed lost children roaming through the ruins and men and women in shock, sitting in the rubble of their homes. It showed heaps of bodies waiting to be cremated. A reporter's voice commented on possible starvation and epidemic. The whole thing hit me hard. I thought about the emptiness the survivors must feel and about how they must feel about the future.

The orientation introduces the main elements. It gives the reader the necessary background information.

"The report featured" begins the complication and gives a concrete description of the report's specifics that relate to the writer's feelings.

"The whole thing hit me hard" begins a sequence of the writer's inner responses.

But life, my life, couldn't stop. My refrigerator and cupboards were empty; I had to work the next day, and there were places to go and people to meet, as the saying goes. So an hour later I was pushing a cart through Ralph's, but I still didn't feel good. Something was eating away at me. I hurried to stock up on groceries for the week—some oranges, apples, a head of lettuce, juice, milk, a chicken, and a pound of beef. I began to notice other people shopping around me: some together, chatting and smiling, and some alone, lifting items from shelves and comparing prices.

"My refrigerator and cupboards were empty" prepares the reader for the next phase and ties back to "But life, my life, couldn't stop."

"So an hour later" is an overt transition into the next supermarket phase. The writer continues to blend in feelings—"I still didn't feel good. Something was eating away at me"— while generating a realistic description of the market.

Pushing the cart toward the checkout stand, I tried to understand the feeling that seemed to be deepening in me. Just foolishness, I thought. I must have become lost in my thoughts, for my cart slammed into another shopper's. I glanced at her. Her eyes sparkled at my mistake. Her tan skin seemed golden, and each eyebrow was perfectly shaped. Then I glanced over her shoulder and saw a poster advertising a charity. The photograph of a lost, half-naked child holding an empty bowl, the eyes pleading, seemed to leap at me. At that moment, the images from the news rose up in my mind—the ruined homes, lost children, starvation—

The phrase "tried to understand the feeling" reminds readers of the main issue and nudges them toward the climax.

"I must have become lost in my thoughts" begins the display of the shopper and starving child that crystallize the writer's personal insight.

The one-sentence resolution gives his insight and reminds readers of details mentioned earlier, thus creating a sense of roundness.

and I felt anger and frustration as I realized how

helpless I was, and how spoiled.

WRITING TASK—RESPONDING TO EXPERIENCE

In 350 to 400 words narrate a meaningful experience. The experience, which may be from the distant or near past, should be one that holds some interest for you, one that brought some insight or new awareness that you can communicate to a reader. To begin, compose a memory list or cluster that includes both inner responses and specific details.

A word of caution: Don't choose a long-term relationship to describe. Relationships are much too complex for such a brief assignment. You might, however, pick just one incident from a complex relationship. Choose a date, an argument, or a chance meeting—an event that embodies the meaning of the relationship.

Remember:

1. Use listing or clustering to compose a prewritten draft.
2. Use a general response to organize your paper.
3. Write a rough draft based on the list or cluster that illustrates your responses with plenty of specific detail.
4. Try to get your reader to visualize the experience.
5. Arrange your material in climactic order, showcasing the most dramatic part at the end.
6. When you write the final draft, imagine a reader looking over your shoulder to help you shape your paper coherently.

GROUP WORK

Group members should feel free to consult each other during each stage of the writing process.

For the final draft, exchange papers and read to identify the orientation, complication, and the resolution. Is this draft developed effectively? Does it have an effective climax?

Part Two
WRITING TASKS

Part Two presents a variety of tasks designed to teach principles of good writing. They range from short paragraphs that emphasize patterns of organization to longer, more complicated essays. Some are accompanied by many examples and thorough discussions that we hope will guide you through the possible pitfalls of the tasks. Others have a minimum of explanation and illustration.

How should you approach this part? That depends on the skill you already have. There's no reason for you to start at the beginning and go to the end. Instead, your teacher will guide you through a sequence of tasks to help develop your writing strengths.

4

Paragraph Structure

Part One contained writing tasks designed to teach you a composing process we hope you will use for all your writing assignments. You practiced the four steps of that process—prewriting, rough draft, editing and revising, and final draft—with assignments that demanded few decisions about organization. We suspect you found it easy to arrange the content you selected from your prewritten lists or clusters because the material fell neatly in chronological or spatial order. But the tasks in the following sections require more conscious choices about structure. In that respect they are typical of the writing you will be expected to do in other courses. Some of the tasks require only one paragraph; some can be better handled in two or three paragraphs; still others will require longer, multiparagraph essays. In any case, as in all prose, the paragraph is the fundamental unit of organization.

Of course paragraphs come in a great variety. In an essay a writer may use one kind of paragraph to introduce the subject and other kinds to develop different portions of the main idea, to summarize evidence presented or arguments made up to a certain part of the essay, to provide a transition between major parts of the essay, or to conclude the essay. If dialogue is included in the paper, paragraphing is used to indicate a change of speaker. The point is that paragraphing is put to a variety of uses in prose writing.

The pages that follow in this chapter, though, concentrate on the most frequently used, the most basic kind of paragraphs—those intended to present one part of an essay's central point; in other words, the paragraphs that serve as major building blocks in the body of an essay (see Deductive Essay, Chapter 14).

A well-structured paragraph consists of several sentences that discuss a single idea. A paragraph can stand alone as a brief work, but usually a paragraph functions as part of a longer piece of writing. Successful, fully developed paragraphs, regardless of differences in plan and content, share three characteristics:

1. *Unity:* All of the sentences in the paragraph contribute to the same idea.
2. *Coherence:* The thought proceeds logically from sentence to sentence.
3. *Adequate development:* The paragraph contains enough information to convey the idea in a reasonably thorough manner.

By studying the following paragraph you can see how Olivia Vlahos, author of *Human Beginnings*, applies the principles of good paragraph structure. Vlahos develops a single idea—in this case, that all living creatures communicate in some form. First, she maintains unity by making every sentence relate to this single idea. Second, she achieves coherence by repeating similar sentence structures, only varying these structures in the closing two sentences. Finally, as the third characteristic of a well-structured paragraph, she adequately develops her subject by listing five examples of how animals, including humans, communicate.

Nearly all living creatures manage some form of communication. The dance patterns of bees in their hive help to point the way to distant flower fields or announce successful foraging. Male stickleback fish regularly swim upside-down to indicate outrage in a courtship contest. Male deer and lemurs mark territorial ownership by rubbing their own body secretions on boundary stones or trees. Everyone has seen a frightened dog put his tail between his legs and run in panic. We, too, use gestures, expressions, postures, and movement to give our words point.

The opening sentence identifies the single topic Vlahos will develop. The topic is developed by several examples.

Using a Topic Sentence

Frequently a writer uses a topic sentence to announce the content of a paragraph to a reader. In the earlier paragraph about communication among living creatures, the topic sentence is a clearly phrased, direct statement that begins the paragraph,

Nearly all living creatures manage some form of communication.

Most topic sentences are direct statements:

The invention of the telephone has influenced the way we live in innumerable ways, some less obvious than others.
Wyoming cowboys have four distinct styles of dress.
Sherlock Holmes and Doctor Watson were the first "buddies" in what was to become a pattern in detective stories.
Vandals affect a community no matter how prepared it is.

Consider how useful a topic sentence can be for readers and writers. For readers, a topic sentence states the main idea of the paragraph (usually at or near the beginning) so they know immediately what the more specific sentences of the paragraph add up to. Imagine the burden you place on a reader if you give several examples but never say directly what the examples have in common.

For writers, a topic sentence serves as a reminder of the boundaries of the paragraph, thereby helping them to stick to the point and develop a unified paragraph. Once you have a clear topic sentence, you will find it easier to complete the paragraph. If you find it difficult to write a topic sentence, perhaps you need to think more about your material. Or you may want to write the other sentences of the paragraph first and phrase the topic sentence later. In any case, what you include in a topic sentence depends on your material and on how you decide to organize it.

What makes an effective topic sentence? An effective topic sentence has the following characteristics:

1. It has a subject and a controlling idea.
2. It is limited enough to be developed in one paragraph.
3. It lends itself to development.

The topic sentence "Good listeners not only hear what is said, but also understand nonverbal messages" has these three characteristics. It has a subject, "listeners," and a controlling idea, "understand nonverbal messages." It is reasonably limited in scope, because the writer has not staked out the entire territory of listening skills. And although it may be true that an expert could write several hundred pages on nonverbal messages, it is also true that a fairly satisfactory discussion could be presented in one paragraph. Finally, the sentence lends itself to development. The writer could follow with examples of such nonverbal messages and interpret them for the reader. That, in fact, is what a reader will probably be expecting after reading this first sentence.

In contrast, the topic sentence "Nonverbal language is interesting" is less focused; and, therefore, it is less clear just what information should follow. Besides that, the tone has changed. The first sentence promises information; the second merely states an attitude. The reader doesn't know what's coming and may be thinking, "Oh, yeah! Not to me!"

How about this sentence: "The guinea pig is a member of the rat family"? You probably noticed right away that this sentence does not meet the third characteristic above. It does not lend itself to further development. It may be a useful fact to know and it could be followed by other facts about guinea pigs, but where is the controlling idea that brings these facts together for a reader? Without a controlling idea, any number of unrelated facts could be included and presented in any order. In short, this example is not a topic sentence at all—just a fact.

As you write topic sentences, ask yourself if they have the three characteristics we have been discussing. For example:

Topic Sentence

Rabies is a real reason to fear wolves.

Subject?	Rabies in wolves
Controlling Idea?	Rabies in wolves is a real threat
Limited?	Yes
Development?	Description of the danger rabid wolves have posed

Topic Sentence

Temporary workers, often referred to as "disposable workers," have legitimate reasons to be angry.

Subject?	Temporary workers
Controlling Idea?	Have legitimate reasons to be angry
Limited?	Yes
Development?	Presentation of reasons for temporary worker anger

Topic Sentence

Writing is a deeply personal process, full of mystery and surprise.

Subject?	Writing
Controlling Idea?	A mysterious, surprising process that reflects individual writers

Limited? | Yes
Development? | Description of the writing process from a personal perspective that emphasizes mystery and surprise

Topic Sentence

Although Anne Rice and Joan Didion are contemporary women fiction writers, the experiences they capture are startlingly different.

Subject? | The fictional experiences that Anne Rice and Joan Didion capture in their work
Controlling Idea? | How these experiences differ
Limited? | Yes
Development? | Contrast Rice's content with Didion's

Topic Sentence

Students interested in a career in landscape architecture often visit the Randolph Nursery to see the miniature replicas of the world's most famous gardens.

Subject? | Students of landscape architecture
Controlling Idea? | Often visit Randolph Nursery
Limited? | Yes
Development? | The writer will have trouble here. The controlling idea—"often visit"—does not lend itself to development very well. It seems to require a list of the times visited—not a very interesting content. Probably the writer intends to describe the miniature gardens. If so, the sentence should be rephrased to make the gardens the subject.

Topic Sentence Rephrased

Randolph Nursery's miniature replicas of the world's most famous gardens are a valuable resource for landscape architecture students.

Now the miniature garden replicas serve as the subject of the paragraph. Their value as a resource for landscape architecture students serves as the controlling idea. The development can include description and a discussion of what can be learned by visiting the gardens.

Placing the Topic Sentence

Jonathan Weiner, in the following paragraph from his book *The Next One Hundred Years*, places his topic sentence squarely at the beginning of the paragraph.

> *Even though ozone is poisonous to breathe, in its proper place, the stratosphere, the gas is vital for our health.* It blocks ultraviolet rays from the Sun that would otherwise damage the DNA molecules in birds, bees, green leaves, and human skin down here on the ground. It is like an invisible membrane between Earth and outer space. About 500 light-years from Earth, in the shoulder of the constellation of Orion, there is a red supergiant star called Betelgeuse, whose diameter is almost a thousand times that of our Sun. Astronomers believe that Betelgeuse is now nearing the end of its life and may be about to explode—perhaps some time in the next few thousands or tens of thousands of years. One astronomer has conjectured that if Betelgeuse explodes into a supernova, it will shower our region of space with such intense ultraviolet light and X-rays that it will strip off Earth's ozone layer. Then the ultraviolet light of our own Sun will fry the biosphere.

By immediately announcing the subject and the controlling idea—ozone is vital for our health—in the opening sentence, Weiner prepares the reader for the specific reasons that follow. Sometimes a writer will structure a topic sentence as a question and place it at the beginning of a paragraph. Phil Donahue in a paragraph from *The Human Animal* begins with a question that serves as a topic sentence.

> *Bees get together and build hives, termites build mounds, beavers build dams, and spiders spin webs, but what other animal can change stone and glass into poetry?* Other animals can alter their environment at the margins, but only we can transform our environment so completely that we reshape our destiny. Alone in the animal kingdom, we can set goals for ourselves and then pursue them. The dream of the medieval craftsmen who built Chartres was to secure a place for themselves in heaven. By lavishing love on their stone and glass, they glorified God and hoped to be rewarded in the next life. But in the process, they changed this life, made it more beautiful and more worth living.

Sometimes the controlling idea of a topic sentence is refined by one or two sentences that follow it, a method Suzanne Gordon uses in the following example:

It is rare to find people who actually like to be single and want to stay that way. What one finds more frequently are men and women who say they adore being single but who spend most of their nonworking time looking for some kind of sexual or romantic attachment. Tony, for example, has a certain image of life with a woman. It includes fidelity, marriage, domesticity. But until he finds the particular woman with whom he can have total communication he won't give up his freedom. He has had several almost-major involvements in the past years. But each time he started measuring the current woman against his mental image. Reality never quite matched the ideal: the woman was too thin; they didn't really have that much in common—there were always objections. And he'd begin to long for his single days again. The last time this had happened, the woman found someone else. And he continued on his rounds of the single life. After a time Tony watched the woman get more and more involved with her new man. He began to rethink his relationship with her. She was actually more intelligent, prettier, and more sexually exciting than he had realized. She would not have been a bad person to spend a life with. He even talked to her about that prospect, but she was too attached to her new beau, and they were thinking of living together.

Although placing a topic sentence at the beginning of a paragraph is sound practice, and we strongly advise you to follow that practice in formal assignments, a writer will sometimes place it in another part of the paragraph or, if the controlling idea can be clearly understood from the discussion, leave it out entirely.

Reporter Robin Roberts places the topic sentence at the end as a conclusion to be drawn from the details that come before it.

If you watch a Little League game, in most cases the pitchers are the most mature. They throw harder, and if they throw accurately very few batters can hit the ball. Consequently, it makes good baseball sense for most hitters to take the pitch. Don't swing. Hope for a walk. That could be a player's instruction for four years. The fun is in hitting the ball; the coach says don't swing. That may be sound baseball, but it does nothing to help a young player develop his hitting. *What would seem like a basic training ground for baseball often turns out to be a program of negative thoughts that only retards a young player.*

If a writer chooses to leave out a topic sentence, then the controlling idea must emerge from the paragraph's details. Robert T. Bakker leaves out the topic sentence in the following paragraph from *The Dinosaur Heresies.*

Humans are proud of themselves. The guiding principle of the modern age is "Man is the measure of all things." And our bodies have excited physiologists and philosophers to a profound awe of the basic mammalian design. But the history of dinosaurs should teach us some humility. The basic equipment of our mammalian class—warm bodies clothed in fur, milk-producing breasts to nourish our young—is quite ancient. These mammalian hallmarks are as old as the dinosaurs themselves. Indeed, the Class Mammalia emerged fully defined, in the world ecosystems just as Dinosauria began their spectacular expansion. If our fundamental mammalian mode of adaptation was superior to the dinosaurs', then history should record the meteoric rise of the mammals and the eclipse of the dinosaurs. Our own Class Mammalia did not seize the dominant position in life on land. Instead, the mammal clan was but one of many separate evolutionary families that succeeded as a species only by taking refuge in small body size during the Age of Dinosaurs. As long as there were dinosaurs, a full 130 million years, the warm-blooded league of furry mammals produced no species bigger than a cat. When the first dinosaur quarry was opened in 1822 at Stonesfield, England, quarry men found the one-ton *Megalosaurus* and a tiny mammal.

The adaptability to environmental conditions of mammals and dinosaurs is the subject of Bakker's paragraph, but the controlling idea, which questions the popular belief that early mammals were more adaptable than dinosaurs, is not directly stated.

CLOSING WITH A CLINCHER

Writers who have begun a paragraph with a topic sentence will often end with a clincher—a sentence or two that restates the controlling idea in different words, summarizes the discussion, or offers the writer's personal response to the material. In the following paragraph from *Illiterate America*, Jonathan Kozol ends with a clincher that dramatically restates his controlling idea in specific detail.

Many illiterates cannot read the admonition on a pack of cigarettes. Neither the Surgeon General's warning nor its reproduction on the package can alert them to the risks. Although most people learn by word of mouth that smoking is related to a number of grave physical disorders, they do not get the chance to read the detailed stories which can document this danger with the vividness that turns concern into determination to resist. They can see the handsome cowboy or the slim Virginia lady lighting up a filter cigarette; they cannot heed the words that tell them that this product is (not "may be") dangerous to their health. Sixty million men and women are condemned to be unalerted, high-risk candidates for cancer.

Developing a Paragraph

How long should a paragraph be? Paragraph length depends on many things: the complexity of the idea; the method of development; the length of adjacent paragraphs if it is part of a longer work; and the age, knowledge, interest, and educational background of its intended audience. Most important, a paragraph should be developed enough to do justice to the controlling idea expressed in the topic sentence.

Short paragraphs are easier to read, but a paper consisting of two- or three-sentence paragraphs may make the entire effort seem immature and underdeveloped. Long paragraphs seem more intellectual and weighty, but too many of them may discourage a reader and make the subject appear more difficult and intricate than it actually is.

The best approach, really, is not to worry much about paragraph length. Instead, concentrate on fully developing the controlling idea in your topic sentence by including enough specific supporting information to avoid skimpy, immature paragraphs, such as the one that follows.

> A number of curious experiences occur at the onset of sleep. A person just about to go to sleep may experience an odd physical sensation, the most common of which is the sense of floating or falling. A nearly universal occurrence at the beginning of sleep (although not everyone recalls it) is a sudden jerk of the body. The onset of sleep is not gradual at all. It happens in an instant.

Obviously, the above paragraph suffers from underdevelopment. The writer needs to add more specific information and concrete details to develop the topic sentence adequately. Now study the original paragraph as Peter Farb wrote it. Notice how the addition of information and specific details (placed in italics in the passage) turns an underdeveloped paragraph into a fully developed one.

> A number of curious experiences occur at the onset of sleep. A person just about to go to sleep *may experience an electric shock, a flash of light, or a crash of thunder*—but the most common sensation is that of floating or falling, *which is why "falling asleep" is a scientifi-*

cally valid description. A nearly universal occurrence at the beginning of sleep (although not everyone recalls it) is a sudden, *uncoordinated jerk of the head, the limbs,* or even the entire body. *Most people tend to think of going to sleep as a slow slippage into oblivion,* but the onset of sleep is not gradual at all. It happens in an instant. *One moment the individual is awake, the next moment not.*

When you find that you have written an underdeveloped paragraph, there is no need to moan and wring your hands. Instead, use prewriting techniques to generate more detail—that is, develop another list or create a new cluster. You can then integrate the detail into a revised version of your paragraph.

Achieving Unity

A paragraph is unified when all the sentences clearly relate to the controlling idea expressed in the topic sentence. Read Lael Morgan's paragraph from "Let the Eskimos Hunt" to see how the supporting information and details relate the idea that many people oppose hunting even where animal populations are dangerously large.

<u>Many Americans mindlessly oppose hunting, even in cases where animal populations are dangerously high.</u> In some areas of Alaska, wolves have become so prolific they are running out of hunting ground and prey heavily on moose, deer, and occasionally dogs. In the past, game managers curbed wolf populations by trapping and aerial hunting without wiping out the species. Still, whenever they propose to do this nowadays, they receive tens of thousands of letters in protest. Growing deer populations in parts of California threaten to starve themselves out. Sea-otter colonies, burgeoning along the Pacific coast, are fast running out of	*Topic sentence* *Establishes that some areas are over-populated.* *Charges that some people oppose even sensibly controlled hunting.* *Shows the dangers of uncontrolled animal population growth.*

fodder, too, as well as putting commercial fisher-

men out of business.

Now read the following paragraph for unity problems. As you read, identify the supporting sentences to see if they relate to the controlling idea in the topic sentence.

(1) Attending this college may be unexpectedly dangerous. (2) Last week in the parking lot my friend Bill accidentally bumped the side of a pickup. (3) Just as he was finishing a note to leave on the windshield, the owner came up, scowled at the grapefruit-size dent, then punched Bill in the nose. (4) He then drove off without looking back or taking Bill's name and address. (5) At least Bill didn't have to pay for the damage. (6) Three days ago a bicyclist wearing portable radio earphones plowed into a psychology instructor, and both went sprawling over the walkway. (7) Yesterday, in the zoology lab, a four-foot snake slipped from its cage. (8) No one noticed until it struck at one student, sending four others into shock. (9) Then the lab technician came in, snatched up the snake, and stuffed it back into the cage. (10) No one plans to sue the college, but those students have a good case if any of them would press it.

No doubt you'll agree that in the following sentences the writer strays from the controlling idea that the college campus may be an unexpectedly dangerous place.

(4) He then drove off without looking back or taking Bill's name and address.
(5) At least Bill didn't have to pay for the damage.
(9) Then the lab technician came in, snatched up the snake, and stuffed it back into the cage.
(10) No one plans to sue the college, but those students have a good case if any of them would press it.

Each of these sentences gives additional information about the incidents, but they digress from the controlling point. While revising the paragraph for unity, the writer will delete some details and subordinate other details so that each sentence clearly relates to the controlling idea in the topic sentence. Revised, the paragraph reads as follows:

Topic sentence

Attending this college may be unexpectedly

dangerous. Last week in the parking lot my friend

Bill accidentally bumped the side of a pickup.

Just as he was finishing a note to leave on the

```
windshield, the owner came up, scowled at the
```
Integrated details

```
grapefruit-size dent, then punched Bill in the

nose before driving off without taking Bill's name

and address. Three days ago a bicyclist wearing
```
Sentence 5 deleted

```
portable radio earphones plowed into a psychology

instructor, and both went sprawling over the walk-

way. Yesterday in the zoology lab a four-foot
```
Integrated details

```
snake slipped from its cage. No one noticed until

it struck at one student, sending four others into

shock before the lab technician came in, snatched

up the snake, and stuffed it back into the cage.
```
Sentence 10 deleted

Maintaining Coherence

A paragraph is coherent when the sentences proceed logically from one to the other. Generally, a writer achieves coherence in one of four ways:

1. By arranging the supporting information in a logical order, such as time order, space order, order of climax, specific-to-general order, or general-to-specific order
2. By using transitional words and phrases to guide the reader overtly
3. By repeating key words and phrases
4. By using parallel structure

When a paragraph is incoherent, it reads as if the sentences are disconnected, making readers feel that they must leap from thought to thought.

Study the following paragraph by Laurence Perrine about the psychological differences between ghost and horror stories and great literary works that evoke horror. Notice how Perrine maintains coherence by contrasting details, arranging them in general-to-specific order, and how he uses parallel structure to emphasize the contrast. Also notice how he uses transitional phrases and restates key ideas.

```
Most of us enjoy the goose flesh and the tingle
```
The second sentence restates in more concrete language the thought expressed in the opening sentence.

```
along the spine produced by the successful ghost

story. There is something agreeable in letting our
```

blood be chilled by bats in the moonlight, gutter-

ing candles, creaking doors, eerie shadows, pierc-

ing screams, inexplicable blood-stains, and weird

noises. But <u>the terror aroused by tricks and</u>

Perrine has placed the topic sentence in the middle of the paragraph.

<u>external "machinery" is a far cry from the terror</u>

<u>evoked by some terrifying treatment of the human</u>

<u>situation.</u> The horror we experience in watching

This sentence is arranged in a parallel fashion.

the Werewolf or Dracula or Frankenstein is far

less significant than that we get from watching the

bloody ambition of MacBeth or the jealousy of

Perrine arranges the closing sentences with contrasting parallel clauses and uses transitional phrases to guide the reader.

Othello. <u>In the first,</u> terror is the end-product;

<u>in the second,</u> it is the natural accompaniment of

a powerful revelation of life. <u>In the first,</u> we are

always aware of a basic unreality; <u>in the second,</u>

reality is terrifying.

Remember, whether you develop a paragraph by contrast, as Perrine does in the preceding example, or whether you use some other method discussed in the following chapters, you must make your sentences proceed logically from beginning to end—you must maintain coherence.

WRITING TASK—PARAGRAPH STRUCTURE

Write a paragraph that reflects the principles of well-written paragraphs as discussed in this chapter. Feel free to use your own subject or use one of the following three assignments.

1. The following topic sentences are either too general or too factual. Revise one of them to make it an effective topic sentence and to reflect your own experiences and interests. After composing a prewritten draft, write a well-structured paragraph that supports the controlling idea of the revised sentence. Remember, write only one paragraph, not one for each topic sentence.
   a. Hollywood films have both good and bad features.

    b. Vandalism is a problem in urban, suburban, and rural areas.

    c. People must assume responsibility for their actions.

    d. Consumer complaint departments are busy in department stores.

    e. Everyone believes that travel is educational.

    f. Grading policies are different for different classes.

    g. Going to college is expensive.

    h. Dieting is the world's fastest-growing sport.

    i. Part-time jobs teach high school students important lessons.

    j. Computers may or may not be tomorrow's teachers.

2. Read the following paragraph, from "How TV Violence Damages Your Children" by Victor B. Cline, which concentrates on the relation between televised violence and real-life violence.

> Much of the research that has led to the conclusion that TV and movie violence could cause aggressive behavior in some children has stemmed from the work in the area of imitative learning or modeling which, reduced to its simplest expression, might be termed "monkey see, monkey do." Research by Stanford psychologist Albert Bandura has shown that even brief exposure to novel aggressive behavior on a one-time basis can be repeated in free play by as high as 88 percent of the young children seeing it on TV. Dr. Bandura also demonstrated that even a single viewing of a novel aggressive act could be recalled and produced by children six months later, without any intervening exposure. Earlier studies have estimated that the average child between the ages of 5 and 15 will witness, during this 10-year period, the violent destruction of more than 13,400 fellow humans. This means that through several hours of TV-watching, a child may see more violence than the average adult experiences in a lifetime. Killing is as common as taking a walk, a gun more natural than an umbrella. Children are thus taught to take pride in force and violence and to feel ashamed of ordinary sympathy.

Do some televised programs and movies teach children to take pride in force and violence as Cline suggests? Perhaps they do and perhaps they don't—you can't be certain. You can be certain of what you observe, though, and perhaps you've seen children imitating televised events and situations in their free play.

Write a paragraph that concentrates on the relation of televised violence to children's play. Whereas Cline deals generally with the problem, you are to deal specifically with it—that is, you are to write from your own observations. Begin by composing a topic sentence that states something to the effect that children model televised violence. Use specific information based on your observations of children, such as a younger brother or sister, neighbors, or schoolchildren. You might even include specific information from your childhood experiences with modeling violent events or situations you had seen televised. To get your paragraph started, compose a prewritten draft of your subject and use it as the basis for your paragraph.

3. Write a paragraph on the subject of "stars," any kind of stars— night stars, movie stars, football, baseball, tennis stars, the little gold stars teachers did or didn't stick to the tops of your school papers, even five-star generals. Set your imagination free (how about "starry-eyed"?) The only restriction is that your final paragraph must embody the principles of a well-written paragraph as we've discussed them in this chapter.

Remember:

1. Begin with prewriting.
2. Organize your paragraph by using a topic sentence that announces the subject and controlling idea, is limited, and lends itself to development.
3. Be sure your paragraph is fully developed.
4. Check to see if it is unified.
5. Be sure it is coherent by applying transitional techniques.

Suggestion: Pay particular attention to the topic sentence. If it is poorly constructed, the entire paragraph might go astray.

GROUP WORK

Work in groups of three. Exchange final drafts and read for the following: Can the topic sentence be developed? Is it clear? Is it limited? Is the draft unified and coherent? Offer helpful advice.

5

Examples

An excellent way to develop paragraphs is through examples, which can transform the facts and assertions of a topic sentence into concrete pictures that stick in a reader's mind. Writers generally use two kinds of examples: typical and specific.

Typical Examples

Typical examples, as opposed to specific examples, are timeless and general (but not overgeneral and vague). Writers often compose typical examples by generalizing from experiences gathered from many specific observations.

Roxanne Arnold, reporting the results of a poll taken among state lottery players, offers typical examples of the strategies that habitual players adopt to increase their chances of winning. She starts with a general introductory sentence about lottery players being a "varied lot," follows with a topic sentence that limits her attention to the "peculiar strategies and gimmicks" players use, and develops her paragraph with several examples of typical behavior.

As might be expected, the poll revealed lot-

tery players to be a varied lot. <u>Much like the</u>

<u>eccentric handicappers found at race tracks, they</u>

<u>have their own peculiar strategies and gimmicks</u>

<u>for bringing them luck.</u> For the most fatalistic

Topic sentence limits the subject and suggests examples will follow.

among them, superstition governs how, when and
where to scratch off the latex-covered tickets.
There are sweeping, single-motion scratches, others who savor the suspense of uncovering the tickets square by square. Some pick their patterns
randomly and others scratch the same sequence
ticket after ticket. There are players who buy in
three's, some who buy in four's or five's. There
are players who carry lucky pen knives or favorite
coins and others who call in pinch hitters to do
their scratching for them. There are pools of
players. In offices, factories and businesses,
workers are teaming up in lottery clubs of 10 and
20, banking on the notion that bigger purchases
improve the odds. But no matter what tactic they
use, nearly all the lottery diehards have the same
aim—to win, and to win big.

Typical examples of scratch-off strate-gies and buying patterns follow.

Clincher ends the paragraph.

The examples Arnold uses are typical; that is, the behaviors are repeated
time after time by a variety of people.

Peter Farb and George Armelagos use typical examples to develop the
following paragraph from *Consuming Passions: The Anthropology of Eating.*
Farb and Armelagos begin the paragraph with three sentences of background
information related to the subject of medieval table manners. In the fourth
sentence they state the paragraph's central idea—by modern standards even
the best of medieval table manners were crude. They then develop the rest of
the paragraph through typical examples.

Among the important societal rules that represent one component of cuisine are table manners.
As a socially instilled form of conduct, they

Opening sentences provide back-ground information related to medieval society's crude table man-ners.

reveal the attitudes typical of a society. Changes in table manners through time, as they have been documented for western Europe, likewise reflect fundamental changes in human relationships.

<u>Medieval courtiers saw their table manners as distinguishing them from crude peasants; but by modern standards, the manners were exactly the opposite.</u> Feudal lords used their unwashed hands to scoop food from a common bowl, and they passed around a single goblet from which all drank. A finger or two would be extended while eating, so as to be kept free of grease and thus available for the next course, or for dipping into spices and condiments—possibly accounting for today's "polite" custom of extending the finger while holding a spoon or small fork. Soups and sauces were commonly drunk by lifting the bowl to the mouth; several diners frequently ate from the same bread trencher. Even lords and nobles would toss gnawed bones back into the common dish, wolf down their food, spit onto the table (preferred conduct called for spitting under it), and blow their noses into the table cloth.

Topic sentence

The topic sentence is developed through a series of typical examples that illustrate the crude table manners of medieval society.

Farb and Armelagos's typical examples of medieval table manners are based on research rather than on direct observation. Often, however, writers generalize about their own personal observations and experience. For example, in the following paragraph a student writer offers her conclusions about the way typical coffee and soap commercials depict housewives. Her analysis is rooted in her own experience.

<u>Many coffee and detergent commercials present degrading images of housewives.</u> Loyal but fearful, the typical housewife in these commercials seems to live in terror of failing to serve her husband a good cup of coffee or get his laundry clean. Coffee commercials often show the husband sipping a cup of her latest brew. Disappointed by the taste, he complains, usually in front of a neighbor. Humiliated publicly, the housewife listens to the neighbor's advice: "Use Brand X, it has robust flavor!" Many detergent commercials create a similarly degrading image. The typical housewife in these commercials faces public humiliation when she fails in her efforts to get her husband's shirts clean. "Ring around the collar! Ring around the collar!" her husband's colleagues whisper among themselves. Moreover, her laundry must look as white, feel as soft, and smell as fresh as the neighbor's, or the entire neighborhood will be sure to break out in song about her failure. Do housewives become as distraught as their harassed counterparts on television? I doubt it. Certainly housewives, and everyone else for that matter, realize that a ring around the collar is not going to strangle anyone and that brewing a weak cup of

The writer opens with a topic sentence.

She adds a sentence that further develops the topic sentence.

A typical example develops one part of the topic sentence.

She uses a transitional sentence to lead the reader into the second typical example, which develops another part of the topic sentence.

At this point, the writer adds some closing thoughts and ends with a clincher.

coffee is not grounds for divorce. <u>To create</u>

<u>commercial images of housewives who appear to</u>

<u>think of nothing else is to degrade housewives in</u>   *Clincher*

<u>general</u>.

Now consider a paragraph from psychologist Erich Fromm. Notice that the examples Fromm uses differ from the other illustrations we've presented in this section. They are not grounded in observation or research. They are logical generalizations about human behavior, sometimes called hypothetical examples. Fromm uses them not as factual information but to impress his reader with the idea that people with different attitudes will view an experience differently.

What is, for example, the attitude of different people toward a forest? A painter who has gone there to paint, the owner of the forest who wishes to evaluate his business prospects, an officer who is interested in the tactical problem of defending the area, a hiker who wants to enjoy himself—each of them will have an entirely different concept of the forest because a different aspect is significant to each one. The painter's experience will be one of form and color; the businessman's of size, number, and age of trees; the officer's of visibility and protection; the hiker's of trails and motion. While they can all agree to the abstract statement that they can stand at the edge of the forest, the different kinds of activity they are set to accomplish will determine their experience of "seeing a forest."

Though Fromm's paragraph is structurally complicated—instead of arranging his examples one after the other he mixes them throughout—he still follows the method of developing his point with typical examples.

Specific Examples

In contrast to typical examples, which are composed by generalizing from extensive research or observation, specific examples capture a single experience, fact, or event, which may also come from research or observation. In the following paragraph from "The Frontier," Richard Shenkman uses specific examples to show that the popular image of the "wild west" is mainly a Hollywood creation.

The popular image of the frontier as a place   *Background information introduces*
                                                        the subject.
of violence is only partly due to the fact that

the place often was violent. Most of it is due to

hype, particularly Hollywood hype. <u>The truth is</u>

<u>many more people have died in Hollywood westerns</u>

<u>than ever died on the real frontier (Indian wars</u>

<u>considered apart).</u> In the real Dodge City, for

instance, there were just five killings in 1878,

the most homicidal year in the little town's fron-

tier history—scarcely enough to sustain a typical

two-hour movie. In the most violent year in Dead-

wood, South Dakota, only four people were killed.

In the worst year in Tombstone, home of the shoot-

out at the OK Corral, only five people were killed.

The only reason the OK Corral shoot-out even

became famous was that town boosters deliberately

overplayed the drama to attract new settlers.

"They eventually cashed in on the tourist boom,"

historian W. Eugene Hollon says, "by inventing a

myth about a town too tough to die."

Topic sentence

The writer develops the paragraph with three factual examples. He uses the common practice of placing the most dramatic example last and the weakest in the middle.

In "Sexism and Language," Aileen Pace Nilsen uses several brief examples to support the following paragraph's controlling idea: The armed forces
disguise jobs traditionally considered to be "women's work" by changing
their titles.

The armed forces, particularly the Marines,

use the positive masculine connotation as part of

their recruitment psychology. They promote the

idea that to join the Marines (or Army, Navy, or

Air Force) guarantees that you will become a man.

But this brings up a problem, because much of the

The subject requires background information to prepare the reader.

work that is necessary to keep a large organization running is what is traditionally thought of as "woman's work." Now, how can the Marines ask someone who has signed up for a "man-sized job" to do "woman's work"? <u>Since they can't, they euphemize and give the jobs titles that are more prestigious or, at least, don't make people think of females.</u> Waitresses are called "orderlies," secretaries are called "clerk-typists," nurses are called "medics," assistants are called "adjutants," and cleaning up an area is called "policing" the area. The same kind of word glorification is used in civilian life to bolster a man's ego when he is doing such tasks as cooking and sewing. For example, a "chef" has higher prestige than a "cook" and a "tailor" has higher prestige than a "seamstress."

The question sets up the topic sentence that follows.

The development is composed of a series of very brief examples.

The writer closes with a clincher that correlates military practice with civilian practice.

Nilsen's specific examples are very brief, each relating a specific fact. Writers also use brief examples to capture moments of experience, like snapshots that freeze a moment in time. These verbal snapshots, when appropriate for a subject, help a reader see the point.

Jane van Lawick-Goodall uses short, visual examples to illustrate the social behavior of chimpanzees she has studied in Tanzania. This paragraph illustrates the technique of presenting examples like photographs in an album. As you read, notice the stress Goodall puts on visual images. Although she uses few overt transitions, notice how she guides the reader into each of the first four examples by beginning them with "I saw" and "I watched." She varies the openings of the last two sentences after she has set the pattern in the reader's mind.

While many details of their [the chimpanzees'] social behavior were hidden from me by the foliage, I did get occasional fascinating glimpses. I saw one female, newly arrived in a group, hurry up to a big male and hold her hand toward him. Almost regally he reached out, clasped her hand in his, drew it toward him, and kissed it with his lips. I saw two adult males embrace each other in greeting. I saw youngsters having wild games through the treetops, chasing around after each other or jumping again and again, one after the other, from a branch to a springy bough below. I watched small infants dangling happily by themselves for minutes on end, patting at their toes with one hand, rotating gently from side to side. Once two tiny infants pulled on opposite ends of a twig in a gentle tug-of-war. Often during the heat of midday or after a long spell of feeding, I saw two or more adults grooming each other, carefully looking through the hair of their companions.

For this particular paragraph the verbal snapshots are effective. These visual examples communicate more than a lengthy discussion would. You might also notice how Goodall varies the lengths of the examples. The shortest is only ten words; the longest, divided into two sentences, is forty-one. In order, they are the longest first; then the shortest; next two of middle length; then one that is quite short; then one of middle length as a close. We aren't suggesting you follow this pattern, but we are suggesting that variety in the length of examples adds to the pleasure of reading the paragraph. Whenever you use several examples in a paragraph, vary their lengths. Variety will help keep your reader interested.

Often writers use examples that can be characterized as incidents or events. The following student writer uses three specific incidents as examples to illustrate a relationship between a particular film and murder.

Is there a direct relationship between murder in Hollywood films and murder in real life? No one knows for sure, but after the opening of a 1980s film about street gangs called "The Warriors," rival gangs clashed in or near some theaters. In Palm Springs during an intermission in the showing of The Warriors, some members of a Fontana motorcycle gang made several sexual comments to a local girl. The Family, a rival gang, came to her rescue. Violence exploded. A member of the Blue Coats killed a nineteen-year-old member of the Family

The writer opens with a question to hook the reader's interest.
The topic sentence suggests a link between films and real acts of violence.

Example 1. Notice how the writer introduces each example with a clear transition that names the city where the event took place.

with a Saturday night special. In Oxnard two gangs
clashed on opening night of <u>The Warriors</u>. When
people crowded into the lobby someone, yet to be
identified, stabbed an eighteen-year-old to death.

Example 2

In Boston several gang members leaving a theater
featuring <u>The Warriors</u> taunted a sixteen-year-old
boy with a line from the script. A brawl broke
out. Someone used a knife. Six hours later the boy
was dead.

Example 3

One effect of these specific examples is that they are convincing. They convince in a way that no abstract discussion ever could. But when you use isolated examples such as the ones relating gang violence to films, you must remember that they are not "proof." Their value lies in their emotional impact.

Often writers develop specific examples more fully than the brief examples represented in the above illustrations. In a paragraph from "Tools of Torture," Phyllis Rose presents five well-detailed examples (sometimes referred to as extended examples) to support the controlling idea that the Middle Ages offered many ways "to torment a person," all of them gruesome.

<u>Even in the Middle Ages, before electricity,</u>
<u>there were many things you could do to torment a</u>
<u>person.</u> You could tie him up in an iron belt that

Topic sentence, brief and to the point.

held the arms and legs up to the chest and left no
point to rest, so that all his muscles went into
spasm within minutes and he was driven mad within
hours. This was the twisting stork, a benign-look-
ing object. You could stretch him out backward

Example 1. Notice how the examples seem to increase in intensity.

over a thin piece of wood so that his whole body
weight rested on his spine, which pressed against
the sharp wood. Then you could stop up his nos-

Example 2

trils and force water into his stomach through his mouth. Then, if you wanted to finish him off, you and your helper could jump on his stomach, causing internal hemorrhage. This torture was called the rack. If you wanted to burn someone to death without hearing him scream, you could use a tongue lock, a metal rod between the jaw and collarbone that prevented him from opening his mouth. You could put a person in a chair with spikes on the seat and arms, tie him down against the spikes, and beat him, so that every time he flinched from the beating he drove his own flesh deeper onto the spikes. This was the inquisitor's chair. If you wanted to make it worse, you could heat the spikes. You could suspend a person over a pointed wooden pyramid and whenever he started to fall asleep, you could drop him onto the point. If you were Ippolito Marsili, the inventor of this torture, known as the Judas cradle, you could tell yourself you had invented something humane, a torture that worked without burning flesh or breaking bones. For the torture here was supposed to be sleep deprivation.

Example 3

Example 4

Example 5

Rose arranges these extended examples with care, knowing that a reader might become distracted by the shocking information and abundant detail. Somewhat like the student writer of the last paragraph, Rose uses parallel construction, that is, she introduces each example with similar phrases, "you could tie," "you could stretch," "you could use," and "you could heat."

Moreover, Rose also ends three of the five examples by naming the particular device, thus bringing each example to a clear close.

Brief narratives often serve as extended specific examples. When using several narrative examples, you must carefully separate them with transitional phrases. In the student paragraph that follows, notice how the three narrative examples are separated by transitional phrases.

<u>Working at the Experimental Farm School, a converted two-story house at the north end of campus, has taught me to expect surprises from preschoolers.</u> Once following an earthquake, a four year old climbed out of a second-story window onto the roof and hid behind the air-conditioning unit while the staff frantically searched the entire house. About a month ago, a group of three year olds during free play decided to make an "experimental cake." When their student observer stepped away to answer the phone, one of the group brought three chicklets from the farm yard and covered them with batter. The episode that shocked me the most, though, took place on a cold, rainy overnight in December. The children had all crawled into their sleeping bags for the night—or so I thought—and the only sounds were the splashing rain and crackling fire. I had first watch, so I sat in an easy chair in front of the fireplace. Slowly, I began to nod into sleep. Wham! Another earthquake? A bomb? World War III? As my heart floated down from my throat, I discovered what I

Topic sentence

Example 1. Notice the overt transition "once" that begins the first example.

Example 2. The transitional phrase "About a month ago" signals that a new example is coming.

Example 3. This is the longest and most dramatic example. The writer uses an entire sentence to serve as a transition.

should have been prepared for. While I was snor-

ing, the kids had crept into the kitchen and

returned with pots and pans, which they happily

banged to wake me up.

These narrative examples are to the point—they clearly illustrate why the writer has learned to expect surprises from preschoolers.

Combining Typical and Specific Examples

Writers often combine typical and specific examples. Sometimes they combine examples in a single paragraph, but at other times they arrange them in separate paragraphs to avoid writing excessively long paragraphs. The following two paragraphs combine typical and specific examples to make a single point about education.

Lower-division courses are far from the ideal

of education. Generally, an ideal education

requires interaction with teachers and other stu-

dents. When a student has difficulty understanding

a mathematical concept, scientific principle, or

literary work, he or she must have the opportunity

to meet with an experienced teacher, one who has

spent years not only learning a subject but also

communicating with students. When a student

encounters new ideas in lectures or reading, he or

she must have the opportunity to explore them in

teacher-guided discussions, not just in rap ses-

sions over coffee in the cafeteria.

During my freshman year, only one of my class-

es was small enough to permit interaction with

The opening sentence serves as the topic sentence.

The writer creates a typical example to illustrate what an ideal education should embody.

This second topic sentence links clearly to the first while indicating that a specific example follows.

students and the teacher, a sprightly woman who loved literature. Each session was devoted to a discussion of a single literary work. One session that dealt with <u>Waiting for Godot</u> turned into a heated debate about the meaning of human activity. She directed the discussion with questions, helping us understand our positions. Out of the discussion came a series of unanswered questions that became the basis for a writing assignment that she individually reviewed with each of us during her office hours. This kind of education is ideal, but it happens only when classes are small enough to allow for person-to-person instruction. It cannot happen in large lecture classes where many students see only the teacher's tiny figure beyond a sea of heads.

A specific example illustrates the writer's experience with ideal education.

The closing sentences serve as a clincher statement.

In this illustration, typical and specific examples work well together. If the writer had presented only what he considered the typical aspects of an ideal education, the example would have been too vague. But by including a specific example, he gives the reader a concrete illustration of what he believes is necessary to achieve an ideal education. He organizes each paragraph around linking topic sentences.

WRITING TASK—EXAMPLES

Write a paragraph that uses examples to support a topic sentence. You may develop your paragraph by composing generalized observations, representative facts, brief narratives, verbal snapshots, or brief incidents, as illustrated in this chapter.

As always, we suggest that you select your own topic, but if you become stumped, we offer the following suggestions.

1. Write a paragraph on one of the following general observations. Compose a clear topic sentence that organizes your paragraph. Use several examples to illustrate the controlling idea in your topic sentence.

   a. Crude language spoken publicly is objectionable.
   b. Crude language spoken publicly is acceptable.
   c. Some films have clear social significance.
   d. Photographs reveal human experience.
   e. Graffiti carry psychological messages.
   f. People display odd behavior in public places, such as elevators, medical offices, public meetings, or on public transportation.
   g. Some commercials suggest that buying a product will bring happiness, security, popularity, or romance.
   h. Part of the national economy, a great deal of which relies on consumption, flourishes because of our vices.
   i. Slasher films have a sexist slant.
   j. Serious matters of public concern have been turned into entertainment.

2. Perhaps you would like to write two paragraphs related to a single topic. If so, try the following writing task:

   In popular magazines such as *Psychology Today, People,* and *Time* or *Newsweek,* study several ads for similar products manufactured by different companies—beer, vodka, whiskey, cigarettes, or cars of comparable price, for example. Determine the common elements, which might include the uses of language and images, that the advertisements use to sell the products. Once you have identified some common elements, list them as a means of prewriting. Next compose a topic sentence that communicates the idea that some companies selling familiar products use similar techniques in their advertisements. Finally, support the topic sentence by using typical and specific examples in your paragraphs. Be sure to develop a linking topic sentence for the second paragraph. You might use the following pattern:

Paragraph Number 1

Topic sentence
Typical examples

Paragraph Number 2

Second topic sentence linking to the first one
Specific example
Clincher statement

Remember:

1. Develop the material through prewriting.
2. Compose a limited topic sentence.
3. Write a rough draft that arranges your examples in an effective pattern and ends with a clincher.
4. Write a final draft with clear transitions between examples.

GROUP WORK

As a group discuss Chapter 5 before starting the writing task. If any areas are confusing, help each other clarify the difficulty. Select a common topic, which all of you can use as a subject for this draft.

Spend some time brainstorming as a group before actually beginning to write. Feel free to use any of the material the group develops.

Finally, distribute copies of the final draft and hold a read around—that is, read your drafts as swiftly as possible. Take no more that three minutes for commentary on each essay.

6

Cataloging

Often writers will use a catalog of very brief examples or descriptive details to develop a paragraph. It might help to think of a catalog as a list. Catalogs, like lists, are easy to make. Without much effort you could catalog the outstanding presidents from American history; your favorite films, songs, television programs, books, or sports figures; or what you want for Christmas. For example, a catalog of prominent black Americans who have changed their given names to African or Islamic names might look like the following:

- Malcolm Little became Malik al-Shabazz.
- Cassius Clay became Muhammad Ali.
- Lew Alcindor became Kareem Abdul-Jabbar.
- Stokely Carmichael became Kwame Ture.
- LeRoi Jones became Amiri Baraka.

Given an appropriate subject, a brief catalog such as this could be used to develop a paragraph. In fact, one student used this catalog to develop a paragraph as part of an essay about racial identity for Americans of African descent. Of course, the writer had to polish this catalog and fit it into his discussion.

What is in a name? Judging from the debate started by civil rights leader Jesse Jackson, a great deal. Jackson says that Americans of African descent should abandon the designation "black"

The opening sentences establish the subject and provide the reader with background information.

just as they once abandoned the designation
"Negro." In its place they should adopt the designation "African American." During the last three
decades, African Americans have also been changing
their given names to African or Islamic names:
political leader Malcolm Little becoming Malik al-
Shabazz, heavyweight boxing champion Cassius Clay
becoming Muhammad Ali, Lakers basketball star Lew
Alcindor becoming Kareem Abdul-Jabbar, activist
Stokely Carmichael becoming Kwame Ture, writer
LeRoi Jones becoming Amiri Baraka. Just as a name
change can be important to an individual's identity, a name change can be important to a group's
identity, too, by accurately reflecting its heritage.

Here's where the catalog begins. Notice how the main clause sets up the pattern.

The paragraph closes with a clincher that stresses the importance of an accurate designation.

Typically, when writers use a catalog to develop a paragraph, they will begin with a topic sentence, follow with any background information the reader might need, and then write a main clause that ends with a colon and sets the pattern in motion. The writer of the next paragraph follows this pattern. As you study this short paragraph, notice how the elements of the catalog follow the colon.

The dominant advertising slogan in the 80s was
"Youth Sells," but the dominant slogan in the 90s
is "Maturity Sells." In television commercials of
the 80s, young people seemed to be the only ones
traveling to exciting places, eating in restaurants, buying cars, and drinking beer. In commercials of the 90s the cast of characters is begin-

This paragraph begins with a topic sentence and several sentences of background information.

ning to change. Now faces in television commer-

cials show lines of age and experience. During any

night of television viewing, you will see mature

adults enjoying the ad writer's vision of the good

life: Eastern Airlines showing a couple in their

sixties cavorting on an exotic beach, McDonalds

featuring a flirtatious seventy-five-year-old man

eyeing an elderly woman, Subaru showcasing an

eighty-year-old woman taking a joy ride, Bud Light

showing two grandparents holding foamy beer mugs.

If television commercials reflect economic reali-

ties, it is safe to assume that more and more con-

sumers with economic clout are entering their twi-

light years.

The main clause ends with a colon, setting up the catalog. Notice that the catalog is composed of four elements: "Eastern Airlines showing . . ."; "McDonalds featuring a flirtatious . . ."; "Subaru showcasing an eighty-year-old . . ."; "Bud Light showing two . . . ."

The paragraph closes with a clincher that suggests the reason for the change.

Notice that the elements that make up the catalog—the examples or descriptive phrases that follow the colon—are not main clauses. If you do use main clauses for the elements in your catalog, be sure to separate them with semicolons; otherwise you will be writing comma splices, an error writing teachers seldom ignore.

A catalog's rapid accumulation of detail demands attention. Writers, therefore, will sometimes use catalogs to thrust a reader into the middle of an experience. For example, read the following paragraph and notice how quickly the writer creates a visual picture of a concert that has gone out of control.

Last summer I attended an out-of-doors concert

that erupted into a riot. From where I sat on a

distant grass-covered knoll, I watched the partic-

ipants, like insane characters in a movie scene,

attack each other: a guitarist smashing a micro-

phone against a fan's head, a herd of drunks hurl-

The topic sentence establishes the time and event the writer will describe.

The opening main clause sets up the pattern by introducing the catalog: (1) guitarist smashing a fan; (2) drunks hurling bottles; (3) girls shaking their fists and shouting; (4) club-waving guards; and (5) bystanders scurrying. Notice that none of the catalog elements are phrased as main clauses.

ing beer bottles at the dodging musicians, a group

of girls dressed in punk rock styles shaking their

fists and shouting for blood, and club-waving secu-

rity guards wading into the crowd as innocent

bystanders scurried for shelter. <u>The whole time, I</u>

<u>thought, this is insane, this is insane, while</u>

<u>overhead, a police helicopter buzzed and in the</u>

<u>distance sirens wailed</u>.

The writer closes with a clincher that states his personal response, making it dramatic by using auditory detail.

Not all catalogs are this emotionally gripping. Sometimes writers use them to tantalize their readers. Catalogs of this sort generate expectations and promise excitement. Paul Theroux uses this technique in a paragraph in *The Great Railway Bazaar*, a book that describes his trip by train across Asia. Theroux uses two catalogs in a single paragraph. The first—which begins "Anything is possible"—creates the atmosphere of the train. The second—which begins "It was my intention"—catalogs the various railroads Theroux will ride during his journey. As you read, notice how Theroux uses a colon to set up each catalog.

<u>Then Asia was out the window, and I was car-</u>

<u>ried through it on these eastbound expresses mar-</u>

<u>veling as much at the bazaar within the train as</u>

<u>the ones we whistled past.</u> Anything is possible on

a train: a great meal, a binge, a visit from card

players, an intrigue, a good night's sleep, and

strangers' monologues framed like Russian short

stories. It was my intention to board every train

that chugged into view from Victoria Station in

London to Tokyo Central: to take a branch line to

Simla, the spur through the Khyber Pass, and the

chord line that links Indian Railways with those

The topic sentence sets the paragraph in motion by suggesting the exotic aspects of the trip both from inside and outside the train.

The first catalog lists the exotic experiences on the train.

The second catalog lists the exotic course of Theroux's train journey from London to Tokyo.

in Ceylon; the Mandalay Express, the Malaysian

Golden Arrow, the locals in Vietnam, and the

trains with bewitching names, the Orient Express,

the North Star, the Trans-Siberian.

Besides generating excitement and building expectations in a reader, a writer can also use the cataloging pattern to present a great deal of information in a condensed form. Barbara W. Tuchman uses this technique in *A Distant Mirror* to give her readers an impression of the fourteenth century's conception of distant places. One of the problems a writer faces when arranging catalogs of this sort (or any sort, for that matter) is how to present the details in an orderly fashion. Tuchman solves the problem by first introducing the catalog with a colon, then beginning each major element with a key word and following it with one or more descriptive details. The key words are *forests, horned pygmies, brahmins, men, cyclopeans, monoceros, Amazons, panthers, trees,* and *snakes.* As you read, study how Tuchman has followed this plan.

> Faraway lands, however—India, Persia, and beyond—were seen through a gauze of fabulous fairy tales revealing an occasional nugget of reality: forests so high they touch the clouds, horned pygmies who move in herds and grow old in seven years, brahmins who kill themselves on funeral pyres, men with dogs' heads and six toes, "cyclopeans" with only one eye and one foot who move as fast as the wind, the "monoceros" which can be caught only when it sleeps in the lap of a virgin, Amazons whose tears are of silver, panthers who practice the caesarean operation with their own claws, trees whose leaves supply wool, snakes 300 feet long, snakes with precious stones for eyes, snakes who so love music that for prudence they stop up one ear with their tail.

So far we have used illustrations by writers who have arranged their catalogs into single sentences. This is the most common practice. But often writers catalog a series of questions. Later in her book, Tuchman uses this pattern to make her readers aware of the kinds of mysterious questions the fourteenth-century mind puzzled over.

> For all the explanations, the earth and its phenomena were full of mysteries: What happens to fire when it goes out? Why are there different colors of skin among men? Why do the sun's rays darken a man's skin but bleach white linen? How do souls make their way to the next world? Where lies the soul? What causes madness? Medieval people felt surrounded by puzzles, yet because God was there

they were willing to acknowledge that causes are hidden, that man cannot know why all things are as they are; "they are as God pleases."

As we said, cataloging is a quick way to involve your readers. It is a pattern that thrusts them into an experience. Its underlying effect is achieved not through logic but through bombardment.

WRITING TASK—CATALOGING

Write a paragraph built on the catalog pattern. Be sure to write a topic sentence that prepares the reader for the catalog and to follow with sentences that set the catalog in motion. Remember, a catalog can deal with almost any subject, but its main purpose is to quickly involve your reader; therefore, you must work to create a strong impression with the material you select. To get you started, here are a few suggestions. Keep in mind that you can shape them to your own purposes.

1. Take a walk down Main Street. Visit some part of the town where you live and record an extended list of physical details you feel convey the dominant feeling of the area. Build the list into a paragraph according to the catalog pattern.
2. Visit a store. Walk through a department, hardware, liquor, shoe, drug, or dime store. Or sit around a pool hall, beauty parlor, bar, cafeteria, library, or street corner. Wherever you visit, record your impressions, then develop them in a paragraph according to the catalog pattern.
3. Sit on a rock. Go to a park, grove of trees, lake, hilltop, bird sanctuary, or empty football field. Record your impressions and build them into a catalog.
4. Review your life. Build a paragraph by cataloging the high or the low points—the peaks and the valleys. Or if questions about your life come to you, build a paragraph out of them.
5. Capture an experience. Record the dominant impressions of an experience you've had, then build the impressions into a catalog.

Try to be as vivid as possible when composing your catalog because you want the reader to become involved. The key thought behind this pattern is bombardment. Bombard your reader with vivid details.

Remember:

1. Begin with a topic sentence and background information your reader might need.

2. Introduce your catalog with a main clause that ends with a colon.
3. Be sure the elements of the catalog that follow the colon are not main clauses that can stand alone.
4. End with a clincher.

GROUP WORK

In subgroups of three, review your catalog paragraphs. Pay particular attention to the following questions: Does the topic sentence effectively indicate that a catalog will follow? Is a colon used correctly? Are the items in the catalog cast in similar grammatical units—that is, are they parallel?

7
Anecdote

An anecdote is a brief narrative that illustrates a point or captures a person's character. Simple enough. But unlike other patterns we've discussed, anecdotes seldom make direct statements. They suggest rather than declare; they need to be interpreted; they are never accepted at face value.

Use an Anecdote to Reveal Character

Often an anecdote that reveals character will be brief. Author Banesh Hoffman, in "My Friend, Albert Einstein," uses the following anecdote to illustrate that simplicity was actually the essence of Einstein's character.

He was one of the greatest scientists the world has ever known, yet if I had to convey the essence of Albert Einstein in a single word, I would choose "simplicity." Perhaps an anecdote will help. Once, caught in a downpour, he took off his hat and held it under his coat. Asked why, he explained, with admirable logic, that the rain would damage the hat, but his hair would be none the worse for its wetting. This knack for going

Hoffman opens with a clear topic sentence that prepares the reader for an illustration of Einstein's simplicity.

This single anecdote captures Einstein's personality.

Hoffman ends with a clincher suggesting that simplicity was at the heart of Einstein's discoveries.

instinctively to the heart of the matter was the

secret of his major scientific discoveries.

Brief as it is, this anecdote shows something about Albert Einstein's simple way of looking at experience. In other words, it does what some anecdotes are supposed to do: It reveals character.

Generally, anecdotes are more complex than the one above. They often require stage setting, which might include background information, description, and even snatches of dialogue. James Phelan uses a complex anecdote in *Howard Hughes: The Hidden Years* to reveal Hughes' capricious character and the fear the multimillionaire's whims triggered in his employees.

During Howard Hughes' years of seclusion in the Desert Inn in Las Vegas, he would demand the same meal every day for lengthy stretches. At one point, according to his long-time aide, Gordon Margulis, he was having two scoops of Baskin-Robbins' banana-nut ice cream with every meal, so his staff kept it constantly on hand.

One day, when the supply needed to be replenished, it was learned that the flavor had been discontinued. Hughes' staff panicked. Someone telephoned the Baskin-Robbins office in California and asked them to make a special batch of banana-nut. They agreed to make up the smallest batch they could on special order—350 gallons. "We still had a few scoops of the old banana-nut when the new banana-nut arrived," says Margulis, "so we felt all set for the rest of Hughes' lifetime."

When the ice cream was served to Hughes the next day, however, he ate it and declared: "That's great ice cream, but it's time for a change. From now on, I want French Vanilla."

The Hughes anecdote is part of a much longer work. This is usually the case with anecdote. Phelan uses it as a quick means to reveal Hughes's character. Speed and impact give it punch. Punch, or surprise, as opposed to reasoned discourse, is characteristic of most anecdotes. The punch may be designed to generate a laugh, such as the banana-nut ice cream caper. Or it may tug at a deeper emotional awareness.

Use an Anecdote to Make a Point

In *Desert Solitaire* Edward Abbey uses an anecdote to make a point about the plight of Navajos living in a world that has little respect for their heritage.

It will not be easy. It will not be easy for the Navajos to forget that once upon a time, only a generation ago, they were horsemen, nomads, keepers of flocks, painters in sand, weavers of wool, artists in silver, dancers, singers of the Yei-bie-chei. But they will have to forget, or at least learn to be ashamed of these old things and to bring them out only for the amusement of tourists.

Abbey begins setting up the anecdote by calling to the reader's mind what the Navajos once were.

Notice how he uses a catalog to work in a great deal of detail.

A difficult transitional period. Tough on people. For instance, consider an unfortunate accident which took place only a week ago here in Arches country. Parallel to the highway north of Moab is a railway, a spur line to the potash mines. At one point close to this road this railway cuts through a hill. The cut is about three hundred feet deep, blasted through solid rock with sides that are as perpendicular as the walls of a building. One afternoon two young Indians—Navajos? Apaches? beardless Utes?—in a perverted Plymouth came hurtling down the highway, veered suddenly to the right, whizzed through a fence and plunged straight down like helldivers into the Big Cut. Investigating the wreckage we found only the broken bodies, the broken bottles, the stain and smell of Tokay, and a couple of cardboard

"For instance, consider an unfortunate accident" announces the anecdote.

Abbey gives some background information that leads up to the incident.

Now he moves directly into the story.

Abbey catalogs the contents of the wreckage to show the reader what today's young Navajos possess: a sharp contrast to the proud possessions of former Navajos. At this point the contrast becomes even more direct—the dreams of drug-store cowboys juxtaposed against the reality of the past.

suitcases exploded open and revealing their former

owners' worldly goods—dirty socks, some underwear,

a copy of <u>True West</u> magazine, a comb, three new

cowboy shirts from J. C. Penny's, a carton of

Marlboro cigarettes. But nowhere did we see any

conchos of silver, any buffalo robes, any bows,

arrows, medicine pouch or drums. Some Indians.

Abbey closes with an ironic comment—"Some Indians"—to show what an insensitive white man's response might be.

The pride of the ancient Navajo has been bartered for the cheap goods of modern society. That may be one way to look at these paragraphs. Or perhaps the criticism goes much deeper. Modern America has sold the goods and the dreams the goods represent to the Indians, thus diminishing their lives. Beyond that, just as the Navajo are diminished, so too are we diminished by the same forces that have driven these Indian boys to the fantasies of Tokay and *True West.*

Remember that anecdotes often speak indirectly. When you read one you must examine it to get the point. When you write one, you must shape it so a reader will get the point.

WRITING TASK—ANECDOTE

Write an anecdote that reveals character or makes a point about a social issue. Keep in mind that anecdotes suggest rather than declare the writer's concern. They also involve some descriptive stage setting so that the reader can visualize the experience. And, most important, they end with some punch that drives the point home.

If you have been doing Daily Writing as described in Part IV of this book, we suggest you reread some of your entries. They may suggest an anecdote to you, especially your entries in Chapter 31, Portraits and Relationships.

If you choose to write an anecdote that illustrates a social issue, be sure to stick to a particular case that suggests the larger issue, as Abbey does in his anecdote of the Navajo youths. For instance, if you're concerned over the health care of the infirm, you might select a particular case from a local convalescent home as the focus for your anecdote. If you're concerned about the behavior of authorities, parents, students or politicians, choose for your focus a particular case from your experience.

Remember:

1. Anecdotes suggest rather than directly state a point.
2. They involve stage setting.
3. They often involve dialogue.

GROUP WORK

Often anecdotes are brief narratives, a story that makes a point or reveals character. Not everyone in your group will be assigned an anecdote, but for those who are, meet and read each other's work. Does the anecdote suggest, rather than directly state a point? Has the writer set the stage? If the writer uses dialogue, is it used correctly?

8

Comparison and Contrast

- "It's a good movie, but I liked the book better."
- "People are all alike."
- "The Chiefs are better than the Browns."
- "Did anyone ever say you look like Kevin Costner?"
- "A vegetarian diet is healthier than a meat diet."

These bits of imaginary conversation all embody comparisons or contrasts. We're sure you've heard such comments many times in your life.

To compare is to point out similarities; to contrast is to point out differences. For the purposes of discussion we use "comparison" to refer to both processes.

Whenever you arrange two subjects for discussion, you will almost always be comparing them. In a comparison paragraph you might discuss only the similarities or only the differences of your subjects. Or you might choose to discuss both the similarities and differences. The choice, of course, depends on the subjects and your purpose for comparing them.

Sometimes writers will include undeveloped, or informal, comparisons that are merely incidental in a longer passage, such as this illustration from a paper on the subject of the human brain.

> Modern computers are fast, accurate, and able to do a wide variety of programmed tasks, but they still lack the flexibility of the human brain.

In a brief comparison such as this, the intention is not to compare the two subjects fully. The writer is merely alluding to one subject in order to place another subject in a familiar context for the reader. A fully developed comparison pattern takes at least an entire paragraph, sometimes several paragraphs, to deal adequately with the two subjects.

When comparing subjects, you, like professional writers, should practice three important principles. First, make sure that there is a sound basis for comparison. In many cases, this means that your subjects should be perceived by most people as belonging together in the same class, or group. For instance, one writer might effectively compare a bee with a snake because both are living creatures. Another writer might effectively compare a bee with a helicopter because both are things that fly. But we doubt that any writer could effectively compare a helicopter with a snake no matter what the purpose. When you employ comparison, therefore, make sure your subjects are logically related. (For an exception, see Chapter 9, Analogy.)

Second, because comparisons involve two subjects, you must quickly orient your reader. In the opening sentences, let your readers know that a discussion of two subjects is to follow. For example, read the opening sentences from newspaper columnist Suzanne Britt's comparison of neat people and sloppy people.

> I've finally figured out the difference between neat people and sloppy people. The distinction is, as always, moral. Neat people are lazier and meaner than sloppy people.

Britt's opening clearly identifies her subjects and lets you know that a comparison will follow. When writing a comparison, you should do likewise or risk confusing your readers.

Third, once the subjects have been clearly introduced in the opening sentences, use clear stylistic techniques to keep your reader from becoming confused while shifting from one subject to the other. Sometimes you may use parallel structure to balance the similarities and differences of the subjects. But more frequently you will use transitional words and phrases, such as *whereas, on the one hand, on the other hand, in contrast, like, unlike,* and *but* to guide a reader through a comparison.

To see these three principles at work, read the following student paragraph taken from a museum report. As you read the paragraph, keep the following in mind:

1. Notice how the writer presents both subjects—elephants and mastodons—in the topic sentence.
2. Examine how the writer uses the topic sentence to lead readers into a comparison-and-contrast pattern.
3. Watch for the brief phrases that remind readers of the comparing and contrasting process: "Like the modern elephant" and "Unlike the elephant."

4. Notice the sentence that pivots the paragraph and moves it from pointing out similarities to pointing out differences between the two beasts.

After you've read the paragraph, we suggest you reread it along with the comments in the margin so that you can more firmly grasp the pattern.

<u>When I first saw the reproduction of the pre-historic mastodon, I thought of elephants I had seen in circuses and zoos.</u> Like the modern elephant, the mastodon is large, with legs that remind me of sturdy tree trunks. The ancient beast had large, floppy ears and a long trunk which he could use as a tool for gathering food. But after a closer look, I saw some major differences between the modern elephant and the prehistoric mastodon. The mastodon's tusks grew longer and curved upward at a sharper angle. Unlike the elephant with its thick, almost hairless hide, the mastodon was matted with long, thick hair. And although the mastodon was large, it was not as tremendous in size as its modern descendant.

The topic sentence sets up the two elements to be compared and contrasted—mastodon and elephant.

Brief presentation of the similarities between the two creatures. Notice the use of "like" to set up the similarities.

"But after a closer look . . ." serves as a pivotal sentence to guide the reader into the contrast section.

Brief presentation of the differences between the two creatures.

The final sentence reminds the reader of the two elements presented.

This writer has discussed both the similarities and differences of elephants and mastodons. But as we mentioned above, you may also choose to concentrate only on similarities or only on differences. In either case the discussion will usually be structured in one of two ways: by block arrangement or by point-by-point arrangement.

Block Arrangement

Block arrangement is quite simple. First you discuss the outstanding points of one subject; then you discuss the outstanding points of the other. Generally, you will close the paragraph with a comment that brings the two subjects back together. For example, study the following paragraph from

Edward T. Hall's *The Hidden Dimension*. Hall uses block arrangement to discuss the differences between Arab and American attitudes toward road rights.

Another silent source of friction between Americans and Arabs is in an area that Americans treat very informally—the manners and rights of the road. In general, in the United States we tend to defer to the vehicle that is bigger, more powerful, faster, and heavily laden. While a pedestrian walking along a road may feel annoyed, he will not think it unusual to step aside for a fast-moving automobile. He knows that because he is moving he does not have the right to the space around him that he has when he is standing still. It appears that the reverse is true with the Arabs who apparently take on rights to space as they move. For someone else to move into a space an Arab is also moving into is a violation of his rights. It is infuriating to an Arab to have someone else cut in front of him on the highway. It is the American's cavalier treatment of moving space that makes the Arab call him aggressive and pushy.

The topic sentence clearly identifies two subjects: American and Arab attitudes toward road rights.

The first block presents American behavior.

This sentence serves as a transition from the first to the second block.

The second block presents Arab behavior.

The closing sentence brings the two subjects back together.

Hall's block arrangement is quite clear. First he presents the American attitude; then he presents the Arab attitude. He lets the reader know he is shifting the discussion from Americans to Arabs with a transitional sentence, "It appears that the reverse is true with the Arabs who apparently take on rights to space as they move." Hall closes with an observation that brings the two subjects together.

Now study student-writer Susan Wo's paragraph also arranged by blocks. She discusses the differences between "negative addicts" and "positive addicts." As you read, notice how Wo swings from one block to the other by using the transitional phrase "In contrast." She also sets up the closing comments with the phrase "In any case."

The word addict is usually used in a negative way, but when used in a positive fashion, it has a different significance. Negative addicts may be people who smoke until their breath grows weak and raspy and their lungs decay. At a greater extreme, they may be hooked on heroin, alcohol, or gambling—or on any compulsion that so dominates their lives that it threatens both their existence and the existence of loved ones. In contrast, positive addicts may be addicted to jogging, swimming, or meditating—activities that sustain health and help people live vigorously. They may be addicted to diary keeping, spending up to two hours a day writing down their experiences and thoughts. Some claim that concentrated reading may be a positive addiction that helps readers sustain intellectual involvement with their own growth and society. In any case, unlike negative addicts who seem bent on destroying themselves and those around them, positive addicts perpetuate life and become better people through their compulsion.

Although the two subjects are not clearly identified in the topic sentence, the writer gives the reader a clear idea of what to expect.

The first block presents details related to the negative addict.

The phrase "In contrast" announces the movement into the second block, which presents details of the positive addict.

The phrase "In any case" announces that the two subjects will be brought together to close the paragraph.

Point-by-Point Arrangement

You will find that the block arrangement is effective for comparing subjects in relatively general terms. But to compare several specific aspects of your subjects, point-by-point arrangement is more effective because it alternately presents each point you consider. When using a point-by-point arrangement, be sure to phrase your sentences so that a reader can follow the shift from one subject to the other. For example, study Gilbert Highet's discussion of the differences between early Greek teachers called sophists and their rival teacher Socrates. Notice how Highet counters one attribute or set of attributes with another, often using a semicolon to signal the shift from subject to subject. Also notice that he begins each main clause with a clear reference to the appropriate subject: "they" refers to the sophists, "he" to Socrates.

<u>To some of his contemporaries Socrates looked like a sophist; but he distrusted and opposed the sophists wherever possible.</u> They toured the whole Greek world; Socrates stayed in Athens, talking to his fellow-citizens. They made carefully prepared continuous speeches; he only asked questions. They took rich fees for their teaching; he refused regular payment, living and dying poor. They were elegantly dressed, turned out like film stars on a personal appearance tour, with secretaries and personal servants and elaborate advertising. Socrates wore the workingman's clothes, bare feet and a smock—in fact, he had been a stonemason and carver by trade, and came from a working-class family. They spoke in specially prepared lecture halls; he talked to people at street-corners and in the gymnasium, where every afternoon the young men exercised, and the old men talked, while they all sunbathed. He fitted in so well there that he sometimes compared himself to the athletic coach,

The topic sentence opens with some background information before suggesting the contrast between Socrates and the sophists.

The first three differences are each presented in one sentence, and the main clauses are separated by a semicolon.

As the description of the differences becomes more complex, the writer divides the details into sentences, beginning with "They were elegantly dressed...." This detailing also adds structural variety to the paragraph.

The writer returns to the semicolon structure.

The writer leaves the contrast to develop Socrates more fully, thus accentuating his method as superior to the sophists'.

who does not run or wrestle, but teaches others
how to run and wrestle better; Socrates said he
trained people to think. Lastly, the sophists said
they knew everything and were ready to explain it.
Socrates said he knew nothing and was trying to
find out.

He closes by bringing the sophists back into the process and suggesting that Socrates is superior.

Structurally, Highet's paragraph is quite simple, yet he effectively works in a great deal of detail about the sophists and Socrates. Of course, his sympathies are clear: He applauds Socrates while making the sophists look like egocentric materialists. In the following paragraph, student-writer Sherry Simon uses the same point-by-point arrangement. The writer compares television sitcom families to real-life families.

Throughout the history of television, families
have appeared in a variety of combinations. There
have been mothers raising children alone; children
raising their grandparents; three bachelors with a
house full of children. There have been black and
white families, blue-collar and white collar families. But the family combination, whether black or
white, blue or white collar, that has endured over
the years is the upper middle class family, featuring a mom and dad, two or three children, which
includes teenagers, and grandparents who occasionally make an appearance. This is the combination
established in the 1950s by "Ozzie and Harriet"
and carried on by "The Bill Cosby Show," America's
most popular family sitcom. Of course, the irony
of the family sitcom success is that sitcom fami-

This writer opens with background information to prepare the reader for the central discussion.

The topic sentence presents the subjects and suggests that a comparison will follow.

lies stand in such contrast to what most people experience in real-life families. Consider the simple experience of laughter. In sitcoms there is a laugh every fifteen seconds; whereas real-life families I know can go for weeks, maybe even years, without experiencing a comical situation. Sitcom parents and teenagers easily "bond" together; yet in real life teenagers may speak fewer than five words a day to parents. For some reason, family sitcoms always showcase siblings disturbed with one another and the parents playing referee. But in reality any family psychologist will say kids casually undermine their parents in a psychological game of "get the grown ups." On a more serious note, the parents in a sitcom family are generally wise and profound. They offer advice the way politicians pass out press releases. In contrast, real-life parents may be living on the emotional edge, struggling for the mysterious codes that will guide their children through a gauntlet of dangers that range from drug use to teenage parenthood. Sure, the illusion family sitcoms create is fun, but the problems that real families face cannot be solved with glib humor in a half-hour time slot.

The first point is that actual families do not find themselves in humorous situations.

The second difference is that parents and teenagers in actual families do not easily "bond."

The third difference is that in actual families children are usually allied in opposition to parents.

The fourth, and most serious, difference, is that actual families must deal with complex problems.

The closing sentence clinches the comparison.

Is the writer unfair in his comparison? After all, do viewers confuse a family comedy series with reality? You can decide that issue for yourself. However, the point-by-point arrangement of this paragraph is effective.

Extended Comparison and Contrast

To avoid excessively long paragraphs, you will sometimes devote two or more paragraphs to a comparison of one aspect of your subject. For example, in the following paragraph from "Sexism in English: A 1990s Update" Aileen Pace Nilsen devotes two paragraphs to the comparison of male and female attitudes toward marriage by examining the way language is used. As you read, notice that the organizational techniques Nilsen uses are the same as the techniques used in one-paragraph comparisons.

In relation to marriage, there is much linguistic evidence showing that weddings are more important to women than to men. A woman cherishes the wedding and is considered a bride for a whole year, but a man is referred to as a groom only on the day of the wedding. The word "bride" appears in "bridal attendant," "bridesmaid," "bridal shower," and even "bridegroom." "Groom" comes from the Middle English "grom," meaning "man," and in this sense is seldom used outside of a wedding. With most pairs of male/female words, people habitually put the masculine word first—"Mr. and Mrs.," "his and hers," "boys and girls," "men and women," "kings and queens," "brothers and sisters," "guys and dolls," and "host and hostess"—but it is the "bride and groom" who are talked about, not the "groom and bride."

The importance of marriage to a woman is also shown by the fact that when a marriage ends in death, the woman gets the title of "widow." A man gets the derived title of "widower." The term is not used in other phrases or contexts, but "widow" is seen in "widowhood," "widow's peak," and "widow's walk." A "widow" in a card game is an extra hand of cards, while in typesetting it is an extra line of type.

Nilsen has used point-by-point arrangement. In the following paragraphs the student-writer uses block arrangement to compare two California communities.

I have lived in only two communities in California, hating both, but for different reasons. Each has its own logic, I suppose, but this young woman from the Midwest would prefer a place less extreme in lifestyle than either Sand Point or the Peaks. Sand Point is a tourist-hating town located next to a beach resort. The attitude of the area is loose and casual. The motto of the Sandy kids is "Have a good time." And they do. There are parties that last the weekend and surfing all day long. The educational goal of most Sandy kids is a semester or two at the local community college. Only the adults in this community are employed, most of them at the nearby docks. Most are committed union members, living in low-cost housing. Cops patrol Sand Point intensively, and it is not unusual to find fugitives hiding beneath Mustangs and Falcons or escaping through a dark alley.

The only evidence of law enforcement you see in the Peaks is an occasional security guard informing someone that the Mercedes or Porsche is parked in the wrong place. The whole environment revolves around stuffy money and finding new ways to show it off. High-class young adults here jog daily on the greenbelts in their designer sweats, and they are never caught without their bottle of Perrier while cooling down. Teenagers from the Peaks have Ivy League Colleges in their futures, sorority and fraternity members all the way. Kids from the Peaks earn "spending" money at local boutiques or ritzy restaurants. Their fathers are land developers and their mothers contribute time to charities, eat lunch at quaint, expensive bistros, and shop at Neiman-Marcus or I. Magnin.

In the space of an hour last week, I saw a Porsche in the Peaks and a beat-up Toyota in Sand Point, both sporting a "Save the American Dream" bumper sticker. If the Peaks and Sand Point are examples of the American Dream, count me out.

The writer devotes a paragraph to each block. The block pattern is effective for these subjects because the writer emphasizes the general nature of her subjects, not specific differences. Also notice that she brings the two subjects together in the brief closing paragraph.

WRITING TASK—COMPARISON AND CONTRAST

Write a comparison of one or more paragraphs. You may concentrate on the similarities, the differences, or the similarities and the differences of your subjects. You may use the block or point-by-point arrangement. Be sure to follow the three principles characteristic of comparisons: select subjects that are related; use clear transitional techniques as you shift from subject to subject; bring your subjects together at the close of the comparison. As a way to get started, we offer the following tasks for your consideration. Select one, narrow it to manageable size, and begin the prewriting process. Also keep in mind that you may create your own writing task or modify any of the following tasks to fit your interests.

1. Compare two historical or literary figures who represent two ways of life or two ways of perceiving the world.
2. Compare two news programs, one broadcast locally and the other broadcast nationally. For this brief assignment, you should concentrate on one or two aspects of the program rather than on the entire program.
3. Compare how two people from different cultures, economic situations, or age groups might perceive the same experience.
4. Compare opposing sides of an argument on a controversial issue, such as capital punishment, gun control, euthanasia, or animal experimentation.
5. Compare two methods of losing weight, two methods of physical conditioning, or two methods of self-defense.
6. Compare two classic films from the same category, such as two westerns, thrillers, musicals, or romances. We suggest you concentrate on one or two aspects of the films, such as plot, leading characters, or atmosphere.
7. Compare two paintings, songs, or poems dealing with similar subjects but created by different artists.
8. Compare the "mythic" character with the actual character of a historical figure who has been featured in popular movies, such as someone from frontier lore like Buffalo Bill Cody or Annie Oakley. This assignment will require some simple research.
9. Compare a stereotype to a reality or an ideal to a reality. For example, compare the stereotype of a politician to an actual politician, the stereotype of a film star to an actual film star, or the stereotype of a male or female athlete to an actual athlete.
10. Read this quotation from cultural critic Robert Grudin:

> Individuals who have, from one cause or another, flirted with genuine self-knowledge, are aware of the curious impulse to become their own opposites. The gentle wish to be bold, the mercurial patient, the industrious lazy, the temperate passionate. Conscious of our own psychological convexities and concavities, we wish to turn ourselves inside out, to taste fresh being at the alien polarity. And those who one way or another achieve these reversals, expecting strange new experiences, are often surprised by the native and intimate familiarity of the forms they have assumed.

Grudin stresses the dual nature of personality. Select a character from fiction, film, or public life and compare the opposite sides of his or her personality. Or compare opposite sides of your personality or opposite sides of the personality of someone you know well. Your purpose should be to make Grudin's general observations more specific.

Remember:

1. Develop a prewritten draft of the similarities and differences of your subjects.
2. Develop a topic sentence that clearly announces your subjects.
3. Use clear transitional techniques throughout your paper as you shift from subject to subject.
4. Bring the two subjects together in a closing statement.

GROUP WORK

Your group should consider the advantage of doing two comparison-and-contrast drafts—one employing block arrangement and the other, point by point—which would give each of you experience with the two dominant strategies. In any case, read each draft to determine if the similarities and differences are balanced. Examine the use of transition from one subject to the other. If reading the block method, ask yourself if there is a clear transition from one block to the other. If reading a draft developed point-by-point, ask yourself if the writer makes effective use of semicolon, parallel structure, and transitional words to shift from point to point.

Try working in pairs—that is, exchange your essay with one group member; read the essays simultaneously; then exchange your observations. After you are finished, switch partners and repeat the process.

9
Analogy

Earlier we said that to write an effective comparison (as well as an effective contrast) pattern, you need to use two subjects which most people would see as belonging to a common group. Analogy, however, is a special kind of comparison that works only when you compare subjects from different groups. In other words, unlike ordinary comparisons that present the similarities of two things very much alike, an analogy presents the similarities of two things basically different. In simple terms, analogy uses something that is widely known to reveal something unknown.

Often writers use analogy descriptively. Read the following paragraph from surgeon Richard Selzer's *Mortal Lessons*. Selzer begins with a quick comparison between a scalpel and the bow of a cello. He then compares the way a scalpel cuts to the movement of a slender fish. Selzer's analogy helps the reader to "feel" the scalpel at work.

> One holds the knife as one holds the bow of a cello or tulip—by the stem. Not palmed nor gripped nor grasped, but lightly, with the tips of the fingers. The knife is not for pressing. It is for drawing across the field of skin. Like a slender fish, it waits, at the ready, then, go! It darts, followed by a fine wake of red. The flesh parts, falling away to yellow globules of fat. Even though I've used it so many times, I still marvel at its power—cold, gleaming, silent. More, I am still struck with a kind of dread that it is I in whose hand the blade travels, that my hand is its vehicle, that yet again this terrible steel-bellied thing and I have conspired for a most unnatural purpose, the laying open of the body of a human being.

Sometimes writers use analogy for the purpose of explanation. For example, the following analogy from *The Shopping Mall High School* explains the underlying nature of American secondary education.

> If Americans want to understand their high schools at work, they should imagine them as shopping malls. Secondary education is another consumption experience in an abundant society. Shopping malls attract a broad range of customers with different tastes and purposes. Some shop at Sears, others at Woolworth's or Bloomingdale's. In high schools a broad range of students also shop. They too can select from an astonishing variety of products and services conveniently assembled in one place that is equipped with ample parking. Furthermore, in malls and schools many different kinds of transactions are possible. Both institutions bring hopeful purveyors and potential purchasers together. The former hope to maximize sales but can take nothing for granted. Shoppers have a wide discretion not only about what to buy but also about whether to buy.

Other times writers will use analogy to illustrate an abstract idea, one that might be difficult for a reader to grasp. Julian Jaynes uses analogy in this fashion when trying to show the limitation of human consciousness.

> Consciousness is a much smaller part of our mental life than we are conscious of. How simple that is to say; how difficult to appreciate! It is like asking a flashlight in a dark room to search around for something that does not have any light shining upon it. The flashlight, since there is light in whatever direction it turns, would have to conclude that there is light everywhere. And so consciousness can seem to pervade all mentality when actually it does not.

By comparing the abstract to specific, concrete, seeable things, a writer can make an abstract concept a little clearer. The same is true of complicated experiences.

A writer might, for instance, decide to communicate the complicated thrill of a love affair. How? Well, the writer might do it by comparing it to a roller coaster ride—by using analogy. Although a love affair and a roller coaster ride are totally different experiences, they do share some general characteristics. Both have moments of heightened anticipation and exhilaration. Both capture a person's full attention. Both provide occasional surprises. And both, perhaps, end too soon. An analogy that is used to explain a complicated experience of this sort would be much longer than the above examples. A writer would develop it in a special pattern by introducing the subjects in the topic sentence.

The following illustration represents such a pattern. In it the writer compares getting a college education to a trip through a car wash. She sets up her subjects in the topic sentence. She then gives a brief description of the aspects of the car-washing experience that she wants to develop in her comparison. Next, she weaves together the experience of being a student with that of a car being scrubbed. Note that she doesn't try to describe every detail of the car-washing experience but instead selects only what she needs to make the connections between the two experiences—no more. We want to stress the importance of selecting appropriate details when writing anything, but especially when writing an analogy. If you include too much description, you may sidetrack your reader.

Like a trip through a car wash, a college education is an unveiling experience. The car arrives, its brilliance dimmed by layers of dust accumulated on the road. Sprayed and brushed repeatedly as it moves down the line, the car begins to regain its true color. So too a student enters the educational process, his potential hidden by inexperience and misconceptions about the world. He may resist at first, but gradually the repeated immersions in course work and the buffeting of his professors will begin to have an effect. He will discover previously unsuspected talents and interests; he will begin to view the world differently; he will become more tolerant of others as he learns of the complexity of human affairs. If he is lucky he will find two or three teachers who seem to speak directly to him, who have the skill and patience to put the final, polishing touches on his education, just as a small group of wash boys clean up the last specks of dirt on an automobile. If all goes well, what

The topic sentence presents two subjects and clearly leads the reader to expect an analogy.

Two sentences about the car wash set up the comparison.

The writer compares the educational process to previous statements about the car wash.

Second similarity between education and car wash.

emerges from the process is a person better

equipped to serve as an example to those who still

labor under their private accumulations of igno-

rance and prejudice.

As you can see from the illustration, analogy differs from ordinary comparison in that the writer focuses more on one subject than the other. She uses the car wash merely to get the reader thinking about a college education in a certain way.

We want to pass on a word of caution here. It's a mistake to carry an analogy too far. If the writer had extended the car wash analogy by comparing the preliminary vacuuming of the car to a college orientation course and a wax job to upper-division art courses (or any other courses, for that matter), the paragraph would have become ridiculous. Remember, the value of analogy lies in its power to suggest. It helps a writer lead the reader to experience something in a different way.

Now, let's examine another pattern built on analogy. Unlike the last illustration, this one relies on suggestion more than on direct comparison. This paragraph, from Donald Hall's "Four Kinds of Reading," compares certain kinds of reading to a narcotizing experience. The paragraph comes after others that discuss reading for information, literary experience, and intellectual awareness. As you read, notice the way Hall suggests the relation between reading and narcotics by using such words as *narcotic, opium, daydream, drug, addict,* and *trip.*

> But most reading which is praised for itself is neither literary nor intellectual. It is narcotic. Novels, stories and biographies—historical sagas, monthly regurgitations of book clubs—are the opium of the suburbs. The drug is not harmful except to the addict himself, and is no more injurious to him than Johnny Carson or a bridge club, but it is nothing to be proud of. This reading is the automated daydream, the mild trip of the housewife and the tired businessman, interested not in experience and feeling but in turning off the possibilities of experience and feeling. Great literature, if we read it well, opens us up to the world, and makes us more sensitive to it, as if we acquired eyes that could see through things and ears that could hear smaller sounds. But by narcotic reading, one can reduce great literature to the level of *The Valley of the Dolls.* One can read Anna Karenina passively and inattentively, and float down the river of lethargy as if one were reading a confession magazine: "I Spurned My Husband for a Count."

Writers will sometimes create dramatic analogies to make a point. Dramatic analogies are not always structured in traditional paragraphs. They may be arranged in narrative form with dialogue and description. For example, the following dramatic analogy opens the preface of Anne and Paul Ehrlich's *Extinction,* a nonfiction work based on the premise that the disappearance of other species shows that human life is also threatened.

As you walk from the terminal toward your airliner, you notice a man on a ladder busily prying rivets out of its wing. Somewhat concerned, you saunter over to the rivet popper and ask just what the hell he's doing.

"I work for the airline—Growthmania Intercontinental," the man informs you, "and the airline has discovered that it can sell these rivets for two dollars apiece."

"But how do you know you won't fatally weaken the wing doing that?" you inquire.

"Don't worry," he assures you. "I'm certain the manufacturer made this plane much stronger than it needs to be, so no harm's done. Besides, I've taken lots of rivets from this wing and it hasn't fallen off yet. Growthmania Airlines needs the money; if we didn't pop the rivets, Growthmania wouldn't be able to continue expanding. And I need the commission they pay me—fifty cents a rivet!"

"You must be out of your mind!"

"I told you not to worry; I know what I'm doing. As a matter of fact, I'm going to fly on this flight also, so you can see there's absolutely nothing to be concerned about."

Any sane person would, of course, go back into the terminal, report the gibbering idiot and Growthmania Airlines to the FAA, and make reservations on another carrier. You never have to fly on an airliner. But unfortunately all of us are passengers on a very large spacecraft—one on which we have no option but to fly. And frighteningly, it is swarming with rivet poppers behaving in ways analogous to that just described.

The rivet poppers on Spaceship Earth include such people as the President of the United States, the Chairman of the Soviet Communist Party, and most other politicians and decision makers; many big businessmen and small businessmen; and, inadvertently, most other people on the planet, including you and us.

Of course you know "Growthmania Airlines" and "rivet poppers" do not exist. The Ehrlichs created them for the purposes of the dramatic analogy—that is, to make the point that like the rivet poppers who are dismantling an aircraft, the world's political and business leaders as well as ourselves are responsible for the slow destruction of the Earth.

When writing an analogy, be cautious. Often an analogy can be flat, confused, or unintentionally comic—usually because the writer hasn't thought through the comparison. So be on guard: think through the comparative points of your two subjects and be sure the analogy reveals the point you want to make.

WRITING TASK—ANALOGY

1. Develop an analogy by using one of the following to illuminate an abstract idea, an experience, or a process. We suggest you begin the writing process by developing four or five rough sentences that show how the familiar subject reveals the less familiar subject. Then build a fully developed paragraph from this rough draft. We encourage you, of course, to modify any of the following suggestions to fit your own interests.

a flowing river	a tornado
a merry-go-round	a dark tunnel
the changing seasons	a bird of prey
the phases of the moon	a slot machine
the passage of the sun	a crap game
the changing tide	ripening fruit
running long distances	an unweeded garden
a spider web	a cluttered room
walking through a desert	a poker hand
mountain climbing	a game of solitaire

2. If you wish to write an extended paper, create a dramatic analogy that illuminates a complex problem. We suggest you review the Ehrlichs' earlier analogy of the "rivet poppers" and consider a topic from the following list.

- The destruction of rain forests
- The desire to succeed at any price
- Enforcing or not enforcing capital punishment
- Lying by political leaders
- World starvation
- Consuming products that deplete the Earth's natural resources
- Allowing or not allowing abortion
- The disposal of toxic waste
- The use of cosmetic surgery for vanity
- The extinction of an animal species

Remember:

The term to which you compare an idea or experience is not the subject of your piece. For instance, when Selzer writes, "One holds the knife as one holds the bow of a cello or tulip—by the stem," he is not writing about a cello or tulip stem, he is writing about the process of surgery that starts with the proper handling of a scalpel. Be sure not to lose sight of your true subject.

GROUP WORK

As a group, select a single subject for your analogy draft—that is, compare a life to a river or develop an analogy to illustrate a point, such as the lying of public officials, the bungling of admission departments, or the role of a teacher.

After the analogies are completed, each of you can read them to the group. Of course each analogy, even though it deals with the same subject, will be different. After each reading, then, the writer might explain his or her approach.

10
Classification

Human beings love to classify—that is, to divide a large subject into components before sorting them into categories according to qualities they share. We speak of lyric poetry and dramatic poetry; farces, comedies, and tragedies; economy cars, sports cars, and luxury cars; and, all too often, the good guys and the bad guys.

A music teacher may sort students according to their voices: soprano, mezzo-soprano, alto, tenor, baritone, and bass. A political science teacher may sort the same students according to their political leanings: radicals, liberals, conservatives, reactionaries, and independents. The college registrar, for statistical purposes, may sort them according to sex, age, major, grade-point average, city, state or country of origin, or future educational plans. A student may be content just to sort members of the opposite sex: fantastic, attractive, passable, and no thanks.

The point is that any subject can be classified in a number of ways depending on the writer's point of view and purpose. For example, in a paragraph from his essay "Fans," Paul Gallico sorts the crowds that attend sports events. He divides them into categories according to what sport they watch and identifies each category by its outstanding characteristics.

> The fight crowd is a beast that lurks in the darkness behind the fringe of white light shed over the first six rows by the incandescents atop the ring and is not to be trusted with pop bottles or other hardware. The tennis crowd is the pansy of all the great sports mobs and is always preening and shushing itself. The golf crowd is the most unwieldy and most sympathetic, and is the only horde given to mass production of that absurd noise written generally as "tsk, tsk, tsk,

tsk," and made between tongue and teeth with head-waggings to denote extreme commiseration. The baseball crowd is the most hysterical, the football crowd the best-natured and the polo crowd the most aristocratic. Racing crowds are the most restless, wrestling crowds the most tolerant, and soccer crowds the most easily incitable to riot and disorder. Every sports crowd takes on the characteristics of the individuals who compose it. Each has its particular note of hysteria, its own little cruelties, mannerisms, and bad mannerisms, its own code of sportsmanship and its own method of expressing its emotions.

Often the terms *division* and *classification* are distinguished from each other, but division and classification work together in the sorting process. Writers usually begin by dividing a subject into categories before they classify the individual components of the subject according to qualities they share. In other words, division breaks one subject into several categories; classification sorts the individual parts of the subject into the appropriate categories. For example, the subject "popular movies" might be divided into the following categories: western, horror, mystery, crime, science fiction, musical, and comedy. Once the subject is divided into several categories, individual movies can be classified within the appropriate categories. Consider the classification of several well-known films: *Unforgiven,* for example, would clearly be classified under western; *Friday the 13th* under horror; *Pulp Fiction* under crime; *The Day the Earth Stood Still* under science fiction; . . . and so on.

Of course, when a subject has disparate components, it may not be easy to classify. Consider *Alien.* Many would automatically classify *Alien* under science fiction because it takes place aboard a spaceship sometime in the future, but the film also concentrates on the crew's battle with a monster, a hideous creature that devours them one at a time. This monster, like Jason in *Friday the 13th,* seems indestructible. Should *Alien* be classified under science fiction or horror? The answer depends on who is doing the classifying and her category descriptions.

Establishing Categories for Classification

Writers tend to use at least three categories when they classify; otherwise, they might inadvertently compare and contrast their two subjects. They may use ready-made categories, as Paul Gallico does above, or create their own categories. For example, student-writer Sarah Collins created an unusual category she calls "car movies." She then divided the category even further and classified several films within a subdivision she named "macho car movies."

American men seem to have had a mystical bond with the automobile since Model Ts began rolling off Henry Ford's assembly line in 1909. Nowhere has the relationship between driver and car been captured as effectively as in "macho car movies," Hollywood films that exploit the psychological relationship between masculinity and sleek, powerful automobiles. Teenage Cruiser Movies clearly relate the theme of becoming a man to the automobile. For example, 1955's Rebel Without a Cause features James Dean, who came to epitomize the concept of "being cool" for teens throughout the country, cruising Los Angeles streets in a tricked-out 1949 Mercury while escaping the influence of his ineffectual parents. This film features a game of "chicken," thus establishing the important link between male courage and the automobile. 1973's cruiser movie American Graffiti features teenagers cruising to the once popular lyrics, "womp-bomp, get around, I get around . . ." while street lights glint off metallic fenders and chrome bumpers. Outlaw Chase Movies stress the relationship between high-speed driving skill and manhood. For example, in 1958's Thunder Road Robert Mitchum, as cool as James Dean, plays a sleepy-eyed moonshine runner who drives a souped-

The opening sentences supply background information and state the general topic, "macho car movies," and the central point, "macho car movies . . . exploit the psychological relationship between masculinity and . . . the automobile."

The writer presents the first category, Teenage Cruiser Movies, and follows with examples.

Presenting the second category, Outlaw Chase Movies, the writer not only gives examples but also includes a departure from the formula.

up roadster during a series of chase scenes that make up most of the film. In 1968 these character-istics are refined in Bullitt, which features a chase that bumped and thumped for almost fifteen minutes over San Francisco hills. The film's most important relationship was between the central character, played by Steve McQueen, and his car, a sleek Mustang. Chase movies such as Smokey and the Bandit offer a variation of this formula. The chase is played for laughs as an inept, redneck lawman pursues the macho outlaw driver.

Professional Racing Movies present a different image of manhood achieved behind the wheel. 1966's Grand Prix features a sophisticated macho man instead of an inexperienced teenager, self-absorbed cop, or mindless outlaw. This character, played by James Garner, is coolly professional on the race track as he maneuvers a high-performance machine over Europe's most prestigious courses. Even though the character is suave, his manhood is still measured by courage and daring behind the wheel. Grand Prix was followed by Winning and Red Line 7000. None, however, can match the sheer glitz of Days of Thunder, in which American stock car racing is nothing more than a backdrop for a young driver, played by screen idol Tom Cruise, to

The writer presents the third cate-gory, Professional Racing Movies, and gives examples.

```
prove his masculinity by "rubbing" fenders at

breakneck speeds on a crowded track.
```

Although this paragraph is organized by one controlling idea, it could have been divided into several shorter paragraphs, each devoted to one category of "macho car movies." If you find yourself writing an excessively long paragraph, consider dividing it at a logical spot. Just make sure the relationship between the parts will be clear to your reader.

The writer of the preceding example wasn't just handed her classes; she created them. She then created labels to identify them for the reader.

Working with existing classes may be tougher than finding new ones. The writer is obligated to offer some new insights into the groups, not merely to pass on commonly known information. For instance, in the following example from *Blood and Money,* Thomas Thompson spends a paragraph describing the different classes of surgeons. To make his material fresh, he describes each group according to its general personal characteristics, thus giving readers a new way of looking at the people who might be plunging scalpels into their flesh.

Among those who train students to become doctors, it is said that surgeons find their niche in accordance with their personal characteristics. The orthopedic surgeon is medicine's carpenter—up to his elbows in plaster of Paris—and tradition holds that he is a gruff, slapdash sort of man whose labor is in a very physical area of healing. Away from the hospital, the orthopedists are often hunters, boaters, outdoorsmen.

The neurosurgeon, classically, does not get too involved with his patients. Or, for that matter, with anybody. They are cool men, blunted, rarely gregarious.

Heart surgeons are thundering egotists, star performers in a dazzling operating theater packed with assistants, nurses, paramedics, and a battery of futuristic equipment which could seemingly lift the room into outer space. These are men who relish drama, who live life on the edge of the precipice.

And the plastic surgeon? He is, by nature, a man of art, and temperament, and sensitivity. "We are the artists who deal in beauty lost, or beauty that never was," said one plastic man at a national convention. "Our stitches are hidden, and so are our emotions."

Arranging a Classification

The arrangement of a classification piece is quite simple. A writer will present the categories in the order that seems most appropriate. We do want to make one hard rule about classification arrangement: Always give the name of the class in the first sentence that starts the group description. The name will help you keep the reader on the right track by announcing that a shift from one group to another will be taking place.

You face one danger here. Often a classification piece will get boring if you merely tick off one category after another. How do you avoid boring your readers? Create some variety. For instance, Thompson begins his first three group descriptions with "The orthopedic surgeon," "The neurosurgeon," and "Heart surgeons." After these three standard openings the reader might react with a ho hum. But Thompson anticipates this response, so he varies the last opening by beginning with a question: "And the plastic surgeon?" It's not a spectacular tactic, but it serves to nudge a drowsing reader. It's unexpected.

Now study the following example in which student-writer Harold Grant classifies the behavior of socially effective children. Notice that Grant mentions the categories in the opening to let the reader know what to expect, a common practice in classification patterns. Like Thomas Thompson's paragraph before, Grant's material is divided into several short paragraphs to avoid writing one excessively long paragraph. As you read, notice how clearly he arranges the classes, first identifying the group, second identifying its chief behavior, and then developing an example of the behavior at work.

Young children who can "read" the instructions and feelings of their peers tend to be more successful in school than children who cannot. On any playground these effective social skills are easily identified and those who possess them can be identified as Leaders, Mediators, and Therapists.

The Leader excels at organizing, coordinating, and maintaining activities. This child might not always initiate a game but will step in to direct it. For example, one child says, "I want to play Martian tribe but nobody else does." The leader will respond, "Okay, you get to choose the chief but you can't choose yourself," thus revealing he or she understands group resistance to the first child's desire to be chief.

The Mediator negotiates solutions and prevents or resolves social conflicts. For example, when one child urges a group to play hide-and-seek, a squabble develops over who will be "it." The mediator will sense everyone's reluctance to be isolated as the outsider and suggest the group be divided into teams so no one child is "it."

The Therapist analyzes emotional situations individual children face, often reflecting another child's feelings much like close friends in an adult relationship. For example, one child falls and hurts an ankle, the other children run away. The therapist stays back, perhaps saying, "Your ankle must really hurt, but it must also hurt to be left alone." No matter what category socially effective children fall into, their skill at "reading" their peers will help them succeed as they advance through the grades.

Grouping and Sorting Classes

You can think of classification as another word for grouping or sorting. You have a large number of instances, too many to discuss individually, and you group, sort, or classify them into a small number of classes according to some principle of similarity that is meaningful for your paper.

It's very much like sorting the mail. When you drop a letter into the slot at the post office, you take the first classification step yourself by dropping your letter in the out-of-town slot instead of the local slot. A mail clerk going through the out-of-town mail conducts further classification by sorting the letters into bags labeled New England, Middle Atlantic, South Atlantic, Midwest, South, Southwest, Northwest, and Pacific Coast. When a bag of letters arrives at a New England depot, it is further sorted by zip code and later still by street address. Only then does the name of the individual addressee become important.

When you want to arrange some information in a classification pattern, you must sort its components into meaningful groups. *Meaningful* is the key word. Consider our post office analogy. For the first clerk to decide to classify the letters alphabetically would not have been to sort them meaningfully. Such a sorting would produce stacks of bags labeled A, B, C, and so on through Z. This system would not serve the post office's purpose of passing mail from senders to receivers. A meaningful classification would be for the clerk to sort the mail by destination, not by alphabet.

In a different situation, the destination of a letter may not be the best way to classify it. Consider the needs of someone in business who receives bundles of mail daily—requests for charitable donations, advertisements, business reports, invitations, demands for business actions, and notes from old friends. Whether formally or informally, the executive will classify the day's mail according to the importance of each letter, perhaps arranging it in categories such as immediate response, eventual response, information only, and junk. Given the executive's situation, these would be meaningful classes.

Once you have your meaningful classes spotted, you need to be sure they're equally general. It wouldn't make much sense to classify bundles of mail headed for the East under the labels New England, Middle Atlantic, Southeast, and Boston. These classes are not equally general. The first three are regions. Boston is a city—in fact, part of New England. Would Thomas Thompson have made much sense if he had classified surgeons under orthopedic surgeons, neurosurgeons, heart surgeons, plastic surgeons, and surgeons in training? Of course not.

Your classes should also be inclusive—they should cover the territory reasonably well. If the postal clerks had forgotten to label a bag Midwest, their system would not cover the territory of the United States. If you classify religions in America by referring only to Catholics, Baptists, Methodists, and Christian Scientists, you have not covered the territory. Of course the word *reasonably* has to operate here. Perhaps your paper can't include every specific instance, and if you think you've covered the territory and someone says, "Hey, how about the Poseidon freaks?" you may be justified in dismissing that person as a crackpot. If you want to avoid leaving yourself open to criticism, you may have to resort to changing your subject to major religions in America and then define the term *major* as you see it. Realistically, such problems won't crop up too often, and if you avoid major omissions, most readers will accept the fact that you are characterizing prominent classes and recognize the logic of your arrangement. Your classes should be exclusive, too, with no overlapping. If the postal clerks have drawn their boundaries well, there will be no doubt that a particular letter belongs in the Middle Atlantic and not the Southeast bag. If you are classifying television programs and you decide to group them as children's, westerns, situation comedies, and educational, your classes are not exclusive. A children's program could be a western or educational. The problem here is in the method of arriving at the classes. Children's is a class arrived at according to age; westerns and situation comedies are classes arrived at according to content; educational is a class arrived at according to purpose. You can't mix methods of classification without confusing your reader.

Hold the following four principles in mind while thinking through a classification piece.

1. Develop meaningful classes.
2. Shape them at the same general level.
3. Make sure they are inclusive enough to cover the territory.
4. Make sure they are exclusive enough not to overlap.

WRITING TASK—CLASSIFICATION

Write a piece developed by classification. Avoid the obvious and the superficial. Don't classify salespeople into the successful and unsuccessful or cars into luxury and economy classes. Such classifications and others like them don't merit your attention or your reader's. They're too obvious.

Here are some general subject areas you might consider classifying. Keep in mind that they need to be focused—that is your job.

teachers	vacations
jobs	restaurants
department stores	boutiques
students	athletes
coaches	lies
police officers	movies
books	disguises
television programs	sports fans
playgrounds	affairs
dates	lovers
doctors	nurses

If these don't work for you, you may want to use one of the following questions to lead you into classification.

1. What are the ways to obtain knowledge?
2. What are the ways to manipulate others?
3. What are the ways to bring joy to others?
4. What are the ways to make big money?
5. What are the ways to stop smoking?
6. What are the ways to get a person to say yes?
7. What are the ways to live without working?
8. What are the ways to cook a good anything?

Remember:

1. Divide your subject into at least three groups.
2. If you develop your own categories and labels, announce them at the beginning of your paragraph.
3. Develop meaningful categories that don't overlap.
4. Keep your reader interested and avoid merely ticking off one category after another.

GROUP WORK

Develop a plan for a classification paper: clearly state the subject, identify the groups you've divided the subject into, and list the items in each group.

In a group meeting, exchange plans and evaluate them. Are there at least three groups in the classifications? Does the division make sense? Do any of the items overlap? Offer any suggestions or point out any areas of confusion.

Once the final drafts are written, submit them for group review. Distribute a copy to each group member. When reading them, pay particular attention to how each classification group is presented. Is the presentation effective? Can each group be easily distinguished from the others? Finally, jot down your observations and return the draft to the writer.

11
Definition

When speaking, many of us toss away words like a gambler throwing quarters at a Las Vegas slot machine. But when writing, most of us try to use words precisely. We live with the knowledge (maybe even the fear) that on a sheet of paper our words can be examined—studied in context and explored in a dictionary; whereas in speech we relax with the knowledge that words melt like cotton candy on a warm tongue.

Trying to use words precisely can be a gut-wrenching business. Some words are so much a part of a specialized vocabulary that only certain occupational or recreational groups know them. Some are used so infrequently that few readers know what they mean. Some are so slippery that people understand them differently. But when you write, you have to struggle to be precise—painfully precise—in overcoming the specialized, the infrequent, the slippery word. Sometimes that means defining, briefly or extensively, any key word you use to make sure the reader understands what you mean.

Brief Definitions

A brief definition will usually do for an obscure or specialized word. A synonym, a short phrase, a brief comparison—that's all you need.

Synonym: When my uncle returned from abroad, he gave each of us a grego, which is a jacket.

Short Phrase: Some historians suggest that the American government during the last century conducted an unofficial pogrom, an organized massacre of helpless people, against Indians confined to reservations.

Comparison: Thallium, a metallic element resembling lead, is rare.

When you give a brief definition, always try to work it into the flow of your piece. Don't stop the movement, announce the word's meaning, then pick up the march. Also avoid misusing when and where in definitions. Don't write something like this:

Gregarious is when people flock or herd together.

Or this:

Gregarious is where people flock or herd together.

Gregarious is neither a time nor a place—it's a mode of social behavior.

Extended Definitions

Brief definitions are easy enough. The real difficulty comes with extended definitions of abstract or general words, words such as *freedom, love, prejudice, equality, delinquency, patriotism, affluence,* or *poverty.* Words such as these have become so slippery you must define them. Usually the definition will be extended—a well-developed paragraph or more in length—so that your reader will have a clear idea of what such a word means to you. For example, Madonna Marsden in a paragraph in "The American Myth" defines her understanding of the American Dream.

> Open almost any magazine and you'll find it—the lavish array of material objects which connote the comfort, the status, and the security, which are the components of the American Dream. For these are the clichés of the American good life—"a chicken in every pot," "a car in every garage," a place where even the person born into poverty can give a tug on his or her bootstraps and have a chance at the Presidency or a seat on the Stock Exchange. And it has happened here. Think of our great political and industrial heroes: Andrew Jackson, Abraham Lincoln, Andrew Carnegie, John D. Rockefeller. Though essentially simple men, they made the most of their native intelligence and natural spunk. They worked hard, rose through the ranks, and were rewarded by fame and/or fortune. And that is the American myth of success. With hard work comes achievement, and with achievement comes the material comforts of the American Dream and sometimes even great riches and a place in history.

Marsden follows a tidy and effective pattern. She opens with a topic sentence that leads readers to expect a definition. She follows with a catalog of examples of clichés associated with the American Dream. She further develops the paragraph with a catalog of men who have actually achieved the Dream. She then closes with a clincher that sums up her concept.

Marsden's paragraph primarily relies on a catalog of brief examples for development (see Cataloging, Chapter 6), but extended definitions can be developed in a variety of ways. You can

1. use synonyms
2. give examples
3. discuss the origin of the word
4. develop comparisons or analogies
5. tell what the word is not
6. create an anecdote to show the word in action

As you have probably noticed, many of these items (examples, anecdotes, comparisons, and analogies) are methods of paragraph development studied in earlier chapters. We don't suggest you try to use all these techniques in any single definition. We listed them to give you an idea of the possibilities.

Extended Personal and Objective Examples

Extended definitions can be purely personal or they can be largely objective. A personal definition, like the preceding one, explains how a writer is using the term—"Never mind what other people think the American Dream means; it means this to me." Such a strategy is useful if your purpose is to get a reader to see a word in a different light or if you are discussing your understanding of the term. Everyone knows, for instance, what *prejudice* means: "prejudging without adequate information." But to a six-year-old, *prejudice* may mean waiting at a candy counter until all the adults are served. It may mean not counting as a real person, tolerated rather than truly listened to. It may mean being discriminated against on the basis of size.

An objective definition, on the other hand, seeks general agreement. It's the kind of definition that applies in all cases at all times. This requires detailing. The word *democracy* means "rule by the people." At this level, most people can agree with the definition without further discussion. But two opposing political forces may need to reach a more detailed agreement if they are to talk together productively. For example, who are the people? Everyone? Voters? Only those over twenty-one? A ruling class that claims to speak in the name of all? It would be meaningless to discuss the value of "democratic elections" without a comprehensive definition of democracy. Objective definitions, therefore, should spell out the details.

First, let's examine an extended personal definition of *patriotism*. Student-writer Max Sheridan starts with a topic sentence that establishes the broad meaning of patriotism. He then spends four sentences exploring what patriotism isn't. He follows with examples—brief ones—of patriotic behavior. He then spends a sentence on the origins of the word before moving into a comparison with parental love. He finishes the paragraph by reminding the reader of his opening thought, thus indicating he has covered the territory.

<u>True patriotism is wishing your country well.</u>

It does not require chest thumping, flag waving, fiery speeches, or parades. We use the word incorrectly when we confine it to ostentatious acts. It is not boasting, but service; not hatred, but love; not loud, but quiet. Quiet, loving service is what a patriot has to offer.

This opening sentence clearly suggests that a definition will follow.

The following four sentences tell what patriotism isn't. Since patriotism is such an abstract concept, the writer tries to give his definition life with image-producing phrases: chest thumping, flag waving, fiery speeches, and so on.

The voter who puts public welfare above private greed is practicing patriotism. The person who expresses his opinion on local, state, and national problems; who dares to criticize elected representatives; whose personal behavior serves as a prod to the conscience of others is practicing patriotism. Those who do these things do so because they care about their country.

Because definitions tend to be inclusive, examples tend to be impressionistic and general, as these are. The last sentence in this series comes back to the central point: wishing your country well.

We get the word <u>patriot</u> from the Latin for "fellow countryman," a term suggesting a loving relationship that is at the heart of patriotic behavior.

Here the writer dips into etymology—word history—to set up the analogy that follows.

One's love for his fellow countrymen and, therefore, his country is not unlike parents' love for their children. Parents want their chil-

This analogy further illustrates what patriotism means to the writer.

dren to realize their potential, to grow, to
become better. They invest time and effort to this
end. They support their children through rough
times, but they also demand certain standards of
behavior. It would be a poor parent who said, "My
child, right or wrong," if that phrase is intended
to convey an unthinking support of whatever the
child wants to do. By the same token the phrase,
"My country, right or wrong," should not be
accepted blindly as a patriotic position. Wishing
your country well is harder and more complicated
than blind loyalty.

*The clincher sentence recalls the
introduction and closes the paragraph.*

Do you agree with this definition? Perhaps not. But agreement isn't what
this writer is after. Instead he seeks understanding. There is no doubt that
you have a strong impression of what he means by *patriotism*.

Now let's examine an objective definition to give you an idea of how to
go about writing one. One dictionary definition of *plagiarism* is "to steal
someone else's ideas or words and pass them off as one's own."

As you define a term in your paper, you may wish to see what a dictionary's definition is, but don't merely quote the dictionary in your paper ("as the
. . . says . . .") and stop with that. Instead make the word yours; discuss it as
you see it and as you want your reader to understand it. The dictionary definition of *plagiarism* is clear, as far as it goes, but a more extended objective definition gives the reader a better understanding of plagiarism and how it happens.

<u>Plagiarism is taking the words or ideas of
another and pretending they are yours.</u> It is a
serious literary crime, a form of dishonesty that,
if discovered, carries heavy penalties. There are
two kinds of plagiarism, the intentional and the
unintentional. Intentional plagiarism is an act of
either defiance or desperation. The defiant student

*The topic sentence is a capsule defini-
tion.*

*The writer amplifies on the capsule
definition.*

*Then he divides the term into two
kinds.*

*He divides the first kind into two
subparts.*

sees no reason to learn about photosynthesis (for example) himself, and so he "rewrites" an article or textbook entry and brazenly submits it to the instructor as his own work. The desperate student probably agrees that the subject is worth knowing about, but he's neglected his studies too long. In panic he also turns in someone else's work, throwing in a few misspellings for authenticity. More often plagiarism is unintentional, a product of ignorance. The student is required to write on a subject he is not expert on. The instructor knows this and expects the student to turn to other written sources for information. Unfortunately, those other sources phrase things so well that the student cannot see any alternative ways of organizing the material. Instead of making the information his and then expressing what he has learned, he produces a patchwork piece of alternating amateur and professional sentences and paragraphs. He's not proud of it, but what can he do? Well, fortunately, there are many things he can do. And in the process of following the tips presented below, he will not only learn his subject well, he will avoid the embarrassment of being charged with plagiarism.

He explains one subpart.

He explains the other subpart.

The writer discusses the second kind of plagiarism.

The final sentences lead to the rest of the paper, discussing ways to avoid plagiarism.

An extended personal definition such as this is usually used as a part of a longer paper, and usually comes near the beginning. In a paper discussing the skill of bullfighting, for example, it may be useful to have a definition of the term *adorno*. Briefly, it means a kind of flowery theatricality by which a bullfighter shows domination over the bull. But an extended definition giving examples of *adorno* in practice would be helpful for the reader of such a paper.

Using a Variety of Methods

As we mentioned before, writers use a variety of methods in definitions. The writer who defined *patriotism* used examples and analogy. The writer who defined *plagiarism* used classification. Keep in mind that patterns seldom appear in pure form. They get mixed together. And nowhere do they get more mixed than in defining terms. So when you write an extended definition, use good horse sense. If you don't know what horse sense is, read the following extended definition by writer Earl Rudolph.

Horse sense is a judgment which reflects sound thinking. It is not a blind jump into a decision which may lead to ruin. Horse sense is not a hasty conclusion which prompts action causing deep regret later. In other words, horse sense is common sense. Anyone possessing this common sense would know better than to wear bathing trunks outdoors in December. He certainly would regret this action while recuperating from pneumonia. A sensible casting machine operator will turn off his machine before he attempts to retrieve a die which has fallen into the mechanism. A thoughtful homeowner carries liability insurance to avoid being sued by someone injured on his property. These people all use horse sense or common sense in mak-

The topic sentence puts the term into a general class. The two sentences that follow tell what it is not.

Next Rudolph gives a synonym.

Then he gives three examples.

Then he makes a summary statement about the examples.

ing important decisions almost every day of their

lives. We see then that horse sense or common

sense often requires sound thinking.

Rudolph's clincher sentence returns to first statement.

There's always a limit to how far a definition can go. We're sure you could sit down and list many more examples of horse sense than Rudolph does. But remember, in definition your goal is to give the reader a clear understanding of the term. That calls for personal judgment. When you've nailed down the term, stop.

WRITING TASK—DEFINITION

You are to write an extended definition of a word or phrase. Develop your definition by using several of the techniques discussed earlier: Use synonyms, give examples, discuss the word's origins, develop comparisons, tell what the word is not, create an anecdote to show the word in action. You may consult a dictionary, but do not use a dictionary quotation as the main part of your definition. You may, however, integrate information you learn from the dictionary into your extended definition. Your task is to make the definition fresh by using your understanding and experience to illuminate the word's meaning.

The following are four options. Choose one of them for this task.

1. You have been assigned to help write a health report for the college medical center. Your primary responsibility is to define a mental health term so that your fellow students will understand it. Select one of the following terms.

stress	burnout
depression	anxiety
apathy	addiction
obsession	workaholic syndrome

2. Stereotypes appear in movies and on television—the good, bad, or tough cop; the kindly doctor; the typical housewife; the private detective; the ideal family; and so on. Isolate a particular stereotype you recognize in several films or shows and define it in a paragraph.

3. Write an extended personal or objective definition for one of the following words or phrases:

glamour	poverty
luck	tyranny
beauty	confidence
abundance	phony
scholar	clever
negligent	tragedy
funny	female liberation
sexual harassment	male liberation
breach of confidence	liberation theology
fiasco	social responsibility
ambition	

4. Write an extended definition of a slang term or phrase. First explain the term, then create several brief situations in which it might be used. You may use a term from the following brief list of current and past slang. But better yet . . . select a current slang term or phrase and define it.

bonehead	scam
geek	heyday
macho	greenhorn
rip-off	shoddy
cool	radical or rad

Remember:

1. You're writing a definition that not only explains how the word is generally used but also explains your understanding of the word.
2. Develop your definition by using patterns such as example, comparison and contrast, analogy, anecdote, and classification.

GROUP WORK

Before a work session, select a term you wish to define. During the session each group member should present a term and propose an approach to its definition. To further develop information for the first draft, the group can spend three minutes brainstorming each term to generate more information.

For the next session, you should return with a draft and several copies. Circulate them among group members for review.

Read each draft silently as a group. After each reading, offer your observations to the writer. Be sure to "test" the definition. Is it precise enough? What has the writer left out? Is it too general?

12
Cause And Effect

An eight-year-old bursts through the screen door, tears running down his cheeks, hand clasped over his nose with a few droplets of blood squeezing between his fingers. Dad puts down the dish towel and turns from the sink with an "I'm an understanding papa" look on his face.

"Sandra hit me," the boy cries. "Right in the nose."

Dad begins to wipe away the blood and tears. The screen door flies open again. The sister storms into the kitchen and shouts, "He threw the baseball at me."

"She tried to horn in on our game. She can't hit."

"I can hit better than you. Look at your nose."

And on and on and on.

At one level this drama illustrates child behavior. At another it illustrates cause-and-effect relationships.

We begin the drama with a clear effect—the bloody nose. We then fall back to a cause—a right cross. At first it all seems simple. We probe deeper: right cross to nose caused by brother tossing baseball at sister.

Hmmmmmm!

The plot thickens: tossed baseball caused by sister trying to join the game.

Here we stop, for we want only to give you an idea of what cause-and-effect patterns involve, not probe the roots of sibling rivalry.

When writers explain why something happened or what could possibly happen or the results of something happening, they are dealing in cause and effect.

Why did Sandra punch her brother? Does violence broadcast on television stimulate violence on the street? Has economic recession changed college programs? Why do so many older Americans revere Clint Eastwood? These are all questions that would lead you into using a cause-and-effect pattern.

Causal Chains

The informal anecdote above illustrates one important characteristic of cause-and-effect relationships: They often occur in a sequence, each event contributing to the following event in a *causal chain.* In other words, a cause triggers an event which in turn becomes the cause of another event. Often a writer will use a causal chain to arrange a cause-and-effect paragraph, or entire essay for that matter, explaining both the causes and effects of an event. In the following paragraph, the writer explains violent teenage encounters in her hometown by using a causal chain.

An adolescent ritual of manhood in Lakeview, my hometown of about 75,000 people, centers on Friday night violence among teenage boys. Parents usually explain the underlying cause of the violence by saying "boys will be boys," suggesting that their children are motivated by mysterious hormonal explosions beyond anyone's understanding. Though the actual details of these violent encounters may vary from one Friday night to another Friday night, the general pattern is always predictable. Typically, an encounter is set in motion during a sports event in which a team from Northwood High School opposes a team from South Hills High School. Since the competition between the two schools is strong, both on and off the playing field, the sports event usually ends with the winners taunting the losers and the losers vowing

The opening sentences provide background information and establish the paragraph's direction.

Strong competition between the schools leads to verbal taunting.

revenge. The rowdier students often withdraw to
beer parties where they continue to brag about the
victory or threaten their arch rivals. As the parties become rowdy, the neighbors complain, and
about midnight the police disperse the teenagers,
ordering them to go home. Many do, but others
gather at their favorite hangouts, Northwood's
Taco Bell and South Hills' Denny's. Eventually, a
boisterous group, usually the winners, will cruise
the opposition's hangout and shout obscenities
from their cars. The losers will typically respond
with obscene gestures, climb into their cars and
give chase. Eventually the two sides will meet up
in a parking lot or community park where they call
each other's manhood into question. The final
result is several broken noses, skinned knuckles,
and expensive dental bills—after all, "boys will
be boys."

Emboldened by the taunting and fueled by beer, the boys' behavior grows rowdy.

The rowdy behavior forces the police to break up the parties.

Sent to the streets, a few boys invade their opponents' territory, and the night ends in a fight.

When identifying the events related in a causal chain, a writer must be aware of the immediate causes and effects, which are the ones occurring near an event, and the remote causes and effects, which are the ones occurring further away in time. In the above paragraph, for example, the rivalry between Northwood and South Hills is the remote cause of Friday night violence; the verbal and physical confrontations are the immediate effects. The writer, we should point out, is also aware that a much more remote cause for the rivalry might be at work—unknown developmental or psychological forces that the parents dismiss by saying "boys will be boys."

When discussing cause-and-effect relationships, you should also be aware of a common fallacy called *post hoc,* short for the Latin phrase *post hoc, ergo propter hoc,* which is translated into English as "after this, therefore because of this" and sometimes referred to as the *false cause* fallacy. A writer commits the false cause fallacy by offering the wrong reasons for the cause of an event: black cats don't cause bad luck; an eighty-year-old who has smoked cigarettes for sixty years does not prove that the effects of smoking are healthful; laziness is not the reason for poverty, and so on.

Since cause-and-effect relationships can be confusing, it might help you to understand them if you think of causes as reasons and effects as results. If, for instance, you answer a "why" question, you will be giving reasons, that is, the causes: Why do such classic horror films as *Friday the 13th, Halloween,* and *The Texas Chain Saw Massacre* still thrill teenage audiences? If you answer a "what" question, you will probably be giving results, that is, the effects: What are the social consequences of film violence? If you answer a compound "why" and "what" question, you will be giving the reasons and results, that is, the causes and effects: Why do slasher films thrill teenage audiences, and what are the social consequences?

You should also know that writers do not always discuss both causes and effects of an event. Often they will concentrate on only the causes or only the effects.

Discussing Causes

When the effect of an event is clear, you will not need to spend much time discussing it, but you will need to discuss its causes. For example, statistics indicate that teenage suicide is increasing. If you were to write about the problem, you would not have to spend much effort substantiating the fact. Rather, you would spend most of your effort discussing the reasons why teen suicide is increasing—that is, the causes.

The pattern for explaining the causes for a known effect is simple. Open with a statement that clearly states the effect. Then list the causes in the body of the paragraph. The following example follows this pattern, but with a twist: the writer opens with a "why" question, thus indicating to a reader that causes will follow.

Why is aerobic exercise a popular activity in southern California? There is no single answer, but there are many possibilities. Perhaps southern Californians live in such a youth-oriented culture that those moving into middle life exercise in a desperate effort to keep what nature is tearing

The opening statement clearly leads the reader to expect causes to follow.

The writer develops three causes.

Cause 1: Exercise is stylish.

from them. Others may exercise to be part of "the

scene," just as some people go to nightclubs to be

part of that scene. Or perhaps there is a deeper

cause. Some enthusiasts, especially joggers, long-

distance walkers, and swimmers, claim that extend-

ed periods of exercise can lead to meditative

trances with all the benefits of quiet sitting.

They see themselves as innovators in the tradition

of "moving meditation," such as that practiced by

Sufi whirling dervishes. Still others claim they

exercise merely to stay fit by burning off extra

servings of cream pie, chocolate cake, ice cream,

and jelly rolls.

Cause 2: Exercise has psychological benefits.

Cause 3: Exercise burns calories.

As you read the paragraph, did you notice how frequently the writer qualified the causes by using words and phrases such as "perhaps," "others may," "some," and "others claim"? Since not everyone who exercises does so for the same reason, the writer wants to be clear about the fact that these are possible causes, thus avoiding the false cause fallacy.

Now study the following paragraph from Sam Keen's *Faces of the Enemys*, which explores the ultimate causes of war, causes buried deep in the human psyche. Earlier in the text he asked why human reason and the destructive power of military technology fail to discourage political leaders from waging wars of aggression. Here he concludes that the problem of lasting peace cannot be solved by reasonable negotiations and arms reduction alone; it can only be solved by understanding the "hardness of our hearts."

The problem seems to lie not in our reason or our technology, but in the hardness of our hearts. Generation after generation, we find excuses to hate and dehumanize each other, and we always justify ourselves with the most mature-sounding political rhetoric. And we refuse to admit the obvious. We human beings are <u>Homo hostilis</u>, the hostile species, the enemy-making animal. We are driven to fabricate an enemy as a scapegoat to bear the burden of our denied enmity. From the unconscious residue of our hostility, we create a target; from our private demons, we conjure a public enemy. And, perhaps, more than anything else, the wars we engage in are compulsive rituals, shadow dramas in which we continually try to kill those parts of ourselves we deny and despise.

Are the ultimate causes of war buried deep in humankind's psychological nature? Keen's observation is interesting, probing beneath what most of us perceive as the immediate causes of war, such as territorial expansion, personal power, religious disagreements, and competing political philosophies.

Discussing Effects

When the causes of an event are clear, you will spend most of your effort discussing the effects. For example, most studies show that many children spend more time watching television than they spend in school. Most people accept the studies as accurate. As a writer, therefore, you would spend your effort explaining the effects of extended television viewing on children.

In the following student paragraph, Ruth Lee discusses the effects of feminism on her college campus. She uses a simple pattern, first introducing the cause for change, then listing the changes—that is, the effects of the causes.

Our campus still benefits from the success of the early woman's movement. First, the Woman's Center is still open to give special attention to older women returning to college and to advise younger women who might have special problems. It was the Woman's Center that began the campus-wide discussion of "date rape" and elevated the discussion beyond legal issues to a discussion of the roles society assigns men and women and how those roles affect values and behavior. Second, women's interests are still reflected in the curriculum. For example, literature courses continue to include many women writers and history courses

The opening sentences effectively establish the feminist movement as the cause of the following effects.

Notice that each effect is introduced by a transition— "first," "second," and "finally."

First effect—opening a woman's center.

Second effect—changing curriculum.

emphasize not only the work of history's outstanding women but also the enduring social contribution of women as reflected in public documents and private journals. Finally, several women hold important campus administrative positions. We currently have a woman president, two women deans, and over 50% of our faculty are women. Of course, these facts make demographic sense because over 55% of our students are women.

Third effect—more female administrators.

In the following paragraph from *The Cinema as Art,* film historian Ralph Stephenson explains the effects film directors can create by manipulating "scale" in their work—that is, using camera techniques to reduce or enlarge a subject.

> Manipulation of scale can imply a comment on what is being shown. Near the beginning of Pakula's *All the President's Men,* the two journalist heroes are seen in the Library of Congress. At first we are shown just them and the dozens of file cards in front of them. Then gradually the camera moves back and upwards to the very top of the vast dome-shaped room, leaving the two men dwarfed below, the magnitude of their task emphasized. In David Lynch's *Blue Velvet* an opening sequence of suburban tranquility is interrupted by the sight of a man suffering a heart attack in his garden. Unexpectedly the camera leaves the stricken figure and plunges deep into the undergrowth, seeking out a colony of tiny beetles until their unceasing activity fills the screen. This eerie shot is the first indication that all is not what it seems beneath the smooth surface of small-town life.

Stephenson's paragraph pattern is straightforward: He opens with a topic sentence that establishes the cause for the effects he will be discussing. He then follows with two examples from widely viewed films. While understanding cause-and-effect relationships might be difficult, setting them out can still be done in simple paragraph patterns.

WRITING TASK—CAUSE AND EFFECT

Respond to one of the following questions, concentrating on cause (reasons), effect (results), or both together. If necessary, narrow the focus of the question so that it can be discussed within a reasonable length. You may also rewrite any of these questions or create your own subject to reflect your particular interests.

1. Is intuition an effective way to solve problems?
2. What have been the indirect effects of a historical figure in your life, someone such as a political leader, an artist, or a philosopher?
3. What have been the effects of a significant public event in your life?
4. Why do some artistic works affect you?
5. Why does a particular television show, song, or film succeed?
6. What are the causes of homelessness, child abuse, gang violence, or other social phenomena?
7. What are the causes of a family, institutional, or social custom?
8. Should children be treated like adults?
9. Why does the burning of the American flag enrage many Americans?
10. What effects does a particular advertisement attempt to create in the minds of consumers?

Remember:

1. Limit your subject and keep to what you know.
2. In the opening sentence, clearly indicate that you will be writing a cause-and-effect piece.
3. Be clear about whether you are dealing with long-term or immediate causes or effects.

GROUP WORK

During a group session, identify a problem on campus or within the community. Brainstorm the problem to get a general picture—that is, try to define its scope, who it involves, who and what it impacts. Between sessions, gather more information. During the next session complete the picture and prepare to write a draft.

Between sessions write a draft. Use the first paragraph to state the problem and its effects. Use the second paragraph to state the causes. Finally, use the third paragraph to offer a solution and what will result from it.

In the next session, read the drafts aloud and hold group responses after each reading. Is the problem clearly stated? Are the effects and causes clear? Is the solution logical and does it clearly indicate the results that will accrue from its implementation?

13
Description

You've already had some experience with descriptive writing in Chapter 2, Getting Started. We've emphasized the value of embedding bits of description in all but the most scientifically objective pieces. Descriptive details will bring life to classifications, comparisons, contrasts, examples—indeed, descriptive details will make all patterns you use more vivid. Moreover, when a descriptive paragraph is mixed with other patterns, it can tug powerfully on the reader's attention. Writers who use description effectively evoke scenes, people, situations, and actions by involving their readers' senses and experiences. But unlike development by examples, comparison and contrast, classification, or analogy, descriptions are not always cast in traditional structures. Writing effective description, therefore, often depends on cunning. Of course, to be cunning the writer must be tuned to what the paper needs and what readers can follow.

Whatever is being described, the writer must use concrete language and specific detail. Without them writers cannot lead their readers to see and feel what they have in mind. Consider the following portion of an essay by Flannery O'Connor describing the way her peacocks greet visitors to her home. Her use of specific detail allows us to accurately visualize the scene.

> The peacock himself is a careful and dignified investigator. Visitors to our place, instead of being barked at by dogs rushing from under the porch, are squalled at by peacocks whose blue necks and crested heads pop up from behind tufts of grass, peer out of bushes, and crane downward from the roof of the house, where the bird has flown, perhaps for the view. One of mine stepped from under the shrubbery one day and came forward to inspect a carful of people

who had driven up to buy a calf. An old man and five or six white-haired, bare-footed children were piling out the back of the automobile as the bird approached. Catching sight of him they stopped in their tracks and stared, plainly hacked to find this superior figure blocking their path. There was silence as the bird regarded them, his head drawn back at its most majestic angle, his folded train glittering behind him in the sunlight.

Maxine Hong Kingston in a memoir, *The Woman Warrior,* uses specific details to create an impression of her mother. She describes her mother in a photographic scroll of her graduating class. After the opening sentence that identifies the scroll, Kingston concentrates on her mother. Notice how she uses images of the other young women in the photograph to clarify her mother's qualities. Besides directly stating that her mother is intelligent, alert, and pretty, Kingston uses the brief comparisons to establish that she was also physically fit, serious, and enduring when the photograph was taken.

> The second scroll is a long narrow photograph of the graduating class with the school officials seated in front. I picked out my mother immediately. Her face is exactly her own, though forty years younger. She is so familiar, I can only tell whether or not she is pretty or happy or smart by comparing her to the other women. For this formal group picture she straightened her hair with oil to make a chinlength bob like the others'. On the other women, strangers, I can recognize a curled lip, a sidelong glance, pinched shoulders. My mother is not soft. My mother is not humorous, not like the girl at the end who lifts her mocking chin to pose like Girl Graduate. My mother does not have smiling eyes; the old woman teacher (Dean Woo?) in front crinkles happily, and the one faculty member in the western suit smiles westernly. Most of the graduates are girls whose faces have not yet formed; my mother's face will not change anymore, except to age. She is intelligent, alert, pretty. I can't tell if she's happy.

Seldom will you write a purely descriptive paper, but you will have the opportunity to use description in many of your papers.

Use Description to Dramatize Experience

A pedestrian piece of prose can be elevated to a more vivid reading experience through a paragraph of description. In the piece that follows, social science major Joyce Brown includes a paragraph of dramatic description in a paper that deals with the psychological requirements of the deadening routine of a detective. She begins by relating clichéd views of what it takes. Then she develops a descriptive paragraph by using typical details from a detective's work life. As you read the illustration, note how the descriptive paragraph paints a vivid picture of a detective's routine work and seems to flow from the opening paragraph.

To be a police detective patrol officers must meet some tough requirements. They must stay alert, keep calm under pressure, and perform their job fairly. These are general requirements—the kind of requirements every citizen expects every cop to meet, somewhat like the Boy Scout motto, "Be Prepared." But there is a much tougher requirement. Anyone who wants to be a detective must think of it as the spine of the job. It has to do with the courage to meet the tedious, unglamorous day-to-day activities all detectives face.

In any year individual detectives will spend hundreds of hours in routine work behind a government-gray desk under the glare of fluorescent lights. They will punch thousands of telephone numbers until calluses form on their fingers tips. They will each get thousands of busy signals and few answers for their trouble. They will individually spend hours filling out reports and sitting in courtrooms waiting to testify in a trial. Often detectives see criminals they have arrested sent home by judges. In a year they will spend endless hours driving crowded streets during a steamy summer and frigid winter. They'll eat pounds of hamburger, salami, and bologna for lunches and wash it all down with enough coffee to kill ten average kidneys. The odds are they will never be shot at, but they will probably get spit on and cursed. No doubt some violent drunk or strung-out junkie will retch on their shoes. A dramatic life—no. Moreover, keep in mind how hard it is to stay alert, calm, and fair in the face of this kind of psychological torture.

The writer continues her essay by exploring the psychological effects of this kind of tedious routine. She develops most of the paper through objective research that supports her points. But without a descriptive paragraph that paints a detective's routine, the information would not have much impact.

The illustration raises an obvious question. Is the description a true one? Yes and no.

It isn't true if you read it as objective information. Not every detective eats pounds of hamburger, salami, and bologna during a year of lunches. Not every detective gets spit on.

But if you read it for the writer's emotional intent, the paragraph is true. The writer wants to generate a feeling in the reader. She's not claiming to be objective. She's clearly biased. She has a point of view and uses a dramatic description to involve her readers in it. She is writing subjectively, not objectively. So, from an inner perspective—from the writer's emotional viewpoint—the illustration reflects a general truth. Moreover, within the context of the entire essay, it is effective.

Use Description to Dramatize the Abstract

Most writing draws from our creative juices, but description seems to draw the most. To use description effectively in your writing, you must be able to use details to your advantage. Nowhere is this more difficult than in attempting to describe the abstract—that level of experience almost impossible to communicate. One way to do it is through analogy. Another, perhaps one that wears better on readers, is to find descriptive details strong enough to make readers see and feel the abstraction.

Michael Herr does it in *Dispatches,* a collection of personal essays about the Vietnam War. Through the use of concrete description he makes the reader feel how sensitive one becomes to sound while in a jungle filled with enemies. Before going on, think for a moment about how you would describe the abstract experience of straining to hear sounds in a world gone silent. Then study Herr's paragraph to see how he does it.

> There were times during the night when all the jungle sounds would stop at once. There was no dwindling down or fading away, it was all gone in a single instant as though some signal had been transmitted out to the life: bats, birds, snakes, monkeys, insects, picking up on a frequency that a thousand years in the jungle might condition you to receive, but leaving you as it was to wonder what you weren't hearing now, straining for sound, one piece of information. I had heard it before in other jungles, the Amazon and the Philippines, but those jungles were "secure," there wasn't much chance that hundreds of Viet Cong were coming and going, moving and waiting, living out there just to do you harm. The thought of that one could turn any sudden silence into a space that you'd fill with everything you thought was quiet in you, it could even put you on the approach to clairvoyance. You thought you heard impossible things: damp roots breathing, fruit sweating, fervid bug action, the heartbeat of tiny animals.

Like the passage describing a police detective's work, this paragraph is subjective. Herr uses as much experience as he needs to make the reader feel the threatening silence. He draws from the past—"I had heard it before in other jungles"—and relates the past to the present he describes. He even draws you into his imaginings to illustrate how the strain of listening leads one to hear the impossible, "damp roots breathing, fruit sweating, fervid bug action, and the heartbeat of tiny animals." Herr touches another abstraction: fear—the fear of being caught unaware by an enemy that moves through the silence.

Use Description in Reports

Sometimes descriptive paragraphs are absolutely necessary for a paper to be effective. This is often the case with reports that involve close observation. For a psychology class one student was asked to visit a preschool and select a child for a day's observation. Then she was to describe the child at school and draw some conclusions about how well the school's program was meeting the child's needs. The whole project took ten paragraphs. Having explained the program in the first paragraph, the writer devoted the second to a description of the child and his behavior.

> At first glance John seems to be a typical four-year-old: scruffy sun-bleached hair, a few freckles, worn cords, short-sleeved shirt, and tattered tennis shoes on his feet. But behind his boyish appearance, he seems to be a loner. During the first fifteen-minute class session, he was the only child who did not raise his hand to answer a question or share an experience. He was attentive at first but soon lost interest. Once he reached out a finger to poke a boy in front, then stopped, perhaps thinking better of it. Finally, his thumb went into his mouth. As soon as the class broke up, he headed for the monkey bars, where he climbed to the highest rung and sat, his eyes staring toward the distant hill. No one tried to approach him; the other children, most of whom chased around the play yard, seemed to respect his wish for privacy. Later, when the class regrouped for story time, John didn't show as much interest as he had during the sharing session. He seemed more interested in tracing the cracks in the wall than in listening to *Frog and Toad Are Friends*.

One last word about description. Often when beginning writers have little to say, their eyes will reach into the mind's landscapes and return with chunks of description. They will then glue them onto their papers. This practice just won't do. Whenever you include a full paragraph of description in an essay, be sure it has a clear purpose.

WRITING TASK—DESCRIPTION

Write a description that evokes a scene, a person, a situation, or an action. Keep in mind that an effective description works to create a predetermined response in a reader. For instance, if you were to write about a teacher you see as absentminded, you would select details that reflect absentmindedness. Remember, too, that description often works indirectly. Don't tell readers; show them. (Review Chapter 2.)

GROUP WORK

Work in pairs. Exchange drafts and review them for the following: Is the language specific? Is there enough detail to create a strong picture? Does the arrangement follow an appropriate pattern? Does the draft create a dominant effect? Share your observations.

14
Deductive Essay

If you are able to develop a paragraph with examples, catalogs, comparisons, contrasts, and so on, you will probably have little trouble writing a brief deductive essay of several paragraphs, which is typical of most college writing. Moreover, with practice you can even master an extended essay of several pages, which is typical of college research projects and professional writing. (See "Drowsy America," page 172.)

An essay is a nonfiction composition about a limited topic. It analyzes or interprets information in a personal way. This does not mean that an essay is about the writer. It could be, but usually it is not. Rather, the sense of personal involvement comes from the writer's thoughts, insights, and values being used in an analysis or interpretation of a topic.

A deductive essay might more precisely be called a *deductively arranged* essay. Deductive reasoning moves from the general to the specific; a deductively arranged essay moves from a generalization, called the *central point,* to the more specific information that develops the key idea of the central point.

It might be helpful to think of the writer of such an essay as a teacher, guide, or expert who has studied a particular topic, collected related material, thought about the material, and organized it for presentation to an audience.

Obviously, such a guide would have examined and thought about the topic carefully. And before writing, he or she would have decided, at least tentatively, on a central point (sometimes referred to as a *thesis* or *controlling idea*) that the essay will develop. This central point is the generalization which begins the deductive arrangement.

Say, for example, that you are preparing an essay on learning a foreign language. You studied both Spanish and Japanese in high school, and you spent a summer vacation in Italy. You have a friend who studied Russian at the Language School in Monterey, and you've talked with her about the methods used there. Reflecting on these experiences and recalling moments of discouragement and of accomplishment, you decide to write in favor of the "total immersion" method of language study. You phrase a tentative central point: *The best way to learn a new language is to live in that language environment twenty-four hours a day.*

You are on your way to a deductively arranged essay.

What you have learned from your experiences in language classrooms, on the streets of Rome, and in your discussions with your friend about her experience, plus whatever additional information you may have, will provide the specific content to support the validity of your central point.

The deductively arranged essay begins with an introduction, generally one paragraph long, but occasionally more. The purpose of the introduction is to arouse readers' interest and prepare for the discussion to follow. It contains a central point that sets the boundaries of the essay just as a topic sentence sets the boundaries of a paragraph.

The introduction is followed by a discussion several paragraphs long. Each paragraph includes a topic sentence and develops a subpoint of the central point in a detailed, thorough manner. The paragraphs are linked by clear transitions, smoothing the way for readers to follow the ideas.

In developing the discussion section, use appropriate strategies for paragraph development you have practiced in earlier writing tasks. In our learning-a-foreign-language example, you might include a paragraph or more of definition, introducing the term *total immersion* and explaining it in detail. Somewhere in the paper you would perhaps contrast typical one-hour-a-day classroom study and total immersion study. You may have had experiences in learning Italian vocabulary which could be presented in a cause-and-effect pattern. Certainly you would use many examples, both specific and typical. The point is that your deductively arranged essay can be shaped through the use of various paragraph strategies.

The essay ends with a conclusion that often restates the central point and provides a sense of completion, or *closure,* to the essay. A typical essay for a college class is between 500 and 750 words, but the length is most appropriately determined by the complexity of the idea and the amount of detailed discussion necessary to support the idea sufficiently.

A simple diagram of a typical deductive essay is given on page 146.

Please don't get the idea that an essay needs to be as mechanical as the diagram might indicate. It doesn't. But we want you to understand that simple essays have the same basic structure. How well writers use the structure depends on their skills.

With the diagram in mind, study the following essay written by Joanne Vega for a class in mass communications. We suggest that you read the essay

Introduction

Opening statement that leads to central point
Central point

Discussion section composed of several paragraphs. The number and the development strategies used vary according to content.

Topic sentence
Development of topic sentence

Topic sentence
Development of topic sentence

Topic sentence
Development of topic sentence

Topic sentence
Development of topic sentence

Conclusion

Thesis restated/Closing comments

through once; then read it a second time along with Vega's observations printed in the margin.

Exploited Desires

Some magazine advertisers often promote products by associating them with powerful desires. Consider jeans, for example. In the past, no-nonsense manufacturers, such as Levi, Lee, and Wrangler, promoted jeans as apparel that would wear like iron. Times, however, have changed. Today, high-fashion manufacturers, such as Calvin Klein, Jordache, and Georges Marciano, promote jeans through sexual association. For instance, a recent Jordache advertisement features a stunningly attractive couple wearing jeans. The setting is a garage in murky light. He is resting his back against a truck in a sexually suggestive pose—legs spread, one hand on a hip and the other brushing his thigh, and open shirt revealing rippled abdominal muscles, his skin glistening with sweat. She crouches catlike at his side, hugging one of his legs as tightly as her jeans hug her hips while she stares at the viewer with a sultry expression. "Wear Jordache," the advertisement suggests, "and fulfill your sexual desires." This Jordache advertisement is typical of high-fashion jeans advertisements-Guess?, Calvin Klein, Buffalo, Versace- all associate their jeans with sexual desire.

Joanne Vega takes her title from the central point: Advertisers exploit consumer desires to sell their products.

Many beginning writers waste time in their introductions. Vega does not. She plunges into the subject—magazine advertisers who appeal to powerful consumer desires—and quickly launches into an example—jeans. She begins by noting how jeans were once marketed, then explains how they are currently marketed.

Vega lists a number of jean manufacturers, but concentrates on one advertisement to show how sexual desire is exploited. She makes effective use of description, juxtaposing the male and female models.

In this paragraph Vega expands the discussion from jean advertisers to advertisers in general. She presents her central point, though not directly: Many advertisers exploit desires to trick consumers into buying their products. The introductory section is ended.

But jeans advertisers are not the only ones to exploit consumer desires, and sexual desire is not the only desire advertisers exploit to trick consumers into buying their products.

Many Americans seem to be obsessed with eating healthy foods, dieting, and exercising. This desire to lead a healthy life has not been lost on advertisers. Many, in fact, are exploiting it. For example, a recent series of milk advertisements in nationally distributed magazines, such as Vanity Fair, Vogue, Bazaar, and Glamour, feature well-known women testifying to the health advantages that come from drinking milk. For example, ice skating champion Kristy Yamaguchi gives milk four 6.0s as an after-sports drink; tennis star Gabriela Sabatini claims milk has more vitamins and minerals per ounce than the leading sports drink, and super-model Kate Moss praises milk for building strong bones. In a comic touch, each celebrity has a milk mustache, the kind most children have playfully made when drinking a glass of milk, thus suggesting the healthy innocence of childhood. Like the producers of milk, Evian has also created a series of advertisements associating good health with drinking Evian "natural spring water," but in contrast to the milk adver-

Ends with a sentence that embodies the central point.

The discussion section begins. The first three sentences focus this paragraph. If they were rewritten as a single topic sentence, it might read as follows: "Advertisers exploit consumer desire to be healthy."

In the first example Vega presents commonly published milk ads that feature celebrities testifying to the health benefits of milk. She assumes that her readers will have seen these ads so it is unnecessary to describe them in detail.

In the second example Vega uses Evian water advertisements that feature ordinary people in healthful activities. Again, these are common ads so Vega does not have to describe them in detail.

tisements, Evian features ordinary men and women who seem to be cooling down after a hard workout. Each Evian advertisement is photographed outdoors and includes the quotation, "Another day, another chance to feel healthy." What do these advertisements have in common? They certainly don't give much information to convince consumers to buy their products; <u>instead they exploit the desire to lead a healthy life by associating their products with images of healthy men and women.</u>

She ends with a clincher, reminding the reader of this paragraph's focus.

Some advertisers create upbeat advertisements, like those that associate products with health, to exploit the desire for adventure. Ford, General Motors, and Jeep associate their four-wheel-drive vehicles with conquering the wilderness. Nike, Wolverine, and Timberline associate their rugged shoes with blazing new territory. <u>Other advertisers exploit the darker side of adventure.</u> For example, a recent Alyssa Ashley advertisement in <u>Glamour</u> associates Musk body scent, with a "good girl's momentary longing to be bad." The advertisement features an attractive young woman straddling the back of a Harley Davidson motorcycle. She rides behind a "typical" biker: tattooed, with long, greasy unkempt hair, an untended beard, sunglasses, fringed leather pants, motorcycle boots,

The first sentence presents a smooth transition from "health" to "adventure." In the next two sentences she identifies several companies that appeal to the desire for adventure in ads. But then she shifts: "Other advertisers exploit the darker side of adventure," thus announcing the primary focus of this paragraph.

Vega presents a single ad to support her point. She describes it in detail because most of her readers would not have seen it. She keeps her description focused, piling detail upon detail to create a picture of being "bad," thus keeping the "desire for forbidden adventure" before her readers. She closes with a quotation from the ad that reflects her point.

and a sleeveless denim jacket with the head of a fox sown on the back. She is turned toward the camera, and stares at the viewer, her face framed with long, brown hair, a naughty pout on her lips. She wears red cowboy boots and a rayon, baby-doll length dress. The hem of the dress is hiked up above one thigh, almost high enough to reveal the bottom of a hip, and her right hand rests on the top of the bare thigh. Apart from the provocative pout and hiked up dress, she looks like any well-groomed young woman who might read a middle-class magazine like <u>Glamour</u>, not a woman who lives on the "wild side." The image dominating the advertisement raises one question: Would the young woman attracted to this advertisement be buying a perfume, or would she be buying a symbolic encounter with the forbidden adventure? <u>The caption that accompanies the Musk advertisement reveals the answer, "Sometimes even good girls want to be bad."</u>

The closing sentence clinches the point.

Advertisers often exploit a desire for economic and social independence. Women are frequently the target for such advertisements. For example, no company has exploited this desire more effectively than Philip Morris in a campaign to sell Virginia Slims cigarettes. Each advertisement

The first two sentences set up the discussion in this paragraph: Advertisers exploit the female desire for economic and social independence. She begins the discussion by referring to Virginia Slims "You've Come a Long Way, Baby" ad campaign.

in the campaign features images of strong, independent women: one riding a motorcycle, another
standing behind a man who is cooking, and yet
another of a woman in a leather jacket, leaning on
a sports car door. Each advertisement is accompanied by a sentence declaring the woman's independence: "I don't necessarily want to run the world,
but I wouldn't mind taking it for a ride"; "Equality comes with no apron strings attached"; and "I
always take the driver's seat." Moreover, each
advertisement features the slogan, "You've Come a
Long Way, Baby."

More particularly, one recent Virginia Slims
advertisement in Vanity Fair exploits the desire
for independence in a male-dominated business
world. The advertisement concentrates on a young
woman dressed in a short-skirted business suit and
walking down a busy street, which suggests she is
out in the world, confronting the challenges of
business life. Her back is to the viewer as she
looks over her shoulder and smiles. The central
image creates the impression of a business woman
on the run. In one hand she carries a briefcase,
and in the other hand, which she is lifting toward
her mouth, she holds a portable phone—details that
further emphasize the woman's independence. Promi-

Vega continues the discussion from the last paragraph. Here, though, Vega is more specific, analyzing a single "You've Come a Long Way, Baby" ad.

She describes the ad in detail, emphasizing the idea of indepen-dence it embodies.

nently featured in the hand that holds the phone is a cigarette. A caption in a red rectangle in the upper right-hand corner says, "Virginia Slims" and beneath that is the dominant campaign slogan, "You've Come a Long Way, Baby." Clearly, the cigarette, the brand name, and the slogan are all associated with the image of the independent business woman. Combined, they suggest that if a woman desires to be viewed as independent, smoking Virginia Slims will help. The quotation attributed to the woman emphasizes the point, "A woman's place is any place her feet will take her."

The last two sentences serve as a clincher.

While this Virginia Slims' advertisement directly exploits the desire many women have for independence, ironically, it also suggests women also desire the opposite of independence. Beneath the surface lurks the suggestion that, yes, this woman is independent but that the business she practices is the "world's oldest profession"—that is, she sells sexual services. For example, the quotation, "A woman's place is any place her feet will take her," tacitly suggests she is a "street walker," a phrase used to refer to a prostitute. Also her holding a telephone suggests the name "call girl," another name for prostitute that suggests she is on call to fulfill a man's sexual

In this paragraph, Vega offers an even deeper analysis of the "You've Come a Long Way, Baby" ad. She points out that on the surface it appeals to the modern woman's active desire to be independent, but in the subtext the ad appeals to the passive desire to be dependent on man.

Vega seems to be having some fun with this subject. Is she serious about this analysis?

desire. Moreover, the dominant image of a woman pursuing a career suggests the term "professional," yet another term for prostitute. The use of "Baby" also suggests that the woman is dependent and immature. Consider, for example, who would call her "Baby." Certainly not other women, especially career women, nor would men who recognize her apparent independence. Only men who feel superior to her would call her "Baby," thus suggesting she is someone who needs to be cared for. Clearly, in a bit of advertising slight-of-hand, Virginia Slims exploits opposite desires—the assertive desire to be independent and the passive desire to be dependent.

She ends this paragraph with a clincher. The discussion section is finished.

Sexual fulfillment, a healthy life, adventurous experiences, or independence—can advertisers actually exploit these desires to trick unwary consumers? When asked if they can, most consumers deny the power of advertisements, claiming they make their purchases rationally. But the power of most advertisements is emotional, operating beneath a consumer's awareness where rational decisions give way to emotional expression. The tactic must work. Why else would advertisers continue to exploit human desires in their campaigns?

The conclusion begins. Vega summarizes the central point and subpoints effectively. She then sets up the question, Do advertisements work? She answers it with a question of her own: "Why else would advertisers exploit human desires?"

Now that you've studied the diagram and a deductive essay, let's look at the process Vega worked through to complete the final draft of her deductive essay. We have divided the writing process into steps for instructional purposes. But the step-by-step process we describe is not as rigid in practice as it might seem in print. While writing your own essays, you will frequently move back and forth between steps as you explore the possibilities of your subject, experiment with content and organization, and decide on the final phrasing of sentences and paragraphs.

Getting Started
SELECTING A SUBJECT

You will write many of your college essays as responses to class assignments. Often these assignments will be open ended—that is, you will have no more than a list of general subjects to choose from. In this situation you should select a subject you already know something about, so look first at your own interests and experiences, such as your work, leisure activities, and reactions to news items, books, television programs, or films. Your personal experiences and observations will enrich an open-ended essay assignment.

You will also write college essays in response to highly specific class assignments. Often these assignments will follow a learning unit and serve as a way of testing how effectively you can apply the unit's key concepts. For example, a history assignment might ask you to discuss the causes of a particular historical event. A philosophy assignment might ask you to analyze the ethical implications of a political act. A psychology assignment might ask you to contrast two theories regarding the structure of the mind.

Joanne Vega wrote the above essay in response to an assignment in mass communications:

> Magazine advertisers seldom give detailed product information. Instead they rely on other approaches to sell their products. In a four-to-five-page essay that indirectly approves or disapproves of this practice, identify one approach advertisers use to sell their products and analyze five or more advertisements to show the approach at work.

Clearly, this is a specific assignment, yet it allows writers to bring their own opinions and research to the essay. Now read how Vega approached this assignment:

> Our class had just finished a unit on tactics advertisers use in mainstream magazine ads. I knew I had to demonstrate what I had learned and also present my knowledge clearly. I faced one major problem—the class had learned a great deal. For instance, we learned about propaganda devices, such as testimonial, plain folks,

transfer, glittering generality, and so on. We also learned how advertisers associate products with appealing lifestyles and how they tug at our emotions. I had pages and pages of notes . . . far too much information to integrate into a single essay.

NARROWING THE SUBJECT

I began by analyzing the writing assignment and decided it had three elements. First, I had to concentrate on one tactic; second, I had to show how it worked in some representative ads; and third, I had to suggest my attitude about its use without stating how I felt directly.

Since most ads usually incorporate several tactics, I had to discipline myself to concentrate on only one, which was not easy since I wanted to show everything I had learned.

I decided to trust my intuition and selected several ads that caught my eye as I thumbed through such magazines as *Vanity Fair, Vogue, Glamour, Elle,* and *Esquire,* all glossy, main-stream magazines. Once I had the ads, and there were plenty of them, I began to sort them into groups and categorize them—adventure, health, independence, sexuality, and so on. Well, it didn't take me long to decide to concentrate on desire, that is, to show how advertisers use desire to sell their products.

At this point, I had met the first two assignment requirements; the next was easy: I decided that these advertisers were exploiting consumer desires to sell their products.

Some writers are fearful about narrowing a subject because they believe that the broader the subject, the more they will have to say about it. But the opposite is true. A writer can find more that is informative and interesting to say about a narrow subject, such as "advertisers exploit desires to trick consumers," than about a more general subject, "how advertisers sell products." A narrow subject allows, even forces, a writer to use specific supporting material. Specific information is always more interesting than general observations. Vega's decision to narrow her subject was a step in the right direction. Her topic would become even narrower after she had collected the details she needed to write the paper.

PREWRITING

Vega's next task was to use prewriting techniques to generate ideas and specific details. She decided on the ads she would use, especially the ones she would discuss in greater detail, and analyzed how they associated a desire with a product. She made a list of specific details for each advertisement by concentrating on the ones that supported her interpretation.

Planning the Essay

PHRASING A CENTRAL POINT

After Vega felt she had enough material for her essay, she turned her attention to phrasing the central point.

But before we discuss the central point, we should mention that the methods of development that you have been practicing in earlier writing tasks are all applicable in one way or another to a deductive essay. For example, an essay may have a paragraph devoted to definition, another to a catalog, others to comparison and contrast, a cause-and-effect relationship, or examples. Or the dominant method of development might be classification while the individual paragraphs are developed by examples, analogies, anecdotes, and descriptions. In other words, an essay is built by selecting a variety of methods appropriate to your essay content and to the central point that organizes the content.

A central point serves the same purpose for an essay that a topic sentence does for a paragraph—it states and imposes limits on a narrowed topic. The central point, stated in one or two sentences, appears in the introduction to a deductive essay, usually at the end. Sometimes a central point also indicates the subparts of the subject and suggests the method of essay development to be used.

A central point is a generalization that indicates the main idea of the paper. It is the idea that all the later paragraphs will support, argue for, or illustrate. It should be broad enough to serve as an umbrella for everything in the essay, while at the same time providing a focus. In other words, it should clearly stake out the territory of the essay.

Because a central point guides both the reader and the writer, it should be phrased carefully. You may find it necessary to revise the sentence containing the central point several times until you are satisfied that it clearly indicates what your content will be. It is probably a good idea to do this early in your planning so you have a clear idea of where the paper is going. Even then, you will probably find yourself changing the wording of the central point from time to time as your essay develops.

Joanne Vega wrote several versions of her central point before she was satisfied:

My first central point was too broad and probably misleading:

Advertisers use our emotions to trick us into buying their products.

I could see right away that this central point promised a paper much bigger than the one I expected to write. It seemed to include all advertisers—television, magazine, billboard, newspaper. It also seemed to include all kinds of emotions, such as love, fear, hate, anger, and jealousy. I did like the word "trick" because it reflected my attitude toward advertisers in general. I decided to keep "trick" and try again:

Magazine advertisers use our desires to trick us into buying their products.

A little better than the first, but not on target. I limited the subject to magazine ads and emphasized "desire," which I saw as being more limited than "emotions." I also kept "trick," but the sentence seemed flat, mainly because of the predicate "use," an undistinguished verb. I needed a stronger word than "use" to reflect my attitude. I also did not like suggesting that this would be told from a subjective point of view, as "our" and "us" suggest. I went back to my scratch pad and came up with the following:

Some magazine advertisers exploit desires to trick consumers into buying their products.

This sentence worked for me. It limited the discussion to "some magazine advertisers," not all of them. The words "exploit" and "trick" reveal my attitude. Moreover, it was a simple, straightforward sentence that expressed exactly what I intended to discuss.

No matter how thoroughly you work at sharpening a central point, you may find that you need to change it again after you have done more planning or after you have started writing the paper. When Vega wrote the final draft of her essay, she had to reword the central point one more time so it would flow with the paragraph. Nevertheless, throughout the planning and writing of her essay, Vega was guided by "Some magazine advertisers exploit desires to trick consumers into buying their products," which is revealed by the close of the introduction.

DECIDING ON PURPOSE AND AUDIENCE

At this point Vega needed to consider what the purpose of and the audience for her essay would be. Every essay should have a dominant purpose, such as to inform, to entertain, to persuade, or to analyze. Of course, an informative essay can have entertaining moments. Conversely, an entertaining essay can inform or persuade. But one purpose will be dominant. Deciding on a purpose is easy and nearly automatic—the phrasing of the central idea and the content you plan to present usually suggests the purpose immediately. Nevertheless, it's a good idea to make a conscious decision because then you will be less likely to mix purposes inappropriately.

Just as you must keep your dominant purpose in mind, you must also imagine your audience. Being aware of your readers will help you make choices about vocabulary and content, especially when it comes to including or excluding background information. For example, if you were writing for an audience of psychologists, you wouldn't have to explain the meaning of "id." But if you were writing for first year psychology students, you would.

Joanne Vega faced an interesting writing situation. Who hadn't seen magazine advertisements? No one. Vega had to take this fact into consideration. She writes,

> My essay's dominant purpose would be analysis: I would analyze several ads to show how advertisers exploit consumer desires. Since my instructor had formed "critique groups," I decided my group members would be my audience. I assumed they, like me, would feel as if they have been bombarded with ads of all kinds, and I guessed that they would also be familiar with most of the dramatic ads I had selected to write about. Indeed, several of us had discussed Guess? and Calvin Klein ads for their provocative content. This assumption helped me make a decision: the important ads, that is, the ones that would carry the weight of my analysis, I could analyze in detail.

Just as Vega's audience influenced her choices, your audience will influence your choices. It is essential, therefore, that before you move too far into the planning of an essay, you should determine who your audience will be.

MAKING A PRELIMINARY PLAN

Vega's next step was to sketch out a plan for her essay by selecting items from her list of descriptive details and observations. She would then arrange them in an appropriate order. Her preliminary plan for "Exploited Desires" looked like this:

Central Point	Some magazine advertisers exploit desires to trick consumers into buying their products.
Subpoint 1	In contrast to traditional makers of jeans, high-fashion makers of jeans associate their products with sex.

- Early makers of jeans, such as Levi, Lee, and Wrangler, emphasized long wear.
- Today's makers of jeans, such as Calvin Klein, Guess?, and so on . . . associate their jeans with sex.

Subpoint 2   Many advertisers associate their products
                                with health.

- Milk industry associates milk with health by using celebrities—
  Kristy Yamaguchi, Gabriela Sabatini, Kate Moss.
- Evian water associates healthy everyday people with their product.

Subpoint 3   Some companies associate their products
                                with adventure.

- Auto companies associate four-wheel-drive vehicles with adventure.
- Alyssa Ashley associates Musk with the adventure of being "bad."

Subpoint 4   Some companies associate their products
                                with independence and its opposite,
                                dependence.

- Philip Morris's Virginia Slims campaign associates smoking cigarettes with independence.
- Philip Morris also associates smoking cigarettes with dependence.

Conclusion   Do ads work? They must . . . why else
                                would advertisers bombard us?

The form your planning takes is up to you. Some writers construct very specific outlines, delineating subpoints and sub-subpoints until they've listed every item to be included in the paper. Others list main subpoints only and informally jot down some ideas under each one. Some write formal outlines in complete sentences. No matter how you go about it, have a plan—that's the message.

While planning, keep in mind one general principle: Start your essay strong and finish stronger. You should present some interesting content early to keep readers interested, but the most emphatic paragraph is generally the last discussion paragraph. In practical terms, unless you have a good reason to do otherwise, hold back the material with the most impact for the end, and present the next strongest early. Weaker or less interesting material should come somewhere in the middle.

Writing the First Draft

Now would be a good time to reread Vega's essay to see how she worked the material from her plan into her final draft. You'll see how she reworded subpoints and filled in detail from her notes and the advertisements them-selves. She wrote a single paragraph introduction that uses her first subpoint to lead to the central point and set up the discussion. You'll also see that her discussion section is organized by three more subpoints, the last subpoint divided into two parts. Each of the first two subpoints in the discussion is developed in single paragraphs, but the last subpoint is developed in three paragraphs that concentrate on a single advertisement. Finally, note how she ended with a conclusion that reminds readers of her central point and subpoints while dealing with the obvious question: Do advertisements work?

INTRODUCTION

Now, with a clearly worded central point and a plan for presenting the subpoints and supporting material, you are ready to begin writing an introduction. For most essays you will be writing, a one-paragraph introduction will be sufficient, although several paragraphs are appropriate for long essays.

Effective introductions do more than offer writers a chance to clear their throats—they must be more than a series of aimless, dull comments. A solid introduction will focus an essay by presenting a central point in a way that draws readers into the discussion. Here is a brief list of some common approaches writers use to develop their introductions:

1. statements of striking examples, facts, or statistics that will surprise readers
2. a brief presentation of an opposing argument or an attack on a commonly held belief
3. a provocative quotation or interesting question
4. an anecdote or narrative closely related to the subject
5. a definition, but not one merely taken from a dictionary

If appropriate for your subject, any one of these can be an effective way to begin a deductive essay. We do want to make one strong suggestion: Always end your introduction with the central point. Why? Like the end of an essay, the end of a paragraph is the dramatic point and, therefore, more easily remembered.

The introduction to "Exploited Desires" takes one paragraph. Vega's strategy is very effective: She develops a specific example to lead to the essay's central point. Here's how she does it.

She opens with a general observation that many advertisers appeal to consumer desires to sell products. She develops this observation by moving the first subpoint to the introduction, claiming that jean manufacturers once emphasized durability but now emphasize sex appeal. She analyzes a specific Jordache advertisement to support her claim. Relying on reader experience with current jean advertisements, she links Jordache's practice to that of other companies. Finally, she closes with the central point, which expands from the conclusions she's drawn from the Jordache analysis—that is, "jean advertisers are not the only ones to appeal to consumer desires, and sexual desire is not the only desire advertisers exploit to trick consumers into buying their products." Stated more directly, as Vega does in her tentative central point, "Some magazine advertisers exploit desires to trick consumers into buying their products."

Some magazine advertisers often promote products by associating them with powerful desires. Consider jeans, for example. In the past, no-nonsense manufacturers, such as Levi, Lee, and Wrangler, promoted jeans as apparel that would wear like iron. Times, however, have changed. Today, high-fashion manufacturers, such as Calvin Klein, Jordache, and Georges Marciano, promote jeans through sexual association. For instance, a recent Jordache advertisement features a stunningly attractive couple wearing jeans. The setting is a garage in murky light. He is resting his back against a truck in a sexually suggestive pose—legs spread, one hand on a hip and the other brushing his thigh, and open shirt revealing rippled abdominal muscles, his skin glistening with sweat. She crouches catlike at his side, hugging one of his legs as tightly as her jeans hug her hips while she stares at the viewer with a sultry expression. "Wear Jordache," the advertisement suggests, "and fulfill your sexual desires." This Jordache advertisement is typical of high-fashion jeans advertisements—Guess?, Calvin Klein, Buffalo, Versace—all associate their jeans with sexual desire. But jeans advertisers are not the only ones to exploit

First sentence sets up the general observation.

Introduces the central claim by briefly contrasting how traditional jean makers promoted jeans to how today's high-fashion jean makers promote jeans.

An analysis of a specific ad to develop her observation.

Creates a transition from Jordache to other manufacturers stating that the appeal to desires is a common practice.

Closes with the central point.

consumer desires, and sexual desire is not the

only desire advertisers exploit to trick consumers

into buying their products.

About her introduction, Vega writes,

> For previous essays I wrote introductions that tended to be general and vague. Why? Because I had been taught to begin with a broad generalization and narrow to a particular aspect of that generalization. Well, I would get essays back with comments about the introduction like, "too broad, focus your thought," "be more specific," and "a wasted paragraph, give me more particulars."
>
> For this introduction, I decided to be as specific as I could by getting right into one of my subpoints. Of course, I had to rework it so it would lead to my central point, but it allowed me to analyze a specific example, thus illustrating for my readers what would unfold in the discussion. Nobody accused me of being overly general.

Whatever method you use in an introduction, keep in mind what you are introducing: the central idea of your essay. Whatever you say in an introduction must establish the content and direction of the discussion. In fact, some writers prefer to write a sketchy draft of their introduction and then write the discussion in more detail. They say the introduction is easier to write when they know exactly what comes next. You may wish to follow their advice, or you may wish to write a detailed introduction first and be prepared to go back and change it if the discussion section takes some unexpected twists. Our experience tells us that if writers develop a clear plan and follow it, then they can write their essays from beginning to end without facing any major revisions.

DISCUSSION

If you can write paragraphs with topic sentences, you should have no trouble putting together a discussion of a central point. If you haven't already done so in the planning stage, you should first rewrite your subpoints into topic sentences. You will then develop these topic sentences into separate paragraphs by expanding the ideas and details you listed in your plan. Develop the subpoints by using examples, catalogs, comparisons, contrasts, causes and effects, classifications, or any combination of methods. In other words, develop the discussion in any way that fits the material and follows the logic of your discussion. Vega developed "Exploited Desires" mainly through examples, but we want to emphasize that different central points require different strategies.

Here are Joanne Vega's comments about writing the discussion of her essay:

> Since I had a detailed plan, writing the discussion was merely a matter of following it—that is, once I decided to and figured out how to integrate my first subpoint into the introduction.
>
> I would begin to write a discussion paragraph by first phrasing a topic sentence. Then I would block out the examples, filling in the details from my observation list and by reexamining the particular ads I had selected. I worked through each subpoint that way until I got to the subpoint that concentrated on the desire for independence, the third in the discussion. I knew this was my strongest point: I felt the Virginia Slims ads were the most dramatic of my examples. They were also the most complex, so I had detailed analysis. Moreover, I had an opposing interpretation. As a consequence, I divided the discussion of the use of independence into two paragraphs, one that concentrated on the general campaign and one that concentrated on a specific ad. The next paragraph in the series, concentrated on the ironic perspective that an ad emphasizing the desire for independence also embodied the desire for dependence. Tricky to structure, but I felt I had found the solution.
>
> Finally, I went back to each paragraph to integrate the topic sentences so that they didn't sound like "announcements," even though that was the purpose I wanted them to serve. For example, in my plan, the subpoint related to health was first phrased,

```
Many advertisers associated their products with the desire
to lead healthy lives to exploit consumers.
```

Once revised to integrate it effectively into the paragraph, it became three sentences, all working together to make a single point,

```
Many Americans seem to be obsessed with eating healthy
food, dieting, and exercising. This desire has not been lost on
advertisers. Many, in fact, are exploiting it.
```

All this was a slow process, but one that got results.

An important difference between writing individual paragraphs and writing a complete essay has to do with the need to use transitions to link all the paragraphs in the discussion and to reflect the central point. In a short essay, transitional markers are usually embedded in the topic sentence in the form of a single word or short phrase that can be repeated in the opening of each discussion paragraph. Notice how Vega embeds key words or forms of key words from the central idea in the opening of each of her discussion paragraphs, especially *desire* and *exploit.*

Central point: Jean advertisers are not the only ones to appeal to consumer *desires,* and sexual *desire* is not the only *desire* advertisers *exploit* to trick consumers into buying their products.

First discussion paragraph opening: Many Americans seem to be obsessed with eating healthy foods, dieting, and exercising. This *desire* to lead a healthy life has not been lost on advertisers. Many, in fact, are *exploiting* it.

Second discussion paragraph opening: Some advertisers create upbeat advertisements, like those that associate products with health, to *exploit* the *desire* for adventure.

Third discussion paragraph opening: Advertisers often *exploit* a *desire* for economic and social independence.

Fourth discussion paragraph opening: More particularly, one recent Virginia Slims advertisement in *Vanity Fair exploits* the *desire* for independence in a male-dominated business world.

Fifth discussion paragraph opening: While the Virginia Slims' advertisement directly *exploits* the *desire* many women have for independence, ironically it also suggests women *desire* the opposite of independence.

Repetition is not the only transitional technique writers use, but it is effective to keep the central point in the reader's mind.

CONCLUSIONS

Finally a successful essay should conclude, not just stop. Conclusions and introductions are important; they stand out as the first and last contact you'll have with readers. Whereas an introduction serves to hook readers and to present the paper's central idea, a conclusion completes the discussion and often echoes the central and supporting points along with their applications or significance.

In other than narrative and descriptive essays, an essay's conclusion usually is contained in a paragraph separate from the discussion. There are several standard ways to develop concluding paragraphs. For instance, an effective conclusion can do the following:

1. Offer an answer to a question, a solution to a problem, or the result of a behavior raised in the introduction and explored in the discussion; or point out that there is no clear answer, solution, or result, thus showing the issue's complexity.
2. Present a quotation, especially one that amplifies the central point or varies another quotation already presented in the introduction.
3. Relate a relevant anecdote that the reader will be likely to remember and that echoes the central point.
4. Rephrase the central and supporting points, followed by a closing sentence or two to turn the reader's mind back to the discussion.

"When I wrote my conclusion," Vega says, "I wanted to answer the obvious question—Can advertisers actually exploit such desires? Responding to this question would also allow me to remind readers of the central point and subpoints. I end with a rhetorical question, since there is no answer to the question I initially posed."

Let us offer a word of caution here. Conclusions must develop from the rest of the essay. Don't shift directions in a conclusion. And don't merely end with, "That's all, Folks!" Try to bring the thought process that unfolded in the discussion to a logical close.

TITLES

Once you've got the introduction, discussion, and conclusion written, all that's left is the title. Vega's title, "Exploited Desires," refers directly to her essay's central idea. "Desire" and "exploited" are two key words she uses in the central point and subpoints. Selecting key words to use as a title is an effective practice. You might also consider using a dramatic phrase from the essay. In any case, apply some thought to a title, but keep it simple.

Whatever you do, don't title an essay "Assignment 3" or any title like that. A title should suggest an essay's content, not its sequence in the course. Also don't underline or put quotation marks around your title. If you use a quotation or a title from another work as part of your title, however, use quotation marks or underlining, whichever is appropriate, for that part.

Revising the First Draft

If you set your essay aside for a few days before you revise, you will be more objective in your evaluation and better able to see its strengths and weaknesses. But if you cannot delay the revision, you must still try to approach the paper from the point of view of a reader. Review the paper slowly, concentrating on its overall clarity. Try doing this while reading aloud. It will help you find confused or inconsistent areas. For this first reading, ask yourself the following questions:

1. Is the central point stated clearly? Does it indicate the scope and direction of the paper?
2. Is the paper unified? Does every sentence and paragraph have a clear relation to the central point?
3. Are the vocabulary and content appropriate for the chosen audience?
4. Is the paper organized logically and effectively?

If you need to make changes, make them and then read the paper again, concentrating on smaller elements by asking yourself the following questions:

1. Are the paragraphs developed with sufficient detail and explanation?
2. Does the paper move smoothly from paragraph to paragraph—that is, is the paper coherent?
3. Is the introduction interesting and to the point? Does it lead naturally to the statement of the central point? Does the concluding paragraph bring the paper to a satisfactory close without being unduly repetitious or introducing a new subject?

During a third reading you should concentrate on even smaller elements. As you do, try reading the essay backward sentence by sentence. By reading each sentence out of context, you may find it easier to answer the following:

1. Are the sentences clear, grammatical, and free from sentence errors?
2. Is the paper consistent with the conventions of punctuation and mechanics?
3. Do the words convey the intended meaning? Are they spelled correctly?

If all this sounds like a lot of work, it is. But excellence is not born in first drafts. It is achieved through thoughtful and painstaking revision.

Student Essay for Further Study

A second student example, a deductive essay written by Elaine Kubo, follows. Kubo's assignment required that she select a subject of historical and national significance. She was to develop a 750- to 1000-word essay about the subject from a "personal" perspective. She selected the Great American Depression of the 1930s, a period of severe economic disruption. Before studying Kubo's deductive essay, read her comments about the assignment and also study her comments printed in the margin.

Deciding to write about the Depression wasn't easy. First, I thought I would write about the Vietnam War, but I had nothing personal to say. There were other subjects I considered—the 60s Free Speech Movement, the Watergate scandal during the Nixon presidency, the assassination of John F. Kennedy, even some recent terrorist activities—but I couldn't find what my instructor called the "personal angle." While browsing through my daily writing entries, I came across a reference to the Depression. I had always been struck by how my grandparents said the Depression, which they lived through, was a frightening period of their lives because of the economic uncertainty. But I also remembered their wonderful stories about the strengths that the Depression experience brought out in them. Their experience along with my parents' experiences as children during that time gave me the personal angle I needed.

Because of all the information I had, the main problem I faced was finding a focus and drafting a central point. I decided to approach the Depression by recognizing that it was a dreadful time for many Americans—who could deny that—but that there were personal sagas worth telling that didn't get put in history books, the kind of stories my family told. This was the start of my focus, but I needed at least three subpoints. After some brainstorming, I decided I could categorize the stories under subpoints that reflected determination, dignity, and sense of community.

Working with family stories caused another problem. I would mostly have to develop my essay through narrative examples. I had, therefore, to summarize the stories without putting in unnecessary detail, and I had to find representative examples, ones that reflected broad experience without being overly general. With all this in mind I began to make lists and to "sketch" the paper before writing the rough draft.

The Thirties: A Personal History

Members of my generation have grown up during a time when the majority of Americans have lived in relative comfort. Nevertheless, we have all seen photographs of the Great American Depression of the 1930s: images of anonymous men in dark suits and tweed caps selling apples on street corners; hollow-cheeked women cuddling infants in front of clapboard shacks; crowds milling before factory gates; hoboes gathered around campfires and eating from tin cans; Model T Fords loaded with chairs, tables, mattresses, and boxes of clothes crawling along desert highways toward the Pacific. These dreadful memories, preserved in history books, seem totally grim. But besides the dreadful memories, there are positive aspects of the Depression that haven't been preserved in history books. These memories are carried by people who suffered yet lived through the thirties.

One positive aspect of the thirties my grandparents remember was the determination to overcome adversity it stirred in them. Like many Kansas

My introductory paragraph was the hardest to write. First, I wanted to establish my perspective—that is, I was a person who had not experienced the Depression. Then I wanted to show my readers that I recognized how terrible the Depression was for most Americans. Here's where I got the idea to use a catalog [see Chapter 6] of Depression photographs that most everyone would have seen. This gave me a chance to recreate the Depression experience in my readers' imaginations. I wanted to make the images vivid; so I used some specific detail in each one. The opening then sets up a contrast with what I have to say about the Depression experience. The last two sentences embody my central point.

I worked in a key phrase—positive aspects—which I repeat in every topic sentence to help my readers recognize that a new subpoint is being introduced.

Paragraph 2 introduces my first subpoint—that the Depression experience helped my grandparents become determined to overcome adversity. Although I use my grandparents as

farmers in the early thirties, they were suffering from the country's sudden economic collapse, but they still had land and raised some crops. Then nature turned against them. Unrelenting winds swept across the plains, destroying crops and swirling away the topsoil. A drought came with the wind and destroyed any chance they might have had to grow a crop. Finally, the bank demanded payment on the farm's mortgage. They couldn't scrape together the money, so they lost the farm. But if economic collapse and a senseless act of nature destroyed them financially, these events toughened their will to overcome adversity. They moved to a small Kansas town. Days, my grandfather worked as a clerk in his uncle's store; nights, he studied law. My grandmother, who had taught before marrying, worked at the local school. By 1938 my grandfather had passed the state examination allowing him to practice law. By the end of World War II my grandmother was school superintendent.

I know there were many less fortunate than my grandparents, many who were fighting poverty all those years, but some people who lived through the thirties remember poverty as being different then. It seems that another positive aspect of the

an example, I also try to show that they represent many people who lived during that time.

This is probably the paragraph I rewrote the most. I wanted to create some drama; that is, life went from bad to worse, but through personal determination life got better. I actually saw this paragraph as a tribute to human courage as embodied in my grandparents.

I open paragraph 3 with a transitional sentence that reminds my readers of the central point. The second sentence is the topic sentence that sets up the second subpoint—"that people could be poor without losing personal dignity."

Depression was that people could be poor without losing personal dignity. My mother has a childhood memory of a gray-haired man who knocked at the kitchen door one day and asked to do some work in return for a meal. Her father refused to allow him to work, but invited him to join the family for a lunch of soup and biscuits. After the meal he whittled little wooden birds for all the kids. My mother says that the whole family gave him the respect they would give any successful artist now. My retired neighbor knew out-of-luck businessmen and bankrupt investors who sold flowers on street corners and caddied at golf courses without losing a sense of personal dignity. Can you imagine such things today? Perhaps because there were so many people broke and hungry, it wasn't considered a failure not to have a regular job. People respected each other anyway.

Another positive aspect some people experienced during the thirties was the sense of community it created in them. Many people carry stories about grocers who supplied out-of-luck neighbors with food on credit and charged no interest. Others talk about going to wedding showers without enough money to buy a nice gift and the guests all digging into their pockets and pooling their

I decided to use one specific example and one typical example to support my subpoint—one from my mother's childhood and one from a neighbor's experience. Since the example in my second paragraph was so long, I wrote shorter ones here to create some variety for my readers.

I round off the third paragraph with a clincher written as a question, and then I answer the question in an attempt to show the difference between today's values and Depression values.

The opening sentence of the fourth paragraph presents my subpoint—that for some people the Depression experience created a sense of community.

To create variety and move my readers along, I created three one-sentence examples of community. Then I used a transitional sentence that begins "But perhaps the most startling example . . ." to set up the most dramatic of my examples. I actually considered making this example a separate paragraph because it is so long; then the topic sentence would have been developed in two short paragraphs instead of one long one.

change to buy a community gift for the bride. My aunt remembers over a hundred people turning out to help repair a neighbor's house that had partly burned down. But perhaps the most startling example of the sense of community I've heard comes from my friend's family experience. Her grandparents were forced to move from the countryside to Boston, where they rented a one-bedroom apartment. At the time, my friend's grandmother was seven months pregnant and started having labor pains. A doctor, selected at random from the phone book, came over immediately, completed a quick examination, then called for hot water. He delivered a healthy, six-pound girl. A week later the new parents got a bill for $7.32, the cost of home delivery. Since the move and rent had taken all their money, they couldn't pay. But when other people living in the building—all of whom had been complete strangers to them until the baby was born—heard of the couple's plight, they chipped in pennies, nickels, dimes, and quarters. They sent the fee to the doctor. Less than three days later, the doctor drove up with a back seat full of groceries. He said his nurse had sent the bill by mistake, so he used the payment to buy groceries for them. <u>At one time I might have seen this</u>

I end the paragraph with a clincher and distinguish the sense of community from charity, which I felt was an important distinction to make.

aspect of the Depression as an act of charity; now
I see it as an act of community.

   Indeed, the historian's portrayal of the
Depression as a grim time for Americans is accurate, but we must remember that a personal history
that doesn't get into books parallels the social
upheaval we've read about. It's the history carried in the minds of people who endured through
that time. Often those memories have some positive
aspects.

In my concluding paragraph I merely restate my central idea by reasserting that the historical view of the Depression is accurate but that another kind of history exists in the memories of people who lived through it.

An Extended Professional Essay for Further Study

Finally, we would like you to examine an essay by Anastasia Toufexis which appeared in *Time* magazine. Toufexis explains that Americans do not get enough sleep, a condition that taxes our emotional and physical well-being. Her essay has an underlying cause-and-effect pattern. After a lengthy introduction, Toufexis describes various effects of sleep loss, then shifts to a discussion of the causes. She ends with an appeal to us to change our habits. As you read, notice that although the overall pattern is cause and effect, she has used other strategies to develop individual paragraphs: specific examples, typical examples, catalog, comparisons, and contrasts. She has also used a technique you may want to consider for some of your essays: brief quotations from doctors and others who have special information and whose opinions therefore add validity to the message.

Drowsy America

At 7 a.m. or 6 or maybe even 5, the blare of
the alarm breaks the night, and another workday
dawns. As an arm gropes to stop the noise and the
whole body rebels against the harsh call of morning, the thought is almost always the same: I have
to get more sleep. That night, after 17 or 18

Topic of sleep is introduced with a dramatic narrative.

hours of fighting traffic, facing deadlines and racing the clock, the weary soul collapses into bed
once again for an all-too-brief respite. And just
before the slide into slumber, the nagging thought
returns: <u>I have to get more sleep.</u>

Millions of Americans make this complaint, but
how many do anything about it? Sleep is a biological imperative, but do people consider it as vital
as food or drink? Not in today's rock-around-the-
clock world. Not in a society in which mothers
work, stores don't close, assembly lines never
stop, TV beckons all the time, and stock traders
have to keep up with the action in Tokyo. For too
many Americans, sleep has become a luxury that can
be sacrificed or a nuisance that must be endured.

To some night owls, the very idea of spending
more than 20 years of one's life in idle snoozing
is appalling. Listen to Harvey Bass. Between a job
as a computer-systems manager in New York City and
free-lance consulting, he gets no more than five
hours of sleep a night and sometimes only two. He
admits that the schedule occasionally leaves him
with a "tingling around my head." Even so, he
says, "If I live a normal life span, I will have
lived 20% more than the average person because I'm
awake."

Second paragraph begins with two rhetorical questions.

Brief catalog of sleep-reducing conditions.

Specific example amplifies general statements of paragraph above.

That may sound like an attractive exchange, but scientists are increasingly making the case that forgoing rest is a foolish and often perilous bargain. In fact, evidence is mounting that sleep deprivation has become one of the most pervasive health problems facing the U.S. Researchers have not proved conclusively that losing sleep night after night directly causes physical illness, but studies show that mental alertness and performance can suffer badly. "Sleepiness is one of the least recognized sources of disability in our society," declares Dr. Charles Pollak, head of the sleep-disorder center at Cornell University's New York Hospital in Westchester County. "It doesn't make it difficult to walk, see or hear. But people who don't get enough sleep can't think; they can't make appropriate judgments; they can't maintain long attention spans."

Central point—"forgoing rest is a foolish and often perilous bargain— implies a cause-and-effect development. Placing central point here sets up a deductive arrangement.

Expert opinion supporting central point.

Such mental fatigue can be as threatening as a heart attack. Recent evidence indicates that drowsiness is a leading cause of traffic fatalities and industrial mishaps. "Human error causes between 60% and 90% of all workplace accidents, depending on the type of job," observes biological psychologist David Dinges of the University of Pennsylvania. "And inadequate sleep is a major factor in human error, at least as important as drugs, alco-

Next two paragraphs present general statements about effect of sleep loss.

Expert opinion.

hol and equipment failure." Other research suggests that sleep loss contributes to everything from drug abuse to poor grades in school.

A typical adult needs about eight hours of shut-eye a night to function effectively. By that standard, millions of Americans are chronically sleep deprived, trying to get by on six hours or even less. In many households, cheating on sleep has become an unconscious and pernicious habit. "In its mild form, it's watching Ted Koppel and going to bed late and then getting up early to get to the gym," says Cornell's Pollak. In extreme cases people stay up most of the night, seeing how little sleep will keep them going. They try to compensate by snoozing late on weekends, but that makes up for only part of the shortfall. Over the months and years, some researchers believe, the deficit builds up and the effects accumulate. "Most Americans no longer know what it feels like to be fully alert," contends Dr. William Dement, director of Stanford University's sleep center. They go through the day in a sort of twilight zone; the eyes may be wide open, but the brain is partly shut down. . . .

Typical example of "cheating on sleep" habit.

Expert opinion.

One sign of sleep deprivation is requiring an alarm clock to wake up. Another is falling asleep within five minutes after your head hits the pil-

Cause-and-effect pattern begins with some common effects of insufficient sleep.

low. Well-rested people drop off in 10 to 15 minutes. A third clue is napping at will. "People
like to boast about their ability to catch 40
winks whenever they want," explains Dement, "but
what it means is that they're excessively sleepy."
On the other hand, when people get enough rest,
they remain awake no matter what the provocation:
droning teachers, boring books, endless roads,
heavy meals, glasses of wine—even articles about
sleep.

Brief catalog.

Perhaps the most insidious consequence of
skimping on sleep is the irritability that
increasingly pervades society. Weariness corrodes
civility and erases humor, traits that ease the
myriad daily frustrations, from standing in supermarket lines to refereeing the kids' squabbles.
Without sufficient sleep, tempers flare faster and
hotter at the slightest offense.

Another effect: irritability.

But there are far grimmer effects. Harrowing
tales are told by interns and residents, many of
whom routinely work 120-hour weeks, including 36
hours at a stretch. Some admit that mistakes are
frighteningly common. A California resident fell
asleep while sewing up a woman's uterus—and toppled onto the patient. In another California case,
a sleepy resident forgot to order a diabetic

Another effect: low job performance.

*Three specific examples of effect of
sleep loss on job performance.*

patient's nightly insulin shot and instead pre-
scribed another medication. The man went into a
coma. Compassion can also be a casualty. One young
doctor admitted to abruptly cutting off the questions of a man who had just been told he had AIDS:
"All I could think of was going home to bed."

The U.S. Department of Transportation reports
that up to 200,000 traffic accidents each year may
be sleep related and that 20% of all drivers have
dozed off at least once while behind the wheel.
Truckers are particularly vulnerable. A long-haul
driver covering up to 4,000 miles in seven to 10
days often averages only two to four hours of
sleep a night. "I've followed trucks that were
weaving all over the road," says Corky Woodward, a
driver out of Wausau, Wisconsin. "You yell, blow
your air horn and try to raise them on the CB
radio. But sometimes they go in the ditch. You ask
what happened, and they can't remember because
they're so tired." . . .

Sleep-deprived workers may resort to alcohol
and drugs as a way to compensate for fatigue. But
the solution only compounds the distress. Many
people wind up on a hurtling roller coaster, pop-
ping stimulants to keep awake, tossing down alco-

Another effect: traffic accidents.

Typical example.

Another effect: relying on drugs to control sleep patterns.

hol or sleeping pills to put themselves out, then swallowing more pills to get up again. . . .

One of the most surprising recent discoveries concerns the sleep needs of adolescents. For years they were urged to get eight hours, the same as adults. No longer. Teenagers appear to require more than 9 1/2 hours. Catskadon found that to be the case when she studied a group of children every summer for seven years, from the time they were ages 10 to 12 until they turned 17 to 19. During the experiments, the youngsters got 9 1/2 hours of sleep each night. In the beginning years of the study, they experienced no problems during the day, but after they reached puberty there was an increase in daytime sleepiness.

Research results used to correct a common misunderstanding about adolescent sleep needs.

Teenagers who are struggling to juggle demanding academic schedules, friendships and dating, and sometimes after-school jobs, are horrified by the idea of nine-plus hours of sleep. "My God, how would I have time to do anything?" protests Kimberly Erlich, 15, of Van Nuys, Calif. "That would mean going to sleep at 8 p.m. I can't imagine that." Kimberly tries to get at least seven hours.

Specific example of resistance to sleep needs.

Others appear to be getting even less. And that is interfering with their ability to learn, contend teachers, who say they are confronting more and more draggy pupils, even in elementary school. Sleepy youngsters are arriving late to class, forgetting assignments, moving at a snail's pace from task to task, and sometimes dropping their head on their desk to catch a few winks.

Brief catalog of effects on young students.

College students are notorious for nodding off in class and hibernating on weekends. Phil Simon, a 20-year-old junior at the University of Oregon in Eugene, is not unusual. During the week, he rises anytime between 7:30 a.m. and 11, depending on his classes, and retires sometime between 1 a.m. and 2:30. He naps whenever he gets a chance, but that does not always work well. "A few weeks ago," he recalls, "I had a break between two morning classes, so I slept. But when I woke up, the morning class I had attended felt like it never happened. It seemed more like a dream." On weekends he heads for bed at 3 a.m. and doesn't get up until 1 p.m.

Specific example.

It was civilization that created the dilemma of sleep loss. The sun presumably dictated the habits of ancient people: when it was up they were awake, and when it went down they slept. Maybe when the moon was full they stayed up a bit later. The discovery of fire probably allowed the first change in that pattern. As flames lit the dark, surely some adventurous souls delayed bedtime. But sweeping change came only a century ago with the

Shift to an ultimate cause: development of artificial lighting.

introduction of the light bulb. Thomas Edison's glowing invention permitted cheap, safe and efficient illumination throughout the darkest nights. By the end of World War II, people were sleeping about eight hours.

Today new cultural and economic forces are combining to turn the U.S. into a 24-hour society. Many TV stations, restaurants and supermarkets operate through the day and night. Business is increasingly plugged into international markets that require around-the-clock monitoring and frequent travel across time zones. As CEO of Intellicorp, a software company, Tom Kehler, 43, regularly works 12-hour days in his Mountain View, California, office and hopscotches the globe. This fall he spent 13 days in Europe, followed by a few days back in California and 10 days in the Orient. Then he flew home and went directly from plane to office. He subsists on four to five hours of sleep a night and occasional 15-minute cat-naps during the day—and unlike most people, he likes it. "Sleep always felt like an interference with life," he says.

Changing family patterns are adding to the national sleep deficit. Working single mothers and two-career families are hard pressed to find time for the children or the household chores. To fit

Typical examples illustrating another cause: demands of modern living.

Specific example.

Another cause: changing family patterns.
Specific example of family lifestyle that reduces sleep opportunities.

everything in parents are extending their waking hours. Financial adviser Ben Sax, 34, commutes to New York City each day from his home in a suburb to the north, where he lives with his wife Holly, a lobbyist, and their two children, ages 4 and 6. The parents get by on four to five hours of sleep. "We're shocked when we call people at 9:30 or 10 at night and they're asleep," says Ben. "Our kids are still up at that time." In fact, many working couples are keeping their youngsters up late simply to see them. . . .

Because so few studies have been done, scientists cannot make definitive comparisons between American sleep patterns and those of other countries. But many researchers believe that all industrialized nations are experiencing sleep-deprivation problems, though usually not as serious as those in the U.S. "The Europeans don't have 24-hour societies like we do," says Henry Ford Hospital's Roth. "If you're in Paris and you're looking for a restaurant at 2 in the morning, you're not going to find one so easily." In Germany most stores close by 6:30 p.m., TV networks usually sign off by 1 a.m., and Sunday remains largely a day of rest.

Comparison: United States and other industrial countries.

If any nation can be said to be suffering greater sleep loss than the U.S., it may be Japan.

Comparison with Japan developed with typical examples.

Officeworkers in Tokyo often commute for an hour or more, arriving at their desks at 9 a.m. and staying until 8 p.m. or later. Then they go out to eat and drink with colleagues, an essential part of the job, and catch the last train home at midnight. Workers get only 113 days off a year, compared with Americans' 134 and Germans' 145. Exhausted Japanese can be seen sleeping everywhere: on subways and trains, in elevators, at concerts and baseball games, and during business meetings. The usual apology: "Well, it's not exactly polite, but it can't be helped."

Many Americans concede nothing to the Japanese in the tirelessness department. "People love to boast about how little sleep they've had," says Dr. Neil Kavey, director of Columbia University's sleep center in New York City. "It's macho and dynamic." Those who run themselves ragged are often hailed as ambitious comers, while those who insist on getting their rest are dismissed as lazy plodders.

Expert opinion.

As long as that attitude persists, the national sleep deficit will not be easy to close. Government and businesses can help by formulating more enlightened work rules and schedules. What is needed most of all, though, is a fundamental change in Americans' thinking about the necessity

Call for a change in sleep habits.

of sleep. A difficult task, yes. But not impossible. Millions of citizens have already shown themselves capable of making far harder decisions once
they realize that their health is at stake. Americans have stubbed out cigarettes, laced up exercise shoes and pushed away plates laden with high-
cholesterol, high-fat foods. By comparison,
choosing to spend some more time abed in blissful
oblivion should be attractive. It is a message
that is becoming unmistakable: Wake up, America—by
getting more sleep.

Comparison: lack of sleep habit with other dangerous habits.

Clincher.

One Last Thought

We have very limited intentions for this chapter. We've tried to give you only the most basic elements of the deductive essay. We're a little fearful that you'll approach the writing of a short deductive essay rigidly. That would be a mistake because within the general framework we've presented, approaches to the deductive essay are as varied as the people who write them. As a writer you have to find the voice and method of development that fit the idea, emotion, knowledge, and experience you wish to communicate. Your choices will vary with your subject matter and your attitude toward it. The more you write, the more choices you will see as possibilities. It's the real challenge writing offers. Enjoy it.

WRITING TASK—DEDUCTIVE ESSAY

Select a subject you feel personally involved in either because you hold strong opinions about it or because it has touched your life directly. Here are a few possibilities, but, as always, feel free to choose a topic of your own.

bank credit cards
health programs
family relationships
MTV
improving education

intelligent animals
truth in advertising
cultural differences
self-discipline
travel

Once you have a subject, write an essay of five or more paragraphs exploring it. You can go about this task in one of two ways. You can take each step to your instructor for review, or you can work through the steps on your own. In either case, we advise you to follow this procedure:

1. Select a broad subject and narrow it until you have a topic that can be treated with specific content in a single essay.

2. Do prewriting exercises to develop ideas and specific details.

3. Phrase a tentative central point that states the topic, limits it, and either implies a method of development or indicates the subparts of the topic.

4. Organize a plan on a separate sheet of paper. Include the central point and subpoints that will make up the discussion paragraphs. Fill in brief phrases to remind yourself what material you will use in the development of the subpoints.

5. Once you have a plan, write an introductory paragraph that presents the central point in the closing sentences. Remember, the introduction should serve a purpose by giving the reader important information related to the central point. Also remember that the central point you started with may need to be reshaped to fit into the introduction.

6. Once the introduction is completed, shape the subpoints into topic sentences and develop the discussion section of your essay. You should have several discussion paragraphs, each built around a subpoint cast in a topic sentence. Also be sure to use clear transitions linking your paragraphs.

7. After you've completed the discussion section, write a conclusion that restates the central point and adequately closes the essay.

8. Write a title—a simple one. Don't put quotation marks around it and don't underline it.

9. Reread your entire essay several times, making revisions and corrections as necessary.

GROUP WORK

The group should review the first essay in steps, allowing about four class sessions to complete the task.

1. If you have not been given a list of subjects, brainstorm your own list. Once you have a list of several subjects, quickly discuss each one to see if it could be explored effectively in a three- to four-page essay. Be sure to record ideas related to each subject.

2. You should all return for the second session with a subject and a working plan, which should include a tentative central idea, subpoints, and any supporting detail you have. Take turns presenting

your work and listen to the observations other group members offer.

3. For this session you all should have a rough draft and a copy for each group member. Spend this session reading the drafts individually and noting your observations. Then as a group review each draft, pointing out what is effective and what would benefit from revision.

4. For this last session, bring your final draft with copies. Break into subgroups of three. Each paper should be reviewed in detail. First, all three group members should read through a paper quickly. Then the writer should read the draft aloud while the other members follow along with their copies. Whenever anyone spots something wrong, stop and discuss the problem. If changes will improve the essay, make notes and then correct the essay during the polishing stage before submitting it to the instructor.

15
Inductive Essay

An inductively arranged essay reverses the arrangement of the deductive essay. As the last chapter explained, the deductive arrangement develops from general statement to specific information. For example, suppose your central point is that the Huntington High School physical education department prepares students physically and emotionally to live healthy lives. In a deductive essay, you would present this point in the introduction and follow with a discussion section showing specific instances of the preparation taking place.

An *inductively arranged* essay, though, moves from specific detail to a generalized central point stated or implied near the end of the paper, usually in the final paragraph. In such an essay you might have a paragraph describing a typical physical education class hour at Huntington High School, another paragraph contrasting this class with others you have observed, a catalog of a semester's units of instruction, an examination of the effects of this instuction on students' lives, and end the essay with a statement of the central point.

Why use an inductive pattern? Sometimes you will not want to reveal your central point in the opening paragraph. You may want to save it for the end so that it will have more impact. Or you may want to develop two sides of an argument before revealing your own position. Instead of assuming the role of a guide to an already announced destination, the writer of an inductive essay becomes more like a fellow explorer, examining the territory and finally reaching a conclusion at about the same time the reader does.

From the following diagram, you can see that an inductively arranged essay gives the writer a great deal of freedom, but if a writer does not have a firm grip on the form, he or she might go astray by failing to link the discussion paragraphs to the central point that appears in the conclusion.

Opening: Suggests the general subject. Does not state the central point.

Discussion: Paragraphs can be developed by examples, catalogs, anecdotes, comparison and contrast, analogy, classification, causes and effects, definitions, or description and narration. Like a deductive essay, an induc -tive essay can be several paragraphs long.

Conclusion: States or implies the central point.

Now examine an inductively arranged essay in which student-writer Tyler Davis discusses the "devious" editorial policies of many women's magazines. As you read, notice the following three principles at work:

1. The general subject—young women smokers—is introduced without being stated as a central idea.
2. The discussion paragraphs detail separate but thematically related information that leads up to and supports the central idea.
3. The conclusion presents the central point.

What follows is Davis's inductive essay. Read it through, then reread it along with the comments in the margin.

Reading Can Be Hazardous to a Woman's Health

The title suggests the subject.

At a time when more and more Americans are giving up smoking, or better yet, never starting to smoke at all, one group of smokers is growing—young women in their teens or early twenties.

The opening sentences give the general subject without stating the central idea.

Smoking affects women more than men by increasing the risk of cervical cancer, miscarriages, and osteoporosis, among other disorders. Yearly at least 125,000 American women have died from the effects of smoking cigarettes. All of these deaths could have been avoided with accurate information about the dangers of smoking. Is there a reason why young women are not getting the message?

The second paragraph advances the essay by establishing the dangers of smoking to women. The writer uses specific detail effectively. The question that closes this paragraph serves as an effective transition to the next.

You might find the answer in glossy women's magazines, such as Mademoiselle, Self, and Cosmopolitan. Many publications directed toward the female reader are paid substantial sums of money by tobacco companies to run advertisements that

The first sentence of this paragraph answers the closing question of the last. The writer advances toward the central point by linking the magazines, which are purportedly concerned with female health issues, to the glamorization of smoking.

glamorize smoking. The advertisements often feature sexy, independent women smoking cigarettes in smart clothing and elegant settings. These magazines also run articles on female health issues. Sometimes the editors even position cigarette advertisements next to articles on health and exercise that feature models that look like the models in the cigarette advertisements, thus creating the illusion that smoking is part of an active, healthy lifestyle. If women rely on these magazines as their only source of health information, they might never know that smoking is harmful.

A quick review of several women's magazines featuring health articles reveals a great deal about the way they fail their readers. During the last seven years, not one featured a full-length article or devoted an editorial to any aspect of the dangers of smoking. Yet during this period lung cancer surpassed breast cancer as the number one cancer killer of women. More than three dozen articles dealing with breast cancer, which is unrelated to smoking, were published, but none on lung cancer, which is directly related to smoking. Two magazines actually published short items associating smoking positively with weight control.

The fourth paragraph opens by announcing that these magazines fail their readers and then the writer documents the failure—an important step toward the central idea.

All, however, ran multiple advertisements in each issue for tobacco companies.

Can tobacco companies influence a magazine's content? Most women's magazines are little more than shopping catalogs, page after page of advertisements enticing women to become avid consumers. What on the surface may seem to be legitimate articles are often disguised advertisements—articles on health and beauty, for instance, with photographs of specific products mentioned. Clearly, these magazines serve one purpose: to make money for their owners. Why risk the wrath of tobacco interests? Of course, tobacco companies cannot directly dictate a magazine's content, but they can cancel an ad campaign if the magazine details the hazards of smoking. Now tobacco companies have become conglomerates so that such major food advertisers as Nabisco and General Foods are owned by cigarette manufacturers. Clearly, lost advertisement money from both food and cigarette interests would be a major economic blow for any women's magazine.

Feminist organizations were outraged when they learned that movie makers accepted advertisement money for featuring characters smoking cigarettes in their films. The Philip Morris Company, for example, paid thousands of dollars to have Lois

The fifth paragraph opens with an obvious question which indicates that the writer is thinking of the reader's responses. The writer does not answer the opening question directly, but the answer is implicit—money talks.

This closing paragraph opens with an unexpected twist. The writer uses the example of cigarette campaigns in popular films because it appears so devious, thus helping the reader to accept the central point: It is devious for women's magazine editors to ignore the health hazards of smoking while accepting millions in cigarette advertisement money.

Lane smoke Marlboros in Superman II. This type of campaign, again directed toward young women, is clearly devious. But it is equally devious for women's magazine editors to ignore the health hazards of smoking while accepting millions in cigarette advertisement money.

An inductive essay is also an effective pattern to use in arranging personal insights. By presenting personal experience and responding to it, you inductively lead a reader to a central point—an "Ah ha!" experience. Often in a personal inductive essay, you will imply your central point rather than state it directly. Such an inferential conclusion draws readers deeper into the essay by allowing them the satisfaction of inferring the meaning.

Now examine a personal inductive essay by student-writer Tom Stevens. He uses the inductive pattern to express his attitude toward development in his community.

Growth

I have become more aware lately of just how much meaning is summed up in the commonplace word *growth*.

Notice how the lead presents the general subject without stating it as a central idea.

After spending August working as a counselor at a YMCA camp in the Sierra Nevada, I headed home to Orange County. Since the thought of a trip through Los Angeles always depresses me, calling up visions of housing tracts pasted together and of jammed freeways that lead to the city's concrete heart where gray towers spear into the afternoon pall, I decided to take the longer but more scenic route north of L.A. and over the Cajon Pass. I was in for a surprise. When I crossed the

The opening sentence in the second paragraph gives some background to help orient the reader.

"Since the thought of" gives a response to past experience and backs it up with specific details.

"I was in for a surprise" prepares the reader for the specific details that follow in the next few sentences.

last ridge just before sunset and began the descent to the coastal plain, I saw that the fields of crops and citrus I remembered having been there had vanished. In their place were housing projects, shopping centers, gas stations, trailer parks, and schoolyards. The whole scene reminded me of a huge bowl heaped with junk and covered over with a layer of haze thick as gauze. I felt I was entering a nightmare. Certainly all this growth couldn't have happened in a single month, but then I remembered I had not traveled this particular route for almost ten years. I wanted to escape the numbing scene, so I stepped on the gas pedal and pointed my VW toward the city of Irvine and my home.

Irvine is a new city being slowly carved from a massive cattle ranch, according to the designs of a master plan. I can remember my parents saying they had moved to Irvine because it would never have the growth that came to Los Angeles.

The morning after I returned home, I was up early. It's my habit to jog just after sunup. I set out on my usual run: an easy jog to a nearby field, then a harder run across a mile of open space to the high school where I usually do four leisurely laps around the track, and then I head for home along a road that takes me to the crest

*"The whole scene reminded me"
begins a response shaped in an image
that suggests all the clutter and pollution the writer has associated with
L.A.*

*"Certainly all this growth" gives the
background of the writer's thought.
Using the key word "growth" is
important here. The writer wants the
reader to associate it with building.*

*"I wanted to escape" begins another
response.*

*Notice how this paragraph and the
preceding paragraph are linked by
"Irvine." The opening sentence of this
paragraph supplies the reader with
more background.*

*"The morning after . . ." sets up the
next sequence that begins with background information related to the
writer's usual run. If he didn't present this information here, he would
have to work it in later.*

*Even though much of this is back-
ground, the writer works in specific
details.*

of a hill and down a path that leads to my back gate. At the field I saw that things had changed. All along its perimeter builders had terraced the hillsides and poured concrete slabs for housing foundations. Ahead, adjacent to the school, they had framed eight apartment buildings. I did four spiritless laps with my view of the field and hills cluttered by the new construction; then I started up the road to the hill's crest. I grew sad as I ran. Just one month earlier, wildflowers, rabbits, squirrels, sparrows, meadowlarks, and ground owls thrived in the field along the road. Now, the builders had scraped the field clean of vegetation. I saw no life. I did see heavy bulldozers and earthmovers, like the gorged offspring of ancient mastodons, standing in the fields. At the hill top, I paused to catch my breath. Below, in the northern half of the city, I saw where builders had cleared other fields for construction and had sawed down whole eucalyptus stands that once protected orange groves from harsh winds. I couldn't get over the thought that all this leveling had happened in a single month. I felt as if I were in the presence of a demonic force whose power I couldn't grasp. It had changed the old growth of flowers, trees, and wildlife into the new growth of houses, apartments, and shopping centers.

"At the field" sets up the specifics that follow.

Notice how he uses guiding words like along and ahead.

This section includes background information mixed with a great deal of detail. The writer contrasts the hills and fields as they were with how they are. Notice how "now" is used to guide the reader from past to present.

Here the writer shapes a response into an image by comparing the machines to prehistoric creatures.

He continues to document the "growth" he sees.

He moves from concrete details to his inner responses.

Here the writer brings out the idea that the old growth of living things has been replaced by a new growth.

That afternoon, while driving to campus, I passed more construction in the part of Irvine set aside as the industrial center. Here, the growth seemed to move upward rather than outward. I drove through the awesome shadows of multistoried buildings with the afternoon sun flashing through the steel skeletons rising in what had once been strawberry fields. I had seen it all before—this part of the city had been under development for years—but after my experiences driving back from the Sierras and jogging through my neighborhood, the growth took on a new meaning. The thoughts from Joni Mitchell's "Big Yellow Taxi" came to me. I had heard the song often, but this time its thought seemed to capture what I was thinking. I recalled the words "they paved paradise and put up a parking lot."

Maybe southern California or Orange County or the city of Irvine fails as an example of paradise, but it seems to me that each field and hillside no matter where it is holds a little bit of paradise. All this new growth was bringing me a sense of loss—not just for my neighborhood but for all neighborhoods that are giving up their bits of paradise to more housing tracts, shopping centers, and industrial complexes. And, finally, the question comes to me: Just as the unchecked growth of

"That afternoon" shows that time has passed and introduces the new sequence of experiences related to observing growth.

"I had seen" presents more background information and pulls together the experiences.

He brings in a quotation. Notice that he gives all the important information related to it—the name of the song and the vocalist. He also places it near the end of the essay because it serves to bring his thoughts together.

Notice how the writer refers to the song by bringing out the idea of paradise. The entire paragraph provides a showcase for insight. He closes by raising a question about the dangers of unchecked growth. But notice how he has tied it to other communities, thus linking his insight to the experience of others.

The final question embodies the central point.

vines will destroy smaller plants by blocking out
the sun, won't the unchecked growth of buildings
smother people who must live in their shadow?

A Professional Inductively Arranged Essay for Further Study

In the following essay, Pulitzer Prize winner George Will discusses public policy. Will begins by briefly mentioning jai alai to introduce the topic of state-sponsored gambling. He then shows how common gambling is, lists reasons given for accepting gambling, discusses its drawbacks, and concludes by condemning it. His central point is directly stated in the last two sentences. Notice that Will's attitude toward gambling is never in doubt. His choice of words and phrases, beginning with the very first sentence, strongly indicates what his attitude is, and the conclusion comes as no surprise.

Lotteries Cheat, Corrupt the People

On the outskirts of this city of insurance companies, there is another, less useful, business based on an understanding of probabilities. It is a jai alai fronton, a cavernous court where athletes play a fast game for the entertainment of gamblers and the benefit of, among others, the state treasury.

The first paragraph introduces the topic of gambling. Notice the phrase "less useful," which establishes the adversarial tone.

Half the states have legal betting in casinos, at horse or dog tracks, off-track betting parlors, jai alai frontons, or in state-run lotteries. Only Connecticut has four (the last four) kinds of gambling, and there is talk of promoting the other two.

Paragraphs 2, 3, and 4 show that state-sponsored gambling is widespread.

Not coincidentally, Connecticut is one of just seven states still fiercely determined not to have an income tax. Gambling taxes yielded $76.4 million last year, which is not a large slice of Connecticut's $2.1 billion budget, but it would be missed, and is growing.

Last year Americans legally wagered $15 billion, up 8 percent over 1976. Lotteries took in 24 percent more. Stiffening resistance to taxes is encouraging states to seek revenues from gambling, and thus to encourage gambling. There are three rationalizations for this:

Will lists three arguments in favor of gambling, but calls them rationalizations, thus casting doubt on their validity.

State-run gambling controls illegal gambling.

Gambling is a painless way to raise revenues.

Gambling is a "victimless" recreation, and

thus is a matter of moral indifference.

Actually, there is evidence that legal gambling increases the respectability of gambling, and increases public interest in gambling. This creates new gamblers, some of whom move on to illegal gambling, which generally offers better odds. And as a revenue-raising device, gambling is severely regressive.

This paragraph answers the first pro-gambling assertion by arguing that legal gambling increases illegal gambling.

Gamblers are drawn disproportionately from minority and poor populations that can ill-afford to gamble, that are especially susceptible to the lure of gambling, and that especially need a gov-

This paragraph argues that gambling revenue is not gained painlessly because it comes mainly from those who can least afford it.

ernment that will not collaborate with gambling entrepreneurs, as in jai alai, and that will not become a gambling entrepreneur through a state lottery.

A depressing number of gamblers have no margin for economic losses and little understanding of the probability of losses. Between 1975 and 1977 there was a 140 percent increase in spending to advertise lotteries—lotteries in which more than 99.9 percent of all players are losers. Such advertising is apt to be especially effective, and cruel, among people whose tribulations make them susceptible to dreams of sudden relief.

Grocery money is risked for such relief. Some grocers in Hartford's poorer neighborhoods report that receipts decline during jai-alai season. Aside from the injury gamblers do to their dependents, there is a more subtle but more comprehensive injury done by gambling. It is the injury done to society's sense of elemental equities. Gambling blurs the distinction between well-earned and "ill-gotten" gains.

Gambling is debased speculation, a lust for sudden wealth that is not connected with the process of making society more productive of goods and services. Government support of gambling gives

Three paragraphs argue that gambling is not "victimless." In the short run it deprives gamblers' dependents of necessities; in the long run it subverts the morals of society by implying that wealth can be amassed without work.

a legitimating imprimatur to the pursuit of wealth without work.

"It is," said Jefferson, "the manners and spirit of a people which preserves a republic in vigor." Jefferson believed in the virtue-instilling effects of agricultural labor. Andrew Jackson denounced the Bank of the United States as a "monster" because increased credit creation meant increased speculation. Martin Van Buren warned against "a craving desire . . . for sudden wealth." The early nineteenth-century belief was that citizens could be distinguished by the moral worth of the way they acquired wealth; and physical labor was considered the most ennobling labor.

Will quotes Jefferson, Jackson, and Van Buren as opponents of undeserved or unearned (speculative) wealth.

It is perhaps a bit late to worry about all this: the United States is a developed capitalist society of a sort Jefferson would have feared if he had been able to imagine it. But those who cherish capitalism should note that the moral weakness of capitalism derives, in part, from the belief that too much wealth is allocated in "speculative" ways, capriciously, to people who earn their bread neither by the sweat of their brows nor by wrinkling their brows for socially useful purposes.

Of course, any economy produces windfalls. As a town grows, some land values soar. And some investors (like many non-investors) regard stock trading as a form of roulette.

This paragraph is a short acknowledgment that some people gain money accidentally or as a matter of luck in any system.

But state-sanctioned gambling institutionalizes windfalls, whets the public appetite for them, and encourages the delusion that they are more frequent than they really are. Thus do states simultaneously cheat and corrupt their citizens.

Will's concluding paragraph states the central point directly.

WRITING TASK — INDUCTIVE ESSAY

Write an inductively arranged essay according to the principles illustrated in this chapter. Begin by selecting a subject in which you are interested and with which others might identify. Next, prewrite the essay using information you have gathered or experience you have had. Sharpen the central idea so that it will guide you during the revision process. Write the final draft for submission.

GROUP WORK

During the first working session, develop a list of interesting subjects in social criticism. Select two or three subjects for the group to address in an inductive essay that may be based on immediate personal experience or observed experience, such as the model essays "Growth" and "Reading Can Be Hazardous to a Woman's Health."

For the second session have complete drafts and circulate copies for review. Read them for inductive structure. Does the essay open with a general observation? Do the discussion paragraphs build toward the central point? Is the central point made clear in the final paragraph? Share your observations.

16
Associational Essay

By this point in *One to One* you would probably have little trouble arranging a paper covering the advantages and disadvantages of a particular job, the effects of the energy shortage on your campus, the process of preparing for an overseas journey, or the reasons for supporting one political candidate over another. This kind of material lends itself to organization reports and traditional essays.

But what of personal growth? What of insight that comes from life's disruptions and joys? How do writers go about exploring feelings involved in ending a relationship, losing a friend, becoming an adult, seeking truth? How do writers deal with feelings about succeeding, failing, aging, and dying? How do writers share insights that come from experiences such as these? They put them in reports, right?

Not likely. Separating, growing, seeking, failing, succeeding, aging, dying—this is the stuff of emotion. More often than not, these subjects can't be handled in formal patterns, but can be handled through less direct means. That's the function of the *associational essay*. This pattern offers the means to explore elusive areas of experience—that is, a way to search through life's nooks and crannies to see what experience has stored there.

This exploration usually involves the intuitive rather than the intellectual part of the mind, for the explorer abandons logical constraints in order to make more creative connections between separate memories drawn from personal experience. These memories often span a writer's life history by associating bits and pieces from the past and present that connect to a subject. Associational essays, then, tend to reflect the flow of psychological time instead of the procession of chronological time.

They often begin with an event or a thought important to the writer's current life, then skip to memories that connect with the present, hop forward to the not-so-distant past to make other connections before returning to the present. They may leap ahead, just as everyone's thought does, to construct a possible future. Sometimes they even include dreams and fantasies, hopes and fears, and, at times, philosophical musings.

At this point you probably sense that the writing of an associational essay requires a more creative touch than the writing of standard patterns. It does. The fact that it does presents a problem. As with most creative forms, the associational essay follows no clear pattern; therefore, we can't give you hard-and-fast rules. What we can do is give you some general guidelines.

Begin by recalling an experience that holds a great deal of emotion for you and that has brought some insight about yourself. Don't worry about whether the experience will seem earthshaking to your readers. Often the slightest experience, while appearing to be ordinary to others, may hold tremendous emotional energy for you. It's your job to show the emotion of the experience to the readers.

Once you've identified the experience and insight, draw together a list by associating memories you connect with the experience. In this prewriting phase, you shouldn't waste time evaluating the associations, you should only record them—no judgment, just writing.

After collecting the raw material, you need to shape the whole essay. Like all finished writing, the associational essay has a beginning, a middle, and an end. But unlike the deductive essay, the beginning of an associational essay merely suggests where the essay is headed. It never sets down a controlling idea.

The middle of the associational essay weaves together memories connected with the central experience, but the bulk of the details will come from the past. The paragraphs, though less organized than traditional patterns, should begin with sentences that give readers a sense of order. Never let readers stumble in disordered associations, but guide them each step of the way.

The end of the essay reveals the insight you've gained from the experience. This revelation, however, should be suggested, not flatly stated as the moral of your experience. Such suggestion is often hard to achieve. To make writing the conclusion easier, we suggest you use an image or thought that circles back into the essay and indirectly captures the point.

One last thought: Since the strength of an associational essay comes through the power of suggestion, the method of development is suggestive description. But before you can use description to suggest, you must have a clear understanding of what you want the reader to feel—a sense of loss; the pain of separation; the joy of discovery; the fear or acceptance of success, failure, aging, death. Once you have a clear understanding of your intent, you can select descriptive details that suggest the feeling. Often you may go through several drafts before you know exactly what it is you're after—that's the nature of creative writing—but before you write the final draft, you should have an exact understanding of what you're doing.

By way of illustration, we offer the following associational essay. Larry Swanson, the writer, relates an experience he had returning to the home and neighborhood where he was born and raised. His parents have moved to a new house, and his former home is to be destroyed. He uses the experience to indirectly communicate his feelings about change and to share an insight that comes to him through the encounter. As you read, notice that Swanson never flatly states a moral or a controlling idea; rather he suggests his feelings by describing early memories he associates with growing up in the old neighborhood. The use of suggestion creates subtle suspense and prepares readers for the final insight.

First read Swanson's opening comment on the essay; then read the entire essay. Finally, reread the essay with his marginal comments.

My goal for this essay was very clear—I wanted to communicate what "home" and "change" mean to me. By "home" I mean all those deep feelings, often confused feelings, that seem to be located just below consciousness. By "change" I mean a sense of loss and separation. I began developing the essay from various daily writing entries. These were bits and pieces of memories I had recorded in the Past Life and Portraits and Relationships chapters. Of course, the daily writing entries were incomplete in themselves; I had to polish and add information to make everything fit. There is one experience I very much liked about writing this essay, a discovery I made while doing the final draft: The use of Allie, Allie Oxen Free in the closing section. In children's games of hide and seek, the phrase means the players can come "home" safely, but in the essay it means that childhood is over.

Allie, Allie Oxen Free

In the middle of my freshman year in college I returned to my hometown to visit the old neighborhood. It was the last time I could go home. Home—the word has a deep meaning for me.

I use the opening sentence to set up the event that will organize the essay and to suggest the direction. I repeat "home" followed by a dash and a short comment on its personal meaning to stress its importance.

Driven out by a severe drought, my parents came from the cornfields of Nebraska to the house where

Here I needed to supply some background that shows my family's connection with the house and neighborhood.

they lived for thirty-five years. I was born in the back bedroom because, as my mother said, "there just wasn't enough time to get to a hospital." My earliest memories center on playing in that house: pushing trucks over the hardwood floors, my pajama knees mopping up the morning dust; rummaging through my mother's pan drawers and banging them on the linoleum; and hiding behind the overstuffed couch whenever I was called for lunch. The backyard seemed to stretch the length of a football field and was the place I would chase my older brother and sisters until I fell down, breathless and sweating. Before I started grammar school, I knew all the neighborhood's marvelous places: the avocado tree where my friends and I used to climb to an ancient tree house that had been built by children before us, the park where the old-timers would sit on benches and laugh at our wild games, the abandoned garage where we used to spy at the neighborhood through knotholes.

I felt I had to catalog a series of memory experiences I associated with the house and neighborhood so that the reader would feel what I was feeling. I arranged them chronologically—from childhood to starting school.

All that came back to me as I drove to pick up my parents for a final visit. You see, my home and the surrounding two blocks were to be destroyed. The City Council, those faceless champions of change, had condemned the neighborhood and planned to replace it with a civic center.

I conceived this paragraph as a bridge. It gives more background and expresses my attitude toward destructive change done in the name of progress. I remembered that social critic Lewis Mumford once said that "Progress does not necessarily mean improvement."

As I turned onto the street where my parents had bought a tract home, I saw my father, a little stooped since retiring after years of hard labor, standing before the recently seeded lawn that was beginning to sprout slivers of grass. In work boots, khaki trousers, and plaid shirt, which had become faded and thin from too much sun and too many washings, he didn't seem to belong to the stucco house packed with all the modern conveniences I knew my parents had avoided most of their lives. I pulled to the curb and he climbed in.

"Where's Mom?" I asked.

"Not coming," he said. "Let's go."

That was all he had to say to make me understand that Mom didn't want to make a final visit to the old place and to make me realize I didn't either.

As we drove, he filled his pipe, lit it, and began puffing—the smoke carrying the smell of Sugar Barrel, a smell I will always associate with him. We chatted about nothing important. "How're classes?" he asked and I answered routinely, knowing that neither of us wanted to say much about losing our home. Then we were on the old street, and the memories seemed to rise in my blood.

In this brief portrait of my father, I wanted to create the feeling that he was out of place in this new environment. Also I wanted to create a contrast: my father who once grew corn in vast fields has been reduced to growing grass and forced into a life of modern conveniences.

I should say I have never written dialogue before. What I learned is that dialogue that works needs to be shaped. You just can't write down what people say. You must "arrange" it, strip it to the essentials. I'm also trying to enlarge the portrait of my father for my reader.

I first saw the store the Hungarian couple used to run. The advertisements were peeling off the walls, the windows had been boarded up, and the screen door dangled stiffly from one hinge—empty, abandoned. But I remembered how I once spent summer afternoons sitting in front of it and playing Monopoly with my friends or chess with old man Jefferson, a retired sailor. The car seats we used to lounge on were still there, but the stuffing had been torn out and only the springs remained.

Then we passed Mr. Salling's house. Tall and bony, Salling was the neighborhood's mysterious figure. The few times I saw him in the sunlight he wore a gray suit and had gray hair and skin. But more often I saw him moving behind the curtains where he paced the darkened parlor or rocked in a creaky chair. I was told he had been "that way" since "losing his wife." He wanted only to be left alone. One morning I learned that he had "left" the night before. I never heard of him again.

We drove past the vacant lot that had been the scene of many of my childhood joys. Each Independence Day the neighborhood fathers would set up a fireworks display and thrill us kids for hours. In the spring we held war games there. Costumed in makeshift army uniforms and wearing

These next three paragraphs come from revised daily writing entries. I added detail and polished the entries. I begin each paragraph with a clear opening sentence to orient my reader. I try to create a contrast between past and present, to suggest death in the Mr. Salling paragraph and to highlight loss through change, especially in the part that refers to Billy.

plastic helmets and carrying plastic rifles, we dodged through the tall grass and dove into fox-holes, shouting "TATATATATA, Gotcha! C'mon you're dead!" During the summer, the lot served as the center for our nightly game of hide-and-seek. As my father and I drove past, I imagined hearing Billy Kieler's voice, the loudest and most melodic among us, echoing throughout the neighborhood, "ALLIE, ALLIE OXEN FREE! ALLIE, ALLIE OXEN FREE!" Billy was the first of my childhood friends to move away. How much had his life changed, I wondered. Yes, how much?

Then we were in front of our old wood-frame home. My father climbed from the car. I looked straight ahead. "Coming?" he said. But before I knew I had made a decision, I said no. I turned in time to see him walk the five steps up to the front porch, unlock the door, and step inside. No, I just could not bring myself to see the house empty, abandoned.

Not going into the house reflects my reluctance to making the journey that I expressed in the opening. I hope the words "empty" and "abandoned" echo the statement about the store.

I sat staring at the front lawn and recalled how I had spent hundreds of Saturday mornings mowing the grass, trimming the hedges, and hoeing around the rose bushes. I had hated to spend my Saturday mornings in such labor since I hadn't inherited my dad's love of growing and caring for things. Now the grass was brown and the hedges and

In this paragraph I weave past with present. I'm trying to suggest my desire for things to stay the same—but, of course, I know they can't.

rose bushes were dying and I missed the unvarying routine those secure Saturday mornings brought.

In a few moments Dad was returning, lugging a heavy toolbox in each hand. I saw he breathed a little heavy. I went to help him.

"Hard going?" I asked.

I use this exchange with my father to set up the final insight.

"It's the last time for me," he said as we hefted the boxes into the car.

At first I didn't make the connection between his words and mine. I had referred to the difficulty he had carrying the boxes. He referred to much more. He referred to the illusion I wished to keep. I glanced up the street to the vacant lot and wished I could hear those comforting words that meant everything was okay, that the game was over and I could return home: ALLIE, ALLIE OXEN FREE!

I wanted to create a sense of loss— very complicated loss—loss of youth, home, neighborhood, and loss through death. I wanted to suggest that life is not a game, unlike the childhood games I've mentioned. Everyone must accept change. There is no Allie, Allie Oxen Free in life.

Did you notice how muted Swanson's essay seems, yet how it still communicates a great deal of emotion? He patiently develops the scene and memories through description that suggests a deeper meaning than he reveals. When he does comment, he doesn't shout; he comments in a quiet way. After rereading the essay Swanson said, "Now 'Allie, Allie Oxen Free' seems to be about growing up, about becoming an adult."

WRITING TASK—ASSOCIATIONAL ESSAY

Write an associational essay. We recommend the following procedure:
1. Select an event that means a great deal to you and that brought you some personal insight.

2. Use your journal to trigger memories you associate with the experience. Collect the raw material in extended lists.
3. Decide what you wish to communicate to readers. Use it as the essay's guiding principle.
4. Write the essay by beginning with the main experience. Follow with a development of the experience while weaving in the associations you've collected.
5. Round off the essay by stating or implying how you feel or what you've learned from the experience.

Remember:

The primary method of development should be description. You will need to work in some background information and responses, but the main intent is to suggest the meaning of the experience, not to explain it.

GROUP WORK

For the first session bring journal entries you feel might serve as a starting point for an associational essay. Read and discuss the entries together. Identify the dramatic moments in the entry.

For the second session have a "fleshed out" sketch of an associational essay. Review the sketches for effective structure. Identify ways the "insight" might be dramatized.

For the third session review the completed drafts. Read closely for the connections between events. Does each essay offer an insight at the close, whether stated or unstated?

17

Do Not Do

Directive Process Analysis

Unlike *informative process analysis,* which explains how something works (see Chapter 18), *directive process analysis* explains how to do something. Directive process analysis, therefore, is a practical kind of writing. You might, for example, explain how to get to a particular place, how to perform an experiment, how to assemble a kit, or how to create a writing project. Directive process analysis is usually based on the assumption that someone will follow the directions to complete a task. The directions may be as simple as instructions on how to take a test or as complicated as instructions on how to fly an airliner.

For example, read the following directions for seeking redress for an insurance claim that has been refused. The writer's purpose is to guide a reader to a predetermined goal by breaking down the steps required to get there.

> When you must deal with an insurance company that refuses to pay for a medical expense or denies part of a claim you believe should be paid in full, don't merely give up your claim. Instead, you can exercise your rights. Remember, the insurance company owes the claim unless it can demonstrate why the claim should not be paid. You the insured do not have to demonstrate why it should pay. Before embarking on a crusade to recover your money, be sure you have properly filled out and submitted the proper forms (by the way, be sure to keep copies for reference). In summary, here are the basic steps to take when you believe an insurance company has erred: First, appeal to a high official at the insurance company and, if you can, include additional documentation for your claim. Second, if

that is unsuccessful, write to your state insurance commissioner (every state has one), enclosing copies of all correspondence between you and the insurer. Third, if the response is still not satisfactory, decide whether the amount you feel you are owed is worth suing for. Whatever you do, don't make the mistake of threatening a local agent with a lawsuit before taking the initial steps. You'll just be wasting your breath and if you follow through, your money. You must follow this simple procedure before any court will consider your claim.

This paragraph embodies several common characteristics of directive process analysis. First, it immediately establishes the writer's purpose. Second, the process is broken down in several steps. Third, the reader is addressed directly as "you." Fourth, like many directive process analyses this paragraph alerts the reader to possible mistakes he or she might make and to their consequences.

Usually a directive process analysis will be composed of several paragraphs. As is usual, both the introduction and conclusion are brief. At the beginning specify the process you are writing about and perhaps comment on the reason for doing it, its level of difficulty, or the overall approach you will present. At the end of the process, a sentence or two to signal a close is all you need. For example, read Delia Ephron's directions for cutting off jeans.

How to Cut off Your Jeans

It seems like the easiest thing to do. Then you do it and somehow one leg comes out shorter than the other. This time you're going to do it right.

A brief introduction gives reasons for following the directions.

The trick is this: cut one leg first, then match the second one to it. Never cut off both legs at the same time and never cut jeans while wearing them.

The writer presents an overview of the process and tells what not to do.

You will need one pair of used jeans, scissors, ruler and a felt-tip pen (like a Pentel).

Specifies materials needed.

Put on the jeans and look in the mirror. With the pen, mark one leg an eyeballed two inches above the knee if you want Bermuda shorts, four

Getting started; the first two steps.

inches above the knee for short shorts. Take off the jeans, lay them flat on a table, and cut off the leg even with the mark. Don't worry if your cutting is a little crooked. You can correct it later.

The next step, with reassuring comment.

Put the jeans back on and look in the mirror. Now you are going to find the length that is you. Experiment by turning under the bottom edge of the cut-off leg and adjusting the material up and down until you find a length you like. You'll know it when you see it, but it's hard to predict ahead of time. It will depend on such things as your taste and the shape of your thigh. When you find the right length, mark it on the cut leg with the pen. Then take off the jeans.

Sequence of steps with comments.

Lay them flat on a table or the floor. Now here's the important part: Place the ruler <u>perpendicular</u> to the side seam and <u>even</u> with the mark and draw a line across the jeans. The ruler must be perpendicular to get a straight line. Cut the leg carefully along the line through both layers of fabric at the same time.

A key step presented with cautions.

Now cut the second leg to match the first. Fold the jeans in half along the fly so that the cut-off leg is on top. Make sure the waistband is even all around. Using the ruler and pen, mark the length of the cut leg on the uncut one. Cut off the sec-

The final steps.

```
ond leg. Align the legs again to make sure they

match.

     The cut edges look unfinished now. If you run

the jeans through a washing machine a few times

the material will unravel into a nice fringe.
```

The writer closes by commenting on the final results.

WRITING TASK—DIRECTIVE PROCESS ANALYSIS

Write a paper, a directive process analysis, giving directions for the successful completion of a specific and limited task. Keep these general principles in mind:

1. Begin with a brief introduction that establishes the purpose.
2. Specify any materials the reader might need to complete the process.
3. Break the process into simple steps.
4. Address the reader as "you."
5. Alert the reader to possible mistakes and their consequences.

Use one of the following subjects or create a subject of your own.

1. How to guide a conversation
2. How to ask the right questions
3. How to tell a story to children
4. How to train a wild animal
5. How to humanely rid a yard of gophers
6. How to play a children's game
7. How to find your way in a wilderness without a compass
8. How to complain effectively
9. How to win at any game or sport
10. How to survive a natural disaster

GROUP WORK

In threes, meet to review your directive process analysis. Read to determine if the steps are logically arranged and clearly stated. Also determine if there is enough information to complete each step. Discuss your observations.

18
Informative Process Analysis

Informative process analysis might explain how the nervous system functions, how birds fly, how a bill passes through Congress, how meat is processed, or how advertising affects consumer buying patterns. Writers of informative process analyses will not expect the reader to do what they're describing (see Chapter 17, Directive Process Analysis), but instead offer information about how something happens or how something works.

For example, in the following paragraph from *Writing with a Word Processor*, professional writer William Zinsser describes one aspect of his writing process.

> One hang-up we visual people share is that our copy must be neat. My lifelong writing method, for instance, has gone like this. I put a piece of paper in the typewriter and write the first paragraph. Then I take the paper out and edit what I've written. I mark it up horribly, crossing words out and scribbling new ones in the space between the lines. By this time the paragraph has lost its nature and shape for me as a piece of writing. It's a mishmash of typing and handwriting and arrows and balloons and other directional symbols. So I type a clean copy, incorporating the changes, and then I take that piece of paper out of the typewriter and edit it. It's better, but not much better. I go over it with my pencil again, making more changes, which again make it too messy for me to read critically, so I go back to the typewriter for round three. And round four. Not until I'm reasonably satisfied do I proceed to the next paragraph.

Zinsser's process paragraph is developed chronologically—that is, the process is presented one step at a time, a characteristic of most informative process analyses. Sometimes, however, a process is too complex to be organized step by step. And when the writer is trying to relate simultaneous processes, the task is even more difficult. For example, John McPhee in *Oranges* describes the process oranges undergo when they are made into concentrated juice. Notice how McPhee uses transitions to guide the reader through the process.

> As the fruit starts to move along a concentrate plant's assembly line, it is first culled. In what some citrus people remember as "the old fresh-fruit days," before the Second World War, about forty percent of all oranges grown in Florida were eliminated at packinghouses and dumped in fields. Florida milk tasted like orangeade. Now, with the exception of the split and rotten fruit, all of Florida's orange crop is used. Moving up a conveyor belt, oranges are scrubbed with detergent before they roll on into juicing machines. There are several kinds of juicing machines, and they are something to see. One is called the Brown Seven Hundred. Seven hundred oranges a minute go into it and are split and reamed on the same kind of rosettes that are in the centers of ordinary kitchen reamers. The rinds that come pelting out the bottom are integral halves, just like the rinds of oranges squeezed in a kitchen. Another machine is the Food Machinery Corporation's FMC In-line Extractor. It has a shining row of aluminum jaws, upper and lower, with shining aluminum teeth. When an orange tumbles in, the upper jaw comes crunching down on it while at the same time the orange is penetrated from below by a perforated steel tube. As the jaws crush the outside, the juice goes through the perforations in the tube and down into the plumbing of the concentrate plant. All in a second, the juice has been removed and the rind has been crushed and shredded beyond recognition.

An informative process analysis is usually longer than a single paragraph. In fact, both Zinsser's and McPhee's paragraphs are excerpted from much longer works. But whether your analysis is brief or extended, you must keep two principles in mind: First, arrange your material in chronological order. Second, use clear transitional techniques to keep your reader on track. For example, study the following informative process analysis published by the Georgia Paramedics Against Drunken Driving. The writer has carefully arranged the material in chronological order, clearly identifying each step.

Little Known Facts

Do you know what happens in the first fatal second after a car going 55 miles an hour hits a solid object?

The writer opens with a question that establishes the purpose.

In the first 10th of the second, the front bumper and grille collapse.

Notice how each happening is presented within the framework of tenth-of-a-second intervals, dramatizing the step-by-step nature of the process.

The second 10th finds the hood crumbling, rising and hitting the windshield as the spinning rear wheels lift from the ground. Simultaneously, fenders begin to wrap themselves around the solid object. Although the car's frame has been halted, the rest of the car is still going 55 miles an hour. Instinct causes the driver to stiffen his legs against the crash and they snap at the knee joint.

Notice that in several incremental steps simultaneous events are taking place. The writer carefully distinguishes them.

During the third 10th of the second, the steering wheel begins to disintegrate and the steering column aims for the driver's chest.

The fourth 10th of the second the driver is impaled on the steering column and blood rushes into his lungs.

By the sixth 10th of the second, impact has built to the point where the driver's feet are ripped out of tightly laced shoes. The brake pedal breaks off. The car frame buckles in the middle. The driver's head smashes into the windshield, as the rear wheels, still spinning, fall

back to the earth.

In the seventh 10th of the second, hinges rip

loose, doors fly open and the seats break free,

striking the driver from behind.

The seats striking the driver do not bother

him, because he is already dead.

Now will you buckle your seat belt?

The final sentence serves as the conclusion and makes the essay's main point.

WRITING TASK—INFORMATIVE PROCESS ANALYSIS

Write an informative process analysis that explains how something works or how something happens. Keep in mind that this essay should not be written to give a procedure for readers to follow but should be written to inform them about a process. We offer the following subjects to get you started. Feel free to reshape them to fit your own interests or to create your own subject.

1. How psychotherapy works
2. How play helps psychological development
3. How a stroke damages the brain
4. How dreams work
5. How snails, ants, wasps, or other creatures battle
6. How to learn from past experience
7. How messages are sent through the galaxies
8. How a kidney machine works
9. How electrocution takes place
10. How an ancient structure was built

Remember:

1. Immediately present the purpose of the essay.
2. Arrange your material in chronological order.
3. Use clear transitions.
4. Clearly separate simultaneous events.

GROUP WORK

In threes, meet to review your informative process analysis. While reading, ask the following: Is the purpose of the analysis clear? Are the elements clearly related? Are the transitions clear, especially when distinguishing simultaneously occurring events?

19

Argumentative Essay

An argumentative essay is distinguished from other types of essays because it has an *argumentative edge*—that is, the writer takes a stand on a controversial issue and attempts to change someone's opinion or move someone to take action.

In theory, writers use two kinds of arguments: *persuasive argument,* which appeals to feelings by using emotional detail and slanted language, and *logical argument,* which appeals to intellect by using reasonable explanations. In practice, however, writers seldom appeal only to emotion or only to reason. Instead, they will usually appeal to both emotion and reason in the same essay.

For example, suppose you set out to convince your readers that children's cartoons depicting violence should be censored. You might begin with a reasonable explanation that most violent cartoons create a dangerously unrealistic world peopled with characters who solve problems with violence and who never actually die but only "play dead." You might then present several observations of children playing violent games learned from cartoons. At this point you might shift to a more emotional argument by giving detailed examples of children who have been influenced by violent cartoons, actually killing other children in "play." Finally, you might close with an emotional portrait of a future society that embraces the values embodied in these cartoons.

In planning an argumentative essay, you should be careful not to be so reasonable that your argument lacks feeling or so emotional that it lacks substance. As a general guideline, we suggest that an argumentative essay should lean toward reason enough to stand up under critical scrutiny.

Assertions and Evidence

The backbone of an argumentative essay is the assertion. An assertion embodies the opinion you want the reader to accept or the action you want the reader to take. When an assertion is formally stated in a sentence, it is often referred to as a proposition. For instance, the assertion that people should not be allowed to own handguns might be stated as the following proposition, "Handguns should not be available to the public." An assertion that smoking is even unhealthful to nonsmokers might be stated as the following proposition, "All public smoking should be banned." Or the assertion that smoking should be allowed wherever people wish to smoke might be stated as "Banning smoking in public places is a violation of personal freedom." You may have noticed that the proposition of an argumentative essay is similar to the central point in other essays (see pages 156–157). However, there is one major difference: Unlike a central point, a proposition has an argumentative edge, clearly indicating the writer's desire to win over the reader. But no matter what the proposition, the writer must support it with evidence.

It is the quality of evidence that convinces the reader to agree with your assertion. Evidence should be specific to be convincing and will come from the following sources:

1. *Personal experiences* can be used to support a proposition. Suppose, for instance, that you want to convince the campus administration to provide more security guards on campus after dark. In your argument you can include your firsthand experience. Three times your car has been broken into while parked in a campus lot. Several times you saw a gang from the local high school rampaging across campus, tipping over trash cans and verbally abusing students. Once your entire night class waited thirty minutes for a security guard to open a classroom door for a substitute teacher. These personal experiences can serve as legitimate evidence to support your proposition.

2. *The experiences of others* can serve as another source of evidence. You might offer an anecdote about a friend whose dorm or apartment was broken into. Perhaps one of your classmates saw nonstudents disrupt the library or computer room. You might even interview a security guard to determine if the night force is understaffed. When you use the experience of others, you must be sure the information is accurate. You are certain your experiences are valid, but you must carefully assess what others claim has happened to them. It is prudent, therefore, to cite more than one account of the same event.

3. *Authoritative sources* offer the strongest evidence in most argumentative essays. Facts, statistics, scientific research—all serve as authorita-

tive evidence. You can consult encyclopedias, dictionaries, hand-books, digests, reports, journals, and newspapers for information to support a proposition. Once again, consider the argument for increasing campus security after dark. You might research campus and city police reports to see if the crime rate is rising on and around campus. You might research college maintenance reports to see if vandalism has increased. You might also review local and campus newspapers to find articles dealing with campus crime. Any information you find could help support your proposition.

Keep in mind that whenever you use authoritative sources, you should clearly identify where you acquired the material—what newspaper, journal, televised interview, and so on. (See the section on Documentation, pages 239–240; 243–248.)

Arrangement

You may arrange an argumentative essay deductively or inductively, depending on whether your strategy is to state the proposition in the introduction or withhold it until the conclusion (see Chapters 14 and 15). But unlike other essays, argumentative essays frequently include a brief recognition of opposing arguments in order to refute them. For example, in the following passage from "Politics and the English Language," George Orwell recognizes and refutes an opposing argument.

> I said earlier that the decadence of our language is probably curable. Those who deny this would argue, if they produced an argument at all, that language merely reflects existing social conditions, and that we cannot influence its development by any direct tinkering with words and constructions. So far as the general tone or spirit of a language goes, this may be true, but it is not true in detail. Silly words and expressions have often disappeared, though not through any evolutionary process but owing to the conscious actions of a minority.

Orwell follows a common pattern. He begins by establishing his position. He then explains the opposing argument and its weakness. Further on in the paragraph, he gives examples that support his opinion.

Although restating an opposing argument in order to refute it is not used by all writers of argumentative essays, it is a frequent and an effective tactic that shows your reader that you have thoroughly considered the issue, thus making your argument all the more convincing.

The paragraphs that most frequently comprise argumentative essays are structured in patterns you have already mastered, such as development by examples, anecdote, comparison and contrast, definition, cause and effect, or process analysis. Of course, argument paragraphs all share a common purpose and a common tone—to advance the argument and to be argumentative.

EXAMPLES

A concrete example from your own experience or someone else's experience or from an authoritative source provides concrete evidence that shocks readers into awareness. In the following paragraph from his essay "A Scientist: I Am the Enemy" pediatrician Ron Karpati responds to accusations made by animal-rights activists with stunning brief examples. Notice how Karpati first summarizes the activists' position before countering it.

> Much is made of the pain inflicted on animals in the name of medical science. The animal-rights activists contend that this is evidence of our malevolent and sadistic nature. A more reasonable argument, however, can be advanced in our defense. Life is often cruel, both to animals and human beings. Teenagers get thrown from the back of a pickup truck and suffer severe head injuries. Toddlers, barely able to walk, find themselves at the bottom of a swimming pool while a parent checks the mail. Physicians hoping to alleviate the pain and suffering these tragedies cause have but three choices: create an animal model of the injury or disease and use that model to understand the process and test new therapies; experiment on human beings—some experiments will succeed, most will fail—or finally, leave medical knowledge static, hoping that accidental discoveries will lead us to the advances.

ANECDOTE

You might think of an anecdote as an extended example, a brief story that makes a point. In the following paragraph from *We Talk, You Listen* Vine Deloria, Jr., a Native American activist, uses an ironic anecdote to advance his argument that white culture has destroyed the natural environment.

> Every now and then I am impressed with the thinking of the non-Indian. I was in Cleveland last year and got to talking with a non-Indian about American history. He said that he was really sorry about what happened to Indians, but that there was good reason for it. The continent had to be developed and he felt that Indians had stood in the way and thus had had to be removed. "After all," he remarked, "what did you do with the land when you had it?" I didn't

understand him until later when I discovered that the Cuyahoga River running through Cleveland is inflammable. So many combustible pollutants are dumped into the river that the inhabitants have to take special precautions during the summer to avoid accidentally setting it on fire. After reviewing the argument of my non-Indian friend I decided that he was probably correct. Whites had made better use of the land. How many Indians could have thought of creating an inflammable river?

COMPARISON AND CONTRAST

Comparison and contrast patterns advance an argument by placing subjects side by side to delineate their differences and similarities. Naturalist Joseph Wood Krutch uses a subject-by-subject pattern to convince his readers that hunting animals for sport is pure evil.

> Most wicked deeds are done because the doer proposes some good to himself. The liar lies to gain some end; the swindler and thief want things which, if honestly got, might be good in themselves. Even the murderer may be removing an impediment to normal desires or gaining possession of something which his victim keeps from him. None of these usually does evil for evil's sake. They are selfish or unscrupulous, but their deeds are not gratuitously evil. The killer for sport has no such comprehensible motive. He prefers death to life, darkness to light. He gets nothing except the satisfaction of saying, "Something which wanted to live is dead. There is that much less vitality, consciousness, and, perhaps joy in the universe. I am the Spirit that Denies." When a man wantonly destroys one of the works of man we call him Vandal. When he wantonly destroys one of the works of God we call him Sportsman.

In "The Futility of the Death Penalty," Clarence Darrow uses a point-by-point pattern to convince his readers that a high homicide rate and the severity of punishment are not related.

> It seems to be a general impression that there are fewer homicides in Great Britain than in America because in England punishment is more certain, more prompt, and more severe. As a matter of fact, the reverse is true. In England the average term for burglary is eighteen months; with us it is probably four or five years. In England, imprisonment for life means twenty years. Prison sentences in the United States are harder than in any country in the world that could be classed as civilized.

ANALOGY

You must be cautious when using analogy in argument because it can be easily dismissed as fallacious. But in a highly charged argument, analogy can stir a reader's emotions. In "Letter from Birmingham Jail," Martin Luther King answers a public statement made by Alabama clergymen who opposed civil rights demonstrations. In the following paragraph, King uses analogy to refute their opinion.

In your statement you assert that our actions, even though peaceful, must be condemned because they precipitate violence. But is this a logical assertion? Isn't this like condemning a robbed man because his possession of money precipitated the evil act of robbery? Isn't this like condemning Socrates because his unswerving commitment to truth and his philosophical inquiries precipitated the act by the misguided populace in which they made him drink hemlock? Isn't this like condemning Jesus because his unique God-consciousness and never-ceasing devotion to God's will precipitated the evil act of crucifixion? We must come to see that, as federal courts have consistently affirmed, it is wrong to urge an individual to cease his efforts to gain his basic constitutional rights because the quest may precipitate violence. Society must protect the robbed and punish the robber.

CAUSE AND EFFECT

You can use cause-and-effect analysis to expose the reasons or the results of an event. In "Why Don't We Complain?," political commentator William F. Buckley argues that Americans have become helpless when faced with unpleasant situations. In the following paragraph from that essay, he argues that the cause of this helplessness is modern technology and centralized power.

I think the observable reluctance of the majority of Americans to assert themselves in minor matters is related to our increased sense of helplessness in an age of technology and centralized political and economic power. For generations, Americans who were too hot, or too cold, got up and did something about it. Now we call the plumber, or the electrician, or the furnace man. The habit of looking after our own needs obviously had something to do with the assertiveness that characterized the American family familiar to readers of American literature. With the technification of life goes our direct responsibility for our material environment, and we are conditioned to adopt a position of helplessness not only as regards the broken air conditioner, but as regards the overheated train. It takes an expert to fix the former, but not the latter, yet these distinctions, as we withdraw into helplessness, tend to fade away.

Educator E. D. Hirsch traces the social effects of literacy in his attempt to convince readers that standard written English should be taught exclusively.

> Why is literacy so important in the modern world? Some of the reasons, like the need to fill out forms or get a good job, are so obvious that they needn't be discussed. But the chief reason is broader. The complex undertakings of modern life depend on the cooperation of many people with different specialties in different places. Where communications fail, so do the undertakings. (This is the moral of the story of the Tower of Babel.) The function of national literacy is to foster effective nationwide communications. Our chief instrument of communication over time and space is the standard national language, which is sustained by national literacy. Mature literacy alone enables the tower to be built, the business to be well managed, and the airplane to fly without crashing. All nationwide communications, whether by telephone, radio, TV, or writing, are fundamentally dependent upon literacy, for the essence of literacy is not simply reading and writing but also effective use of the standard literate language. In Spain and most of Latin America the literate language is standard written Spanish. In Japan it is standard written Japanese. In our country it is standard written English.

DEFINITION

Sometimes a key word will be important in an argumentative essay. When this is the case, the writer will often define it for the reader, not only for clarification but also to highlight its importance. In most cases the writer will first define the word briefly, then link it directly to the purpose of the essay. In "The Penalty of Death," H. L. Mencken defines *katharsis* to emphasize its importance in understanding his proposition that capital punishment should be legal.

> I borrow a better term from Aristotle: *katharsis*. *Katharsis*, so used, means a salubrious discharge of emotions, a healthy letting off of steam. A school boy, disliking his teacher, deposits a tack upon the pedagogical chair; the teacher jumps and the boy laughs. This is *katharsis*. What I contend is that one of the prime objects of all judicial punishments is to afford the same grateful relief (a) to the immediate victims of the criminal punished, and (b) to the general body of moral and timorous men.

PROCESS ANALYSIS

Sometimes in a course of an argument, you will want to explain how something works to support your argument. In the following paragraph from "Concerning Abortion: An Attempt at a Rational View," Charles Harshrone analyzes the function of a fertilized egg to refute the view that the egg in this early stage is a human being.

> The fertilized egg is an individual egg, but not an individual human being. For such a being is, in its body, a multicellular organism, a *metazoan*—to use the scientific Greek—and the egg is a single cell. The first thing the egg cell does is to begin dividing into many cells. For some weeks the fetus is not a single individual at all, but a colony of cells. During its first weeks there seems to be no ground for regarding the fetus as comparable to an individual animal. Only in possible or probable destiny is it an individual. Otherwise it is an organized society of single-celled individuals.

Before you begin an argumentative essay, we suggest you review Chapter 14, Deductive Essay, and Chapter 15, Inductive Essay. This review will reacquaint you with the patterns and processes of effective writing. But as you review essay arrangements, keep in mind that the writer of an argumentative essay always takes a clear stand on a controversial subject and attempts to convince readers to change their opinion or move them to take action.

WRITING TASK—ARGUMENTATIVE ESSAY

This task challenges you to write an argument essay without a fully developed example essay as a model. Instead of closely examining a model argument essay, we examined the principles of argumentative writing and demonstrated how paragraph patterns you already know can be developed with an argumentative edge. Keep in mind that structurally, an argumentative essay follows the same essay structures you have already used. Your task, then, is to apply these principles and use the appropriate paragraph patterns to write an argumentative essay dealing with a controversial subject about which you have a strong opinion.

If the subject you choose has undergone extensive public debate, such as gun control, abortion, and capital punishment, assume your reader is familiar with the general debate and then develop evidence based on your own personal experience, observation, and reading. Consider subjects from the following list as a way of getting started. All these subjects, like others we've offered, must be limited so that you can deal with them in a college essay. Feel free to reshape them in any way that fits your purpose or to develop your own subject.

1. Vegetarian diet
2. Violence in films or on television
3. "Skin" magazines, such as *Playboy, Playgirl,* or *Penthouse*
4. Birth control advice for teenagers
5. Home education
6. Public profanity or rowdiness
7. Censorship
8. Hidden messages in heavy-metal music
9. Propaganda in political advertising
10. Film ratings

Respond to one of the following problems.

11. You know of a person or group that is being denied some privilege. In an argumentative essay, take up the cause by arguing to change the injustice.
12. Go to the library and read several articles from recent back newspaper issues related to a single subject. Using information selected from the articles take a stand and develop an argumentative essay advocating your position.
13. Write an argument that supports or attacks the assertion that people have a right to decide when and how they wish to die.
14. Write an argument that supports or attacks the assertion that willing prisoners should be encouraged to volunteer for scientific experiments in order to reduce their sentences.
15. For many Vietnam veterans the war never ended. Many veterans came home fighting depression, drug addiction, chronic anger, alienation, and suicidal desires. The federal government estimates that over 800,000 veterans who served in Vietnam still suffer psychological wounds called post-traumatic stress disorder. Write an argument that supports or attacks the assertion that Vietnam veterans should be given special recognition for the sacrifices they have made.

Remember:

1. Develop an assertion with an argumentative edge.
2. From the assertion formulate and write a clear proposition.
3. Select evidence from personal experience, the experience of others, and authoritative sources.
4. Account for opposing arguments.
5. Develop paragraphs that advance your argument.

GROUP WORK

For the first session come with a list of controversial topics. Combine your lists and explore each item's potential as the subject of an argumentative essay. Narrow the selection and develop an assertion with an argumentative edge for each one. Break up into subgroups by topic.

In your subgroup review the chapter together to be sure you understand the nature of evidence. See if the group shares first-hand experience that might serve as evidence for part of an essay. Brainstorm opposing arguments. Then develop a plan for your essay.

For the next session, have complete rough drafts and copies to circulate among your subgroup. Review the drafts for strengths and weaknesses and discuss your observations.

For the next session return with a final draft. Exchange essays with another subgroup that was working on a different topic. Review those essays. Note your observations in the margin. Finally, meet with the other subgroup to discuss your observations.

20

Report

DO NOT DO

In classes other than English, you may be asked to write reports on places you visit. The kind of place will depend on the class—perhaps tide pools for marine biology, museums or galleries for art history, child-care centers for developmental psychology, or even night spots for social anthropology. Generally, although outside reports deal with different kinds of experiences, your instructors will want you to communicate both your observations and your interpretations.

The obligation to observe and interpret seems clear enough, but sometimes beginning writers go astray when doing reports. Some seem to believe their only obligation is to fill up two or three pages that generally describe what they saw and did—a kind of let-me-tell-you-what-I-did-last-Saturday paper. They may include details of what they observed, but they leave the meaning of the observations to the imagination. This is shoddy practice and will usually be rewarded with a low grade.

An effective report includes not only a writer's observations but also an interpretation of them—that is, not merely a record of what was seen but also the meaning of what was seen. But how? you may ask. Simple. By showing the connection between your observations and the material you have learned in class through lectures, discussions, and readings. A report is another means for you to demonstrate and apply the knowledge you've acquired during the semester.

For example, imagine for a moment that you're taking a sociology class. You've been studying nonverbal behavior as it can be observed in public settings. For a final project, you've been asked to write a report based on personal experience with nonverbal behavior. You decide to study waiters and waitresses in a local restaurant. Fine. Probably a good choice. You go to the restaurant and sit in an unobtrusive spot that gives you a clear view of most of the tables and the counter. You select two or three subjects to study. You record every significant gesture, body stance, facial expression. You leave with a notebook full of raw material, much more than you'll need for the full report. At home you sift through the material and organize it into rough form. Now you're ready to write. When you write the paper, you not only describe your observations but also interpret their meaning based on information you've gained from your classroom study of nonverbal behavior. This final step of responding to the material from an informed viewpoint is what the instructor will be looking for when evaluating your paper.

Now study the following paragraph. It is a discussion paragraph taken from a report generated by the sociology assignment. As you read, notice how the writer mixes interpretation with observations. Although the paragraph is developed mainly through concrete description, the bits of interpretation focus the details.

> I noticed that the waiter would nonverbally expose his interest in young female customers and his disinterest in middle-aged female ones. I watched him wait on two women in their early twenties. When he took their orders, he leaned forward and glanced with them at the menus as if he were acting as a friendly advisor. After collecting the menus, he paused for a moment to chat, although neither one's facial expression showed much interest in what he was saying. While he talked and the women sipped from their water glasses, he dangled the menus at his side as if to suggest that he was ready to receive their interest. Later, when he waited on three older women, perhaps in their late thirties, he stood erect, like a private during a military inspection, and hardly looked at them as he wrote on an order pad. He didn't lean forward or try to start a conversation, even though the women seemed friendly. When one called him back to request another item, he stood with the menus held before him as if they served as a protective barrier.

The topic sentence sets up the interpretation of this writer's observations—the waiter nonverbally exposes his interest and disinterest. The writer then details his observations to support his interpretations. He slips in fragments of interpretation, such as "acting as a friendly advisor," "ready to receive their interest," and "the menus held before him as if they served as a protective barrier"—which help focus the details. This is an effective paragraph that not only reports what the writer saw but also demonstrates some understanding of nonverbal expression.

Sometimes you may be assigned to do a report that doesn't require a specific application of what you've learned during a class. Instead it may involve appreciation. No matter, because your obligations are the same: you must deliver a detailed rendering of your observations and your responses to them. The difference is that your responses will be more subjective—they will come out of personal awareness rather than out of a body of knowledge you've mastered.

The following paragraph is taken from a report on a photography exhibit. After giving a general description of the exhibit and the background of the photographer, the writer presents her responses to particular works. She begins this discussion paragraph with a topic sentence that identifies a quality of one photograph, then follows with a detailed description before presenting her response to it.

> Harold Chan's photograph "Night Wood" has a haunting quality. Fog rolls through the pines, but the fog looks more like steam. Leaning against a tree, a man dressed in black and wearing a white mask stares directly at the observer. With fog swirling around him, he seems ghostly, perhaps demonic. I thought of nightmare images. I felt pinned by his round black eyes. I felt almost as if I had been caught in a horrible dream and was unable to awaken. It seems that Chan is depicting the strange forces that exist in the mind's forests where the sleeper may helplessly stumble.

This writer has carefully combined her observations with responses. Concrete description helps the reader see the experience, but the interpretation of the experience helps focus the piece.

There will be two distinct phases in writing a report. First, you'll set out to prewrite the report the way you would any task. We suggest you avoid going to one of your regular hangouts. An atmosphere you are already familiar with may dull your powers of observation. You collect the raw material to use in the final draft by capturing concrete details and your responses to the experience. This note taking is an active part of the assignment. Don't try to write a report from memory. Such reports usually turn out inaccurate and dull.

After you've made your visit and collected notes, you begin the second phase—the actual writing. Begin by sifting through your material. Reread your notes. Reflect on what you've recorded. Is there anything to add? Do you see a general shape? Is there an outstanding point you might use to organize your report?

The general structure of a report is much like that of a deductive essay. Begin with an introduction that gives the instructor some background information and presents a central point. In this case the central point will capture the general point of your paper—the conclusion you've drawn from the experience. For instance, the report from which we took the first example has this central point:

Waiters and waitresses expose their attitudes toward customers through nonverbal behavior.

The report from which the second example came has this central point:

Harold Chan's black-and-white photographs have a haunting theme.

Once you've decided on a central point, you will be able to cut excess detail from your paper and focus your thought.

With the central point chosen and the introduction written, you need merely to organize the remaining material into a discussion. Remember, be sure to include not only detail but your interpretation of the detail. Keep in mind, too, that the discussion paragraphs can be built on any of the patterns you've mastered—development by example, comparison, contrast, analogy, classification, and so on.

The conclusion of a report is usually short, perhaps a brief reminder of the central point or a further observation that grows out of the experience and relates to the class you've been writing it for.

A final thought. When you write a report, don't spend any time writing about why you went where you went. Don't include information that isn't related to the task at hand.

WRITING TASK—REPORT

Use deductive essay structure (Chapter 14) to write a report. We suggest you select a subject that would be appropriate for one of your other classes. If you have not been assigned a report in another class, you might visit a museum, job site, nursery school, an art exhibit, or even another college to use for a report.

Remember

1. Select a place to visit that will provide a learning experience. Avoid familiar hangouts.
2. Make your visit and compile ample notes that include both details and responses.
3. Use deductive essay structure to organize your material.
4. Write an introduction that gives your instructor any pertinent background information.
5. Write a discussion several paragraphs long giving the particulars of your report. Be sure to combine your observations with interpretation. Keep in mind that this is a chance to show your instructor that you can apply some information you've learned during the course.
6. End the report with a brief conclusion.

21
Research Essay

Doing research means investigating a subject to find out more about it. You probably did research when you were deciding on your present course of study or when you last made a major purchase, such as buying a car or a television set. Remember the last time you selected grocery items by reading their labels closely and comparing ingredients? You were doing limited research: gathering information, assessing it, and drawing a conclusion. The kind of research you do for a research essay is not very different, except that you gather information from more sources and write up your conclusions for others to read.

A research essay, the product of your investigation of a topic, is like the deductive essay you studied in Chapter 14. Such an essay moves from a generalization, called the central point, to more specific information that illustrates its appropriateness or validity. For a research essay, the central point is called a thesis, and you support the thesis with specific information in the form of examples, quotations from experts, statistics, or other evidence. The paper proceeds from an introduction that states the thesis, to several paragraphs of information supporting the thesis, and then to a conclusion. Along the way, you indicate your sources for the specific information you have presented, and you also list those sources on a *works cited* page at the end of the essay.

Expressing Your Own Ideas

Many students resist writing a research essay because they fear that doing the research will overwhelm their own ideas and sense of involvement with

231

the topic. True, a research essay can do that, but it doesn't have to. Rather than allow the need to give evidence and cite sources to bury your thoughts about a topic, you can use such evidence and sources to enhance your involvement.

For example, study the following paragraph from the sample essay by Irene Islas. The paragraph demonstrates how a research essay can integrate an author's own ideas on a topic with specific information gathered elsewhere to support those ideas. The paragraph begins with a topic sentence declaring Irene's observation about what motivates graffiti artists. Examples from Irene's research illustrate and support the topic sentence; their sources are cited in parentheses.

Like the early humans who left their hand	*Topic sentence*
prints on the walls of the Lascaux cave in France	
20,000 years ago (Reisner 24-25), modern graffiti	*Source cited*
artists seem to seek an affirmation of self and	
personality in their work. They are drawn by the	
immortality that graffiti offers. "A-One," "Crash,"	*Example*
"Daze," "Dondi," "Lee"—names of writers from the	
1970s, the heyday of graffiti art—ring in the minds	
of younger writers who hope someday to make names	
for themselves. As Lee himself testifies, "When I	*Example*
was young, I thought my name would run forever.	
Writing was my life" ("Buffed Out" 38).	*Source cited*

As you begin working toward writing a research essay, keep in mind that it is really not very different from other deductive essays you have written. You will use the same development strategies you practiced in earlier chapters, but you will also draw upon other resources for information and examples. (See the model for a deductive essay in Chapter 14.)

Steps in Writing a Research Essay: An Overview

An organized, step-by-step approach to writing a research essay is usually the most effective method to follow, but many writers work best by synthesizing or even reordering the traditional steps. The following discussion describes what student writers typically do to produce a successful college research essay. Depending on your own research skills, your topic, or your instructor's advice, you may find it productive to complete the steps described in another order or combination than that which is discussed here.

STEP 1: SELECT A SUITABLE TOPIC

Your initial determination of a research topic establishes the foundation and direction of a successful essay. Select a topic that is both practical for the assignment and interesting to you.

Begin with the understanding that a good topic allows you to say something of your own about it. A political controversy, a neglected social problem and its possible solution, research on your own family history, even a case study of a uniquely interesting place or individual can give you opportunities for fresh comment and analysis. Avoid purely descriptive topics ("What is AIDS?"), subjects that would take too long to learn enough about to be able to add new ideas to ("The Causes of the Civil War"), or complete biographies ("The Life of John Lennon"). Look for more manageable areas—perhaps subtopics of such subjects as those above—which are open to discussion and which lend themselves to the kind of fresh analysis or insight that you will be able to offer once you have done your research.

"Graffiti," for example, is far too broad a subject. "Graffiti art" is less broad, but still too general for adequate treatment in a research essay. "The continuing problem of graffiti art," on the other hand, is a suitable topic to research and write about because it focuses on the continuation of graffiti art and the problems that it creates.

Of course, a topic can be so narrow that you would be unable to track down enough research sources to view it in a larger context. A topic that is too local or too current to be written about anywhere but in the local newspaper ("The graffiti on Lincoln Avenue," for instance) may not provide you with enough material to meet your instructor's goals for the research assignment. As you examine possible research topics, then, look for ways to make them focused but be sure they are broad enough to treat competently in a research assignment.

Finally, one last important characteristic of a good research topic is that it must genuinely interest you. You will do your research and write more effectively when you care about a topic than when it bores you. Think of subjects you enjoy reading about, the sources you elect to take in college, or personal experiences that give you special insight to a topic.

Since you will be working with your research essay topic for several weeks, take time to select the right one for yourself. You may not even be ready to select a suitable research topic right away. For most writers, selection of a topic (Step 1) and investigation of sources (Step 2) actually occur at the same time. That way you can discover potential topics or match your personal interests with materials you know are available for research.

STEP 2: INVESTIGATE AVAILABLE SOURCES

Investigate your library's resources to find out about topics that may interest you and to learn whether or not there are enough available sources on them. As you do so, begin to establish a working bibliography of potential and available sources (for example, books and magazine or newspaper articles). You can list the sources for the working bibliography on a sheet of paper, but it will be more helpful to record each source on a separate three-by-five-inch note card. That way you can easily eliminate or add sources as necessary. Use the working bibliography as a way to gauge the number and types of available sources, as well as a reference from which you can later cite the sources in your text or list them on the works cited page at the end of the essay.

Beginning your resource search with encyclopedias is a good idea. These comprehensive works give you a broad overview of a topic and often provide brief bibliographies of relevant sources that you can seek in your own library. Next, consult your library's indexes for periodical articles and check the card or on-line catalog for books. Look for a variety of sources with different viewpoints and approaches to your subject. A working bibliography with articles only, for example, may not provide you with enough in-depth analysis of your topic. On the other hand, if no current articles are used as source material, your report may be out of date. Try to obtain sources with different slants on your chosen topic. Too many sources with one point of view will not give you a balanced understanding of the topic's major issues.

At this stage your goal is not to read every potential source thoroughly. Skim articles and books to see if they might be suitable for your purpose. Once you have selected a suitable topic to investigate and have a good idea of what sources are available, you will be ready to begin reading closely and taking notes on what you read.

STEP 3: TAKE NOTES

Read your sources with your topic and a potential thesis in mind. As your reading on the topic progresses, you will gradually begin to recognize a major idea that you will want to develop in your paper. Take notes on key ideas or examples, quotations from authorities, and illustrative statistics that would aid a discussion of that major idea.

Using three-by-five-inch cards for note taking will allow you the flexibility to add, delete, and rearrange notes as you write the paper. Give each card a major heading (such as "Causes of illiteracy" or "Cost of education"), making sure to write down the last name (and, if necessary, the first initial) of the source's author and a page number with each note. (The title of the source and publication facts will already be listed in the working bibliography.) Many students use a different size or color of index card for the notes to avoid confusion of sources and notes.

STEP 4: ORGANIZE YOUR MATERIAL

Once you have consulted enough sources to understand the topic well and to develop a discussion about a key issue, review your research notes and begin planning the paper. Formulate your thesis and check to see that you have enough material to develop and support it in the paper. Organize your research note material around the thesis by listing the paper's major sections, such as introduction, discussion section, and conclusion, and then grouping supporting facts and ideas under each section heading. If you prefer, or if your instructor requires you to do so, you can also use a formal outline to plan the essay.

STEP 5: WRITE THE ESSAY

Plan to write the essay over a period of at least two or three days. This will give you time for revising drafts, checking the documentation, and typing and proofreading the final version. Write with your notes and the working bibliography close at hand. Starting with an introduction that clearly states the thesis will help to focus your writing and guide your use of relevant research material. Keep the thesis firmly in mind as you write each section.

Develop the essay by supporting each paragraph topic sentence with examples, quotations, or other relevant information. Cite the sources for such information in your text, as described on pages 239–240. Be careful, however, not to let your essay sound like a mere collection of research notes. Be sure that your paragraph topic sentences develop the thesis and that you analyze, compare and contrast, or otherwise comment on the material from your research sources. Integrate quotations smoothly into your writing, and use transition words and phrases to show how ideas and paragraphs relate.

The conclusion of the research essay should sound conclusive and not as if you were starting a new discussion on another topic. Make the conclusion useful by reemphasizing the thesis and offering a final analysis, overview, or persuasive statement.

STEP 6: REVISE, EDIT, AND PROOFREAD

Take time to revise and edit the essay carefully before typing it. The goal of revision is to strengthen the essay's content, organization, and thesis while it is still in the draft stage. Review the content of the essay. Is more material necessary for adequate support of the thesis? Is some material irrelevant, and should it be deleted? Revise wordy sentences or add transition words and phrases as necessary. Check to see that the essay's content flows smoothly and that it logically develops the discussion in support of the thesis. If certain sections need more examples, or if one section should actually precede rather than follow another, make such changes at this stage. If necessary, reword the thesis statement so that it more accurately reflects the essay's content and organization.

Editing an essay involves checking small but very important features such as grammar, punctuation, mechanics, and spelling. Pay particular attention to verb tenses, pronoun references, and adjective and adverb forms. Have you used capital letters, the apostrophe, commas, and semicolons correctly? Look closely at all uses of quotation marks as well. Check to see that the forms for in-text citations and entries on the works cited page are accurate and correct. Use a dictionary to verify any spelling you are not certain about. Double-check any difficult names or special terms to see that you have spelled them correctly throughout the paper.

Once the final version is typed, you will need to proofread it for minor typing errors. Read each sentence carefully, making any necessary corrections by hand in ink. Neatly cross out unwanted words or letters, and write in corrections and additions above the text line. Retype any page that requires many corrections or appears messy.

Resources for Research

Research involves gathering information about a topic from a variety of available resources. Interviews with experts, opinion polls you conduct yourself, or information you collect from state or community resources can be useful sources. Most effective research, however, eventually draws upon the resources of a college or university library to find out what is already known about a subject or to access information not available elsewhere.

Using the right library sources at the appropriate stage of your research can save you a lot of time and work, as well as ensure the comprehensives of your investigations and, ultimately, the soundness of your conclusions. The following section describes library resources that are indispensable for writing most college research essays. After you have consulted several of them or even while you are still investigating some, you can begin to use nonlibrary resources to supplement your research.

ENCYCLOPEDIAS

Use encyclopedias at the start of your research to get a general understanding of a subject and to find out what is known about it. College level series like *Encyclopedia Britannica* or *Encyclopedia Americana* usually provide up-to-date, comprehensive coverage of most researchable topics. You can use the bibliography at the end of an encyclopedia article to find other resources that address your subject in more detail. Special subject encyclopedias such as *Encyclopedia of American History* or *The Encyclopedia of the Biological Sciences* can also provide detailed introductory information on a subject.

INDEXES

Reference works that list publication information about magazine or journal articles are called indexes. An index tells you the title of a published article (and some books), who wrote it, where it appears, and when it was published. Special subject indexes, such as *Agricultural Index, Book Review Index,* or *Play Index,* catalog articles on a particular subject or in a particular medium. If you looked up the topic of "divorce" in the 1990 volume of *Legal Periodicals Index,* for example, you would find a listing of articles about divorce which were published in legal journals for that year.

General indexes, which differ from the specialized kind, tell you where your topic is discussed or included within another work, say in a chapter or just a few paragraphs. Often the referenced work is one whose title alone would not have led you to consult it. Looking up a subject like "voodoo" in *Essay and General Literature Index,* for example, might direct you to a section in a book titled *The Great Explorers.* Another common general index is *Biography Index,* a good source for finding parts of books or articles that talk about famous people.

One of the most useful indexes is *Readers' Guide to Periodical Literature,* which lists articles appearing in over 200 magazines and journals. Newspaper indexes such as *The New York Times Index* or the *Wall Street Journal Index* provide contemporary information about a subject. You can also use the dates one index gives to locate information in other, nonindexed newspapers. In addition to these and hundreds of other general and specialized indexes, your library may have on-line databases accessible through a computer terminal. Comprehensive on-line systems such as InfoTrac, ERIC, or DIALOG can save you from having to consult several different indexes on a subject. Check with your librarian to find out whether or not the college library has such services available.

BOOKS

Use your library's card or on-line catalog to locate general reference works as well as fiction and nonfiction books. When you first begin your research, skim a book's table of contents or its index to determine its potential as a research source. Once you begin reading and taking notes from all your sources, you can study the book's contents more closely. Make a point of writing down the call number, as well as the title, author, and publication data for any book you search out. You may need the information if you return for the book or later cite it in your paper. (See pages 243–247 for in-text citation and works cited forms for books.)

PERIODICALS

Publications appearing at regular intervals, such as magazines, journals, and newspapers, are called periodicals. Periodicals are useful for getting current information on a topic or finding out about a subject that is too specialized to be written about in books. Most periodical articles are listed in a general or specialized index such as those described above in the section on library indexes. To find out which periodicals your library receives, consult the periodicals list that is usually available in the reference section or at the library's main desk. (See page 245 for in-text citation and works cited forms for periodicals.)

INTERVIEWS

Talking to individuals with first-hand or in-depth knowledge about a topic can add extra dimension to your research paper's discussion. However, be careful about interviewing someone merely because he or she has an opinion on or a little experience with your research topic. Select interview subjects who can supplement your research with unique information or informed insights not available from published sources. Depending on the individual's availability, you can conduct an interview in person, by telephone, or through written correspondence. (See page 247 for the in-text citation and works cited forms for an interview.)

OTHER SOURCES

You can include any kind of information, regardless of its source or form, in your research and in your paper. Pamphlets and fliers, public addresses, lectures, advertisements, theater or concert performances, or city and government documents are just a few of the many research sources you can locate outside the library. If you cite such sources in your paper, list them in the works cited section also. You can generally adapt the form for more common kinds of entries to these less usual ones by including the author's (or performer's) name, the title of the work, and relevant publication facts.

Citing Sources in the Text

You must give credit in the paper to any source that you quote or cite as an authority or from which you borrow information that is not common knowledge (that is, not usually known to people even generally informed about the subject). For example, the fact that Albert Einstein spent his last years at Princeton University would be common knowledge to anyone familiar with his life and work. That Einstein also often referred to God as the "Old One" is probably not so well known. You would need to cite the source of that information if you included it in your text.

Citing a source means giving credit by naming a source's author and the page number(s) where the information you borrowed can be found. In keeping with the research essay style established by the Modern Language Association (MLA), which sets the standard for essays in the field of English, you should cite all your sources in the essay's text.

To cite a source in text when the author's name is part of your own sentence, you usually need give only the page number where the ideas or language you have borrowed appears in the original. Place the page number in parentheses immediately after the borrowed material:

> Calder points out that Einstein often showed his own religious inclinations by referring to God as the "Old One" (138).

Another way to cite a source in text is to place the author's name and the page number for the borrowed material together in parentheses:

> Einstein often showed his own religious inclinations by referring to God as the "Old One" (Calder 138).

If a source has no author attributed to it, cite the work by a shortened version of its title, followed by the page number of the borrowed material. An anonymous work titled "America's Future in Space," for example, might be cited this way:

> These problems were noticed by inspection crews even before the spacecraft left the launching pad ("America's Future" 21).

Place a parenthetical citation as close as you can to the content to which it refers. Often, as in the examples above, that will be at the end of the sentence containing the borrowed material. In some cases, for example, if material from two different sources is included in the same sentence, the parenthetical citation may not be at the end. Also make sure that each source you cite in the paper gets listed in the works-cited section.

The Parts of a Research Essay

A research essay is generally six to ten pages in length, depending on its subject and the purpose for which it is written. In addition to author, title, and date, only this text section and a works cited page (or pages) must be included in all research essays, no matter what their length or intended audience. Other parts, such as a separate title page and an outline, are optional. Very long or complex research essays may include a "notes" section containing additional information about certain parts of the text. Some research essays will provide an appendix for illustrations or for supporting tabular data. It is unlikely, however, that a lower division college essay would need either a notes section or an appendix.

The following sections discuss the title, the optional outline, the text, and the works cited page.

TITLE

Although the Modern Language Association recommends no title page, the decision on whether to include a separate title page will depend on the requirements of your instructor and the format of your essay. If there is prefatory material such as an abstract or an outline, the title is generally put on a separate page that precedes the rest of the essay.

If you do not use a title page, the first page of your essay should look like this:

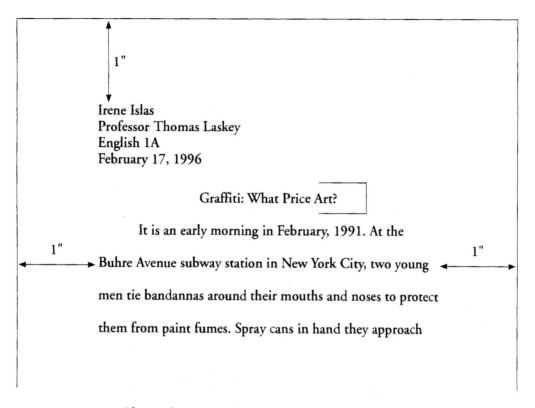

If you do use a title page, it should include the title, your name as author, your professor's name, the name of the class for which you wrote the essay, and the date on which you submit it.

Devise a title that describes the general topic as well as the essay's more particular focus. "Strengthening Education Requirements for Police Personnel" is an effective title because it declares both the topic and the writer's approach to it. "Graffiti: What Price Art?" is also effective. Notice how the subtitle introduces the essay's more specific focus within the broad subject of graffiti. Had one of these titles been simply "Education Requirements for Police Personnel" or "Graffiti," a reader would not be sure what particular aspect of those subjects the essay addressed.

OUTLINE

If your instructor requires a formal outline with the research essay, organize the paper's content into sections of various levels, moving from general to more specific areas of the essay. The following example shows an outline for an essay comparing television programs and audiences:

I. Television Sit-Coms	*First major heading*
A. Adult-Oriented Shows	*First major subheading*
1. Subjects and situations	
2. Character types	*Minor subheadings*
3. Language	
B. Child-Oriented Shows	*Second major subheading*
1. Subjects and situations	
2. Character types	*Minor subheadings*
3. Language	
II. Made-for-Television Dramas	*Second major heading*

Your own outline may not need the same number of major or minor subheadings as this example shows. Notice, however, that an outline divides material into parts; consequently, each part must have a matching part. This means that you should have at least two of each kind of heading in the outline, that is, every *I* should have a *II*, every *A* should have a *B*, and so on.

TEXT

Starting with page 1 of your text, or page 2 if you have no title page, count and number all pages consecutively with Arabic numerals–1, 2, 3, and so on. The page numbers are preceded by your last name. If you have an outline, count and number the title page and outline pages separately, using small roman numerals (i, ii, iii, iv), beginning with ii for the first page of the outline. The title page is counted in the sequence, but the number *i* should not appear on the page.

Type the essay double-spaced throughout, including quotations that are set off from the text and the works cited section. (Note that a quotation of four or more lines should be set off from the text, or displayed, by typing it indented in from the left margin.)

WORKS CITED PAGE

List and describe every source mentioned in the essay in the works cited page(s). Do not include any sources you may have consulted during your research but did not cite in the essay.

Describe each source bibliographically by giving the name of the author or authors, the title, the place of publication, the publisher, and the date of publication, in that order. Give the author's last name first, followed by the rest of the name and any initials in normal order and as given in the source. The following sample entry demonstrates the general form to follow, including punctuation and indentation:

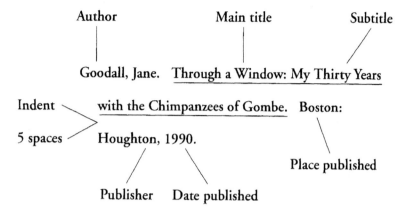

Note: Always allow two spaces between the main elements of the entry, that is, after the names of the author(s) and between the title and the publishing information.

Citation Forms Recommended by the Modern Language Association

The examples that follow demonstrate the forms recommended by the Modern Language Association (MLA) for listing commonly used sources in the works cited page. Following several sample entries is the form for citing that particular source parenthetically in the text. These sample entries vary from the citation method explained in "Citing Sources in the Text" (pages 239–240).

A Book with One Author

Calder, Nigel. <u>Einstein's Universe.</u> New York:

    Viking, 1979.

A Book with Two Authors

Jacobson, Gary C., and Samuel Kernel. <u>Strategy and</u>

    <u>Choice in Congressional Elections.</u> 2nd ed. New

    Haven: Yale UP, 1983.

In-text citation form: (Jacobson and Kernel 112).

Note: Notice that for an entry with more than one author, only the first author's name is reversed. For the name of a university press, use the abbreviation "UP" in place of "University Press," as in the example above.

A Work with Three Authors

```
Poizner, Howard, Edward S. Klima, and Ursula Bel-

    lugi. What the Hands Reveal about the Brain.

    Cambridge, MA: MIT Press, 1987.
```

In-text citation form: (Poizner, Klima, and Bellugi 54).

Note: Use the postal ZIP code abbreviation for a state when the city of publication is not well known or ambiguous (as with Cambridge, England, and Cambridge in Boston, for instance). Also see the following example.

A Work with More than Three Authors

For works with more than three authors, list the first author (last name first) followed by a comma and the abbreviation "et al." (meaning "and others") without quotation marks or underlining.

```
Kevane, Eugene, et al. Ancient Man and Information

    Exchange. Vol. 1. Woodbridge, VA: Tekakwitha

    Institute, 1985.
```

In-text citation form: (Kevane et al. 76)

A Book with No Author, but with an Editor or Editors

```
Erdoes, Richard, and Alfonso Ortiz, eds. American

    Indian Myths and Legends. New York: Pantheon,

    1984.
```

In-text citation: (Erdoes and Ortiz 44).

An Anonymous Book

List a work with no indicated author by its full title, but ignore the articles *a, and,* and *the* at the start of such titles as you alphabetize them, like this:

```
Woolf, Virginia, A Room of One's Own, New York:

    Harcourt, 1957.
```

The World of Learning 1975-76. 26th ed. London:

    Europa, 1975.

In-text citation: (World of Learning 76).

Note: Notice that the short form of the publisher is used: "Harcourt" instead of "Harcourt Brace Jovanovich."

A Signed Article in a Weekly or Monthly Magazine

Griggs, Lee. "Digging Out, Looking Back." Time 22

    Oct. 1990: 38-40.

A Signed Article in a Journal

Schaffner, Paul. "Competitive Admissions Practices

    When the SAT is Optional." Journal of Higher

    Education 56 (1985): 55-72.

A Signed Article in a Newspaper

DeYoung, Josephine. "Air Raid Adolescence." Los

    Angeles Times 17 Feb. Orange County ed. 1991:

    E1.

No page number is given in the text citation if the source is on a single page.

An Unsigned Article in Any Periodical (Magazine, Journal, or Newspaper)

"Giving the PC a Home." U.S. News & World Report 8

    Oct. 1990: 75-76.

In-text citation form: ("Giving" 75).

Note: Except for May, June, and July, abbreviate the names of months: Jan., Feb., Mar., Apr., Aug., Sept., Nov., Dec.

An Advertisement

"The First Powder with the Power of Light." Con-

    noisseur Oct. 1990: [4].

In-text citation form: ("First Powder").

Note: Use brackets to show that no page number appeared in the source.

A Performance

For any kind of performance (a concert, play, ballet, or opera), first give the title of the work, followed by the names of major contributors, such as a performer, writer, director, or producer. End the citation with the theater name, the city (and abbreviated state name if necessary), and then a period, followed by the performance date:

Hamlet By William Shakespeare. Dir. Lesley Greer.

    With Alan Carpenter and Susan McIntosh. West-

       view Arts Plaza, Hollings, CA. 1989.

You can emphasize the contribution of a particular individual by putting that person's name first in the entry:

Greer, Lesley, dir. Hamlet. By William Shake-

    speare. With Alan Carpenter and Susan McIn-

    tosh. Westview Arts Plaza, Hollings, CA. 1989.

A Film

List a film by its title, followed by the name of the director, distributor, and the year. As with an entry for a performance, you can also list the names of other contributors after the title. If you are emphasizing a particular person's contribution, list that person's name first.

Sleeping with the Enemy. Dir. Joseph Ruben.

    Screenplay by Ronald Bass. With Julia Roberts

    and Patrick Bergin. 20th Century Fox, 1991.

Roberts, Julia, actor. Sleeping with the Enemy.

    Dir. Joseph Ruben. Screenplay by Ronald Bass.

    With Patrick Bergin. 20th Century Fox, 1991.

A Television Program

Underline the title of the program, but if you also cite an episode, list its title first, in quotation marks. Include the network (for example, "CBS"), the local station, and the broadcast date.

Donahue, Phil. The Phil Donahue Show. NBC. KNSD,

    San Diego, 23 Aug. 1990.

"AIDS." Oprah Winfrey. With Oprah Winfrey. ABC.

    KABC, Los Angeles, 5 Mar. 1991.

Information from CD-ROM and Other Databases

Provide the information as you would for an article or a book. Then add the title of the database, the publication medium, the name of the vendor is available, and the electronic publication date.

Benta, Harriette. "Japanese-American Internees."

    New York Times 1 April 1995, late ed.: C3. New

    York Times Ondisc. CD-ROM. UMI-Proquest. May

    1995.

Information from an Online Source

Cite a source obtained through a database or information service as you would normally, but include identifying technical information after the end of the entry.

Lines, Patricia. "An Overview of Home Instruc-

    tion." Phi Delta Kappan 68 (1987): 510-17.

    ERIC. Online. 1 Dec. 1992.

An Interview

Stephen Salk. Personal Interview. 6 Oct. 1990.

A Lecture

Calvert, John. "The Reagan Years." South County

    Republicans Conference. Wilmont, TX, 19 Nov.

    1988.

Shorter, Beatrice. "AIDS Prevention." Citrus Com-

munity College. Covina, CA: Mar. 3, 1991.

A Sample Research Essay

The following essay by student Irene Islas demonstrates the use of research materials and documentation to develop the discussion of a research topic. Read the essay at least twice. The first time read to get a sense of its thesis, organization, and content. Then read it a second time to study how Irene integrates examples and quotations from her research with her own ideas.

Irene Islas

Professor Thomas Laskey

English 1A

May 17, 1995

Graffiti: What Price Art?

It is an early morning in February, 1991. At the Buhre Avenue subway station in New York City, two young men tie bandannas around their mouths and noses to protect them from paint fumes. Spray cans in hand, they approach the smooth, stainless steel sides of two cars and proceed to spell out their "tags," or signatures, in huge colorfully ballooned letters. One of them uses black spray paint to write "I love the M.T.A.," "Scrub harder!" and "Bomb trains" inside the letters (Strom). During this same month, at New York's

Present tense examples introduce the paper's topic.

Definition of "tags."

Museum of Modern Art, works of spray-painted graffiti go on sale for thousands of dollars apiece.
The artist is a former gang graffitist whose exhib-
ited work critics hail as "vital" (Patton 138).
Welcome to America, the land of opportunity and
graffiti.

Until recently the most dominant form of graffiti has been the traditional wall writing one
might see in public rest rooms or scrawled across
the walls, billboards, and signposts of large
cities: "Cure Virginity!" "Imperials rule," "Vaco   *Examples of graffiti.*
6911" "Here I sit broken-hearted. . . . '' Written
graffiti has not declined, but today it shares
space with a gaudy new version of itself: spray-
can art. Graffiti artists, known as "writers" on   *Definition of "writers."*
the street, now cover whole sides of buildings,
sidewalks, or subways and train cars nightly with
their gaudy work. Such writers cause literally
millions of dollars of damage every year to create
what many of them insist is art and most of the
public view as outright vandalism. Unfortunately,
whether viewed as art or vandalism, such graffiti
is not going to disappear soon, if at all. In   *Thesis statement.*
fact, today's spray-can graffiti has assumed a new
social status that may make it more irrepressible
than ever.

Part of the blame for the widespread use and destructiveness of graffiti generally today has simply to do with technology. The word <u>graffiti</u> itself comes from Italian and means "little scratchings" or "scribblings," and it originally referred to the small markings earlier ages etched or wrote on hard surfaces (Sagarin). Modern ball-point pens, felt-tipped markers, and especially spray paint cans, however, have taken graffiti far beyond small scribbles. Not only do today's surfaces make writing and drawing easier, but a single can of spray paint, for example, can literally cover most of an entire wall. In addition to being an eyesore, ink and paint contain acids that can stain most surfaces, including tiles and strong plastics. Over time, walls covered by thick layers of enamel or acrylic paint cannot "breathe" and begin to corrode, crack, or discolor ("Graffito").

The result of such destruction is a multi-million dollar business in graffiti-resistant sealants and millions more spent for labor to remove graffiti before it does permanent damage. In 1990, for example, the New York Transit Authority's anti-graffiti campaign kept 1,000 city workers busy scrubbing graffiti off subway cars at an annual cost of $52 million. Some cars were so covered by

Underlining and quotation marks used to define a term.

Citation of a single-page source.

Statistical examples in this and the next two paragraphs.

graffiti or their surfaces so ruined that they were scrapped entirely ("Fade to Gray").

While any graffiti may be ugly and damaging to some extent, spray-paint graffiti exceeds all other types in the extensiveness of its use and the costs it inflicts. Spray-paint artists, or "writers," can cover hundreds of square feet of surface in a single night of painting, sometimes using 40 or more cans of paint to perfect their work (Strom). During the 1980s a now-legendary writer known as "A-One" became famous for painting entire subway cars, top to bottom, in just a few nights of work ("Buffed Out" 37). During three months of 1990, in California, two rival writers known as "Ozone" and "Chaka" managed together to leave their "tags," or signatures, 15,000 times across the city of Los Angeles (Beaty).

Nationwide, taxpayers will spend nearly $4 billion in 1991 to prevent or remove graffiti, with California cities alone spending $100 million for clean-up (Beaty). How much of that may be spray-paint graffiti is not known, though figures for large cities and states can provide a rough picture of the problem. Thus, in 1990 the New York City subway system endured 46,000 graffiti "hits," many of them spray-painted. Some 700 of those hits covered such large areas that cars had to be taken out of service for extensive cleaning and repair (Strom). In Los Angeles, authorities will spend $28 million next year to coat buildings with special graffiti-resistant paint (Beaty).

To the authorities who have to prevent or remove the graffiti, spray-can writers "are vandals and nothing more than vandals" (Strom). According to researchers Ernest Abel and Barbara Buckley, however, there are also those who see the graffiti artist as someone who brightens "a drab area and adds color to the mind-dulling blandness of the inner city" (139). Johnny Sandoras, a local spray-can artist whose tag is "Jax," agrees. Sandoras claims his work and that of others represents a unique part of his community's culture:

> When I put up a piece, it gives the area something for people to look at and come and see. We've had reporters and art people coming around to look at some of the stuff the writers put up. I'm not saying we're doing great art. What I'm saying is, it's art you don't see at the museum. It's as much a part of the community identity as the signs in Chinese you see all over Chi-

Source authors named in the text.

Interview source.

Indent quotations of four lines or more.

natown. People know this is the place to
see real graffiti art.

Like the early humans who left their hand
prints on the walls of the Lascaux cave in France
20,000 years ago, modern graffiti artists seem to
seek an affirmation of self and personality in
their work (Reisner 24–25). They are drawn by the
immortality that graffiti offers. "A-One," "Crash,"
"Daze," "Dondi," "Lee"—names of writers from the
1970s, the heyday of graffiti art—ring in the minds
of younger writers who hope some day to make names
for themselves. As Lee himself testifies, "When I
was young, I thought my name would run forever.
Writing was my life" ("Buffed Out" 38).

Such lofty, philosophical attitudes give
spray-can art its vitality as well as its irrepressible persistence. For older writers like Lee,
graffiti art is "a kind of masochism"; Daze knows
only that he "had to do it again night after
night." For A-One, writing was a kind of vital
competition:

> You'd paint all night, sleep two hours,
> maybe three, then you'd race to the
> writer's bench [where writers gathered to
> watch each other's work appear on the pass-

A colon introduces the indented quo-tation following an independent clause.

ing trains]. When that train came by, you'd
act cool, but you wouldn't be cool. Your
heart would be racing. What would you hear?
Would they say "That is a fresh burn" or
nothing? ("Buffed Out" 38) [Original
emphases]

Younger writers of today echo the same dedica-
tion. In Los Angeles, writers risk death climbing
over freeway overpasses or dodging high-speed
traffic to leave their tags or do a "piece," as a
small mural is called. Los Angeles graffitist
"Ozone" describes writing as "an obsession ("Chris
Coogan"). In New York, a 20-year-old named Alan,
who has already been arrested once for writing,
continues because he cannot stop thinking about
"being out there every night, hitting trains that
are just sitting around out of service" (Strom).

The fundamental force behind spray-can art is
the same as that behind all graffiti: A chance to
say "I am here!" and the opportunity for immortality—however fleeting. "You do a piece somewhere and
people see your name. If it's good art, then they
give you respect. They know who you are," says
Johnny Sandoras, or "Jax."

Though writers use tags instead of their real
names, their identities are known to their

Brackets explain that underlining was in original.

A quotation integrated with text.

friends, and they also get a certain amount of pleasure in having a kind of double identity, a further extension of their sense of immortality (Reisner 86). Referring to spray-can art done on a freeway divider, a harried Los Angeles official adds, "They know their names will be up there for months because the state department of transportation has to shut down the freeway to paint [it] over" (Beaty).

Brackets indicate an alteration of the original.

Ironically, the very "success" of spray-can art may also be the ultimate cause of its demise. States and cities are gearing up to fight a war against graffiti of all types, especially the spray-paint variety. Attendance at nation-wide conferences and heavy use of such organizations as the National Graffiti Information Network are becoming common for every city. California has already passed a (much ignored) law forbidding sales of aerosol paint cans to minors, and the governor is considering signing a new bill that would revoke the driver's license of any convicted graffitist (Beaty). Many cities are following the example set by New York City's highly successful 1984 anti-graffiti campaign. To reduce the nightly spray painting of subway cars by gang writers, the Transit Authority systematically removed every car

with writing on it for cleaning each day before it
went out. The practice was so successful in
depriving writers of their hoped-for fame that the
number of "hits" fell to 160 in 1989 from a high
of 2,612 in 1984 (Strom).

Despite all these efforts, however, no one
expects to end graffiti in any form completely. The
tagging urge may be too great and the rewards too
promising. The spray-can art of writers like
"Crash" and "Daze" became hot-selling gallery
items during the '70s, and the trend continues
today, especially among European collectors
("Buffed Out" 37). In January of 1991, the New
York Museum of Modern Art opened a new show titled
"High and Low: Modern Art and Popular Culture" in
which it featured the "raw, outlaw drawing" of
graffiti art (Patton 142). The exhibit not only
reawakened the public's interest in spray-can art,
it also reaffirmed the hopes of young writers
across the nation that their work is something
more than vandalism ("Upstairs" 95).

The argument may never be settled as long as
the need to create graffiti exists and writers seem
only to hear mixed messages from the public about

their work. After spending millions of dollars each year to eliminate spray-can graffiti, even New York transit authorities were not above acknowledging its merit. In order to raise money a few years ago, they auctioned off some of the most decorated train panels (Strom). As long as they see themselves as artists, writers may never be deterred. "A vandal," says New York graffiti artist A-One,

> is somebody who throws a brick through a window. An artist is somebody who paints a picture on that window. A great artist is somebody who paints a picture on the window and then throws a brick through it.
>
> ("Buffed Out" 38)

The writer uses a quotation as the occasion for a final comment.

No one is denying that some spray-can graffiti has artistic merit. It's the question of who pays for the window that A-One and other writers seem to forget.

Works Cited

Abel, Ernest L., and Barbara E. Buckley. <u>The Hand-</u>
    <u>writing on the Wall: Toward a Sociology and</u>
    <u>Psychology of Graffiti.</u> Westport, CT: Green-
    wood, 1977.

A book with two authors

Beaty, Johnathan. "Zap! You've Been Tagged!" <u>Time</u>
    10 Sept. 1990: 43.

A signed periodical article

"Buffed Out." <u>New Yorker</u> 26 Feb. 1990: 37-38.

Unsigned periodical articles listed by title

"Chris Coogan, Ex-Vandal Vows to Remove L.A.'s
    Ozone Layer," <u>People</u> 23 Sept. 1990: 87.

"Fade to Gray in Gotham." <u>U.S. News & World Report</u>
    22 May 1989: 12.

"Graffito Ergo Sum." <u>Economist</u> 16 Dec. 1989: 66.

Patton, Phil. "'Hi and Low': Modern Arts Meets
    Popular Culture." <u>Smithsonian</u> Nov. 1990:
    138-49.

A book with one author

Reisner, Robert. Graffiti: <u>Two Thousand Years of</u>
    <u>Wall Writing</u>. New York: Cowles Book Company,
    1971.

Sagarin, Edward. "Graffiti." <u>Encyclopedia Ameri-</u>
    <u>cana.</u> 1985.

A signed encyclopedia article

Sandoras, Johnny. Personal interview. 3 Feb. 1995.

Personal interview

Strom, Stephanie. "Subway Graffiti (Art? Mess?)
    Rising as New York's Transit Budget Falls."
    <u>The New York Times</u> 11 Feb. 1991, natl. ed.:
    A16.

A signed newspaper article in a specific edition.

"Upstairs and Downstairs at MOMA." <u>Time</u> 22 Oct.

  1990: 94–95.

A Narrative of Irene Islas's Research Essay

The following is a summarized account of how Irene Islas completed her essay.

SELECTION OF A TOPIC

Irene began her selection of a research topic by listing several that interested her: women in sports, the problem of graffiti, the role of television during the war in the Persian Gulf, and AIDS research. After spending time in the library finding out more about each of these, she chose the problem of graffiti as the topic.

Irene had several good reasons for her choice. The topic of women in sports did not offer much opportunity to write about anything new, and the other two subjects seemed to have too much written about them for her to research in the time she had. Even more importantly perhaps, Irene had more reason to be personally interested in the problem of graffiti and spray-can art. She saw it every day all over the walls of her own neighborhood, and she was puzzled by the different opinions people seemed to have about it. A student Irene had attended high school with, Johnny Sandoras, was well known as a spray-can artist, and he was also attending Irene's college. She decided to investigate graffiti art and use Johnny Sandoras as one of the sources.

INVESTIGATING SOURCES

Irene consulted encyclopedias, indexes, and her library's card catalog while she was trying to select a topic. Once she had selected her topic, she began reading sources and taking notes on them. Irene's working bibliography listed a number of books with "graffiti" in their titles, but very few of them addressed the social impact of graffiti or the spray-can type she wanted to focus her essay on. An encyclopedia article gave Irene some history of the word *graffiti* itself, and she finally located four books that discussed graffiti generally and also described its use by spray-can artists. After reading and taking notes from the four books, however, Irene realized that only two of them would be of use to her when she wrote the essay. She eventually drew upon the work by Reisner for general facts about graffiti and borrowed other information or quoted from the book by Abel and Buckley in several places.

Because her specific topic, spray-can graffiti, was a current social issue,

Irene found a number of magazine and newspaper articles about it. She used the *Readers' Guide to Periodical Literature* to find recent magazine articles such as the *New Yorker* interview titled "Buffed Out" and the report on the Museum of Modern Art's graffiti exhibit reported in *Smithsonian*. A quick search through *The New York Times Index* provided the newspaper article "Subway Graffiti," from which Irene derived the anecdote that makes up the bulk of the paper's opening paragraph. Her use of current periodicals provided Irene with plenty of information and examples to illustrate and support the essay's thesis.

Irene interviewed Johnny Sandoras after she had completed most of her other reading and research. She waited until then because she wanted to use information he might give her to further illustrate what more authoritative sources told her. Irene quoted Sandoras, but wisely limited her use of his insights to aspects of the topic he was qualified to discuss.

WRITING THE ESSAY

Irene wrote her essay over a period of five days, including one evening spent in planning it. She found that getting the exact wording of her thesis took more time than she expected, but she eventually plunged into the writing, later revising the thesis slightly to better match her essay's content. She lost one day of writing when she had to return to the library for a source she had read but had not taken notes from earlier. While writing the essay, Irene found that she was not actually able to use all of the sources she had researched. This is a common outcome of thorough research and one you should expect in your own work.

Once she had a completed draft, Irene spent one full evening revising and editing the final draft before typing. Because her instructor had emphasized that the essay should be well written as well as properly researched, Irene's revisions included changes made for the purpose of improving the organization and writing style. She also reviewed the form for each in-text citation and its accompanying listing on the works cited page. Irene checked the spelling and punctuation, being especially careful about hyphenated words like "spray-can art" and authors' names. She exchanged her final manuscript with that of a classmate so they could help each other with the task of proofreading. Using an ink pen, Irene carefully corrected two small typing errors. Finally, she put the research essay in a folder, ready to hand in to her instructor by the due date.

WRITING TASK—RESEARCH ESSAY

You may have a research assignment already pending in one of your other classes. If so, the advice and illustrations in this chapter should be of help to you. One caution, though. The in-text citations and works cited format shown here follow the Modern Language Association (MLA) guidelines for research documentation. Classes in disciplines other than English may use different styles. Be sure you know which style your instructor requires before you begin a working bibliography.

If you do not have a research assignment for another class, follow this procedure:

1. Write a research essay of 1000 to 1250 words using the Modern Language Association (MLA) guidelines for in-text citations and a works cited page.

2. Select a suitable topic that focuses on a specific aspect of a broader subject. Select a topic you have interest in—the essay may be tedious to complete otherwise. As a general rule, avoid those topics that immediately leap to mind when the word *research* is mentioned: capital punishment, abortion, euthanasia, gun control, and so on. These topics have been done, done, and redone, so it is difficult to find something new to say. Furthermore, chances are you already know where you stand on these highly charged, emotional issues. If so, you may be tempted to hunt for information that supports a conclusion you have already reached. You may profit more from objective research on a subject you are curious to explore further.

3. Spend library time investigating the availability of sources on your topic. You will need both books and magazines as a minimum but be alert for audio cassettes, videos, pamphlets, picture collections, recorded lectures—whatever you can find.

4. Develop a working bibliography to guide your research and to serve as a record of the information you will need for your final works cited page.

5. Take notes on three-by-five-inch cards so you can easily add, drop, or rearrange information as your essay develops.

6. As you review your notes, develop a thesis (central point) and make sure you have enough information about each aspect of your thesis.

7. When you have sufficient appropriate material, organize it and write a first draft.

8. Revise your first draft(s) for clarity, accuracy, and thoroughness of presentation.

9. Type the final draft and read for errors in grammar, punctuation, mechanics, and spelling. If errors are few, correct them in ink. If many, retype the essay.

22

Additional Writing Tasks

In this chapter we offer writing tasks for extended essays. At the very least we hope some of these suggestions will solve the nagging question, "What Should I Write About?" But beyond this practical purpose we hope some will genuinely stir your curiosity. All, of course, are merely suggestions. Feel free to shape them to your own interests.

Starting with a Title

This assignment turns essay writing upside down by making what is usually the last step in essay writing—that is, titling an essay—the first step.

Begin by selecting one of the following essay titles (many of which have been taken from frequently anthologized essays). Your selection should suggest a topic to you. Once you've made your selection, it will become the title of the essay you write.

"Beauty and the Beast"
"The Stone Man"
"Truth and Fiction: An Examination of the News"
"You're Asking Me What Poverty Is?"
"Photographs of My Family"
"Politics and the English Language"
"A Hanging"
"Why We Don't Complain"
"Trapped in Another Life"
"A Definition of Malice"

"The American Way of Death"
"Three Kinds of Discipline"
"Shades of Black"
"In Praise of Idleness"
"The War Room"
"Female Athletes: They've Come a Long, Long Way, Baby"
"The Battle of the Ants"
"A New Game for Teachers to Play"
"It's Time to Stop Playing Indians"
"Kids in the Mall"
"Finding the Fury"
"How Books Helped Shape My Life"
"The Plot Against People"
"About Men"
"About Women"
"Violent Reactions"
"Don't Blame Television"
"Homemaking"
"The Language of Advertising"
"MTV's Message"
"Stripping Down to Bare Happiness"
"It Isn't Working"
"What on Earth Are You Doing?"
"Shame"
"Black Men in Public Space"
"A Few Words about Beasts"
"For My Child"
"An Officer and a Feminist"
"Why I Quit Watching Television"

WRITING TASK—STARTING WITH A TITLE

Keep in mind that your task is not to explain the title, but to write an essay using the title as a creative stimulus. An important part of your task is to shape your choice so that it is limited in scope and reflects your knowledge and interests. Your discussion should reflect appropriate development strategies, such as a mixture of examples, catalogs, anecdotes, comparison and contrast, definition, cause and effect, classification, description, and narration. Once the final draft is finished, the title that triggered your essay should be clearly appropriate.

Writing from Research

We offer the following assignments as prompts to get you started. Feel free to develop them in ways that interest you, keeping in mind that there is no correct or incorrect approach. These prompts will require limited research. While gathering your material be sure to keep track of the sources and document them in your paper.

1. In 1987 journalist Katherine Dieckmann wrote the following:

> Kitsch-as-lifestyle is for sale everywhere now—from restaurants to movies to countless other mock-rural replicas. It's a dominant cultural posture of our time found in everything from the hokey Bartles & Jaymes wine cooler TV spots to the contemporary American lit market dominated by what the British journal *Granta* has dubbed "Dirty Realism." Writers like the late Raymond Carver, Bobbie Ann Mason, and Frederick Barthelme concoct stories populated by suburbanites and rural dwellers who are hopelessly removed from their feelings in a world dominated by commodities, TV, cheesy magazines, *Reader's Digest,* and too much time spent hanging around the mall. The poetics of the Tastee-Freez offers its audience kitsch-culture landmarks that are familiar enough, and yet not too familiar. Those people are hopelessly inarticulate, while readers of these stories have the power to sit back and contemplate this art born of muteness (secure in the notion that they'll never write about us).

WRITING TASK—KITSCH

Your task is to develop a full definition of *kitsch* and explain its role in American Society today.

2. In his essay on prize fighter Benny Paret, who was killed in the ring, Norman Cousins uses physiological details to show the danger of boxing.

> Benny Paret was killed because the human fist delivers enough impact, when directed against the head, to produce a massive hemorrhage in the brain. The human brain is the most delicate and complex mechanism in all creation. It has the lacework of millions of highly fragile nerve connections. Nature attempts to protect this exquisitely intricate machinery by encasing it in a hard shell. Fortu-

nately, the shell is thick enough to withstand a great deal of pounding. Nature, however, can protect man against everything except man himself. Not every blow to the head will kill a man—but there is always the risk of concussion and damage to the brain. A prize fighter may be able to survive even repeated brain concussions and go on fighting, but the damage to his brain may be permanent.

WRITING TASK—VIOLENT SPORTS

Develop an argumentative essay that takes a position against any sport you believe could be life-threatening and devote part of your essay to the presentation of physiological details, as Cousins does, to support your position.

3. Many people feel frustrated in the face of the destruction of the Earth's ecological system. They see the destruction of the environment as being beyond their individual influence and, as a consequence, are reduced to helplessness. For example, tropical rain forests, all located in a narrow range near the equator in Central and South America, Africa, and Asia, are being destroyed so fast that by this century's end, 80 percent will be gone. According to scientific estimates, in a typical 4 square miles of rain forest, there will be over 750 species of trees, over 1500 different kinds of flowering plants, 125 different mammals, 400 kinds of birds, 100 kinds of reptiles, 60 different kinds of amphibians, and countless insects. Moreover, only 1 percent of these species will have been studied. What can any single person do to resist this destruction?

WRITING TASK—THREATENED EARTH

In an essay describe the scope of one threat to the Earth's ecological system. Explain its projected effects. Then suggest actions that individuals can take to reverse the threat, although they may be far removed from the actual problem. Remember, concentrate on a single threat: describe it; point out its effects; suggest actions to reverse it.

4. America's social life used to take place in streets and town squares, but now people spend much of their time in shopping malls. Malls are often

referred to as "the downtown" of our society, a place where people not only shop but also go for dinner, fashion shows, movies, and dances. A 1991 film, *Scenes from a Mall,* satirizes the importance of malls in contemporary life by featuring a couple celebrating their sixteenth wedding anniversary. They reveal infidelities; they break up; they make up; and they examine the worst and best times of their marriage—all in a Beverly Hills shopping mall.

WRITING TASK—MALLS

It is certainly easy to generalize about the social significance of malls (we all have our pet opinions), but what do the experts say? This is your chance to find out. In a fully developed deductive essay, present several informed views of the social significance of malls.

5.   In *The White Album,* novelist and essayist Joan Didion offers the following insight about human behavior.

> We tell ourselves stories in order to live. The princess is caged in a consulate. The man with candy will lead the children to the sea. The naked woman on the ledge outside the window on the sixteenth floor is the victim of *accidie,* or the naked woman is an exhibitionist, and it would be "interesting" to know which. We tell ourselves that it makes some difference whether the naked woman is about to commit a mortal sin or is about to register a political protest or is about to be, the Aristophanic view, snatched back to the human condition by the fireman in the priest's clothing just visible in the window behind her, the one smiling at the telephoto lens. We look for the sermon in the suicide, for the social or moral lesson in the murder of five. We interpret what we see, select the most workable of the multiple choices. We live, especially if we are writers, by the imposition of a narrative line upon disparate images, by the "ideas" with which we have learned to freeze the shifting phantasmagoria which is our actual experience.

WRITING TASK—STORIES

Research the importance of stories in helping people to understand life's mysteries. Define and narrow your subject so that it can be covered in a well-developed essay. Write the essay, documenting your sources.

Charting Your Current Life

If you've been doing Daily Writing, during the second week you collected raw material from your current life. You began by writing an overview that captured this period's dominant activities, impressions, and fantasies. On the following days of that week, you focused your writing by enlarging individual aspects of your current life. You described where you live, personal possessions, important activities, and special places. You also recorded your personal associations with these aspects of your life. Although roughly written, these entries probably come together as part of an account of who you are. We hope that they serve as a first step in achieving what Henry David Thoreau asks of every writer: "a simple and sincere account of his own life, and not merely what he has heard of other men's lives."

To go beyond the general knowledge you've acquired from family, friends, and society at large—to go beyond what you "have heard of other men's lives"—is to approach a deeper understanding of how you fit into the world, an understanding of who you are and what you want to be. Now, after the entries reflecting your current life have had time to incubate, we suggest you write a polished account of your current life—one that not only communicates the details of this period but that also communicates your personal insights.

WRITING TASK—CHARTING YOUR CURRENT LIFE

Write an inductive, associational, or deductive essay that gives an account of your current life. We recommend that you begin by reviewing your Daily Writing entries to stimulate more thoughts. Record your thoughts. As you read and record new thoughts, make a general observation about your recent experience. Shape the generalization into a central idea and use it to select material for your essay. Then, once you've selected the material, use the central idea to organize the paper's development.

Remember, whereas the Daily Writing entries may be rambling, the finished essay should be organized and developed with focused paragraphs. Never set your reader adrift in unfocused material. Your central idea, although not necessarily stated, should be clear to any attentive reader.

Exploring Your Dreams

Sigmund Freud, the founder of psychoanalysis, described dreams as forbidden wishes symbolically disguised to preserve the dreamer's sleep. But

Freud drew his conclusions from limited information. He didn't know, as today's researchers know, that virtually all mammals dream. What forbidden wishes, one may wonder, could birds and infants have?

Since Freud's time, researchers have taken a new attitude toward dreams. They reject the notion that a set of standardized interpretations can be applied to them. They maintain that each person creates individual meaning from dream experience. For instance, if ten people were to dream of wandering through a strange city, the dream would have ten different meanings, one for each dreamer.

These contemporary researchers also maintain that dreams serve as bridges between our conscious and unconscious experience. Many researchers maintain that dreams sometimes indicate the dreamer's destiny by pointing out unrecognized aspects of the dreamer or by focusing on another person who embodies the dreamer's potential. Sometimes dreams provide what is missing in the dreamer's waking life—love, friendship, success, adventure, travel, or freedom. Dreams can sometimes serve as a release from tension, pain, fear, or other emotions that can interfere with waking life. Finally, today's researchers point out the practical nature of dreams. Just as dreams have sometimes helped artists and inventors solve problems in their work, they sometimes serve the same purpose in every dreamer's life.

If you've been recording dreams as part of your Daily Writing, then perhaps you've made connections between your dreams and aspects of your waking life. If so, you might like to develop "dreams" as a subject for an essay.

WRITING TASK—EXPLORING YOUR DREAMS

Begin by rereading your Daily Writing entries on dreams. Have any dreams given you an insight into your life? Have any offered a solution to a problem you've faced? If so, shape a central point from your observation and use it to develop an essay that deals with your dream experience as related to your waking experience.

Responding to Quotations

The Writing Tasks given on the next few pages ask you to respond in some fashion to the words of others. Each task begins with one or more quotations expressing an attitude, insight, or personal opinion. You should read the quotations carefully, relate them to your own experience or knowledge, then write an essay responding in some way to this stimulation.

These tasks are open-ended. We are not asking that you agree or disagree with the quotations. Your paper shouldn't be limited to either an answer to or an amplification of the ideas expressed. Rather, you should let your mind speculate about the quotations and see where your thoughts lead.

Perhaps the quotation will arouse emotions, bring to mind nostalgic memories, or lead to philosophical thoughts. Take, for example, a short quotation from the writing of George Santayana:

> *To me it seems a dreadful indignity to have a soul controlled by geography.*

How could you respond in writing to this quotation? You would begin, of course, with prewriting—jotting down the thoughts that go through your mind as you read it.

- The cliché—travel broadens the mind. Is it true? My aunt and uncle's trip to Europe just reinforced all their prejudices against foreign things.
- Haven't traveled much myself, so can't support or deny the cliché from personal experience.
- Why "soul"? More important than the mind, I guess. Harder to pin down than thought. He's not talking about knowledge in the sense of facts and stories to relate, but about something more fundamental, something closer to the self.
- A soul controlled by geography would be a person imprisoned in some fashion—tied down rather than soaring free—missing out on full potential—the fullness of experience.
- Americans are criticized for this—being provincial—not willing to see the value of other ways of life.

  Example—languages. We think everyone should speak English. I've read that this is a problem in our diplomatic relations—not only do our reps not speak the language, they ignore customs too. What do we miss when we travel and can't speak with the people? All we have for the experience is a lot of slides.

- The other word I wonder about is *indignity.* What does it mean here? Being insulted is an indignity, or having pie shoved in your face—not exactly what he means. Here it is more personal—something you do to yourself—a kind of failure to reach potential again.
- Even if we don't travel we can learn about other ways of doing things.

Example—influx of refugees gives us a chance to relate to another culture, probably in a better way than a whirlwind tour. Trouble is we sit back and wait for them to adopt our ways (and language). How do they manage to study in American colleges?

- The world is becoming Americanized, they say. Coca-Cola in Egypt and McDonald's everywhere. I read that the most successful McDonald's stand is in Japan. And rock music—is that an American export or just a world phenomenon of the times? Is it a way to get beyond the limits of geography?
- Jeans and T-shirts. I saw a picture of a little boy in Cambodia wearing a Butterfinger T-shirt. Where did he get it?

This line of thinking has taken us quite a way away from Santayana's original words, but the journey has suggested any number of possible papers:

- How your aunt and uncle's trip was wasted—what they failed to get out of it
- Where you would like to go and why
- The intangible benefits your own travels have given you
- Your experiences with the language barrier
- Your experiences with people from other countries now settled in your community
- Your failure to learn from newly arrived immigrants
- The good and bad aspects of Americanizing the whole world

Note that it doesn't matter if any of the suggested topics speak directly to what Santayana had in mind. Santayana's words served as stimuli only. Similarly, the quotations in the next section should serve as springboards for your own creative thinking.

Extended Quotations

This section contains eleven quotations from various sources. Each quotation is followed by a writing task with a series of questions designed to get you into the prewriting portion of the task. We hope the questions will be helpful, but ignore them if you don't need them. In no case should you assume that you should write in direct response to any of these questions. Open up your responses. Allow your mind to wander over the entire landscape of possibilities.

After you have chosen a quotation and done some prewriting exploration as we have suggested, your task is to write an essay of your own design (it may be deductive, inductive, personal, or associational) that grows from your consideration of the quotation and the questions that follow it. In your essay you need not mention the quotation at all unless you find some good reason for doing so. Remember, its purpose is only to stimulate your thinking. If you do mention it, make it an integral part of your essay by quoting it in full or in part and including the name of the author. Do not assume that your readers have read the quotation before.

The quotations themselves tend to be general in phrasing; they are statements of attitudes, insights, or personal opinions. The specifics that support such statements are missing. But your paper should include such specifics. If, for example, you were responding to the Santayana quotation given earlier by writing about the benefits you have gained from your travel experiences, you would not just say they have helped you appreciate the customs of others; you would get specific by giving readers the anecdotes and the individual experiences that illustrate the point.

1. MAY SARTON

The reasons for depression are not so interesting as the way one handles it, simply to stay alive. This morning I woke at four and lay awake for an hour or so in a bad state. It is raining again. I got up finally and went about the daily chores, waiting for the sense of doom to lift—and what did it was watering the house plants. Suddenly joy came back because I was fulfilling a simple need, a living one. Dusting never has this effect (and that may be why I am such a poor housekeeper!), but feeding the cats when they are hungry, giving Punch clean water, makes me suddenly feel calm and happy. Whatever peace I know rests in the natural world, in feeling myself a part of it, even in a small way.

WRITING TASK—MAY SARTON

Write an essay that grows from your consideration of the quotation from May Sarton. You may use the following questions as a way of generating material for your essay.

Does this quotation arouse emotions in you? Do you envy the writer's apparent ability to find joy in such simple things? Do you reject the idea? Do you have your own ways of fighting depression? How big a role does the "natural world" play in your daily living? What simple things bring you peace and calm? Or do you really prefer excitement and a more hectic pace? Do you have friends or neighbors who might make interesting studies of either the simple life or the high-pressure one?

2. e. e. cummings

To be nobody-but-yourself in a world which is doing its best, night and day, to make you everybody else—means to fight the hardest battle which any human being can fight

---

WRITING TASK—e. e. cummings

Write an essay that grows from your consideration of the quotation from e. e. cummings. You may use the following questions as a way of generating material for your essay.

What are some of the victories and defeats you have had in what cummings describes as the battle to be "nobody-but-yourself"? Are you still fighting the battle or do you find it more comfortable to be "everybody else"? In what ways does the world (society, family, friends, teachers, the media, the government) try to make you like everyody else?

---

3. JEFFERS, DOSTOYEVSKI, MONTAIGNE

The following three short quotations each make substantially the same point. Consider them together.

Robinson Jeffers

I have never been ambitious, but it seemed unpleasant just the same to have accomplished nothing, but exactly nothing, along the only course that permanently interested me. There are times when one forgets for a moment that life's value is life; any further accomplishment is of very little importance comparatively.

Fyodor Dostoyevski

Perhaps the only goal on earth toward which mankind is striving lies in the process of attaining, in other words in life itself, and not in the things to be attained.

Michel de Montaigne

The great and glorious masterpiece of man is to live to the point. All other things—to reign, to hoard, to build—are, at most, but inconsiderable props and appendages.

WRITING TASK—JEFFERS, DOSTOYEVSKI, MONTAIGNE

Write an essay that grows from your consideration of the quotations from Robinson Jeffers, Fyodor Dostoyevski, and Michel de Montaigne. You may use the following questions as a way of generating material for your essay.

All three of these quotations stress the importance of process (living) over product (accomplishments). How much do we judge others and ourselves on the basis of product? Competitive sports at all levels are one obvious example. Can you think of others? Can you think of times in your life when the experience itself turned out to be more important or worthwhile than the end result? Is the pursuit of a goal as important as the achievement? Or is lack of achievement really failure? How should success in life be measured?

4. MARK KRAM

All of this brings us down to marbles, not the argot for brains but the real thing: perfectly round; so smooth; brilliantly colored; as precious to generations of children as any diamond. Has anyone seen a marble lately? Has anyone seen a marble in the hand of a kid? Most likely the answer is no, for the only things kids carry these days are transistor radios, slices of pizza and tickets to rock concerts. The marble belongs to a time that now seems otherworldly, when trees lined big city blocks as far as the eye could see, when barley soup was supper three times a week, when children had secret places.

WRITING TASK—MARK KRAM

Write an essay that grows from your consideration of the quotation from Mark Kram. You may use the following questions as a way of generating material for your essay.

Have things changed much since you were a kid? What did you do for fun when you were eight, or ten, or twelve? What did you do finally on "Mommy-there's-nothing-to-do" days? Schoolchildren used to survive the year by moving mysteriously through a cycle of ill-defined seasons—marble season, jacks season, mumblety-peg season, bottle-cap season—all without the aid of any adult direction or organization. Now, even the very young, boys and girls alike, get involved in soccer season, football season, basketball season, baseball season, camping organizations, and "lessons" of all kinds. Old-timers will tell you that something valuable has been lost because of all this organization, carried out under constant adult supervision. What do you think? Should kids be left alone more? Should they be allowed to invent their own activities? Are their lives too scheduled? What's the difference, as you see it, between carrying a bag of marbles and carrying a transistor radio?

---

5. JOHN HOLT

From the very beginning of school we make books and reading a constant source of possible failure and public humiliation. When children are little we make them read aloud, before the teacher and other children, so that we can be sure they "know" all the words they are reading. This means that when they don't know a word, they are going to make a mistake, right in front of everyone. Instantly they are made to realize that they have done something wrong. Perhaps some of the other children will begin to wave their hands and say, "Ooooh! O-o-o-o!" Perhaps they will just giggle or nudge each other, or make a face. Perhaps the teacher will say, "Are you sure?" or ask someone else what he thinks. Or perhaps, if the teacher is kindly, she will just smile a sweet, sad smile—often one of the most painful punishments a child can suffer in school. In any case, the child who has made the mistake knows he has made it, and feels foolish, stupid, and ashamed, just as any of us would in his shoes.

WRITING TASK—JOHN HOLT

Write an essay that grows from your consideration of the quotation from John Holt. You may use the following questions as a way of generating material for your essay.

Have you ever felt humiliated in a classroom? By a teacher? By classmates? Can you recall details of the experience and how you felt? Have incidents of this nature influenced how you feel about being in classrooms even now? How do you feel about being in classrooms? Comfortable? Uneasy? If allowed your choice, where do you sit? Why? Do you prefer an active or passive role as a student in a classroom? Do you prefer lectures or class discussions? Why? Can you recall particular classes at any level of your schooling that you either looked forward to or dreaded? Can you bring to mind details of the scene and specifics about how you felt while there? Do you agree with John Holt that having students read aloud is a poor teaching method? If you were a teacher at any level of schooling, what would you do differently than your teacher at that level did? Have teachers or have fellow students had more to do with your attitudes and behavior in classes? Have you ever done anything really stupid in class? Can you tell about it without embarrassment? What punishments are the most effective? The least?

6. ALISON LURIE

For thousands of years human beings have communicated with one another first in the language of dress. Long before I am near enough to talk to you on the street, in a meeting or at a party, you announce your sex, age, and class to me through what you are wearing—and very possibly give me important information (or misinformation) as to your occupation, origin, personality, opinions, tastes, sexual desires and current mood. I may not be able to put what I observe into words, but I register the information unconsciously; and you simultaneously do the same for me. By the time we meet and converse we have already spoken to each other in an older and more universal tongue.

WRITING TASK—ALISON LURIE

Write an essay that grows from your consideration of the quotation from Alison Lurie. You may use the following questions as a way of generating material for your essay.

What do your clothes reveal about you? Do you make conscious choices designed to say something to others? Do your clothes influence your mood, your behavior? Do you judge others by their clothing? How important are clothes in your life? Do changes in fashion reflect changes in public attitudes or are they just the whims of fashion designers? Would you expect to see changes in fashion in a time of great prosperity? A time of economic difficulty? Wartime?

7. JOSEPH L. BRAGA AND LAURIE D. BRAGA

Whether you die at a young age or when you are older is less important than whether you have fully lived the years you have had.

One person may live more in eighteen years than another does in eighty. By living, we do not mean frantically accumulating a range and quality of experience valued in fantasy by others. Rather, we mean finding a sense of peace and strength to deal with life's disappointments and pain while always striving to discover vehicles to make accessible, increase, and sustain the joys and delights of life. One such vehicle is learning to focus on some of the things you have learned to tune out—to notice and take joy in the budding of new leaves in the spring, to wonder at the beauty of the sun rising each morning and setting each night, to take comfort in the smile or touch of another person, to watch with amazement the growth of a child, and to share in children's wonderfully "uncomplexed," enthusiastic, and trusting approach to living. To live.

WRITING TASK—JOSEPH L. BRAGA AND LAURIE D. BRAGA

Write an essay that grows from your consideration of the quotation from the Bragas. You may use the following questions as a way of generating material for your essay.

Do you really believe that one person can live more in eighteen years than another in eighty? Is there value in "accumulating a range and quality of experience"? What are your personal "joys and delights of life"? Are there aspects of life that you "tune out" but feel you shouldn't? What are they? What is your definition of "living"? In other words, what is important? What gives you pleasure? What gives you peace and strength?

8. CARL SAGAN

Every major power has some widely publicized justification for its procurement and stockpiling of weapons of mass destruction, often including a reptilian reminder of the presumed character and cultural defects of potential enemies (as opposed to us stout fellows), or of the intentions of others, but never ourselves, to conquer the world. Every nation seems to have its set of forbidden possibilities, which its citizenry and adherents must not at any cost be permitted to think seriously about. In the Soviet Union these include capitalism, God, and the surrender of national sovereignty; in the United States, socialism, atheism, and the surrender of national sovereignty. It is the same all over the world.

WRITING TASK—CARL SAGAN

Write an essay that grows from your consideration of the quotation from Carl Sagan. You may use the following questions as a way of generating material for your essay.

Does war become more likely or less likely as nations invent and stockpile new weapons? Is there any way to avoid the kind of confrontations Sagan writes about? Is conflict between nations inevitable? Do you think individuals and citizen groups can influence government defense policy? Or do you feel that individuals are essentially powerless in this situation? How would you justify the defense expenditures of the United States in a debate? How would you argue against those expenditures?

9. SHARON CURTIN

I am afraid to grow old—we're all afraid. In fact, the fear of growing old is so great that every aged person is an insult and a threat to the society. They remind us of our own death, that our body won't always remain smooth and responsive, but will someday betray us by aging, wrinkling, faltering, failing. The ideal way to age would be to grow slowly invisible, gradually disappearing, without causing worry or discomfort to the young. In some ways that does happen. Sitting in a small park across from a nursing home one day, I noticed that the young mothers and their children gathered on one side, and the old people from the home on the other. Whenever a youngster would run over to the "wrong" side, chasing a ball or just trying to cover all the available space, the old people would lean forward and smile. But before any communication could be established, the mother would come over, murmuring embarrassed apologies, and take her child to the "young" side.

WRITING TASK—SHARON CURTIN

Write an essay that grows from your consideration of the quotation from Sharon Curtin. You may use the following questions as a way of generating material for your essay.

What are some of the ways our culture separates the old from the young? What are some of the ways we honor old people? What are some of the ways we take away their dignity? Have you ever avoided contact with an old person? Can you explain why? Are you uncomfortable around them? What is the source of the discomfort? Are there old people who are important in your life right now? In what way? Are you afraid of growing old? What do you fear most about it?

10. MORTON HUNT

The record of man's inhumanity to man is horrifying, when one compiles it—enslavement, castration, torture, rape, mass slaughter in war after war. But who has compiled the record of man's kindness to man—the trillions of acts of gentleness and goodness, the helping hands, smiles, shared meals, kisses, gifts, healings, rescues? If we were no more than murderous predators, with a freakish lack of inhibition against slaughtering our own species, we would have been at a terrible competitive disadvantage compared with other animals; if this were the central truth of our nature, we would scarcely have survived, multiplied and become the dominant species on earth. Man does have an aggressive instinct, but it is not naturally or inevitably directed to killing his own kind. He is a beast and perhaps at times the cruelest beast of all—but sometimes he is also the kindest beast of all. He is not all good and not perfectable, but he is not all bad and not wholly unchangeable or unimprovable. This is the only basis on which one can hope for him; but it is enough.

WRITING TASK—MORTON HUNT

Write an essay that grows from your consideration of the quotation from Morton Hunt. You may use the following questions as a way of generating material for your essay.

Humans are very critical of humanity. Why is this so? Why are newspapers and newscasts so full of man's inhumanity to man? Why do history textbooks consist largely of records of conflict? Is anything accomplished by all this attention to our failures? Is kindness boring? Why not make a contribution to the record Hunt calls for, "the record of man's kindness to man"? When did you last see an instance of human love freely given? What examples come to mind of people helping other people? Do you know of instances where one human risked his comfort or life for another? Do you recall an incident where you made yourself feel good by showing thoughtfulness to another? How about recording the time your day was brightened by the smile or kind words of someone else? Can you do it? Can you make such a paper interesting? Can you make it real rather than sentimental?

---

11. ECCLESIASTES

To every thing there is a season, and a time to every purpose under the heaven:

A time to be born, and a time to die; a time to plant, and a time to pluck up that which has been planted;

A time to kill, and a time to heal; a time to break down, and a time to build up;

A time to weep, and a time to laugh; a time to mourn, and a time to dance;

A time to cast away stones, and time to gather stones together; a time to embrace, and a time to refrain from embracing;

A time to get, and a time to lose; a time to keep, and a time to cast away;

A time to rend, and a time to sew; a time to keep silence, and a time to speak;

A time to love, and a time to hate; a time of war, and a time of peace.

WRITING TASK—ECCLESIASTES

Write an essay that grows from your consideration of the quotation from Ecclesiastes. You may use the following questions as a way of generating material for your essay.

What is meant by "time"? What are the contradictions in the quotation? Does the quotation capture aspects of your life? What is the "philosophical attitude" expressed in the quotation? If you find a message in the quotation, what is it? How is the quotation helpful in putting experience in perspective?

Brief Quotations

Following are twenty quotations without comments or questions. Your task is to write an essay using one or more of the quotations as an integral part of your paper. Perhaps the quotation itself will become your title; it may be your first or your last sentence; or it may be quoted elsewhere in your essay. In any case, the essay will be written in illustration of the meaning of the quotation. Notice we said "in illustration." You should not explain the quotation by saying "This quotation by Benjamin Franklin means . . ." Nor should you say "I agree with Somerset Maugham's idea" or "I disagree with Jessica Mitford's statement." These approaches are likely to result in uninteresting papers. Instead, you should describe situations, present information, or discuss your opinions with the intent of rounding out the meaning of the quotation and then use the quotation as a sort of summing up or punch line for your essay.

Some of the quotations here are quite simple and direct; others are more figurative and should not be taken literally. For example, John F. Kennedy's statement "A child miseducated is a child lost" is a simple, direct sentence that starts us thinking about the importance of education. There is no need for interpretation. But when Stephen Leacock says "Personally, I would rather have written *Alice in Wonderland* than the whole *Encyclopaedia Britannica*" he is not talking directly about these works. He is, instead, using them to represent different worlds—one of imagination and wonder and the other of fact and knowledge. In this quotation at least, he sees these worlds in opposition and says, indirectly, that the world of imagination is of more value to him. Kennedy's quotation would lead you to a paper on education. Leacock's quotation could lead you to a much broader range of possibilities. It is more open-ended, more challenging, and therefore, probably, more fun.

> Today the real test of power is not capacity to make war but capacity to prevent it.
>
> —Anne O'Hare McCormick

> The family you come from isn't as important as the family you're going to have.
>
> —Ring Lardner

> This will never be a civilized country until we spend more money for books than we do for chewing gum.
>
> —Elbert Hubbard

> Beauty is the promise of happiness.
>
> —Stendhal

> The real danger is not that computers will begin to think like men, but that men will begin to think like computers.
>
> —Sydney J. Harris

> I like men to behave like men—strong and childish.

—Françoise Sagan

To find a friend one must close one eye—to keep him, two.
—Norman Douglas

The man who strikes first admits that his ideas have given out.
—Chinese proverb

We cannot defend freedom abroad by deserting it at home.
—Edward R. Murrow

We can destroy ourselves by cynicism and disillusion just as effectively as by bombs.
—Kenneth Clark

Intelligent discontent is the mainspring of civilization.
—Eugene V. Debs

The secret of education is respecting the pupil.
—Ralph Waldo Emerson

Science may have found a cure for most evils; but it has found no remedy for the worst of them all—the apathy of human beings.
—Helen Keller

I'd rather have roses on my table than diamonds on my neck.
—Emma Goldman

Man is what he believes.
—Anton Chekhov

Man prefers to believe what he prefers to be true.
—Francis Bacon

A good laugh is sunshine in a house.
—William Makepeace Thackeray

To be wronged is nothing unless you continue to remember it.
—Confucius

Never let a fool kiss you or a kiss fool you.
—Joey Adams

You grow up the day you have the first real laugh—at yourself.
—Ethel Barrymore

We always find something to give us the impression we exist.
—Samuel Beckett

WRITING TASK—BRIEF QUOTATIONS

Write an essay of your own design illustrating the idea expressed in one of the preceding short quotations.

Remember:

1. Do not explain the quotation directly or make direct statements agreeing or disagreeing with its message.
2. Include the quotation somewhere in your paper, perhaps as a summing up or punch line for your essay.
3. As always, be specific. Use details and examples to support your statements.

Part Three

READINGS FOR WRITERS

Part Three begins with a single writing task designed to introduce you to some strategies writers use when writing about what they have read. Following this introductory task is a collection of fifteen essays written by professional writers. These essays cover a wide variety of subjects, ranging from a description of a typical night in a hospital emergency room to an argument opposing the use of animals in scientific experimentation. Each of the essays is followed by two writing tasks, one that directly relies on the essay that precedes it and one that uses the essay as a beginning point for your own writing.

How should you approach this part? More than likely your writing instructor will assign the readings and direct you how you should use them. But if you're self-motivated, we suggest you read some of the essays to see how writers use the strategies presented in Part Two, such as development by examples, definition, and classification. This means you'll be reading like a writer reads—that is, reading to analyze another writer's strategies and practices not merely to analyze the content. Finally, after you've completed your first full essay, you might want to respond to one of the writing tasks that follow an essay you like.

23

Writing About Written Works

Much of your college writing will be in response to written texts. For example, in history you might read a significant government document and write an analytical essay to explore the assumptions that underlie its intent. In psychology you might read two conflicting views of the mind's structure and write a comparison essay to show how they are similar and different. In literature you might read a novel and write an interpretive essay to explain the central character's behavior.

Even though the content of such works is very different, the strategies for writing about written works always apply, no matter what the content.

The structure, for example, can reflect deductive essay structure. The central point will embody the purpose of your essay, and the discussion paragraphs will be organized around topic sentences, each of which develops one subpoint of the central point. The conclusion, as in all essays, should end the paper in a satisfying way.

Simple, right? Yes, the structure is simple, but within this structure you should adhere to several practices common to essays about written works.

Write an Introduction That Represents the Work

Unless you are absolutely certain that your readers are familiar with the written work you are responding to, use your introduction to introduce it. The most efficient way is to summarize it.

Your summary should be brief, perhaps no longer than ten or twelve sentences. When summarizing, don't get bogged down in tedious detail, which will only distract your readers. Instead, select the main elements that support the writer's purpose and use them to create an overview with just enough detail to make your readers feel comfortable as they enter the discussion part of your essay.

To represent the work effectively, you must read it carefully, not just once but several times, taking notes as you go. Once you understand the writer's purpose, you're ready to begin a summary. While writing the summary, follow several common practices.

1. In the first sentence state the author, the title, and the author's main purpose.
2. Follow the opening sentence with a quotation that supports your interpretation of the author's purpose.
3. Attribute quotations to the author in the summary section and wherever appropriate in the discussion and conclusion.
4. Use the historical present—that is, the present tense of verbs—in the summary section and throughout the essay.
5. After stating the author's full name in the opening, use only the last name in the summary section and throughout the essay.
6. End the introduction with the central idea you plan to develop.

For example, student-writer John Beck's opening paragraph for a paper that discusses George Simpson's writing techniques in "The War Room at Bellevue" presents a quick summary of the essay (see pages 365–370).

> George Simpson in "The War Room at Bellevue" describes a typical Friday night in the Bellevue Hospital to show why its emergency team is so highly respected. Simpson writes, "Why do injured cops drive by a half-dozen other hospitals to be treated at Bellevue? They've seen the Bellevue emergency team in action." The emergency team's shift begins at 9:00 p.m. and goes on into the early morning hours. In vivid detail, Simpson describes the dramatic events that unfold in the emergency room and the parade of characters who populate its corridors—that is, the victims of accidental injuries, poisonings, suicide attempts, miscarriages, overdoses, stabbings, and shootings. From the beginning when "An ambulance backs into the receiving bay, its red and yellow lights flashing . . ." to the end when "blood spatters on the floor" from a knife wound, Simpson captures the grinding pace and traumatic conditions doctors and nurses face while they maintain a stoic professionalism. Although few, if any, of Simpson's readers may ever step inside the Bellevue emergency room, all his readers will leave his essay with a powerful sense that they have been there because of Simpson's vivid use of descriptive techniques.

In his summary, John Beck followed the six practices writers often use to begin an essay about a written text. He states the author's full name, the title, and the central purpose in the first sentence. He keeps to the present tense, attributes quotations directly to the author, and uses only the author's last name after the opening sentence. He ends by stating his central point—that is, Simpson successfully uses descriptive techniques to recreate a Friday night in the Bellevue emergency room.

Write a Discussion That Develops the Central Point

The discussion section of an essay about a written work, is like the discussion section of any well-constructed deductive essay—that is, it should be developed around subpoints expressed in topic sentences. For example, Beck's second paragraph in his essay on "The War Room at Bellevue" begins the discussion.

> Simpson's eye for specific detail and use of vivid language helps to recreate the emergency room experience for readers. For example, a stabbing victim is rushed into the trauma room: Simpson creates a vivid linguistic portrait of the event, "A doctor draws blood for the lab . . . a nurse begins inserting a catheter . . . and continues to feed in tubing until [it] reaches the bladder . . . another nurse records pulse and blood pressure." The victim's face is "bloodied" but has not been slashed. His body "shivers" but the room is hot. A nurse asks him questions, but he can only mumble answers. Drunk, he is disconnected from the emergency process. Then Simpson closes the sequence with a startlingly vivid simile:
>
> His left side is swabbed with yellow disinfectant and a doctor injects a local anesthetic. After a few seconds another doctor inserts his finger into the wound. It sinks in all the way to the knuckle. He begins to rotate his finger like a child trying to get a marble out of a milk bottle. The patient screams bloody murder.
>
> Specific language makes this image "realistic," at least realistic enough to make a reader cringe when the "doctor inserts his finger into the wound" and "the patient screams bloody murder."

Beck has organized this discussion paragraph with a clear purpose in mind—to show how Simpson uses specific detail and vivid language to recreate the emergency room experience—which he announces in a topic sentence. The discussion part of the paragraph supports his assertion.

Write a Conclusion That Revisits the Central Point and Discussion

Since your intent in writing about a written work is to represent what the author has achieved, you will probably be wise to remind the reader of your central point and subpoints. This reminder can be done in three or four sentences followed by a brief quotation that brings finality to the essay. Beck used this method to write the conclusion to his essay.

By using vivid language, by carefully arranging events in a stimulus/response structure, and by implying an image of a chaotic world just beyond the emergency room doors, all these descriptive techniques help Simpson create a lasting impression of what the Bellevue emergency team must face during Friday night duty. Is it shocking? Not according to one nurse, who says, "This is nothing, about normal, I'd say. No big deal."

Beck's conclusion is quick and to the point—a wise practice when writing about a written work.

A Student Essay for Examination

Now read Beck's essay, "Friday Night Chaos," as an example of an essay written in response to a written work. Notice that he follows the six guidelines listed above and structures his work with a clear introduction, discussion and conclusion. Also notice that his essay is more than a mere summary of Simpson's "The War Room at Bellevue," it is an analysis of the use of three descriptive techniques.

Friday Night Chaos

George Simpson in "The War Room at Bellevue" describes a typical Friday night in the Bellevue Hospital emergency room to show why its emergency team is so highly respected. Simpson writes, "Why do injured cops drive by a half-dozen other hospitals to be treated at Bellevue? They've seen the

Title: Establishes the atmosphere of Simpson's "Bellevue" essay and the subject of Beck's last discussion paragraph.

The opening sentence embodies three of the six common writing-about-written-works practices: (1) names the author; (2) names the work; and (3) states the work's purpose.

Beck gives a broad summary of Simpson's "Bellevue." Notice that he follows two other common practices: (4) keeps to the present tense; and (5) refers to author by last name only.

Bellevue emergency team in action." The emergency team's shift begins at 9:00 p.m. and goes on into the early morning hours. In vivid detail, Simpson describes the dramatic events that unfold in the emergency room and the parade of characters who populate its corridors—that is, the victims of accidental injuries, poisonings, suicide attempts, miscarriages, overdoses, stabbings, and shootings. From the beginning when "An ambulance backs into the receiving bay, its red and yellow lights flashing . . ." to the end when "blood spatters on the floor" from a knife wound, Simpson captures the grinding pace and traumatic conditions doctors and nurses face while they maintain a stoic professionalism. Although few, if any, of Simpson's readers may ever step inside the Bellevue emergency room, all his readers will leave his essay with a powerful sense that they have been there because of Simpson's effective use of description techniques.

Ends with a central point—that is, Simpson effectively uses description techniques to recreate the emergency room experience—thus following the last common writing-about-written-works paracptice: (6) end the introduction with your essay's central idea.

Simpson's eye for descriptive detail and use of vivid language helps to recreate the emergency room experience for readers. For example, a stabbing victim is rushed into the trauma room. Simpson creates a vivid linguistic portrait of the event, "A doctor draws blood for the lab . . . a

First topic sentence: Sets up the following discussion of Simpson's use of descriptive detail and vivid language.

Beck develops this discussion paragraph by quoting specific phrases and one long passage.

nurse begins inserting a catheter . . . and continues to feed in tubing until [it] reaches the bladder . . . another nurse records pulse and blood pressure." The victim's face is "bloodied" but has not been slashed. His body "shivers" but the room is hot. A nurse asks him questions, but he can only mumble answers. Drunk, he is disconnected from the emergency process. Then Simpson closes the sequence with a startlingly vivid simile:

> His left side is swabbed with yellow disinfectant and a doctor injects a local anesthetic. After a few seconds another doctor inserts his finger into the wound. It sinks in all the way to the knuckle. He begins to rotate his finger like a child trying to get a marble out of a milk bottle. The patient screams bloody murder.

Specific language makes this image "realistic," at least realistic enough to make a reader cringe when the "doctor inserts his finger into the wound" and "the patient screams bloody murder."

Simpson builds dramatic energy in his essay by developing stimulus/response structures. A stimulus incites a reaction which then becomes a stimulus that incites another reaction, and so on. For

Second topic sentence: Sets up discussion of stimulus/response structure. Beck then follows with an extended explanation of stimulus/response. He then presents a sequence from Simpson's "Bellevue" to show the technique at work.

example, imagine a silent movie. A hungry tramp
wanders into a butcher shop where the butcher is
wrapping a string of frankfurters. The tramp, giving in to his hunger, grabs the frankfurters and
races from the door. The butcher shouts and gives
chase, knocking over a delivery man as he charges
into the street. The delivery man, who has dropped
a case of soda, leaps to his feet and runs after
the butcher and the tramp. . . . By the end of the
sequence, most of the town is chasing the tramp
through back alleys and down side streets, causing
havoc as they go. And thus, a stimulus/response
generates action. Simpson uses this technique to
activate his description. For instance, he starts
one sequence with the following stimulus, "An
ambulance backs into a receiving bay, its red and
yellow lights flashing." He follows with a
response, "A split second later, the glass doors
burst open as a nurse and an attendant roll a
mobile stretcher into the lobby," which in turn
becomes a stimulus, when "a nurse screams 'Emergent!'" The stimulus/response continues:

> The lobby explodes with activity as the
> way is cleared to the trauma room. Doctors
> arrive from nowhere and transfer the blood-
> ied body of a black man to the treatment

table. Within seconds his clothes are

stripped away, revealing a stab wound.

This technique creates a dramatic intensity

that adds energy to a descriptive passage that

might otherwise be static.

Perhaps the most powerful technique Simpson

uses to recreate events in the emergency room is

through implication. Without stating a judgment

directly, Simpson creates an unstated image of a

chaotic world. It is in the Bellevue emergency

room that victims with holes blown into their

chests or knives stuck into their backs stagger

from the darkness of angry city streets into the

bright lights of the treatment center. Men and

women of all races and colors have suffered the

unpredictable horrors of city life at night. For

example, from out of the night a black man appears

with a stab wound in his side. A young Hispanic

man brings in his pregnant girl friend who is

bleeding heavily from her vagina. Two police offi-

cers deliver a middle-aged white woman who has

escaped from a psychiatric center and jumped off a

bridge. Ambulance attendants bring in a Hispanic

man with a gapping shotgun wound. A black man who

has drunk poison walks through the doors. This

trauma is inexplicable, the result of random vio-

Third topic sentence: Sets up a discussion of the implied image of chaos.

Beck offers several brief specific examples of the horrors of city life to support his interpretation.

lence or quirks of nature that can only take place in a unpredictable world swept forward by chaotic energy. In contrast to this dark chaos stands the brightly lit emergency room. It is there that doctors and nurses work methodically to repair and save these ravaged bodies. It is there that reason in the form of medical practice brings some order, no matter how temporary, to these disrupted lives.

By using vivid language, by carefully arranging events in a stimulus/response structure, and by implying an image of a chaotic world just beyond the emergency room doors, all these descriptive techniques help Simpson create a lasting impression of what the Bellevue emergency team must face during a Friday night. Is it shocking? Not according to one nurse, "This is nothing, about normal, I'd say. No big deal."

Conclusion: Restates central point and reminds readers of the subpoints. Ends with a quotation that refers back to the entire evening in the Bellevue emergency room.

We'll close with a brief reminder: When writing about a written work, you must do more than merely summarize the work. You must make a point. The summary and quotations you use should support that point.

WRITING TASK—WRITING ABOUT WRITTEN WORKS

Select an essay from "A Collection of Essays" and respond to it in writing. Your response should analyze one aspect of the essay, such as the writer's main point or writing strategies.

Follow the structure explained above—that is, have a clear introduction, discussion, and conclusion, all organized by a central point and subpoints.

GROUP WORK

As a group select an essay to write about. Read the essay and meet to discuss it. First develop a general understanding of the essay. Then analyze the parts to see how they relate to the whole. Finally, identify some possible approaches to writing an essay in response to it.

Come to the next session with a complete draft and copies. Circulate the copies, review the groups' essays, and then share your observations.

24

A Collection of Essays

This chapter is devoted to the essays of fifteen professional writers. Two writing tasks follow each essay, each designed to provide you an entrance into writing your own essay. In other words, these essays are starting places where you can begin to formulate your own responses to experience.

If you have been meeting in work groups, we urge you to continue. Discuss your readings. Develop topics. Review the completed drafts before submitting them for your instructor's evaluation.

Your instructor may assign particular essays to read and respond to, but if yours doesn't then we suggest you begin by browsing the essays to find a writer and subject that holds your attention.

Readings

WHY A DISASTER BRINGS OUT THE BEST IN PEOPLE
Geoffry Cowley

> *"When Dr. James Betts crawled into the smoking ruins of Oakland's collapsed Nimitz Freeway, he had no grounds for assuming he would come out alive."*

TOXINS IN THE MOTHER TONGUE
David James Duncan

> *"By no stretch of the imagination or Bible could that language be considered 'obscene'."*

MATCH TO THE HEART
Gretel Ehrlich

"I have been struck by lightning and I am alive."

SHAMELESS TALK SHOWS
C. Eugene Emery, Jr.

"'No one seriously attempted to correct their inaccurate rendering of historical events, or challenge their reliance on pseudo-biology during their diatribes against Jews and other, unrelated minority groups.'"

BECOMING DESENSITIZED TO HATE WORDS
Ellen Goodman

"The NRA attacked federal agents as 'jackbooted government thugs' who wear 'Nazi bucket helmets and black storm trooper uniforms.'"

IF I WERE A BLACK MAN
Cynthia Heimel

"Would it be a kick to inspire fear just by my very presence?"

THE NEW GENERATION GAP: THIRTEENERS
Neil Howe and William Strauss

"Ads target them as beasts of pleasure and pain who have trouble understanding words longer than one syllable, sentences longer than three words."

THE ELOQUENT SOUNDS OF SILENCE
Pico Iyer

"Silence is something more than just a pause; it is that enchanted place where space is cleared and time is stayed and the horizon itself expands."

IN PRAISE OF GORE
Andrew Klaven

"But enough about me, let's talk about death. Cruel death, sexy death, exciting death: death, that is, on the page and on the screen."

A RESCUE WITHOUT CHEERS
Peter K. Kramer

"Last summer, I was granted a privilege rarely vouchsafed a psychiatrist: I felt a human being return to life under my hands."

IN DEFENSE OF PREJUDICE
Jonathan Rauch

> *"An enlightened and efficient intellectual regime lets a million prejudices bloom, including many that you or I may regard as hateful or grotesque."*

ANATOMY OF AN ASSAULT
Bruce Shapiro

> *"On the evening of August 7, 1994, I was among seven people stabbed and seriously wounded in a coffee bar a few blocks from my house. . . ."*

THE WAR ROOM AT BELLEVUE
George Simpson

> *"Bellevue. The name conjures up images of an indoor war zone: the wounded and bleeding lining the halls, screaming for help while harried doctors in blood-stained smocks rush from stretcher to stretcher, fighting a losing battle against exhaustion and the crushing number of injured."*

BLACK MEN AND PUBLIC SPACE
Brent Staples

> *"My first victim was a woman—white, well dressed, probably in her late twenties."*

SINS OF THE FLESH
Sallie Tisdale

> *"There was never a meal without meat: every afternoon the house filled with the scents of frying oil and roasting flesh."*

Why a Disaster Brings Out the Best in People
GEOFFREY COWLEY

When Dr. James Betts crawled into the smoking ruins of Oakland's collapsed Nimitz Freeway, he had no grounds for assuming he would come out alive. The Bay Area earthquake had slammed the upper span of the two-deck highway onto the lower one, crushing dozens of cars. What remained of the ruined structure was teetering in the aftershocks. Undeterred, Betts and several others inched through the narrow gap to reach 6-year-old Julio Berumen, who lay trapped by the corpse of his mother's friend. The rescue took several hours and involved not only dismembering the corpse with a chain saw but amputating the child's right leg at the knee. Yet Betts insists he never thought twice about going in or staying there.

Nor, it seems, did the scores of bystanders and uniformed rescue workers who combed through collapsed structures seeking signs of life. Nor the Oakland residents who rushed to the freeway to prop it up with makeshift supports. Every human disaster seems to create heroes along with its victims. Their courage sometimes appears more glandular than intentional ("I just did what I had to do," 28-year-old Lenny Skutnik explained after diving into an ice-strewn Potomac River to rescue a drowning plane-crash victim in 1982). But even the most prolonged nightmares spawn astonishing acts of benevolence. A Dutch civilian named Miep Gies risked her life daily for more than two years to feed and shelter the Frank family during the Nazi Holocaust. The 3,000 peasants of Le Chambon, a Huguenot village in south-central France, took similar risks to help Jewish refugees flee the occupation.

Maybe Adam Smith had it right when he remarked that "there seem to be principles in man's nature which interest him in the fortunes of others, and render their happiness necessary to him." But what are those principles? What drives human beings to risk so much for one another? Social scientists think a lot about such questions. Their approaches to human altruism, even their definitions of it, are often disparate, and their findings sometimes raise more questions than they answer. No one can fully explain what propels individuals toward particular acts of bravery. But the research provides a broad framework within which an "interest in the fortunes of others" begins to make sense.

Samuel and Pearl Oliner are concerned specifically with the beneficence of gentiles who sheltered Jews in Nazi Europe. For their 1988 book *The Altruistic Personality*, the two social scientists interviewed several hundred rescuers and compared their testimony to that of "nonrescuers." The rescuers, they found, were more likely to recall having Jewish co-workers, belonging to a Resistance group or having parents who stressed the value of caring for others. So the Oliners conclude that altruism is fueled by "empathy, allegiance to their group or institutional norms, or commitment to principle."

Fine, but what actually motivates people to act on their empathy or allegiances or principles? Social psychologists have developed at least three competing hypotheses. According to the "empathy altruism" model, altruists have no motive beyond the welfare of the person in need. By contrast, the "negative-state relief" model holds that seeing someone in distress causes sadness. Getting involved serves to relieve the sadness, even if it does nothing for the recipient. Finally there's the "empathic joy" hypothesis. Like the sadness-relief model, it assumes that altruistic acts serve to enhance one's own state of mind. But according to this theory, the psychic payoff lies not in trying to help but in witnessing the effect.

Larger riddle: The third model got a boost recently, from an experiment conducted at the University of Washington. Researchers had students watch a taped interview in which a freshman describes her trouble adjusting to college life. Each subject got a chance to tape some words of advice for the distraught student. But they tended to offer help only when assured that she would make another tape, describing the effect of the advice. (According to the other two theories, such feedback shouldn't have mattered.) So perhaps empathetic people act altruistically because they like to see the results. But that raises the question of why seeing the results is so gratifying.

Evolutionary biologists approach the larger riddle from the premise that basic human preferences, like those of other animals, have been shaped over the centuries by the dictates of survival. Contrary to popular belief, Darwinian survival is not a purely competitive struggle among individuals. It consists of *genetic* survival, which can entail *individual* sacrifice. Evolutionary theory says nothing about why some people are more inclined to sacrifice than others. But it does help explain our shared capacity for moral heroism. To understand how, you have to start with what it says about cooperation generally.

From an evolutionary perspective, you would expect to find people charitably inclined toward their kids and other genetic relatives: when kin tend to one another's survival, they tend to their own. Evolutionary theory predicts altruism among non-relatives, too, as long as they have a fair expectation of being repaid. A monkey would further its own survival interest by picking ticks from a companion's back if the companion returned the favor.

Computer models can show how such reciprocal altruism might arise within populations of genetically self-interested individuals. Game theorists start by placing imaginary characters in a situation known as a prisoner's dilemma. Suppose that Jack and Mack are hunter-gatherers. Jack picks berries and Mack kills rabbits. Obviously, both will eat a little better if they share their food. And one may win big if he takes from the other without giving in return. But if both try that trick, neither gains anything.

To see how creatures predisposed to cooperation (C) or defection (D) would fare in a given population, you simply program a computer to spit out strings of Cs and Ds on behalf of generations of Macks and Jacks. The indiscriminate altruists (all C) thrive as long as they're surrounded by others of their kind, but they make easy targets for defectors. Indeed, defectors spread like vermin in a population of these forgiving souls. But once the uncritical altruists are gone, the defectors die out themselves, for lack of anyone to prey on. The most stable strategy is that of the *reciprocal* altruists. Because they're never first to defect, they reap all the rewards of cooperation. But because they play tit-for-tat as soon as they're burned, they're well protected from defectors.

Reciprocity obviously permeates human relationships, bearing on everything from wedding vows to arms control and dinner invitations. But does it shed any light on acts of moral heroism? Would natural selection preserve a tendency to risk one's life for strangers who are unlikely ever to return the favor? Yes and yes, according to Richard Alexander, an evolutionary biologist at the University of Michigan. Reciprocity can take many different forms, he notes in his book *The Biology of Moral Systems.* Helping a stranger might bring status, or even material rewards from others in society. Consider the case of Mark Smith, the Bay Area resident who won a $15,000 sports car in a radio contest but donated it to the Red Cross earthquake fund. Not only did he become an instant folk hero—the radio station matched his gift and gave him another car. Dead heroes don't drive sports cars. But as Alexander observes, their sacrifices can still pay off for their relatives. In many societies, there is a difference between being "a member of the family of a dead hero and being a member of the family of a living [or dead] coward."

Ancient impulses: John Tooby, an anthropologist at Stanford's Center for Advanced Study in the Behavioral Sciences, places a slightly different twist on the riddle of the hero. The question isn't whether a heroic impulse pays off in a modern setting, he says, but how it might have paid off in an ancestral one. Homo sapiens evolved in small hunter-gatherer bands, not in anonymous cities. There was no such thing as a stranger. Averting death by starvation, predation and sickness was the business of daily life, and each group member depended on the others. In evolutionary terms, individuals were under "selective pressure" to increase the likelihood of being rescued. By the logic of reciprocal altruism, those perceived as the best and most loyal rescuers would have stood the greatest chance.

It's only logical, by Tooby's analysis, that we should retain "a spontaneous motivation to help people who are in deep trouble." That the impulse evolved by the cold mechanics of natural selection doesn't make it any less noble. Just ask Julio Berumen.

WRITING TASKS—GEOFFREY COWLEY

1. Write an extended definition of *heroism.* Give yourself time to do prewriting exercises to explore the many types of heroism there may be. Then review the chapter on definition for guidelines to writing the paper.

2. Heroic acts, such as that of Dr. James Betts after the Bay Area earthquake, rightfully receive a good deal of publicity. But for every act like this that captures the attention of the world, countless less dramatic, less well-known acts of heroism or self-sacrifice take place every day. Write an essay about heroism using several less well-known examples. Include your personal definition of heroism early in the paper.

Toxins in the Mother Tongue
DAVID JAMES DUNCAN

1. CENSORED

I was invited, a few years back, to speak to 60 or so high school English students in a small town neither geographically nor demographically far from Sweet Home, Oregon—from whence the Oregon Citizens Alliance and its now nationally famous, selective-Leviticus-quoting anti-homosexual agenda sprang into the national headlines. I was buried in work at the time, but I chose to visit anyhow, when the English teacher who'd invited me mentioned that her students were being forced to read a version of my first novel, "The River Why," from which hundreds of words had been purged by a team of parents armed with indelible black felt pens.

My novel had already been assigned, the teacher explained, and her class was halfway through it, when the mother of a student happened to pick the book up and discover my protagonist's use of language. By no stretch of the imagination or Bible could that language be considered "obscene." Using the Hollywood rating, I believe my novel would receive a PG-13—and I'm embarrassed to add that a G would be more likely than an R. The passages this mother nevertheless proceeded to underline, Xerox and distribute to all comers at a PTA meeting nearly caused the book to be banned outright. But at this same meeting, a couple of brave English teachers stood up and tenaciously defended the morality of my novel's overall aims, and a compromise—which of course satisfied neither side—was reached. The book was called back from the students, duly purged by the parents, reassigned and, as some sort of finale (and, I think, a small act of teacherly revenge upon the vigilantes), I was invited to visit.

The first thing I did upon arriving at the school was paw through an excised copy to see just how black my prose had been deemed to be—and more than a few pages, it turned out, looked rather as if Cajuns had cooked them. But what interested me far more than the quantity of black marks was the unexpected difficulty of the whole censorship endeavor. Hard as these parents had tried to Clorox my prose, a myopic focus on "nasty words" at the expense of attention to narrative flow had resulted in a remarkably self-defeating arbitrariness. They'd taken care, for instance, to spare their big, strapping logging-town teen-agers my protagonist's dislike of the Army Corps of Engineers by converting the phrase "God damn dams" to "God ███ dams." Yet when the same protagonist, one Gus Orviston, told a story about an inch-and-a-half-long scorpion his kid brother lost inside his fly-fishing-crazed family's house, not a word was blackened out of Gus' sur-mise that the lonely creature had ultimately "found and fallen in love with one of my father's mayfly imitations and died of lover's nuts trying to figure out how to screw the thing." Along similar lines, Gus was allowed, in a scene when his lady-love rejected him, to describe himself as a "blubbering Sasquatch . . . my beard full of lint, my teeth yellow, my fly open and undershorts showing there the same color as my teeth, and thick green boogers clogging both my nostrils." Yet when he attempted moments later to describe the bottom of a river as "the place where the slime and mud-suckers and fish-shit live," student innocence had to be protected by the prophylactic "fish-███"

The pattern grew obvious: While my protagonist had been allowed to piss, puke and fornicate, to insult door-to-door evangelists and even to mis-read and reject the Bible with impunity, every time he tried to use an old-fashioned four-letter word—even the innocuous likes of "hell," "damn" or "ass"—down came the indelible markers. Some kind of "suitable-for-mixed-company" politeness was, then, what my censors were out to impose. It always seems to dumbfound and offend the promulgators of such cleanlinesses when the makers and defenders of literature declare even purges like theirs to be not just ineffective but dangerous.

The students' reactions to being censored in this way were mild com-pared to the teachers' reactions and to my own. Most of them considered it an embarrassment—but less of an embarrassment, probably, than a dozen other inescapable facets of high school, small-town and family life. When I read to them the single most censored scene—an exposé of the greed and stupidity of two drunken fishermen—with the missing words restored, the students, on a show of hands, unanimously preferred their drunks to sound like drunks, not Sunday-school teachers. They also agreed unanimously that the purge had been utterly ineffective. But most of them, I felt, were no more able that the parent-censors themselves to perceive any genuine dan-ger in the laundering of their curriculum or literature.

A parable on the danger:

When I was a kid and picked raspberries for pocket money, some of the teen-age boys in the fields used to defy the heat, boredom and row-bosses (most of whom were staid Christian housewives) by regaling us with a series of formulaic, ad-libbed yarns they called "The Adventures of One-Eyed Dirk." To a casual listener, One-Eyed Dirk's were some of the dullest adventures ever endured. We pickers listened with bated breath, though, knowing that it was actually our teen raconteurs, not Dirk, who were hav-ing the adventure. The trick to a One-Eyed Dirk story was to juxtapose strategic verbs and modifiers with names of common objects in a way that enabled you, through the magic of metaphor, to spout pure analogical pornography within the hearing of everyone, yet to proclaim your literal innocence if confronted by an offended adult. An example might go: "Stunned by the size of the musk melons she'd offered him, One-Eyed Dirk groped through his own meager harvest, found the bent green zucchini, sighed at the wormhole in the end, but, with a shy smile, drew it out and thrust it slowly toward her. . . ."

Silly as this kind of thing may be, it underscores the fact that there is virtually nothing a would-be censor can do to guarantee the purity of language, because it is not just words that render language impure. Even "dirty" words tend to be morally neutral until placed in a context—and it is the individual human imagination, more than individual words, that gives a context its moral or immoral twist. One-Eyed Dirk's G-rated zucchinis and wing nuts and valve jobs drive home the point that a bored kid out to tell an off-color yarn can do it with geometry symbols, nautical flags or two rocks and a stick if he wants. The human imagination was designed (by its Designer, if you like) to make rapid-fire, free-form, often-preposterous connections between shapes, words, colors, ideas, desires, sounds. This is its weakness, but also its wondrous strength. The nature of the imagination itself is, at bottom, why organized censorship never works. And it is also why every ferociously determined censorship effort sooner or later escalates into fascistic political agendas, burnings at the stake, dunking-chairs, gulags, pogroms and other literal forms of purge. Obviously, the only fail-safe way to eliminate impurities from human tongues, minds and cultures is to eliminate human life itself.

2. A LIBERAL INCONSISTENCY

The censors of my novel achieved a laughable inconsistency by zeroing in on "four-letter words" and letting the narrative imagery ride. But there seems to me to be a culturally accepted yet comparable inconsistency practiced by some of our most respected publications. Scores of nationally important newspapers and magazines refuse to print some of the very words purged from my novel by small-town parents belonging to the Oregon Citizens Alliance. The national publications characterize their own refusal as "editorial policy." The same publications characterize the Alliance parents' refusal as "religious fanaticism" or "fascism."

How to work it out?

We must begin, I think, by admitting that an editorial policy is, in fact, a kind of fascism. In the litigious context of today's censorship wars, the admirable editorial gentility of, say, a William Shawn is, unfortunately, an indefensible inconsistency. I'm reminded of Austrian novelist Heimito von Doderer's lines: "Weapons that we have not loaded are forced into our hands. And still we fire the shot." Anyone who believes that censorship tends toward fascism is logically forced to admit that the urbane Mr. Shawn used to unwittingly duplicate the small-town vigilantes' "fascistic tendencies" by refusing to print the "s" or "f" words. And those who can't accept this—those who choose to believe that such a word in Shawn's New Yorker would have served no compelling purpose, would have offended many readers and would have cost the publication subscription money—must also admit that there is no compelling reason for small-town parents not to wade through their children's school libraries eliminating "offensive" words and "non-compelling" books.

I am not suggesting that all periodicals and newspapers must print such words. I am suggesting that the average citizen's desire to improve the quality of language or art is born, in rural Oregon as it is in Manhattan, of an increasingly desperate concern for the health of the culture; that, given the rampant decay of the quality of American life, this concern is not about to leave us; that big-city editors, small-town parents, gay artists, unemployed loggers, Baptist preachers and working novelists express their desperation in different ways; and that we are united—and should, I think, be humbled—by our own inconsistencies.

But, as Krishna tells the reluctant archer, Arjuna, in the Bhagavad Gita, we also have our own individual dharmas to follow. Loggers need trees to remain loggers; preachers need full pews and offering plates; and writers need unexpurgated bookstores, libraries and lexicons. When Arjuna balked on the eve of battle, seeing that the opposing army included beloved old teachers, relatives and friends, Krishna told him that our hopes are vain and our labours futile till we see ourselves one with the Maker of the million faces. But Krishna also advised that, with this Oneness at heart, Arjuna should go forth and play his archer's role to the best of his devastating ability. That said, I feel that I—as a novelist engaged in the ongoing fight for every writer's and reader's freedom—must now do my best to destroy, in argument, even a few beloved old teachers, relatives and friends.

3. THE MORALITY OF LITERATURE

Ever since the advent of the printing press, there have been readers who slip from enthusiasm for a favorite text into the belief that the words in that text embody truth: do not just symbolize it, but literally embody it. Not till the past few decades, though, has an alliance of American "conservative Christians" declared that this slip is, in fact, the true Christian religion, that a single bookful of words is Truth, and that this Truth should become the sole basis of the nation's political, legal and cultural life. The growing clout of this faction does not change the uncological aberrance of its stance: Fundamentalists defy the written word in a way that—in light of every Scripture-based Wisdom Tradition in the world, including Christianity's 2,000-year-old own—is not just naive. It is idolatrous. Words in books can remind us of truth, and occasionally help awaken us to it. But in themselves words are just paint, and writers are just painters—Old Testament and Gospel writers, bhakti and Sufi saints, Tibetan lamas and Zen masters included. There are, of course, crucial differences between Scripture and belles-lettres, and between inspired and merely inventive prose. But the authors of both write with human hands, and in human tongues. Let's not overestimate the power of literature.

Let's not underestimate it either. As readers we are asked on Page One to lay our hand upon the back of an author's as he or she begins to paint a world. If the author's strokes somehow repel or betray our trust, if our concentration is lax or if we're biased or closed in some way, then no hand-in-hand magic can occur. But when a great word-painter is read with reciprocally great concentration and trust, an incredible thing happens. First, the painter's hand disappears. Then so does our own. Till there is only the living world of the painting.

This disappearance, the way we lose ourselves in the life of a story, is, I believe, the greatest truth in any literature, be it discursive or dramatic, sacred or secular. It is at any rate the greatest describable truth, because for the duration of the disappearance we possess no *I* with which to describe anything outside the text in which we're lost. Like all great truths, it is simultaneously a sacrifice (of the reader's ego) and a resurrection (of the world, the characters and the ideas in the text). And like all great truths, it is not brought about by any kind of mental computations upon literal meanings of sentences or words. All that's required is a willing immersion of imagination and mind in the dynamic pulse and flow of written language.

In light of this great truth, the most valid form of censorship is that practiced by authors themselves. It is the duty of all writers to scrupulously destroy or revise any or all writing that fails to let them vanish into the life of their own language. What authors are morally obligated to censor from their work is their own incompetence. Nothing more, nothing less. Simple as it sounds, it keeps most of us more than busy. Ezra Pound was quoted as saying, "Fundamental accuracy of statement is the one sole morality of literature." If, in other words, a story requires that its writer create a mountain and further requires that this mountain be imposing, the immoral mountain is not the one with the pair of unmarried hikers copulating on a remote slope. It is the mountain that fails to be imposing. The "sole morality of literature" demands that an author contemplate his peak till frozen clouds begin to swirl round its summit; till the bones of lost climbers and mountain goats appear deep in its crevasses; till its ice and stone mass haunts and daunts us like a cold moon rising not in some safe distance but from the scree at our very feet.

And the same goes—with all due apologies to literary inquisitors everywhere—for the imposing penis. This is not to say that all penises are, according to Pound's dictum, moral. Indeed, a gratuitously shocking penis, an extraneous-to-our-story penis, a hey-look-at-me-for-the-sake-of-nothing-but-me penis, however imposing, is literarily immoral (that is, incompetent), because by jarring the reader from the narrative or argumentative flow into a mood of "What's this stupid penis doing here?" the author has undermined the greatest truth of his tale; i.e., our ability to immerse ourselves in it. But once the dramatic demands of the story itself have requested of its author an imposing penis, it is the one-pointed, apoplectic-veined archetype, the one that has us crossing imaginary legs before we know it (or opening them, as the literary case may be), that is the moral penis, and it is the church, quasi-religious political cult or government agency that seeks to zip a zipper over it that is immoral.

"But how could the decision of male members, filthy language, perversion, sadomasochism, sexual violence and so on ever be wrong? Why, in God's name, shouldn't we censor literature, art and human behavior itself in order to safeguard the purity of our children and our culture?" These are the fundamentalist questions—the Helms, Falwell and Robertson questions. Those who ask them seem to some of us to pride themselves on their amnesia, considering how recently the likes of Stalin, Hitler, McCarthy and Khomeini have asked the same sort of questions. But it's a widespread amnesia. So here are two more answers to the questions—one civil and American, one literary and Christian. First the civil:

All citizens of this country possess a constitutional right to detest the work of any writer or artist they choose to detest—and to criticize that writer or artist, in public and in private, in the most filthy language they are able to devise. I, to cite the handiest possible example, found the few pages of Bret Easton Ellis' "American Psycho" that I was able to read to be as crassly sensationalistic and literarily incompetent, despite a glib facility with sentence-making, as anything I've ever read. But to say that much satisfies me. And it's all the fun the Constitution allows: To carry my disgust further, to try to summon the courage, compose the propaganda, induce the paranoia and generate the political clout that would let me and my ideological clones ban or purge one overpaid hack is simply not the way that people in this tenuously free country long ago agreed to do things.

"The old Irish bards, when asked to recite certain stories, would sometimes say to their audience: " 'Tis an evil tale for telling. I canna' make it." And hearing this, their listeners would request a different tale. I believe Ellis, and Americans in general, are dying for a dose of this bardic wisdom. Yet sickening stories are an unavoidable byproduct of a sick culture, and a crucial diagnostic tool for anyone who seeks a cure. Writers need the freedom to invoke body parts, mayhem and twisted visions for many profound reasons, among them (jumping metaphors) the same reason that chefs need the freedom to invoke curry, garlic, extreme heat and many other things we can't tolerate in straight doses. There is no mention of jalopeño peppers in the Christian Scriptures, and neither the average child nor the average televangelist can handle them. That's no reason to legislate them clean out of our *huevos rancheros.*

Now the literary and Christian argument: In the slender classic, "An Experiment in Criticism," the non-literalistic but indefatigably Christian professor of literature, C. S. Lewis, wrote that our access to a diverse and uncensored literature is spiritually crucial because "We demand windows. [And] literature . . . is a series of windows, even of doors. . . . Good reading . . . can be described either as an enlargement or as a temporary annihilation of the self. But that is an old paradox: 'he that loseth his life shall save it.' We therefore delight to enter into other men's beliefs . . . even though we think them untrue. And into their passions, though we think them depraved. . . . Literary experience heals the wound, without undermining the privilege, of individuality. . . . In reading great literature I become a thousand men and yet remain myself. . . . Here, as in worship, in love, in moral action, and in knowing, I transcend myself; and am never more myself than when I do."

4. WHY NO ARGUMENT AGAINST FUNDAMENTALIST CENSORSHIP WORKS

My home state, Oregon, according to its Library Association was third in the nation in 1992 in the number of challenges to the printed word in schools, libraries and bookstores. The vast majority of these challenges were made by people who consider themselves fundamentalist Christians. I've just provided two arguments against such challenges. But I don't for a minute believe that either of my arguments—nor any conceivable argument resembling them in category—will persuade a single committed fundamentalist that censorship is an ineffective or negative or potentially deadly cultural strategy. The only way to convince a fundamentalist of such a thing would be with a fundamentalist argument. And there are none. Fundamentalism and censorship have always gone hand in hand.

My aim here is literary, not theological. But for literary reasons I am compelled to point out that a theologically motivated, politically powerful cult is out to simplify and "improve" our literature, art, science, sexual choices. Constitution and souls. And I see no effective choice, in defending all of the above, but to confront the theological basis of the cult itself. When I see poets and authors capable of making crowds weep at the beauty of their words reduced to explaining to some half-sentient TV news hound that they are trying to defend freedom of expression, not the freedom of pedophiles, I feel that some huge strategic error is being committed.

Literary people, being comparatively deep, are often mystified and stymied by the relentless shallowness of the fundamentalist attacks. But the beligerent mind-set and self-insulating dogmas that enable this cult to thrive are neither complicated nor invulnerable to criticism. To treat the earth as disposable and the Bible as God, turn that God into a political action committee, equate effrontery with "evangelism," disingenuous televised prattle with "prayer" and call the result "Christianity" is hardly an invincible position. Evangelists such as Pat Robertson subsidize their organizations by manufacturing a series of carefully designed "moral emergencies" that threaten "us," or better yet "our children." Rather than defending various scapegoats over the din of fundamentalist alarms and media sirens, I'd like to take a brief look at the manufacturers themselves.

5. AMERICAN FUNDAMENTALISM

All of the famous televangelists, all the leaders of the contemporary Bible-based political alliances and most of the recent censors of school libraries, crusaders against homosexuality and politically active fundamentalists in general share a conviction that their political and social causes and agendas are approved of, if not inspired, by no less a being than God. This enviable conviction is less enviably arrived at by accepting on faith, hence as fact, that the Christian Bible, pared down into American TV English is God's "word" to mankind, that this same Bible is "His" only word to mankind, and that the fundamentalist's unprecedentedly literalistic slant on this Bible is the one true slant.

The position is remarkably self-insulating. Possessing little knowledge of and no respect for the world's many rich spiritual, literary and cultural traditions, these people have no conceptions or models of love and compassion but their own and can therefore honestly, even good-heartedly, say that it is out of "Christian" compassion and a sort of "tough love" for others that they seek to impose on all others their God, Bible, and slant.

The position is also far from unprecedented. Well-known variations on the theme include the Inquisitor's tough love for heretics, the conquistador's tough love for Incans, Aztecs and Mayans, the Puritan's tough love for witches, the white Western settler's tough love for Native Americans, and so on. Every Bible-reifying crusader group from the European prototype to my home state's Citizens Alliance has seen itself as fighting to make its own or some other community more "Christian." The result, among contemporary non-fundamentalists, has been a growing revulsion toward anything that chooses to call itself "Christian." Yet to this day, I see no more crucial text, in defusing fundamentalist crusades, than the four books of the Gospels, and no more important question to keep asking all such crusaders than whether there is anything truly Christian—that is, anything compassionate, self-abnegating, empathetic and enemy-loving—about their various crusades.

This being a literary essay, it's only fair to point out that fundamentalists are book lovers, too. They just happen to have invested so much brittle love in the first three (Genesis, Exodus, Leviticus) and final (Revelations) books of the one black-covered volume that their ability to enjoy, comprehend or even tolerate other volumes has been drastically curtailed. But another question—again, both literary and theological—that needs to be asked is: How brittle can one's love become before it ceases to be love at all?

The ex-Dominican priest and writer Matthew Fox answers this question by calling contemporary evangelical fundamentalism "Christofascism." But when I've tried to deploy this term, it has felt noxious upon my tongue. What's the difference between Fox or me shouting "Christofascist!" at fundamentalists and Rush Limbaugh shouting "feminazi!" at feminists? Both coinages are a calculated descent into the realm of name-calling. Of course, in the escalating verbal and political warfare between fundamentalism and arts and letters, name-calling has become so difficult to avoid that even actual names have become a form of name-calling. If you want to attack conservative Christianity, for instance, you describe the shenanigans of the Jimmys Bakker and Swaggart; and if you want to demonstrate the decadence of literature and art, you describe the imaginative abominations of Bret Easton Ellis and rectal bullwhips of Robert Mapplethorpe. But with "Christofascism" supposedly lurking to the right of us, and "feminazism" to the left, I am inclined to place Mahatma Gandhi front and center, warning: "Be careful of the means you use to fight the fascist, lest you become fascists yourselves."

The fundamentalist right is outspoken in its desire to simplify and control my vocabulary, my profession and my spirituality. What I feel compelled to do in response is insist upon a distinction. There is a complex 2,000-year-old religious and cultural tradition that calls itself Christianity. There is a plethora of comparatively new factions of Bible-idolizing literalists who call themselves by the same name. But they are not the same. To refer to Origen, Oral Roberts, Dante, Billy Graham, St. Francis, Jerry Falwell, Pat Robertson and Lady Julian of Norwich all as "Christians" stretches the meaning clear out of the term. The word "humanoid" is as helpful. The gulf between traditional Christianity and American fundamentalism is vast. A Francis Schaeffer text used to instruct Baptist seminarians all over the United States on the world's supposed cults, doctrinal blunders and "other religions" defines and illustrates the concept and history of what it calls "mysticism" by analyzing the writings of Henry Miller. To teach that mysticism equals Henry Miller is not teaching at all. It's an attempt to churn out ideological clones who want no "windows," no insight into others, no enlargement or effacement of self—clones content to read and idolatrize their one book, willfully misread all others and deliberately use the resulting curtailment of comprehension, pleasure and tolerance as a unifying principle.

6. SHAME AND REVERENCE

That fly-fishing protagonist of my censored novel, Gus, voiced some serious reservations about the being fundamentalists so possessively refer to as "God." But a literary morality problem that Gus (and I) ran into in telling his story was that, after a climactic all-night adventure with a river and a huge chinook salmon, he had a sudden, transrational (or, in the old Christian lexicon, "mystical") experience that left him too overwhelmed to speak with Pound's "fundamental accuracy of statement," yet too grateful to speak not at all. The paradox this presented my protagonist was, and is, autobiographical. As the recipient of several such detonations, I felt bound by gratitude to speak. But as a lifelong victim of the pollution of the Christian lexicon, I felt compelled to speak in non-Christian terms. Gus' account of his ineffable experience did not once invoke the word *God*. But it did speak of transcendent love, and of a being so God-like that in the end he dubbed it "the Ancient One."

Reader reactions to this climax have been neatly divided. Those who have experienced analogous detonations have sometimes been so moved by the scene that their eyes filled as they thanked me for writing it; and those who have experienced no such detonation have as often asked why I ruined a dang good fishin' yarn with mystical mumbo jumbo. Odd as it may sound, I agree with both reactions. Both are perfectly honest. What more should a writer want from a reader? What more, for that matter, can mortals—be they skeptic or mystic—offer the Absolute? A French novelist/philosopher, Rene Daumal, describes the paradox I faced perfectly. He wrote:

"I swear to you that I have to force myself to write or to pronounce this word: God. It is a noise I make with my mouth or a movement of the fingers that hold my pen. To pronounce or to write this word makes me ashamed. What is real here is that shame. . . . Must I never speak of the Unknowable because it would be a lie? Must I speak of the Unknowable because I know that I proceed from it and am bound to bear witness to it? This contradiction is the prime mover of my best thoughts."

Another word for this shame, in my opinion, is reverence. And American fundamentalists, speaking of the Unknowable, too often lack this quality. Their preachers proudly pronounce the word "God," define it, worship their own definition, impose it upon all adherents, offer an eternal reward for this arrogance, promise eternal torment to all who fail to agree. What an abyss between this and the self-giving Christianity of a Francis, an Eckhart, a Martin Luther King, Jr. What a gulf, too, between this and the contemporary Amish—who practice no evangelism, who tease those who quote the Bible too often (calling them "Scripture smart") and who consider it laughable to pronounce oneself "saved," since God alone is capable of making such weighty decisions.

And what a gulf between fundamentalism and American literature. If the latter arrives at any general theological conclusion as to what we owe to a divinity, it is probably this: Better to be honest to God—even if that means stating one's complete lack of belief in any such being—than to force one's imagination and mind into the mold of a ready-made dogma. In literature,

as in life, there are ways of disbelieving in God that are more compassionate, and in that sense more "Christian," than many forms of orthodox belief.
There are atheists, for example, who believe as they do because the general
state of the world and of humanity makes it impossible for them to conceive
of a creator who is anything but compassionless, remiss or cruel. Rather
than consider God cruel, they choose disbelief. To my mind this is a back-
handed form of reverence; a beautiful kind of "shame."

It seems to upset many fundamentalists that literature's answer to the
God question is virtually the same as the Constitution's. There is also no
doubt that the openness that our literature and form of government encourage results in a theological cacophony and mood of irritable independence
that bear no resemblance to the unison docility that reigns in the average
church. But America is a country, and America's a literature that stakes its
life on the belief that this cacophony and independence are not only legal,
but essential to our ultimate health.

Edward Abbey remains welcome in our libraries, as he will never be in
our churches, to say, "God is Love? Not bloody likely!" Goethe remains
welcome to reply to him: "As a man is, so is his God; therefore God is often
an object of mockery." And readers remain welcome to draw their own
conclusions.

My mother tongue, the language my parents and grandparents used to
draw me from virtual non-being into the naming of and engagement with
life, is English. And there are only so many English words with which to
describe the eternal verities and the journey of the soul. One of the irre-
placeable words in this language is *God.* Yet the God of organized fundamentalism, as advertised daily through a variety of mass media, is a supra-
mundane Caucasian male as furious with humanity's failure to live by a few
arbitrarily chosen lines from the Book of Leviticus as He is oblivious to His
spokepersons' failure to live by the militant compassion of the Gospels.

As surely as I feel love and need for my wife and children, I feel love
and need for a God. But this feeling has nothing whatever to do with supra-
mundane Caucasian males. And I am not troubled by this. If the fundamentalists' God were indeed the One and Only, the likes of Gandhi and Mother
Teresa, Tolstoy and Dostoyevsky, Jung and Merton, Black Elk and Chief
Joseph, Thoreau and John Muir, Rumi and Hafiz, John of the Cross and
Julian of Norwich, Lao-tzu and Bodhidharma, Kabir and Mira Bai, Shunryu
and D. T. Suzuki, Valmiki and Socrates, Dogen and Dante, would all be
heretics, atheists and infidels—because the Absolute they all worship is an
infinitely different being.

I suspect the situation to be rather different. I suspect the odd "evangelical" truth of the matter to be that fundamentalists need non-fundamentalists of all stripes—be they mystics, agnostics, Amish, artists, writers, scientists, believers, nonbelievers—in such a big way that it may not be going
too far to say they need us for their salvation. As Mark Twain pointed out a

century ago, the only really prominent Christian community that fundamentalists have ever managed to establish in any of the worlds is hell.

WRITING TASKS—DAVID JAMES DUNCAN

1. The question of censorship is always with us. Although most of us profess a strong belief in freedom of speech as protected by the First Amendment to the U.S. Constitution, there may be times when we are repelled, sickened, or outraged by the words of a book, article, film, or song, or the images in a work of art. At such times, we may feel that enough is enough and be willing to see the First Amendment as just a guiding principle rather than an absolute prohibition of censorship. We might be willing to compromise in order to eliminate the offensive words or images. Write an essay exploring your thoughts on such a situation. For preparation, read section 3 of Duncan's essay again and spend some time making a prewriting list of your honest thoughts about Duncan's arguments as applied to your own experience.

2. In recent years we have seen widespread efforts by some groups to purify the speech of the marketplace and the campus by aggressively discouraging the use of derogatory words referring to gender, ethnic group, race, physical ability, physical appearance, and so on. Duncan expresses a different view in paragraph 8: "Obviously, the only fail-safe way to eliminate impurities from human tongues, minds and cultures is to eliminate human life itself." In other words, it's impossible. Write an essay in which you defend either side of this argument.

From *Match to the Heart*
GRETEL EHRLICH

Deep in an ocean. I am suspended motionless. The water is gray. That's all there is, and before that? My arms are held out straight, cruciate, my head and legs hang limp. Nothing moves. Brown kelp lies flat in mud and fish are buried in liquid clouds of dust. There are no shadows or sounds. Should there be? I don't know if I am alive, but if not, how do I know I am dead? My body is leaden, heavier than gravity. Gravity is done with me. No more sinking and rising or bobbing in currents. There is a terrible feeling of oppression with no oppressor. I try to lodge my mind against some boundary; some reference point, but the continent of the body dissolves . . .

A single heartbeat stirs gray water. Blue trickles in, just a tiny stream. Then a long silence.

Another heartbeat. This one is louder, as if amplified. Sound takes shape: it is a snowplow moving grayness aside like a heavy snowdrift. I can't tell if I'm moving, but more blue water flows in. Seaweed begins to undulate, then a whole kelp forest rises from the ocean floor. A fish swims past and looks at me. Another heartbeat drives through dead water, and another, until I am surrounded by blue.

Sun shines above all this. There is no pattern to the way its glint comes free and falls in long knives of light. My two beloved dogs appear. They flank me like tiny rockets, their fur pressed against my ribs. A leather harness holds us all together. The dogs climb toward light, pulling me upward at a slant from the sea.

I have been struck by lightning and I am alive.

Before electricity carved its blue path toward me, before the negative charge shot down from cloud to ground, before "streamers" jumped the positive charge back up from ground to cloud, before air expanded and contracted producing loud pressure pulses I could not hear because I was already dead, I had been walking.

When I started out on foot that August afternoon, the thunderstorm was blowing in fast. On the face of the mountain, a mile ahead, hard westerly gusts and sudden updrafts collided, pulling black clouds apart. Yet the storm looked harmless. When a distant thunderclap scared the dogs, I called them to my side and rubbed their ears: "Don't worry, you're okay as long as you're with me."

I woke in a pool of blood, lying on my stomach some distance from where I should have been, flung at an odd angle to one side of the dirt path. The whole sky had grown dark. Was it evening, and if so, which one? How many minutes or hours had elapsed since I lost consciousness, and where were the dogs? I tried to call out to them but my voice didn't work. The muscles in my throat were paralyzed and I couldn't swallow. Were the dogs dead? Everything was terribly wrong: I had trouble seeing, talking, breathing, and I couldn't move my legs or right arm. Nothing remained in my memory—no sounds, flashes, smells, no warnings of any kind. Had I been shot in the back? Had I suffered a stroke or heart attack? These thoughts were dark pools in sand.

The sky was black. Was this a storm in the middle of the day or was it night with a storm traveling through? When thunder exploded over me, I knew I had been hit by lightning.

The pain in my chest intensified and every muscle in my body ached. I was quite sure I was dying. What was it one should do or think or know? I tried to recall the Buddhist instruction regarding dying—which position to lie in, which direction to face. Did the "Lion's position" taken by the Buddha mean lying on the left or the right? And which sutra to sing? Oh yes, the Heart Sutra . . . gaté, gaté, paragaté . . . form and formlessness. Paradox and cosmic jokes. Surviving after trying to die "properly" would be truly funny, but the chances of that seemed slim.

Other words drifted in: how the "gateless barrier" was the gate through which one passes to reach enlightenment. Yet if there was no gate, how did one pass through? Above me, high on the hill, was the gate on the ranch that lead nowhere, a gate I had mused about often. Now its presence made me smile. Even when I thought I had no aspirations for enlightenment, too much effort in that direction was being expended. How could I learn to slide, yet remain aware?

To be struck by lightning: what a way to get enlightened. That would be the joke if I survived. It seemed important to remember jokes. My thinking did not seem connected to the inert body that was in such terrible pain. Sweep the mind of weeds, I kept telling myself—that's what years of Buddhist practice had taught me. . . . But where were the dogs, the two precious ones I had watched being born and had raised in such intimacy and trust? I wanted them with me. I wanted them to save me again.

It started to rain. Every time a drop hit bare skin there was an explosion of pain. Blood crusted my left eye. I touched my good hand to my heart, which was beating wildly, erratically. My chest was numb, as if it had been sprayed with novocaine. No feeling of peace filled me. Death was a bleakness, a grayness about which it was impossible to be curious or relieved. I loved those dogs and hoped they weren't badly hurt. If I didn't die soon, how many days would pass before we were found, and when would the scavengers come? The sky was dark, or was that the way life flew out of the body, in a long tube with no light at the end? I lay on the cold ground waiting. The mountain was purple, and sage stirred against my face. I knew I had to give up all this, then my own body and all my thinking. Once more I lifted my head to look for the dogs but, unable to see them, I twisted myself until I faced east and tried to let go of all desire.

When my eyes opened again I knew I wasn't dead. Images from World War II movies filled my head: of wounded soldiers dragging themselves across a field, and if I could have laughed—that is, made my face work into a smile and get sounds to discharge from my throat—I would have. God, it would have been good to laugh. Instead, I considered my options: either lie there and wait for someone to find me—how many days or weeks would that take?—or somehow get back to the house. I calmly assessed what might be wrong with me—stroke, cerebral hemorrhage, gunshot wound—but it was bigger than I could understand. The instinct to survive does not rise from particulars: a deep but general misery rollercoasted me into action. I tried to propel myself on my elbows but my right arm didn't work. The wind had swung around and was blowing in from the east. It was still a dry storm with only sputtering rain, but when I raised myself up, lightning fingered the entire sky.

It is not true that lightning never strikes the same place twice. I had entered a shower of sparks and furious brightness and, worried that I might be struck again, watched as lightning touched down all around me. Years before, in the high country, I'd been hit by lightning: an electrical charge had rolled down an open meadow during a fearsome thunderstorm, surged up the legs of my horse, coursed through me, and bounced a big spark off the top of my head. To be struck again—and this time it was a direct hit—what did it mean?

The feeling had begun to come back into my legs and after many awkward attempts, I stood. To walk meant lifting each leg up by the thigh, moving it forward with my hands, setting it down. The earth felt like a peach that had split open in the middle; one side moved up while the other side moved down and my legs were out of rhythm. The ground rolled the way it does during an earthquake and the sky was tattered book pages waving in different directions. Was the ground liquifying under me, or had the molecular composition of my body deliquesced? I struggled to piece together fragments. Then it occurred to me that my brain was torn and that's where the blood had come from.

I walked. Sometimes my limbs held me, sometimes they didn't. I don't know how many times I fell but it didn't matter because I was making slow progress toward home.

Home—the ranch house—was about a quarter of a mile away. I don't remember much about getting there. My concentration went into making my legs work. The storm was strong. All the way across the basin, lightning lifted parts of mountains and sky into yellow refulgence and dropped them again, only to lift others. The inside of my eyelids turned gold and I could see the outlines of things through them. At the bottom of the hill I opened the door to my pickup and blew the horn with the idea that someone might hear me. No one came. My head had swollen to an indelicate shape. I tried to swallow—I was so thirsty—but the muscles in my throat were still paralyzed and I wondered when I would no longer be able to breathe.

Inside the house, sounds began to come out of me. I was doing crazy things, ripping my hiking boots off because the bottoms of my feet were burning, picking up the phone when I was finally able to scream. One of those times, someone happened to be on the line. I was screaming incoherently for help. My last conscious act was to dial 911.

Dark again. Pressing against sore ribs, my dogs pulled me out of the abyss, pulled and pulled. I smelled straw. My face was on tatami. I opened my eyes, looked up, and saw neighbors. Had they come for my funeral? The phone rang and I heard someone give directions to the ambulance driver, who was lost. A "first responder," an EMT from town who has a reputation with the girls, leaned down and asked if he could "touch me" to see if there were any broken bones. What the hell, I thought. I was going to die anyway. Let him have his feel. But his touch was gentle and professional, and I was grateful.

I slipped back into unconsciousness and when I woke again two EMT's were listening to my heart. I asked them to look for my dogs but they wouldn't leave me. Someone else in the room went outside and found Sam and Yaki curled up on the porch, frightened but alive. Now I could rest. I felt the medics jabbing needles into the top of my hands, trying unsuccessfully to get IVs started, then strapping me onto a backboard and carrying me out the front door of the house, down steps, into lightning and rain, into what was now a full-blown storm.

The ambulance rocked and slid, slamming my bruised body against the metal rails of the gurney. Every muscle was in violent spasm and there was a place on my back near the heart that burned. I heard myself yell in pain. Finally the EMT's rolled up towels and blankets and wedged them against my arms, shoulders, hips, and knees so the jolting of the vehicle wouldn't dislodge me. The ambulance slid down into ditches, struggled out, bumped from one deep rut to another. I asked to be taken to the hospital in Cody, but they said they were afraid my heart might stop again. As it was, the local hospital was thirty-five miles away, ten of them dirt, and the trip took more than an hour.

Our arrival seemed a portent of disaster—and an occasion for comedy. I had been struck by lightning around five in the afternoon. It was now 9:00 P.M. Nothing at the hospital worked. Their one EKG machine was nonfunctional, and jokingly the nurses blamed it on me. "Honey, you've got too much electricity in your body," one of them told me. Needles were jammed into my hand—no one had gotten an IV going yet—and the doctor on call hadn't arrived, though half an hour had elapsed. The EMT's kept assuring me: "Don't worry, we won't leave you here." When another nurse, who was filling out an admission form, asked me how tall I was, I answered: "Too short to be struck by lightning."

> *"Electrical injury often results in ventricular fibrillation and injury to the medullary centers of the brain. Immediately after electric shock patients are usually comatose, apneic, and in circulatory collapse. . . ."*

When the doctor on call—the only doctor in town, waddled into what they called the emergency room, my aura, he said, was yellow and gray—a soul in transition. I knew that he had gone to medical school but had never completed a residency and had been barred from ER or ICU work in the hospitals of Florida, where he had lived previously. Yet I was lucky. Florida has many lightning victims, and unlike the doctors I would see later, he at least recognized the symptoms of a lightning strike. The tally sheet read this way: I had suffered a hit by lightning which caused ventricular fibrillation—cardiac arrest—though luckily my heart started beating again. Violent contractions of muscles when one is hit often causes the body to fly through the air: I was flung far and hit hard on my left side, which may have caused my heart to start again, but along with that fortuitous side effect, I sustained a concussion, broken ribs, a possible broken jaw, and lacerations above the eye. The paralysis below my waist and up through the chest and throat—called kerauno-paralysis—is common in lightning strikes and almost always temporary, but my right arm continued to be almost useless. Fernlike burns—arborescent erythema—covered my entire body. These occur when the electrical charge follows tracings of moisture on the skin—rain or sweat—thus the spidery red lines.

> *"Rapid institution of fluid and electrolyte therapy is essential with guidelines being the patient's urine output, hematocrit, osmolality, central venous pressure, and arterial blood gases. . . ."*

The nurses loaded me onto a gurney. As they wheeled me down the hall to my room, a front wheel fell off and I was slammed into the wall. Once I was in bed, the deep muscle aches continued, as did the chest pains. Later, friends came to visit. Neither doctor nor nurse had cleaned the cuts on my head, so Laura, who had herded sheep and cowboyed on all the ranches where I had lived and whose wounds I had cleaned when my saddle horse dragged her across a high mountain pasture, wiped blood and dirt from my face, arms, and hands with a cool towel and spooned yogurt into my mouth.

I was the only patient in the hospital. During the night, sheet lightning inlaid the walls with cool gold. I felt like an ancient, mummified child who had been found on a rock ledge near our ranch: bound tightly, unable to move, my dead face tipped backwards toward the moon.

In the morning, my regular doctor, Ben, called from Massachusetts, where he was vacationing, with this advice: "Get yourself out of that hospital and go somewhere else, anywhere." I was too weak to sign myself out, but Julie, the young woman who had a summer job on our ranch, retrieved me in the afternoon. She helped me get dressed in the cutoffs and torn T-shirt I had been wearing, but there were no shoes, so, barefoot, I staggered into Ben's office, where a physician's assistant kindly cleansed the gashes in my head. Then I was taken home.

Another thunderstorm slammed against the mountains as I limped up the path to the house. Sam and Yaki took one look at me and ran. These dogs lived with me, slept with me, understood every word I said, and I was too sick to find them, console them—even if they would have let me.

The next day my husband, who had just come down from the mountains where he worked in the summer, took me to another hospital. I passed out in the admissions office, was loaded onto a gurney, and taken for a CAT scan. No one bothered to find out why I had lost consciousness. Later, in the emergency unit, the doctor argued that I might not have been struck by lightning at all, as if I had imagined the incident. "Maybe a meteor hit me," I said, a suggestion he pondered seriously. After a blood panel and a brief neurological exam, which I failed—I couldn't follow his finger with my eyes or walk a straight line—he promptly released me.

> "Patients should be monitored electrocardiographically for at least 24 hours for significant arrhythmias which often have delayed onset. . . ."

It was difficult to know what was worse: being in a hospital where nothing worked and nobody cared, or being alone on an isolated ranch hundreds of miles from decent medical care.

In the morning I staggered into the kitchen. My husband, from whom I had been separated for three months, had left at 4:00 A.M. to buy cattle in another part of the state and would not be back for a month. Alone again, it was impossible to do much for myself. In the past I'd been bucked off, stiff and sore plenty of times but this felt different: I had no sense of equilibrium. My head hurt, every muscle in my body ached as if I had a triple dose of the flu, and my left eye was swollen shut and turning black and blue. Something moved in the middle of the kitchen floor. I was having difficulty seeing, but then I did see: a rattlesnake lay coiled in front of the stove. I reeled around and dove back into bed. Enough tests of character. I closed my eyes and half-slept. Later, when Julie came to the house, she found the snake and cut off its head with a shovel.

My only consolation was that the dogs came back. I had chest pains and all day Sam lay with his head against my heart. I cleaned a deep cut over Yaki's eye. It was half an inch deep but already healing. I couldn't tell if the dogs were sick or well, I was too miserable to know anything except that Death resided in the room: not as a human figure but as a dark fog rolling in, threatening to cover me; but the dogs stayed close and while my promise to keep them safe during a thunderstorm had proven fraudulent, their promise to keep me alive held good.

WRITING TASKS—GRETEL EHRLICH

1. Write an essay describing an incident you experienced. Before doing your prewriting draft, review Ehrlich's essay. Notice how she

weaves the events going on in the world around her (the dog's presence, the doctor's arrival, her friends' aid) together with her own thoughts and emotions. The incident you choose doesn't have to be as traumatic as being struck by lightning. In fact, the weaving together of external events and internal thoughts is a difficult enough challenge with even an ordinary incident. Choose something you remember well though, because a successful paper will require lots of detail. Perhaps you should make two prewriting lists, one involving your thoughts and emotions during the experience and one involving the things going on around you. Then, as you create your first written draft, move back and forth between the lists selecting your content.

2. Write an essay telling how an incident from your past influences your beliefs or behavior today. Begin the paper with the incident. Describe it fully, using many details to recreate the incident in your reader's mind. When you are finished relating the incident, explain why it is important to you and how it has influenced your life.

Shameless Talk Shows
C. EUGENE EMERY, JR.

> I dated Siamese twins.
> I slept with Bigfoot, too.
> Get me on Sally Jessy.
> Put me on Donahue.
> 'Cause I wanna tell the world about it
> Right now.*

Vicki Abt vividly recalls the first time she tuned in to the "Sally Jessy Raphael" talk show. Abt found the hostess warning viewers that her program that day was not for the squeamish. Abt, a not-so-squeamish social psychologist at Penn State University, stuck around.

"As I'm watching, she's showing a videotape of a murder," said Abt. "The kid was taped to a pole, they were shooting him, they tortured him, and they shot him to death. The second time they shot him, he moaned and I knew it was real. I freaked out. I was screaming. I was crying. I said, 'I can't believe that she's showing this. What is the point of this?'"

The more Abt thought about it—not just the violent images but the absence of a constructive motive for showing the tape—the angrier she

---

*Song lyrics by "Weird Al" Yankovic

became. "It gets people upset, but it doesn't tell them what to do prosocially afterwards, except to turn to a commercial for Nutri/System so you can worry about your diet," said Abt.

She tried to do something. Abt wrote a two-page letter to Raphael "outlining exactly what was wrong with what she was doing and how dangerous it was." Abt never got a response.

Talk-show hosts like to say they get viewers interested in important issues facing society. Raphael's show did exactly that. Abt, who studies how moral principals are shaped by society and the media, got interested in Raphael and her ilk.

> *My dog's a narcoleptic.*
> *My mom's a circus freak.*
> *I gotta get a spot on Geraldo's show this week.*
> *'Cause I wanna tell the world about it*
> *Right now.*

Using that two-page letter to Raphael as an outline, Abt began a content analysis of 60 hours of television talk shows. The result was "The Shameless World of Phil, Sally and Oprah: Television Talk Shows and the Deconstructing of Society," an essay written with Penn State colleague Mel Seeholtz and now published in the *Journal of Popular Culture*, 28 (no. 1), Summer 1994.

"I thought maybe this (the Raphael show) was a fluke," said Abt, who also looked at how such hosts manipulate their audiences and how they make the shows work.

She discovered it was no fluke. She concluded that talk shows:

- Consistently play up the freakish nature of human existence, giving it national prominence and desensitizing viewers to its social implications. As long as they are willing to talk, child molesters, people with sexual quirks, folks with criminal records become recast on these shows as "victims," who can instantly amend for their sins by publicly confessing and apologizing to their victims.
- Provide a voyeuristic look at the deepest personal secrets of dysfunctional relationships or criminal acts, often without giving viewers the opportunity or a feeling of obligation to help. While some talk-show hosts passionately argue that they improve society by forcing the public to confront uncomfortable issues that should be tackled, Abt says the argument is shallow and self-serving. Real-life problems are solved when flesh-and-blood people (who can't escape a problem by changing channels) get involved in the solution. "The abstract concept of altruism is grounded either in experiences that evoke empathy or in real physical consequences. Television talk shows create an ersatz community, without any of the social and personal responsibilities that are attached to real life."

- Provide little or no reliable information to help viewers put what they are seeing into a rational, intellectually honest context. In a program featuring "skinheads," she wrote, "No one seriously attempted to correct their inaccurate rendering of historical events, or challenge their reliance on pseudo-biology during their diatribes against Jews and other, unrelated minority groups."

Thus, Abt warned, talk shows are helping to misshape our culture by misleading viewers.

"Television talk shows create audiences by breaking cultural rules, by managed shocks, by shifting our conceptions of what is acceptable, by transforming our ideas about what is possible, by undermining the bases for cultural judgment, by redefining deviance and appropriate reactions to it, by eroding social barriers, inhibitions and cultural distinctions," she said in the opening paragraph of her essay.

It was a powerful, topical, controversial attack on some of the nation's best-known celebrities and the role they play in society. It wasn't surprising that Abt would be invited to get a first-hand look at life on a talk show.

> My wife ran off with Elvis.
> My boss shaved off my hair.
> I've got a thing for poodles
> And rubber underwear.
> And I wanna tell the world about it
> Right now.

Abt knew better than to expect a reserved, thoughtful debate of the issues between the experts when she agreed to discuss the points she raised on "The Oprah Winfrey Show." She wasn't mistaken.

Instead of an intellectual dialogue, Oprah turned the program into the typical talk-show spectacle, with too many guests and too little time for them to provide anything more than soundbites.

Joining Abt for the two-hour show, aired September 12 and 13, 1994, were *Washington Post* TV critic Tom Shales (who called talk shows "the new pornography of our time" because they turn the audience into voyeurs), *People* magazine TV critic David Hiltbrand (who called Abt's conclusions "preposterous" and argued that "people watch TV with a built-in moral sense"), and groups of viewers from San Francisco, Atlanta, and Boston. Members of Oprah's Chicago audience alone had collectively watched 647 hours of talk shows in one week.

Some audience members said they simply watch such shows to be entertained. Others said they liked the programs because they believe the shows provide important information.

One teenager who expressed the latter view went on to criticize how the shows portray teenagers as "all drug addicts, dropouts, pregnant, or what have you." It didn't seem to dawn on her that if talk shows distort reality in an area where she has some personal experience, the genre might be giving unreliable information in other areas as well.

With Abt pressing for talk shows to feature more debates among experts who actually know what they're talking about, and Shales saying he'd "like to see more smart people on TV, fewer ordinary people and more extraordinary people," Winfrey closed the show by lamenting that "a lot of times when it comes down to what people actually watch, the very programs they criticize are the ones that get the highest ratings."

> *I had a close encounter.*
> *I never chew my food.*
> *I got eleven nose jobs.*
> *I yodel in the nude.*
> *And I wanna tell the world about it*
> *Right now.*

Abt has not been alone in her criticisms.

When "20/20" took a behind-the-scenes look at talk shows, the ABC-TV news magazine (aired September 16, 1994) revealed how one couple, Jennifer and Uriel Soto, managed to get on three different shows with three different stories in a matter of weeks. On "The Ricki Lake Show," they lied by billing themselves as married cousins. Jennifer Soto said the show's producers never asked any questions.

The "20/20" show also featured three men who had pretended to be a gay love triangle during a different Lake show. They alleged that a producer fed them titillating lines to use on the program, a claim the show denies.

Even when the shows have reason to suspect that a guest is lying, it doesn't matter. On "The Montel Williams Show," Jerome Stanfield, a man who later claimed that a producer for the show had encouraged him to lie, told Williams that he was a serial rapist. Although police were unable to confirm Stanfield's story, Williams aired the show anyway. He billed it as an "exclusive," explaining to his audience that, although questions had been raised about the honesty of the guest, "we have no information at this time that leads us to believe he is *not* telling the truth. And because of that we feel it is our duty and our responsibility to broadcast the program out of concern for public safety."

> *I have no genitalia.*
> *I sold my kids for cheese.*
> *I love my blow-up doll so*

Bring out those cameras, please.
'Cause I wanna tell the world about it
Right now.

Despite the criticisms and the exposés of the way these programs stretch the truth, there's little evidence that things have changed in the trashy world of TV talk shows.

Self-proclaimed psychics, promoters of quacky medical treatments, miracle mongers, and UFO enthusiasts usually get to tell their stories on these shows with a minimum of criticism.

For example, hostess and fitness guru Susan Powter spent part of February fawning over the "psychic" Char, showing how a box of burning herbs placed on the abdomen can help premenstrual syndrome sufferers, and trying to scare parents away from getting their children vaccinated.

In another case, talkmeister Jerry Springer brought a woman named Shannon onto his show so her husband could shock her on national TV with the news that he had a long-standing affair with the baby-sitter of the couple's two children. Then, with Shannon already weeping, Springer brought on Cindy, the baby-sitter, who went into further detail about her ongoing relationship with Shannon's husband.

But Shannon, her husband, and the babysitter turned out to be three Toronto-based comedians who reported that "The Jerry Springer Show" had misled Shannon in an effort to humiliate her on national television. Then a Springer spokeswoman had the nerve to threaten to sue the comics for breaking a written promise to tell the truth on the program.

"If I had really been this woman," Suzanne "Shannon" Muir told the *Toronto Star*, "they would have ruined my life."

And in a case that brought haunting echoes of the video that originally prompted Abt to examine what talk shows do to society, police in Michigan charged Jonathan Schmitz with murder after "The Jenny Jones Show" brought Schmitz, 24, on the program and told him he would get the chance to meet a secret admirer on national TV.

The secret admirer of Schmitz, a heterosexual, turned out to be a man—32-year-old Scott Amedure. As the show was being taped, Schmitz was stunned to learn that he was the object of a homosexual crush.

Three days later, after also reportedly receiving an anonymous sexually suggestive note, Schmitz bought a shotgun, went to Amedure's house, and shot him twice, according to police. Jones and her organization have denied any responsibility for Amedure's death. The program never aired.

The murder may make talk-show hosts and their producers reexamine what they're doing, but probably not for long.

Jones's program began getting good ratings only after she began trying to shock viewers and guests. The lesson isn't lost on the industry, which seems ready to do almost anything to raise the level of sensationalism in hopes of attracting a bigger share of the audience.

With 15 talk shows already on the air, television executives hawking new programs are promising even more sensational fare when the new season begins in September.

"There are going to be 20 or so new shows that are worse than the ones I was criticizing," says Abt. "These days, saying you had sex with your father gets almost no reaction. Now you have to have had sex with three fathers. I think the public thinks these shows are telling them something relevant, but the audience has been so brutalized, they need more and more to get outraged."

"The reason these talk shows are so popular is you don't have to educate people to be voyeurs, you don't have to educate people to love gossip, to like freak shows," comments Abt, adding that the same thing holds true for programs featuring psychics, UFO abductees, and the like.

In the end, it's more than the fault of the producers and hosts. The problem lies with the people who choose to watch and believe such shows.

"Oprah's argument to me was that every time she does a public-interest show, her ratings go down the toilet. She's certainly right. But that doesn't excuse it," says Abt. "You can also make a lot of money selling crack cocaine, but I don't do it."

> *I'm just a cross-dressin'*
> *alcoholic neo-Nazi*
> *Porno star, as you may have guessed.*
> *And I'm really gonna feel*
> *a whole lot better*
> *If you let me get this thing off my chest.*
> *Talk Soup. Talk Soup.*
> *Listen to me, listen to me, listen to me.*

WRITING TASKS—C. EUGENE EMERY, JR.

1. In paragraph 13, Emery quotes Vicki Abt to reveal the ways talk shows mislead viewers:

   - By breaking cultural rules
   - By including managed shocks
   - By shifting our conceptions of what is acceptable
   - By transforming our ideas about what is possible
   - By undermining the bases for cultural judgment

- By redefining deviance and appropriate reactions to it, and
- By eroding social barriers, inhibitions, and cultural distinctions

Watch at least three one-hour talk shows, taking notes about moments when one or more of the above charges apply. Then write one of the following essays:

a. Show that one or more of the charges in the list are true for the shows you watched.

b. Compare two or more shows on several items on the list.

Whichever topic you select, identify each show by name, name the host of the show, name the topic(s) discussed, and remember to be as specific as possible about what was said and by whom.

2. Write an essay in defense of talk shows, either arguing that they are educational or that they are harmless entertainment. Examine Emery's essay so that you can answer his (and Abt's) arguments against talk shows, and be sure to back up your argument with evidence and logic.

Becoming Desensitized to Hate Words
ELLEN GOODMAN

The ceremonies are over, but I would like to suggest one last way to commemorate the golden anniversary of the defeat of the Nazis. How about a moratorium on the current abuse of terms like storm trooper, swastika, Holocaust, Gestapo, Hitler? How about putting the language of the Third Reich into mothballs?

The further we are removed from the defeat of the Nazis, the more this vocabulary seems to be taking over our own. It's become part of the casual, ubiquitous, inflammatory speech Americans use to turn each other into monsters. Which, if I recall correctly, was a tactic favored by Goebbels himself.

The NRA attacked federal agents as "jackbooted government thugs" who wear "Nazi bucket helmets and black storm trooper uniforms." In the ratcheting up of the rhetorical wars, it wasn't enough for the NRA to complain that the agents had overstepped their bounds; they had to call them Nazis.

Twice more in recent days, Republican congressmen have compared environmentalist agencies with Hitler's troops. On May 16, Pennsylvania's Bud Shuster talked about EPA officials as an "environmental Gestapo." Before that, Missouri's Bill Emerson warned about the establishment of an "eco-Gestapo force."

On the Democratic side, Sen. John Kerry recently suggested that a proposed new kind of tax audit, on "lifestyles," would produce an "IRS Gestapo-like entity." And John Lewis and Charles Rangel compared silence in the face of the new conservative agenda to silence in the early days of the Third Reich. They didn't just disagree with conservatives; they Nazified them.

Then there are the perennial entries on the Hitler log. Anti-abortion groups talk about the abortion holocaust—comparing the fetuses to Jews and the doctors to Mengele.

Much of the time, the hurling of "Nazi" names is just plain dumb. As dumb as the behavior of punk groups, who think they can illustrate their devotion to anarchism with symbols of fascism. Singers like Sid Vicious, groups like the Dead Boys once sported swastikas without realizing that in Hitler's time and place, they would have been rounded up as enemies of the Reich.

As for pinning the Nazi label on the supporters of abortion rights, the propagandists surely know that Hitler was a hardline opponent of abortion. (Did that make him pro-life?) In "Mein Kampf" he wrote, "We must also do away with the conception that the treatment of the body is the affair of every individual." A woman's body wasn't hers; it belonged to the state.

Even when Nazi-speak is not historically dumb, it's rhetorically dumb. The Hitlerian language has become an indiscriminate shorthand for every petty tyranny.

In this vocabulary, every two-bit boss becomes a "little Hitler." Every domineering high school principal is accused of running a "concentration camp." Every overbearing piece of behavior becomes a "Gestapo" tactic. And every political disagreement becomes a fight against evil.

Crying Hitler in our time is like crying wolf. The charge immediately escalates the argument, adding verbal fuel to fires of any dimension, however minor. But eventually, yelling Nazi at environmentalists and Gestapo at federal agents diminishes the emotional power of these words should we need them.

In time, these epithets even downgrade the horror of the Third Reich and the immensity of World War II. They cheapen history and insult memory, especially the memory of the survivors.

It's one reason George Bush was so quick to take offense at the NRA's Nazi-isms. As a veteran of World War II, he still knows a Nazi when he sees one and knows the difference between the Gestapo and a federal agent.

Exactly 50 years ago this spring, his generation liberated the concentration camps. Americans learned then, with a fresh sense of horror, about the crematoriums, about man's inhumanity, about the trains that ran on time to the gas chambers.

This was Nazism. This was the Gestapo. This was the Holocaust. This was Hitler. If you please, save the real words for the real thing.

WRITING TASKS—ELLEN GOODMAN

1. In recent months, talk radio hosts have come under fire for engaging in, or allowing their callers to engage in, hate speech similar to what Goodman describes. Listen to a few talk radio shows and then write an essay in which you discuss the experience. Did you spot a similar use of emotional labels to discredit people or ideas? If so, what were some of these labels? After a general discussion, focus on one or two specific examples of the use of emotional words that you heard. Explain in what context they were used, and what you think their intended effect was. Then evaluate the examples. Explain how a more reasoned opposition to the person or idea being considered might be phrased. Perhaps the talk shows you listened to were relatively free of emotional labels. If so, write a paper presenting some of the topics discussed and how the host and his callers discussed them.

2. Goodman argues that the use of hate words relating to Nazism and fascism is not only grossly inaccurate to describe events in the United States today, but also "adds verbal fuel to fires . . . however minor." Have you personally experienced moments when emotional labels or "name-calling" added "fuel to the fire?" Using specific examples, write an essay describing one or more such moments. Be sure to have a clearly stated central idea and a concluding paragraph that brings the paper to a proper close.

If I Were a Black Man
CYNTHIA HEIMEL

People would be scared of me. I just might like that. Now I walk down the street all soft and white and dawdling in front of Barneys windows while the Barneys doorman smiles and beckons, cracking the door, inviting me into an air-conditioned wonderland of three-hundred-dollar pillows, three-thousand-dollar suits and a five-thousand-dollar piece of pottery you don't even know what the fuck it is.

What would it be like to instead be a hard-bodied male and gleaming dark and people stepping out of my way or across the street even, grabbing tight to their purses and their shopping bags from the Pottery Barn containing teapots shaped like cabbages? The Barneys doorman would nervously pretend I was invisible. Korean grocers would see me at the salad bar and hope their surveillance cameras were working.

Would it be a kick to inspire fear just by my very presence?

I could walk down the street and not even worry about being raped. Even at three in the morning. Women of every size and age would scurry like ants in my wake, even if I wore a nice suit and wingtips and carried an umbrella. Of course, I might get shot.

And it might be hard to get a cab.

Would I feel odd reading books where white men are simply men but black men are black men? Or in old books Negro men, in new books Afro-Americans or persons of color? Would I feel singled out and special?

Would I feel battered by white people's hatred and fear? Would their constant attitude that I am not only inferior but expendable, that I am stupid and violent, seep into my soul and destroy my opinion of myself? Would I become full of festering self-loathing and get depressed and crave Prozac or Valium or heroin?

Or would I simply get angry, let the anger fuel me to be bigger and better and faster and scary and cynical and separate from everyone? Would I be clever, closed off and seething with hatred and distrust?

I guess I'd be both. I feel both ways now, even in my present incarnation as an invisible white woman, presumed to be incompetent and dependent, someone to bring the coffee. Even in my present soft white incarnation, I often dawdle down the streets with self-loathing and violence in my heart, lucky that heroin makes me puke, often awash with Valium to assuage the rage.

Now. If I were a black man, I'd have one of those pesky penises. And all its accoutrements. Testosterone for one, a stringently demanding hormone: I must compete. I must conquer. I must protect my loved ones, my home, my food, my possessions.

Plus I'd be inoculated from birth with America's rigid definition of masculinity: Be Arnold Schwarzenegger. Free and wild, chanting *"Hasta la vista,* baby" and "I'll be back," wasting bad guys with nary a blink.

But I'd be thwarted and betrayed. Testosterone and Arnold, it turns out, are property of white guys. A black guy may not protect or defend or say *"Hasta la vista."* He's supposed to be the cute roly-poly cop who eats doughnuts while Bruce Willis saves a whole building. Emasculated. Preferably wearing an anchorman hairdo.

I don't know if I'd like being a black man all that much.

But hey, whoa, hold the phone, what if I became a famous black man? Like an idol? A hero?

Say I started out my life living in my grandmother's brothel, or, I don't know, in the projects in San Francisco. A place where white people never go. Poor neighborhoods become exponentially more isolated every day that passes. No supermarkets or movie theaters. No interaction with the outside. An "us" and "them" mentality. A place portrayed as teeming with welfare cheats and junkies, not humans, certainly not potential friends. A place where young boys kill their brothers, where they implode.

And so if suddenly, through careening fate, I became everyone's darling? Everyone's beloved? On TV every minute? What if even the most poisonous bigot made an exception for me? What if when I walked down the street I would see the fear, scurrying and clutching of purses, then suddenly the shock of recognition and then I was everybody's hero?

Then I'd have it made, right? I'd be vindicated, happy.

But wait a minute. I had a soft, dawdling, fleeting brush with semi-fame a few years ago. I went to bed. If anything, fame hurt me. I was led to expect I would suddenly be completely different. I was still me.

So how would it be, being a megastar, getting everything anybody is ever supposed to want, which is all meaningless, and superimposing that on an incredibly damaged and battered ego? I might talk about myself in the third person. I might set fire to myself. I might bash in a car with a baseball bat.

If I were a black man, I don't think I could cope. Although could I be Patrick Ewing for just one day?

WRITING TASKS—CYNTHIA HEIMEL

1. In the manner of Heimel, write an "if I were . . ." essay. You may use one of the people in the list below or one of your own choosing. As Heimel does, put your person in a number of ordinary daily situations and let what you say about her or him reveal your understanding of these experiences.

prisoner	single mother
politician	recent immigrant
senior citizen	gang member
AIDS victim	welfare recipient
celebrity	pregnant teenager

2. Write an essay about a group which you believe is misunderstood by others. Begin with a thorough examination of the misunderstanding and how you know it exists. Then discuss the damage this misunderstanding does to individual members of the group and end with a plea to your reader to treat this group in a more informed way.

The New Generation Gap: Thirteeners
NEIL HOWE AND WILLIAM STRAUSS

As they shield their eyes with Ray-Ban wayfarer sunglasses, and their ears with Model TCD-D3 Sony Walkmen, today's teens and twentysome-things present to Boomer eyes a splintered image of brassy looks and smooth manner, of kids growing up too tough to be cute, of kids more com-fortable shopping or playing than working or studying. Ads target them as beasts of pleasure and pain who have trouble understanding words longer than one syllable, sentences longer than three words. Pop music on their Top 40 stations—heavy metal, alternative rock, rap—strikes many a Boomer ear as a rock-and-roll end game of harsh sounds, goin'-nowhere melodies, and clumsy poetry. News clips document a young-adult waste-land of academic nonperformance, political apathy, suicide pacts, date-rape trials, wilding, and hate crimes.

Who are they, and what are they up to? On the job, Thirteeners are the reckless bicycle messengers, pizza drivers, yard workers, Wal-Mart shelf-stockers, health-care trainees, and miscellaneous scavengers, hustlers, and McJobbers in the low-wage/low-benefit service economy. They're the wan-dering nomads of the temp world, directionless slackers, habitual nonvoters. In school they're a group of staggering diversity—not just in ethnicity but also in attitude, performance, and rewards. After graduation they're the ones with big loans who were supposed to graduate into jobs and move out of the house but didn't, and who seem to get poorer the longer they've been away from home—unlike their parents at that age, who seemed to get richer.

In inner cities Thirteeners are the unmarried teen mothers and uncon-cerned teen fathers, the Crips and Bloods, the innocent hip-hoppers grown weary of watching white Boomers cross the street to avoid them. In suburbs they're the kids at the mall, kids buying family groceries for busy moms and dads, kids in mutual-protection circles of friends, girding against an adoles-cent world far more dangerous than anything their parents knew, kids strug-gling to unlink sex from disease and death.

In them lies much of the doubt, distress, and endangered dream of late-twentieth-century America. As a group they aren't what older people ever wanted but rather what they themselves know they need to be: pragmatic, quick, sharp-eyed, able to step outside themselves and understand how the world really works. From the Thirteener vantage point, America's greatest need these days is to clear out the underbrush of name-calling and ideology so that simple things can work again. Others don't yet see it, but today's young people are beginning to realize that their upbringing has endowed them with a street sense and pragmatism their elders lack. Many admit they *are* a bad generation—but so, too, do they suspect that they are a *necessary* generation for a society in dire need of survival lessons.

When they look into the future, they see a much bleaker vision than any of today's older generations ever saw in their own youth. Polls show that Thirteeners believe it will be much harder for them to get ahead than it was for their parents—and that they are overwhelmingly pessimistic about the long-term fate of their generation and nation. They sense that they're the clean-up crew, that their role in history will be sacrificial—that whatever comeuppance America has to face, they'll bear more than their share of the burden. It's a new twist, and not a happy one, on the American Dream.

Trace the life cycle to date of Americans born in 1961. They were among the first babies people took pills not to have. During the 1967 Summer of Love they were the kindergartners who paid the price for America's new divorce epidemic. In 1970 they were fourth-graders trying to learn arithmetic amid the chaos of open classrooms and New Math curricula. In 1973 they were the bell-bottomed sixth-graders who got their first real-life civics lesson watching the Watergate hearings on TV. Through the late 1970s they were the teenage mall-hoppers who spawned the Valley Girls and other flagrantly non-Boomer youth trends. In 1979 they were the graduating seniors of Carter-era malaise who registered record-low SAT scores and record-high crime and drug-abuse rates.

In 1980 they cast their first votes, mostly for Reagan, became the high-quality nineteen-year-old enlistees who began surging into the military, and arrived on campus as the smooth, get-it-done freshmen who evidenced a sudden turnaround from the intellectual arrogance and social immaturity of Boomer students. They were the college class of 1983, whose graduation coincided with the ballyhooed *A Nation at Risk* report, which warned that education was beset by "a rising tide of mediocrity." In 1985 they were the MBA grads who launched the meteoric rise in job applications to Wall Street. And in 1991 they hit age thirty just when turning "thirtysomething" (a big deal for yuppies in the 1980s) became a tired subject—and when the pretentious TV serial with that title was yanked off the air.

Like any generation, Thirteeners grew up with parents who are distributed in roughly equal measure between the two prior generations (Silent and Boom). But also like any generation, they were decisively influenced by the senior parental cohort. Much as GIs shaped the *Sputnik* 1950s for Boomers, the Silent Generation provided the media producers, community leaders, influential educators, and rising politicians during the R-rated 1970s, the decade that most Thirteeners still regard as their childhood home.

And what did Thirteeners absorb from that generation and that era? Mostly they learned to be cynical about adults whom they perceived to be sensitive yet powerless, better at talking about issues than solving problems. For the Silent Generation, then hitting midlife, the cultural upheaval of the 1970s meant liberation from youthful conformism, a now-or-never passage away from marriages made too young and careers chosen too early. But for Thirteeners just growing up, the 1970s meant something very different: an adult world that expressed moral ambivalence where children sought clear answers, that expected children to cope with real-world problems, that hesitated to impose structure on children's behavior, and that demonstrated an amazing (even stupefying) tolerance for the rising torrent of pathology and negativism that engulfed children's daily life.

When they were small, the nation was riding high. When they reached adolescence, national confidence weakened, and community and family life splintered. Older people focused less on the future, planned less for it, and invested less in it. A Consciousness Revolution that seemed euphoric to young adults was to Thirteeners the beginning of a ride on a down escalator. The public debacles of their youth fostered the view that adults were not especially virtuous or competent—that kids couldn't count on adults to protect them from danger.

From Boom to Thirteenth, America's children went from a family culture of *My Three Sons* to one of *My Two Dads*. As millions of mothers flocked into the work force, the proportion of preschoolers cared for in their own homes fell by half. For the first time, adults ranked automobiles ahead of children as necessary for "the good life." The cost of raising a child, never very worrisome when Boomers were little, suddenly became a fraught issue. Adults of fertile age doubled their rate of surgical sterilization. The legal-abortion rate grew to the point where one out of every three pregnancies was terminated. Back in 1962 half of all adults agreed that parents in bad marriages should stay together for the sake of the children. By 1980 less than a fifth agreed. America's divorce rate doubled from 1965 to 1975, just as first-born Thirteeners passed through middle childhood.

The pop culture conveyed to little kids and (by 1980) teenagers a recurring message from the adult world: that they weren't wanted, and weren't even liked, by the grown-ups around them. Polls and social statistics showed a sharp shift in public attitudes toward (and treatment of) children. Taxpayers revolted against school funding, and landlords and neighborhoods that had once smiled on young Boomers started banning children. The Zero Population Growth movement declared the creation of each additional infant to be a bad thing, and the moviegoing public showed an unquenchable thirst for a new cinematic genre: the devil-child horror film. The same year Boomers were blissing out at Woodstock, the baby that riveted America's attention had a mother named Rosemary (*Please* don't have this baby, millions of viewers whispered to themselves).

From the late 1960s until the early 1980s America's pre-adolescents grasped what nurture they could through the most virulently anti-child period in modern American history. Ugly new phrases ("latchkey child," "throwaway child," and "boomerang child") joined the sad new lexicon of youth. America's priorities lay elsewhere, as millions of kids sank into poverty, schools deteriorated, and a congeries of elected politicians set a new and distinctly child-hostile course of national overconsumption. Then, when Thirteeners were ready to enter the adult labor force, the politicians pushed every policy lever conceivable—tax codes, entitlements, public debt, unfunded liabilities, labor laws, hiring practices—to tilt the economic playing field away from the young and toward the old. The results were predictable.

Since the early 1970s the overall stagnation in American economic progress has masked some vastly unequal changes in living standards by phase of life. Older people have prospered, Boomers have barely held their own, and Thirteeners have fallen off a cliff. The columnist Robert Kuttner describes Thirteeners as victims of a "remarkable generational economic distress. . . . a depression of the young," which makes them feel "uniquely thirsty in a sea of affluence." Ever since the first Thirteeners reached their teens, the inflation-adjusted income of all adult men under age thirty-five has sunk—dropping by more than 20 percent since as recently as 1979. Twenty years ago a typical thirty-year-old male made six percent more than a typical sixty-year-old male; today he makes 14 percent less. The same widening age gap can be observed in poverty rates, public benefits, home ownership, union membership, health insurance, and pension participation. Along the way, this is becoming a generation of betrayed expectations. Polls show that most teenagers (of both sexes) expect to be earning $30,000 or more by age thirty, but in 1990 the U.S. Census Bureau reported that among Americans aged twenty-five to twenty-nine there were eight with total annual incomes of under $30,000 for every one making more than $30,000.

Welcome, Thirteeners, to contemporary American life: While older age brackets are getting richer, yours is getting poorer. Where earlier twentieth-century generations could comfortably look forward to outpacing Mom and Dad, you probably won't even be able to keep up. If, when you leave home, you have a high school degree or better, there's a 10 percent chance you'll "boomerang" back to live with your parents at least once. (Today more young adults are living with their parents than at any other time since the Great Depression.) When you marry, you and your spouse will both work—not for Boomerish self-fulfillment but because you need to just to make ends meet. If you want children, you'll have to defy statistics showing that since 1973 the median real income has fallen by 30 percent for families with children which are headed by persons under thirty. And you'd better not slip up. Over the past twenty years the poverty rate among under-thirty families has more than doubled. Your generation, in fact, has a weaker middle class than any other generation born in this century, which means that the distance is widening between those of you who are beating the average and those who are sinking beneath it.

Everywhere they look, Thirteeners see the workplace system rigged against them. As they view it, the families, schools, and training programs that could have prepared them for worthwhile careers have been allowed to rot, but the institutions that safeguard the occupational livelihood of mature workers have been maintained with full vigor. Trade quotas protect decaying industries. Immigration quotas protect dinosaur unions. Two-tier wage scales discriminate against young workers. Federal labor regulations protect outmoded skills. State credential laws protect overpriced professions. Huge FICA taxes take away Thirteener money that, polls show, most Thirteeners expect never to see again. And every year another incomprehensible twelve-digit number gets added to the national debt, which Thirteeners know will someday get dumped on them. Whatever may happen to the meek, they know it's not their generation that's about to inherit the earth.

Like warriors on the eve of battle, Thirteeners face their future with a mixture of bravado and fatalism. Squared off competitively against one another, this mélange of scared city kids, suburban slackers, hungry immigrants, desperate grads, and shameless hustlers is collectively coming to realize that America rewards only a select set of winners with its Dream— and that America cares little about its anonymous losers. Sizing up the odds, each Thirteener finds himself or herself essentially alone, to an extent that most elders would have difficulty comprehending. Between his own relative poverty and the affluence he desires, the Thirteener sees no intermediary signposts, no sure, step-by-step path along which society will help him, urge him, congratulate him. Instead, all he sees is an enormous obstacle, with him on one side and everything he wants on the other.

And what's the obstacle? Those damn Boomers.

WRITING TASKS—NEIL HOWE AND WILLIAM STRAUSS

1. Near the end of this essay, the authors say, "America rewards only a select set of winners with its Dream—and . . . cares little about its anonymous losers." Consider this statement in the light of your own knowledge, observation, and experience. Create a prewriting sheet that notes specific situations or facts. Then write a paper agreeing or disagreeing with the statement. Choose a narrow focus. Don't try to cover the whole picture of life in the United States; select only a small portion of the possibilities: a law, a program, a volunteer group, or an educational opportunity that helps people avoid being losers or a law, a community attitude, or an economic condition that shows that America "cares little about its

anonymous losers." You can get many hints about appropriate content from a re-reading of Howe and Strauss's essay.

2. Howe and Strauss call the period from the 1960s to the early 1980s "the most virulently anti-child period in modern American history." Do you agree? Is America still anti-child? We have a high divorce rate, an increasing juvenile crime rate, and reductions in educational budgets. We also have record enrollments in childrearing classes, a proliferation of sports opportunities for the young, and an entertainment industry which pays increasing attention to children. So where do we stand? In an essay examine the world of the present-day American child. Is it good; not so good; bad; good for some, bad for others; good in some ways, bad in other ways? If you have information, compare it to the life of children in other countries. You may draw on Howe and Strauss's essay, your own observation, your own experience, and information from books and periodicals.

The Eloquent Sounds of Silence
PICO IYER

Every one of us knows the sensation of going up, on retreat, to a high place and feeling ourselves so lifted up that we can hardly imagine the circumstances of our usual lives, or all the things that make us fret. In such a place, in such a state, we start to recite the standard litany: that silence is sunshine, where company is clouds; that silence is rapture, where company is doubt; that silence is golden, where company is brass.

But silence is not so easily won. And before we race off to go prospecting in those hills, we might usefully recall that fool's gold is much more common and that gold has to be panned for, dug out from other substances. "All profound things and emotions of things are preceded and attended by Silence," wrote Herman Melville, one of the loftiest and most eloquent of souls. Working himself up to an ever more thunderous cry of affirmation, he went on. "Silence is the general consecration of the universe. Silence is the invisible laying on of the Divine Pontiff's hands upon the world. Silence is the only Voice of our God." For Melville, though, silence finally meant darkness and hopelessness and self-annihilation. Devastated by the silence that greeted his heartfelt novels, he retired into a public silence from which he did not emerge for more than 30 years. Then, just before his death, he came forth with his final utterance—the luminous tale of Billy Budd—and showed that silence is only as worthy as what we can bring back from it.

We have to earn silence, then, to work for it: to make it not an absence but a presence; not emptiness but repletion. Silence is something more than just a pause; it is that enchanted place where space is cleared and time is stayed and the horizon itself expands. In silence, we often say, we can hear ourselves think; but what is truer to say is that in silence we can hear ourselves not think, and so sink below our selves into a place far deeper than mere thought allows. In silence, we might better say, we can hear someone else think.

Or simply breathe. For silence is responsiveness, and in silence we can listen to something behind the clamor of the world. "A man who loves God, necessarily loves silence," wrote Thomas Merton, who was, as a Trappist, a connoisseur, a caretaker of silences. It is no coincidence that places of worship are places of silence: if idleness is the devil's playground, silence may be the angels'. It is no surprise that *silence* is an anagram of *license*. And it is only right that Quakers all but worship silence, for it is the place where everyone finds his God, however he may express it. Silence is an ecumenical state, beyond the doctrines and divisions created by the mind. If everyone has a spiritual story to tell of his life, everyone has a spiritual silence to preserve.

So it is that we might almost say silence is the tribute we pay to holiness; we slip off words when we enter a sacred space, just as we slip off shoes. A "moment of silence" is the highest honor we can pay someone; it is the point at which the mind stops and something else takes over (words run out when feelings rush in). A "vow of silence" is for holy men the highest devotional act. We hold our breath, we hold our words; we suspend our chattering selves and let ourselves "fall silent," and fall into the highest place of all.

It often seems that the world is getting noisier these days: in Japan, which may be a model of our future, cars and buses have voices, doors and elevators speak. The answering machine talks to us, and for us, somewhere above the din of the TV; the Walkman preserves a public silence but ensures that we need never—in the bathtub, on a mountaintop, even at our desks— be without the clangor of the world. White noise becomes the aural equivalent of the clash of images, the nonstop blast of fragments that increasingly agitates our minds. As Ben Okri, the young Nigerian novelist, puts it, "When chaos is the god of an era, clamorous music is the deity's chief instrument."

There is, of course, a place for noise, as there is for daily lives. There is a place for roaring, for the shouting exultation of a baseball game, for hymns and spoken prayers, for orchestras and cries of pleasure. Silence, like all the best things, is best appreciated in its absence: if noise is the signature tune of the world, silence is the music of the other world, the closest thing we know to the harmony of the spheres. But the greatest charm of noise is when it ceases. In silence, suddenly, it seems as if all the windows of the world are thrown open and everything is as clear as on a morning after rain. Silence, ideally, hums. It charges the air. In Tibet, where the silence has a tragic cause, it is still quickened by the fluttering of prayer flags, the tolling of temple bells, the roar of wind across the plains, the memory of chant.

Silence, then, could be said to be the ultimate province of trust: it is the place where we trust ourselves to be alone; where we trust others to understand the things we do not say; where we trust a higher harmony to assert itself. We all know how treacherous are words, and how often we use them to paper over embarrassment, or emptiness, or fear of the larger spaces that silence brings. "Words, words, words" commit us to positions we do not really hold, the imperatives of chatter; words are what we use for lies, false promises and gossip. We babble with strangers; with intimates we can be silent. We "make conversation" when we are at a loss; we unmake it when we are alone, or with those so close to us that we can afford to be alone with them.

In love, we are speechless; in awe, we say, words fail us.

WRITING TASKS—PICO IYER

1. When you need silence, where do you go? To your room? To the country-side? To the mountains? Write a descriptive essay about a place that you have used as a retreat from the world, a place where you can find silence when you need it. Spend prewriting time recalling as many specific aspects of the place as you can so you will have a richness of detail to draw upon. As you write, use the details to convey a sense of why the place is important to you.

2. Silence has its uses, but so does sound. We find many sounds pleasurable, comforting, and emotionally satisfying. Write an essay in praise of certain sounds. First, make a list of sounds you like to hear—the roar of a football crowd, the cooing of a baby, the crackle of fireworks, the purring of a fine engine, the voice of a loved one. Try to get a list of at least twenty. Somewhere in the early portion of your paper use several of the sounds from your list in a catalog of pleasurable sounds. In the rest of your paper select two or three sounds to discuss fully.

In Praise of Gore
ANDREW KLAVEN

I love the sound of people screaming. Women screaming—with their clothes torn—as they run down endless hallways with some bogeyman in hot pursuit. Men, in their priapic cars, screaming as the road ends, as the fender plummets toward fiery oblivion under their wild eyes. Children? I'm a little squeamish about children, but okay, sure. I'll take screaming children too. And I get off on gunshots—machine gun shots goading a corpse into a posthumous jitterbug; and the coital jerk and plunge of a butcher knife, and axes; even claws, if you happen to have them.

Yes, yes, yes, only in stories. Of course; in fictions only: novels, TV shows, films. I've loved the scary, gooey stuff since I was a child. I've loved monsters, shootouts, bluddy murther; women in jeopardy (as they say in Hollywood); the slasher in the closet; the intruder's shadow that spreads up the bedroom wall like a stain. And now, having grown to man's estate, I make a very good living writing these things: thriller novels like *Don't Say a Word*, which begins with a nice old lady getting dusted and ends with an assault on a child, and *The Animal Hour*, which features a woman's head being severed and stuffed into a commode.

Is it vicious? Disgusting? Sexist? Sick? Tough luck, it's my imagination—sometimes it is—and it's my readers' too—always, for all I know. And when they and I get together, when we dodge down that electric alleyway of the human skull where only murder is delight—well then, my friend, it's showtime.

But enough about me, let's talk about death. Cruel death, sexy death, exciting death: death, that is, on the page and on the screen. Because this is not a defense of violence in fiction; it's a celebration of it. And not a moment too soon either.

Hard as it is for a sane man to believe, fictional violence is under attack. Again. This year's list of would-be censors trying to shoulder their way to the trough of celebrity is hardly worth enumerating: Their 15 minutes might be up by the time I'm done. Film critic Michael Medved says cinematic violence is part of a pop culture "war on traditional values": Congressman Edward Markey says television violence should be reduced or regulated; some of our less thoughtful feminists tried to quash the novel *American Psycho* because of its descriptions of violence toward women and even some of the more thoughtful, like Catharine MacKinnon, have fought for censorship in law, claiming that written descriptions of "penises slamming into vaginas" deprive actual human beings of their civil rights.

It's nonsense mostly, but it has the appeal of glamour, of flash. Instead of trying to understand the sad, banal, ignorant souls who generally pull the trigger in our society, we get to discuss the urbane cannibal Hannibal Lecter from *The Silence of the Lambs*. Ice-T, penises, vaginas. It makes for good sound bites, anyway—the all-American diet of 15-second thoughts.

But Britain—where I've come to live because I loathe real guns and political correctness—is far from exempt. Indeed, perhaps nowhere has there been a more telling or emblematic attack on fictional violence than is going on here right now. It is a textbook example of how easily pundits and politicians can channel honest grief and rage at a true crime into a senseless assault on the innocent tellers of tales.

It began here this time with the killing of a child by two other children. On February 12, Jamie Bulger, a 2-year-old toddler, was led out of a Merseyside shopping mall by two 10-year-olds—two little boys. The boys prodded and carried and tugged the increasingly distraught baby past dozens of witnesses who did not understand what they were seeing. When they reached a deserted railroad embankment, the two boys tortured, mutilated, and finally killed their captive for no reasons that anyone has been able to explain.

The nation's effort to understand, its grief and disgust, its sense of social despair, did not resolve themselves upon a single issue until the trial judge pronounced sentence. "It is not for me to pass judgment on their upbringing," Mr. Justice Morland said of the boys. "But I suspect exposure to violent video films may in part be an explanation."

No one knew why he said such a thing. There had been speculation in some of the papers that *Child's Play 3* (with its devil doll, Chucky), which had been rented by one of the killers' fathers, had given the son ideas. But there was no testimony at the trial, no evidence presented showing that the boy had seen it or that it had had a contributing effect. It didn't matter. As far as journalists were concerned, as far as public debate was concerned, "video nasties," as they are called here, became the central issue of the case.

We finally know what we are seeing when we look upon the rampaging fire of violence in our society: We are seeing the effects of fiction on us. Got it? Our moral verities are crumbling by the hour. Our families are shattering. Our gods are dead. The best lack all conviction while the worst are full of passionate intensity.

And it's all Chucky's fault.

The instinct to censor is the tragic flaw of utopian minds. "Our first job," said Plato in his classic attack on the democratic system, "is to oversee the work of the story writers, and to accept any good stories they write, but reject the others." Because the perfectibility of human society is a fiction itself, it comes under threat from other, more believable fictions, especially those that document and imply the cruel, the chaotic, the Dionysian for their thrills.

For me to engage the latter-day Platos on their own materialist, political terms would be to be sucked in to a form of dialogue that does not reflect the reality I know—and know I know. Because personally, I understand the world not through language but through an unfathomable spirit and an infinite mind. With language as a rude tool I try to convey a shadow of the world my imagination makes of the world at large. I do this for money and pleasure and to win the admiration of women. And when, in an uncertain hour, I crave the palliative of meaning, I remind myself that people's souls run opposite to their bodies and grow more childlike as they mature—and so I have built, in my work, little places where those souls can go to play.

The proper response to anyone who would shut these playgrounds down for any reason—to anyone who confuses these playgrounds with the real world—is not the specious language of theory or logic or even the law. It's the language of the spirit, of celebration and screed, of jeremiad and hallelujah. Of this.

Now, I would not say that my fictions—any fictions—have no effect on real life. Or that books, movies, and TV are mere regurgitations of what's going on in the society around them. These arguments strike me as disingenuous and self-defeating. Rather, the relationship between fiction and humanity's unconscious is so complex, so resonant, that it is impossible to isolate one from the other in terms of cause and effect. Fiction and reality do interact, but we don't know how, not at all. And since we don't understand the effect of one upon the other—whence arises this magical certainty that violence in fiction begets violence in real life?

The answer seems to come straight out of Psychology IA, but that doesn't negate the truth of it: Pleasure that is unknowingly repressed is outwardly condemned. The censor always attacks the images that secretly appeal to him or her the most. The assault on violent fiction is not really an attempt to root out the causes of violence—no one can seriously believe that. The attempt to censor fictional violence is a guilt-ridden slap at ourselves, in the guise of a mythical *them*, for taking such pleasure in make-believe acts that, in real life, would be reprehensible. How—we seem to be asking ourselves—how, in a world in which Jamie Bulger dies so young, can we kick back with a beer at night and enjoy a couple of hours of *Child's Play 3?*

How can we enjoy this stuff so much? So very much.

Not all of us, perhaps. I'm forever being told that there are people who'd rather not take violence with their fiction—although I wonder how many would say so if you included the delicate violence of an Agatha Christie or the "literary" violence of, say, Hemingway and Faulkner. But even if we accept the exceptions, even if we limit the field to real gore, it does seem to me that the numbers are incredible, the attraction truly profound.

Once I picked out what looked like a cheap horror novel by an author I'd never heard of. For months afterward, I asked the readers I knew if they had heard of the book, *Salem's Lot*, or its author, Stephen King. None of them had. Later, the movie *Carrie* helped launch what has to be one of the most successful novelistic careers since Dickens. But even before that, readers were steadily discovering the nausea and mayhem and terror of the man's vision.

The moral, I mean, is this: To construct a bloodsoaked nightmare of unrelenting horror is not an easy thing. But if you build it, they will come. And so the maker of violent fiction—ho, ho—he walks among us in Nietzschean glee. He has bottled the Dionysian whirlwind and is selling it as a soft drink. Like deep-browed Homer, when he told of a spear protruding from a man's head with an eyeball fixed to the point, the violent storyteller knows that that gape of disgust on your respectable mug is really the look of love. You may denounce him, you may even censor him. You may just wrinkle your nose and walk away. But sooner or later, in one form or another, he knows you'll show up to see and listen to him. Fiction lives or dies not on its messages, but on the depth and power of the emotional experience it provides. An enormous amount of intellectual energy seems to have been expended in a failed attempt to suppress the central, disturbing, and irreducible fact of this experience: It's fun. Like sex: It's lots of fun. We watch fictional people love and die and screw and suffer and weep for our pleasure. It gives us joy.

And we watch them kill too. And this seems to give us as much joy as anything.

All right. I suppose you can talk about the catharsis of terror, or the harmless release of our violent impulses. Those are plausible excuses. I guess. It doesn't take a genius to notice how often—practically always—it's the villain of a successful piece of violent art who becomes its icon. Hannibal Lector and Leatherface. Freddy Krueger and Dracula—these are the posters that go up on the wall, the characters that we remember.

So I suppose, if you must, you could say these creatures represent our buried feelings. Whether it's Medea or Jason (from *Friday the 13th*), the character who commits acts of savage violence always has the appeal of a Caliban: that thing of darkness that must be acknowledged as our own. Not that people are essentially violent, but that they are violent among other things and the violence has to be repressed. Some emotions must be repressed, and repressed emotions return via the imagination in distorted and inflated forms: That's the law of benevolent hypocrisy, the law of civilized life. It is an unstated underpinning of utopian thought that the repressed can be eliminated completely or denied or happily freed or remolded with the proper education. It can't. Forget about it. Cross it off your list of things to do. The monsters are always there in their cages. As Stephen King says, with engaging simplicity, his job is to take them out for a walk every now and then.

But again, this business of violent fiction as therapy—it's a defense, isn't it, as if these stories needed a reason for being. In order to celebrate violent fiction—I mean, *celebrate* it—it's the joy you've got to talk about. The joy of cruelty, the thrill of terror, the adrenaline of the hunter, the heartbeat of the deer—all reproduced in the safe playground of art. A joy indeed.

When it comes to our messier, unseemly pleasures like fictional gore, we are downright embarrassed by our delight. But delight it is. Nubile teens caught out *in flagrante* by a nutcase in a hockey mask? You bet it's erotic. Whole families tortured to death by a madman who's traced them through their vacation photos? Ee-yewwww. . . . Delightful stuff.

And we've always been that way. The myths of our ancient gods, the lives of our medieval saints, the entertainments of our most civilized cultures have always included healthy doses of rape, cannibalism, evisceration, and general mayhem. Critics like Michael Medved complain that never before has it all been quite so graphic, especially on screen. We are becoming "desensitized" to bloodshed, he claims, and require more and more gore to excite our feelings. But when have human beings ever been particularly "sensitized" to fictional violence? The technology to create the illusion of bloodshed has certainly improved, but read *Titus Andronicus* with its wonderful stage direction, "Enter a messenger with two heads and a hand," read the orgasmic staking of Lucy in *Dracula,* read de Sade, for crying out loud. There were always some pretty good indications of which way we'd go once we got our hands on the machinery.

Because we love it. It makes us do a little inner dance of excitement, tension, and release. Violent fiction with its graver purposes, if any, concealed—fiction unadorned with overt message or historical significance—rubs our noses in the fact that narratives of horror, murder, and gore are a blast, a gas. When knife-fingered Freddy Krueger of the *Nightmare on Elm Street* movies disembowels someone in a geyser of blood, when Hannibal Lecter washes down his victim with a nice Chianti—the only possible reason for this nonreal, nonmeaningful event to occur is that it's going to afford us pleasure. Which leaves that pleasure obvious, exposed. It's the exposure, not the thrill, the censors want to get rid of. Again: Celebration is the only defense.

And yet—I know—while I celebrate, the new, not-very-much-improved Rome is burning.

Last year sometime, I had a conversation with a highly intelligent Scottish filmmaker who had just returned from New York. Both of us had recently seen Sylvester Stallone's mountaineering action picture *Cliffhanger.* I'd seen it in a placid upper-class London neighborhood; he'd seen it in a theater in Times Square. I had been thrilled by the movie's special effects and found the hilariously dopey script sweetly reminiscent of the comic books I'd read as a child. My friend had found the picture grimly disturbing. The Times Square theater had been filled with rowdy youths. Every time the bad guys killed someone, the youths cheered—and when a woman was murdered, they howled with delight.

I freely confess that I would have been unable to enjoy the movie under those circumstances. Too damned noisy, for one thing. And, all right, yes, as a repression fan, I could only get off on the cruelty of the villains insofar as it fired my anticipation of the moment when Sly would cut those suckers down. Another audience could just as easily have been cheering the murder of Jews in *Schindler's List* or of blacks in *Mississippi Burning*. I understand that, and it would be upsetting and frightening to be surrounded by a crowd that seemed to have abandoned the non-negotiable values.

Michael Medved believes—not that one film produces one vicious act—but that a ceaseless barrage of anti-religion, anti-family, slap-happy-gore films and fictions has contributed to the erosion of values so evident on 42nd Street. I don't know whether this is true or not—neither does he—but, as with the judge's remarks in the Bulger case, it strikes me as a very suspicious place to start. Surely, the Scotsman's story illustrates that the problem lies not on the screen but in the seats, in the lives that have produced that audience. Fiction cannot make of people what life has not, good or evil.

But more to the point: Though the Times Square crowd's reaction was scary—rude, too—it was not necessarily harmful in itself, either to them or to me. For all I know, it was a beneficial release of energy and hostility, good for the mental health. And in any case, it took place in the context of their experience of a fiction and so (outside of the unmannerly noise they made) was beyond my right to judge, approve, or condemn. Nobody has to explain his private pleasures to me.

Because fiction and reality are different. It seems appalling that anyone should have to say it, but it does need to be said. Fiction is not subject to the same moral restrictions as real life. It should remain absolutely free because, at whatever level, it is, like sex, a deeply personal experience engaged in by consent in the hope of anything from momentary release to satori. Like sex, it is available to fools and creeps and monsters, and that's life; that's tough. Because fiction is, like sex, at the core of our individual humanity. Stories are the basic building blocks of spiritual maturity. No one has any business messing with them. No one at all.

Reality, on the other hand, needs its limits, maintained by force if necessary, for the simple reason that there are actions that directly harm the safety and liberty of other people. They don't merely offend them; they don't just threaten their delicate sense of themselves; they *hurt* them— really, painfully, a lot. Again, it seems wildly improbable that this should be forgotten, but Americans' current cultural discussions show every evidence that it has been. Just as fictions are being discussed as if they were actions, actual crimes and atrocities are being discussed as if they were cultural events, subject to aesthetic considerations. Trial lawyers won a lesser conviction for lady-killer Robert Chambers by claiming his victim was promiscuous: columnists defended Lorena Bobbitt, saying it might be all right to mutilate a man in his sleep, provided he was a really nasty guy. The fellows who savaged Reginald Denny during the Los Angeles riots claim they were just part of the psychology of the mob. And the Menendez brothers based much of their defense on a portrayal of themselves as victims, a portrayal of their victims as abusers. These are all arguments appropriate to fiction only. Only in fiction are crimes mitigated by symbolism and individuals judged not for what they've done but because of what they represent. To say that the reaction to fiction and the reaction to reality are on a continuum is moral nonsense.

Fiction and real life must be distinguished from one another. The radical presumption of fiction is play, the radical presumption of real life is what Martin Amis called "the gentleness of human flesh." If we have lost the will to defend that gentleness, then God help us, because consigning Chucky to the flames is not going to bring it back.

One of the very best works of violent fiction to come along in the past few years is Thomas Harris' novel *The Silence of the Lambs*. The story, inspired, like *Psycho,* by the real-life case of murderer Ed Gein, concerns the hunt for the serial killer Jame Gumb, a failed transsexual who strips his female victims' flesh in order to create a woman costume in which he can clothe himself.

When Harris introduces the killer's next victim—Catherine Martin—he presents us with a character we aren't meant to like very much. Rich, spoiled, arrogant, dissolute. Catherine is admirable only for the desperate cleverness she shows in her battle to stay alive. But for the rest of the novel—the attempt to rescue Catherine before it's too late—Harris depends on our fear for her, our identification with her, our deep desire to see her get out of this in one piece. He relies on our irrational—spiritual—conviction that Catherine, irritating though she may be, must not be killed because . . . for no good reason: because she Must Not. Harris knowingly taps in to the purely emotional imperative we share with the book's heroine, Clarice Starling, the FBI agent who's trying to crack the case: Like her, we won't be able to sleep until the screaming of innocent lambs is stopped. Harris makes pretty well sure of it.

At the end, in the only injection of auctorial opinion in the book, Harris wryly notes that the scholarly journals' articles on the Gumb case never use the words *crazy* or *evil* in their discussions of the killer. The intellectual world is uncomfortable with the inherent Must Not, the instinctive absolute, and the individual responsibility those words ultimately suggest. Harris, I think, is trying to argue that if we don't trust our mindless belief in the sanctity of human life, we produce monsters that the sleep of reason never dreamed of. *The Silence of the Lambs,* as the title suggests, is a dramatization of a world in which the spirit has lost its power to speak.

We live in that world, no question. With our culture atomizing, we think we can make up enough rules, impose enough restrictions, inject enough emptiness into our language to replace the shared moral conviction that's plainly gone. I think all stories—along with being fun—have the potential to humanize precisely because the richest fun of them is dependent on our identification with their characters. But stories can't do for us what experience hasn't. They're just not that powerful. And if some people are living lives in our society that make them unfit for even the most shallow thrills of fiction, you can't solve that problem by eliminating the fiction. By allowing politicians and pundits to turn our attention to "the problem of fictional violence," we are really allowing them to make us turn our backs on the problems of reality.

After a crime like the Jamie Bulger murder, we should be asking ourselves a million questions: about our abandonment of family life, about our approach to poverty and unemployment, about the failures of our educational systems—about who and what we are and the ways we treat each other, the things we do and omit to do. These are hard, sometimes boring questions. But when instead we let our discussions devolve, as they have, into this glamour-rotten debate on whether people should be able to enjoy whatever fiction they please, then we make meaningless the taking of an individual's life. And that's no fun at all.

WRITING TASKS—ANDREW KLAVEN

1. While many people are wringing their hands in despair at the amount of violence in fiction, films, and television and demanding that somebody do something, Klaven celebrates such violence and gore and seems to want even more. He is careful, though, to separate the world of fiction from the real world. He argues that reality "needs its limits, maintained by force if necessary," but that fiction "is not subject to the same moral restrictions as real life." The question in the minds of many is whether or not the two worlds of "reality" and "fiction" can be so clearly separated. Do fictional presentations affect the real world? This is not an easy question to answer with certainty. But what do you think? Do you ever find your own behavior or that of others you know influenced by fiction, movies, television programs and music? Collect your thoughts by doing an extensive prewriting based on your own experiences and observations. Phrase a central point that captures where you stand on this issue. Divide the central point into subpoints. You may wish to make your paper an argument, an associational, or a deductive essay.

2. Write a review of "the best horror movie (or book) I have ever seen." Give an overview of the book in your introduction, and dis-

cuss specific characters, descriptive passages, or situations in the body of your paper.

A Rescue Without Cheers
PETER K. KRAMER

Last summer, I was granted a privilege rarely vouchsafed a psychiatrist: I felt a human being return to life under my hands. The moment—haunting, humbling—immediately turned bittersweet.

The setting was a New England pond, one my family has visited over many years. Though open to the public, the pond's beach tends to attract locals, largely middle-class whites, drivers of station wagons and jeeps. On that summer's day, the parking lot overflowed with campers and Cadillacs with out-of-state tags. I asked the kid who checks stickers what was up. "Company picnic."

"I hope they're not all in the water," I said, and he gave me a funny look. I soon understood why. The employees were all black; the kid thought I was making a racist remark.

The park felt crowded. Boom boxes were at full blast, and the pond, which we had chosen for its innocuousness—we were hoping to make our youngest more comfortable in the water—was roiled by splashing limbs. Suddenly the lifeguard raced into the pond.

"This is for real," I told my wife, and I headed to the water's edge. From only five yards out, the guard dragged the limp body of a boy. As soon as the victim hit the beach, a competent-looking woman checked for respiration and blew two breaths into his mouth. She announced herself as a cardiac nurse, and I felt immense relief. It's been some time since I've had my hands on a lifeless body. I felt for a pulse—there was none—and began pumping the chest. The lifeguard helped to steady the man's neck. Someone ran to a car phone.

The crowd was agitated around us, but I saw only the body. A short teen-age boy, skin purplish brown with a sickly, pale cast. Counting, thrusting, listening to the nurse. And then a pulse, not the subtle kind you search for in the arteries, but a big thump-thumping right under my hand.

Not until the heartbeat returned did I give a thought to race. But as the young man began to groan and sputter, I felt self-conscious about my white hands on this dusty maroon chest, and the whiteness of the nurse and lifeguard, and the angry energy—for they did, I now realized, sound hostile—of the crowd. It was as if I were doing something of dubious worth in an alien culture, rather than something of unquestioned worth in my own.

We had been through six cycles of breathing and pumping, under a minute. It had seemed interminable. The flood of impressions was as you might imagine: the youth of the boy, the vibes from the crowd, the steadiness of the nurse—I was immensely grateful to her—and the vulnerability of the lifeguard, who was huge and sturdy and terribly shaken over this having happened on his watch.

The police arrived with oxygen. The young man tried to vomit but could not. Then came the rescue squad. How long was he under, they wanted to know? Three minutes, the crowd said. Having just endured an interminable 60 seconds, I knew this estimate might be wrong. It was then that I understood how we looked.

The crowd believed that the lifeguard had acted too slowly because he was inattentive to black voices, because black lives do not matter, because no one wants black swimmers in the white man's water. The estimate of his delay began to rise. Five minutes, a woman said. I showed you where he was in the water, and I called five minutes before you came.

What with the noisy waterfront, might someone have shouted unheard for five minutes? For three? Unlikely—the strand is 20 yards wide. What was clear is what is too often clear, the incompatibility of divergent perspectives.

The aftermath was telling. No one thanked us. How stunning to save a life in the sight of dozens of a boy's friends and receive not a word of thanks. The crowd dispersed angrily, regathered at a barbecue pit.

Anger with the lifeguard was perhaps understandable. And when there is so much emotion—death, life—people do vent by arguing and accusing. But what about the nurse, fortuitously tending her children at this spot? In the age of drug-resistant tuberculosis and heaven knows what else, she pressed her mouth to a stranger's and gave him breath.

White bystanders praised the guard belligerently. Splendid rescue. The lifeguard, the nurse and I were a group apart, comrades, trusting only one another. He looked shattered. I said that in emergencies you rarely do things just the way you wish. Now and then you do well enough. At any other time in history, before the dissemination of CPR techniques, before car phones, before police departments with oxygen, this young man would have been dead. Now he was alive. This was one of the good stories.

I would say, upon reflection, that it is an American story, one tainted, as American stories are, by racial division. How did the many African-American observers see the rescue? Filtered, surely, through awareness that a large black presence is unusual on most New England beaches, through concern that a youth was at risk for unknown reasons (because he had not been taught to swim? because past medical care had failed him?), through resentment that the rescuers were to a person white. And the lifeguard, why had he not interrupted the bathers' horseplay, quieted the radios, since they made his job impossible? At the crucial moment, did he assume that just any level of shouting is normal for blacks?

I have thought of that day repeatedly in the past year. The murder of abortionists brings back that scene, and the grousing of dismissed O.J.

jurors, and the intensity of the Michigan militia. We are a nation plagued by irreconcilable perspectives. Our capacity for resentment and mistrust seems limitless.

America's forte is allowing difference to flourish, through tolerance. Today we are in civic imbalance and lack the tolerance needed to contain our diversity. The road back, if any can be found, is via attention to perspective. But it is hard to be sanguine when our starting points are so distant, when what to me is one of life's most hopeful moments is to you, and quite legitimately from your vantage, only further cause for cynicism and despair.

WRITING TASKS—PETER K. KRAMER

1. In this essay Kramer relates an incident that should have ended in relief, joy, and thankfulness but was instead tainted with suspicion and silence. This incident, along with others, leads him to declare, "We are a nation plagued by irreconcilable perspectives. Our capacity for resentment and mistrust seems limitless." Write an essay supporting this statement. Draw examples from whatever areas of human behavior you find appropriate.

   Or, argue that his statement fails to consider the numerous ways in which we do trust each other and cooperate in even tension-filled situations. Use examples to support your thesis.

2. Kramer tells a story and then offers his thoughts about its significance in the last three paragraphs. Write a narrative essay about a personal experience or an incident you observed. In the concluding paragraphs offer your thoughts about the significance of the narrated event.

In Defense of Prejudice
JONATHAN RAUCH

The war on prejudice is now, in all likelihood, the most uncontroversial social movement in America. Opposition to "hate speech," formerly identified with the liberal left, has become a bipartisan piety. In the past year, groups and factions that agree on nothing else have agreed that the public expression of any and all prejudices must be forbidden. On the left, protesters and editorialists have insisted that Francis L. Lawrence resign as president of Rutgers University for describing blacks as "a disadvantaged population that doesn't have that genetic, hereditary background to have a higher average." On the other side of the ideological divide, Ralph Reed, the executive director of the Christian Coalition, responded to criticism of the religious right by calling a press conference to denounce a supposed outbreak of "name-calling, scapegoating, and religious bigotry." Craig Rogers, an evangelical Christian student at California State University, recently filed a $2.5 million sexual-harassment suit against a lesbian professor of psychology, claiming that anti-male bias in one of her lectures violated campus rules and left him feeling "raped and trapped."

In universities and on Capitol Hill, in workplaces and newsrooms, authorities are declaring that there is no place for racism, sexism, homophobia, Christian-bashing, and other forms of prejudice in public debate or even in private thought. "Only when racism and other forms of prejudice are expunged," say the crusaders for sweetness and light, "can minorities be safe and society be fair." So sweet, this dream of a world without prejudice. But the very last thing society should do is seek to utterly eradicate racism and other forms of prejudice.

I suppose I should say, in the customary I-hope-I-don't-sound-too-defensive tone, that I am not a racist and that this is not an article favoring racism or any other particular prejudice. It is an article favoring intellectual pluralism, which permits the expression of various forms of bigotry and always will. Although we like to hope that a time will come when no one will believe that people come in types and that each type belongs with its own kind, I doubt such a day will ever arrive. By all indications, *Homo sapiens* is a tribal species for whom "us versus them" comes naturally and must be continually pushed back. Where there is genuine freedom of expression, there will be racist expression. There will also be people who believe that homosexuals are sick or threaten children or—especially among teenagers—are rightful targets of manly savagery. Homosexuality will always be incomprehensible to most people, and what is incomprehensible is feared. As for anti-Semitism, it appears to be a hardier virus than influenza. If you want pluralism, than you get racism and sexism and homophobia, and communism and fascism and xenophobia and tribalism, and that is just for a start. If you want to believe in intellectual freedom and the progress of knowledge and the advancement of science and all those other good things, then you must swallow hard and accept this: for as thickheaded and wayward an animal as us, the realistic question is how to make the best of prejudice, not how to eradicate it.

Indeed, "eradicating prejudice" is so vague a proposition as to be meaningless. Distinguishing prejudice reliably and nonpolitically from nonprejudice, or even defining it crisply, is quite hopeless. We all feel we know prejudice when we see it. But do we? At the University of Michigan, a student said in a classroom discussion that he considered homosexuality a disease treatable with therapy. He was summoned to a formal disciplinary hearing for violating the school's policy against speech that "victimizes" people based on "sexual orientation." Now, the evidence is abundant that this particular hypothesis is wrong, and any American homosexual can attest to the harm that the student's hypothesis has inflicted on many real people. But was it a statement of prejudice or of misguided belief? Hate speech or hypothesis? Many Americans who do not regard themselves as bigots or haters believe that homosexuality is a treatable disease. They may be wrong, but are they all bigots? I am unwilling to say so, and if you are willing, beware. The line between a prejudiced belief and a merely controversial one is elusive, and the harder you look the more elusive it becomes. "God hates homosexuals" is a statement of fact, not of bias, to those who believe it; "American criminals are disproportionately black" is a statement of bias, not of fact, to those who disbelieve it.

Who is right? You may decide, and so may others, and there is no need to agree. That is the great innovation of intellectual pluralism (which is to say, of post-Enlightenment science, broadly defined). We cannot know in advance or for sure which belief is prejudice and which is truth, but to advance knowledge we don't need to know. The genius of intellectual pluralism lies not in doing away with prejudices and dogmas but in channeling them—making them socially productive by pitting prejudice against prejudice and dogma against dogma, exposing all to withering public criticism. What survives at the end of the day is our base of knowledge.

What they told us in high school about this process is very largely a lie. The Enlightenment tradition taught us that science is orderly, antiseptic, rational, the province of detached experimenters and high-minded logicians. In the popular view, science stands for reason against prejudice, open-mindedness against dogma, calm consideration against passionate attachment—all personified by pop-science icons like the magisterially deductive Sherlock Holmes, the coolly analytic Mr. Spock, the genially authoritative Mr. Science (from our junior-high science films). Yet one of science's dirty secrets is that although science as a whole is as unbiased as anything human can be, scientists are just as biased as anyone else, sometimes more so. "One of the strengths of science," writes the philosopher of science David L. Hull, "is that it does not require that scientists be unbiased, only that different scientists have diferent biases." Another dirty secret is that, no less than the rest of us, scientists can be dogmatic and pigheaded. "Although this pigheadedness often damages the careers of individual scientists," says Hull, "it is beneficial for the manifest goal of science," which relies on people to invest years in their ideas and defend them passionately. And the dirtiest secret of all, if you believe in the antiseptic popular view of science, is that this most ostensibly rational of enterprises depends on the most irrational of motives—ambition, narcissism, animus, even revenge. "Scientists acknowledge that among their motivations are natural curiosity, the love of truth, and the desire to help humanity, but other inducements exist as well, and one of them is to 'get that son of a bitch,'" says Hull. "Time and again, scientists whom I interviewed described the powerful spur that 'showing that son of a bitch' supplied to their own research."

Many people, I think, are bewildered by this unvarnished and all too human view of science. They believe that for a system to be unprejudiced, the people in it must also be unprejudiced. In fact, the opposite is true. Far from eradicating ugly or stupid ideas and coarse or unpleasant motives, intellectual pluralism relies upon them to excite intellectual passion and redouble scientific effort. I know of no modern idea more ugly and stupid than that the Holocaust never happened, nor any idea more viciously motivated. Yet the deniers' claims that the Auschwitz gas chambers could not have worked led to closer study and, in 1993, research showing, at last, how they actually did work. Thanks to prejudice and stupidity, another opening for doubt has been shut.

An enlightened and efficient intellectual regime lets a million prejudices bloom, including many that you or I may regard as hateful or grotesque. It avoids any attempt to stamp out prejudice, because stamping out prejudice really means forcing everyone to share the same prejudice, namely that of whoever is in authority. The great American philosopher Charles Sanders Peirce wrote in 1877: "When complete agreement could not otherwise be reached, a general massacre of all who have not thought in a certain way has proved a very effective means of settling opinion in a country." In speaking of "settling opinion," Peirce was writing about one of the two or three most fundamental problems that any human society must confront and solve. For most societies down through the centuries, this problem was dealt with in the manner he described: errors were identified by the authorities—priests, politburos, dictators—or by mass opinion, and then the error-makers were eliminated along with their putative mistakes. "Let all men who reject the established belief be terrified into silence," wrote Peirce, describing this system. "This method has, from the earliest times, been one of the chief means of upholding correct theological and political doctrines."

Intellectual pluralism substitutes a radically different doctrine: we kill our mistakes rather than each other. Here I draw on another great philosopher, the late Karl Popper, who pointed out that the critical method of science "consists in letting our hypotheses die in our stead." Those who are in error are not (or are not supposed to be) banished or excommunicated or forced to sign a renunciation or required to submit to "rehabilitation" or sent for psychological counseling. It is the error we punish, not the errant. By letting people make errors—even mischievous, spiteful errors (as, for instance, Galileo's insistence on Copernicanism was taken to be in 1633)— pluralism creates room to challenge orthodoxy, think imaginatively, experiment boldly. Brilliance and bigotry are empowered in the same stroke.

Pluralism is the principle that protects and makes a place in human company for that loneliest and most vulnerable of all minorities, the minority who is hounded and despised among blacks and whites, gays and straights, who is suspect or criminal among every tribe and in every nation of the world, and yet on whom progress depends: the dissident. I am not saying that dissent is always or even usually enlightened. Most of the time it is foolish and self-serving. No dissident has the right to be taken seriously, and the fact that Aryan Nation racists or Nation of Islam anti-Semites are unorthodox does not entitle them to respect. But what goes around comes around. As a supporter of gay marriage, for example, I reject the majority's view of family, and as a Jew I reject its view of God. I try to be civil, but the fact is that most Americans regard my views on marriage as a reckless assault on the most fundamental of all institutions, and many people are more than a little discomfited by the statement "Jesus Christ was no more divine than anybody else" (which is why so few people ever say it). Trap the racists and anti-Semites, and you lay a trap for me too. Hunt for them with eradication in your mind, and you have brought dissent itself within your sights.

The new crusade against prejudice waves aside such warnings. Like earlier crusades against antisocial ideas, the mission is fueled by good (if cocksure) intentions and a genuine sense of urgency. Some kinds of error are held to be intolerable, like pollutants that even in small traces poison the water for a whole town. Some errors are so pernicious as to damage real people's lives, so wrongheaded that no person of right mind or goodwill could support them. Like their forebears of other stripe—the Church in its campaigns against heretics, the McCarthyites in their campaigns against Communists—the modern anti-racist and anti-sexist and anti-homophobic campaigners are totalists, demanding not that misguided ideas and ugly expressions be corrected or criticized but that they be eradicated. They make war not on errors but on error, and like other totalists they act in the name of public safety—the safety, especially, of minorities.

The sweeping implications of this challenge to pluralism are not, I think, well enough understood by the public at large. Indeed, the new brand of totalism has yet even to be properly named. "Multiculturalism," for instance, is much too broad. "Political correctness" comes closer but is too trendy and snide. For lack of anything else, I will call the new antipluralism "purism," since its major tenet is that society cannot be just until the last traces of invidious prejudice have been scrubbed away. Whatever you call it, the purists' way of seeing things has spread through American intellectual life with remarkable speed, so much so that many people will blink at you uncomprehendingly or even call you a racist (or sexist or homophobe, etc.) if you suggest that expressions of racism should be tolerated or that prejudice has its part to play.

The new purism sets out, to begin with, on a campaign against words, for words are the currency of prejudice, and if prejudice is hurtful then so must be prejudiced words. "We are not safe when these violent words are among us," wrote Mari Matsuda, then a UCLA law professor. Here one imagines gangs of racist words swinging chains and smashing heads in back alleys. To suppress bigoted language seems, at first blush, reasonable, but it quickly leads to a curious result. A peculiar kind of verbal shamanism takes root, as though certain expressions, like curses or magical incantations, carry in themselves the power to hurt or heal—as though words were bigoted rather than people. "Context is everything," people have always said. The use of the word "nigger" in *Huckleberry Finn* does not make the book an "act" of hate speech—or does it? In the new view, this is no longer so clear. The very utterance of the word "nigger" (at least by a non-black) is a racist act. When a *Sacramento Bee* cartoonist put the word "nigger" mockingly in the mouth of a white supremacist, there were howls of protest and 1,400 canceled subscriptions and an editorial apology, even though the word was plainly being invoked against racists, not against blacks.

Faced with escalating demands of verbal absolutism, newspapers issue lists of forbidden words. The expressions "gyp" (derived from "Gypsy") and "Dutch treat" were among the dozens of terms stricken as "offensive" in a much-ridiculed (and later withdrawn) *Los Angeles Times* speech code. The University of Missouri journalism school issued a *Dictionary of Cautionary Words and Phrases,* which included "*Buxom:* Offensive reference to a woman's chest. Do not use. See 'Woman.' *Codger:* Offensive reference to a senior citizen."

As was bound to happen, purists soon discovered that chasing around after words like "gyp" or "buxom" hardly goes to the roots of the problem. As long as they remain bigoted, bigots will simply find other words. If they can't call you a kike then they will say Jewboy, Judas, or Hebe, and when all those are banned they will press words like "oven" and "lampshade" into their service. The vocabulary of hate is potentially as rich as your dictionary, and all you do by banning language used by cretins is to let them decide what the rest of us may say. The problem, some purists have concluded, must therefore go much deeper than laws: it must go to the deeper level of ideas. Racism, sexism, homophobia, and the rest must be built into the very structure of American society and American patterns of thought, so pervasive yet so insidious that, like water to a fish, they are both omnipresent and unseen. The mere existence of prejudice constructs a society whose very nature is prejudiced.

This line of thinking was pioneered by feminists, who argued that pornography, more than just being expressive, is an act by which men construct an oppressive society. Racial activists quickly picked up the argument. Racist expressions are themselves acts of oppression, they said. "All racist speech constructs the social reality that constrains the liberty of nonwhites because of their race," wrote Charles R. Lawrence III, then a law professor at Stanford. From the purist point of view, a society with even one racist is a racist society, because the idea itself threatens and demeans its targets. They cannot feel wholly safe or wholly welcome as long as racism is present. Pluralism says: There will always be some racists. Marginalize them, ignore them, exploit them, ridicule them, take pains to make their policies illegal, but otherwise leave them alone. Purists say: That's not enough. Society cannot be just until these pervasive and oppressive ideas are searched out and eradicated.

And so what is now under way is a growing drive to eliminate prejudice from every corner of society. I doubt that many people have noticed how far-reaching this anti-pluralist movement is becoming.

In universities: Dozens of universities have adopted codes proscribing speech or other expression that (this is from Stanford's policy, which is more or less representative) "is intended to insult or stigmatize an individual or a small number of individuals on the basis of their sex, race, color, handicap, religion, sexual orientation or national and ethnic origin." Some codes punish only persistent harassment of a targeted individual, but many, following the purist doctrine that even one racist is too many, go much further. At Penn, an administrator declared: "We at the University of Pennsylvania have guaranteed students and the community that they can live in a community free of sexism, racism, and homophobia." Here is the purism that gives "political correctness" its distinctive combination of puffy high-mindedness and authoritarian zeal.

In school curricula: "More fundamental than eliminating racial segregation has to be the removal of racist thinking, assumptions, symbols, and materials in the curriculum," writes theorist Molefi Kete Asante. In practice, the effort to "remove racist thinking" goes well beyond striking egregious references from textbooks. In many cases it becomes a kind of mental engineering in which students are encouraged to see prejudice everywhere; it includes teaching identity politics as an antidote to internalized racism; it rejects mainstream science as "white male" thinking; and it tampers with history, installing such dubious notions as that the ancient Greeks stole their culture from Africa or that an ancient carving of a bird is an example of "African experimental aeronautics."

In criminal law: Consider two crimes. In each, I am beaten brutally; in each, my jaw is smashed and my skull is split in just the same way. However, in the first crime my assailant calls me an "asshole"; in the second he calls me a "queer." In most states, in many localities, and, as of September 1994, in federal cases, these two crimes are treated differently: the crime motivated by bias—or deemed to be so motivated by prosecutors and juries—gets a stiffer punishment. "Longer prison terms for bigots," shrilled Brooklyn Democratic Congressman Charles Schumer, who introduced the federal hate-crimes legislation, and those are what the law now provides. Evidence that the assailant holds prejudiced beliefs, even if he doesn't actually express them while committing an offense, can serve to elevate the crime. Defendants in hate-crimes cases may be grilled on how many black friends they have and whether they have told racist jokes. To increase a prison sentence only because of the defendant's "prejudice" (as gauged by prosecutor and jury) is, of course, to try minds and punish beliefs. Purists say, Well, they are dangerous minds and poisonous beliefs.

In the workplace: Though government cannot constitutionally suppress bigotry directly, it is now busy doing so indirectly by requiring employers to eliminate prejudice. Since the early 1980s, courts and the Equal Employment Opportunity Commission have moved to bar workplace speech deemed to create a hostile or abusive working environment for minorities. The law, held a federal court in 1988, "does require than an employer take prompt action to prevent . . . bigots from expressing their opinions in a way that abuses or offends their co-workers," so as to achieve "the goal of eliminating prejudices and biases from our society." So it was, as UCLA law professor Eugene Volokh notes, that the EEOC charged that a manufacturer's ads using admittedly accurate depictions of samurai, kabuki, and sumo were "racist" and "offensive to people of Japanese origin"; that a Pennsylvania court found that an employer's printing Bible verses on paychecks was religious harassment of Jewish employees; that an employer had to desist using gender-based job titles like "foreman" and "draftsman" after a female employee sued.

On and on the campaign goes, darting from one outbreak of prejudice to another like a cat chasing flies. In the American Bar Association, activists demand that lawyers who express "bias or prejudice" be penalized. In the Education Department, the civil-rights office presses for a ban on computer bulletin board comments that "show hostility toward a person or group based on sex, race or color, including slurs, negative stereotypes, jokes or pranks." In its security checks for government jobs, the FBI takes to asking whether applicants are "free of biases against any class of citizens," whether, for instance, they have told racist jokes or indicated other "prejudices." Joke police! George Orwell, grasping the close relationship of jokes to dissent, said that every joke is a tiny revolution. The purists will have no such rebellions.

The purist campaign reaches, in the end, into the mind itself. In a lecture at the University of New Hampshire, a professor compared writing to sex ("You and the subject become one"); he was suspended and required to apologize, but what was most insidious was the order to undergo university-approved counseling to have his mind straightened out. At the University of Pennsylvania, a law lecturer said, "We have ex-slaves here who should know about the Thirteenth Amendment"; he was banished from campus for a year and required to make a public apology, and he, too, was compelled to attend a "sensitivity and racial awareness" session. Mandatory re-education of alleged bigots is the natural consequence of intellectual purism. Prejudice must be eliminated!

Ah, but the task of scouring minds clean is Augean. "Nobody escapes," said a Rutgers University report on campus prejudice. Bias and prejudice, it found, cross every conceivable line, from sex to race to politics: "No matter who you are, no matter what the color of your skin, no matter what your gender or sexual orientation, no matter what you believe, no matter how you behave, there is somebody out there who doesn't like people of your kind." Charles Lawrence writes: "Racism is ubiquitous. We are all racists." If he means that most of us think racist thoughts of some sort at one time or another, he is right. If we are going to "eliminate prejudices and biases from our society," then the work of the prejudice police is unending. They are doomed to hunt and hunt and hunt, scour and scour and scour.

What is especially dismaying is that the purists pursue prejudice in the name of protecting minorities. In order to protect people like me (homosexual), they must pursue people like me (dissident). In order to bolster minority self-esteem, they suppress minority opinion. There are, of course, all kinds of practical and legal problems with the purists' campaign: the incursions against the First Amendment; the inevitable abuses by prosecutors and activists who define as "hateful" or "violent" whatever speech they dislike or can score points off of; the lack of any evidence that repressing prejudice eliminates rather than inflames it. But minorities, of all people, ought to remember that by definition we cannot prevail by numbers, and we generally cannot prevail by force. Against the power of ignorant mass opinion and group prejudice and superstition, we have only our voices. If you doubt that minorities' voices are powerful weapons, think of the lengths to which Southern officials went to silence the Reverend Martin Luther King Jr. (recall that the city commissioner of Montgomery, Alabama, won a $500,000 libel suit, later overturned in *New York Times* v. *Sullivan* [1964], regarding an advertisement in the *Times* placed by civil-rights leaders who denounced the Montgomery police). Think of how much gay people have improved their lot over twenty-five years simply by refusing to remain silent. Recall the Michigan student who was prosecuted for saying that homosexuality is a treatable disease, and notice that he was black. Under that Michigan speech code, more than twenty blacks were charged with racist speech, while no instance of racist speech by whites was punished. In Florida, the hate-speech law was invoked against a black man who called a policeman a "white cracker"; not so surprisingly, in the first hate-crimes case to reach the Supreme Court, the victim was white and the defendant black.

In the escalating war against "prejudice," the right is already learning to play by the rules that were pioneered by the purist activists of the left. Last year leading Democrats, including the President, criticized the Republican Party for being increasingly in the thrall of the Christian right. Some of the rhetoric was harsh ("fire-breathing Christian radical right"), but it wasn't vicious or even clearly wrong. Never mind: when Democratic Representative Vic Fazio said Republicans were "being forced to the fringes by the aggressive political tactics of the religious right," the chairman of the Republican National Committee, Haley Barbour, said, "Christian-bashing" was "the left's preferred form of religious bigotry." Bigotry! Prejudice!

"Christians active in politics are now on the receiving end of an extraordinary campaign of bias and prejudice," said the conservative leader William J. Bennett. One discerns, here, where the new purism leads. Eventually, any criticism of any group will be "prejudice."

Here is the ultimate irony of the new purism: words, which pluralists hope can be substituted for violence, are redefined by purists *as* violence. "The experience of being called 'nigger,' 'spic,' 'Jap,' or 'kike' is like receiving a slap in the face," Charles Lawrence wrote in 1990. "Psychic injury is no less an injury than being struck in the face, and it often is far more severe." This kind of talk is commonplace today. Epithets, insults, often even polite expressions of what's taken to be prejudice are called by purists "assaultive speech," "words that wound," "verbal violence." "To me, racial epithets are not speech," one University of Michigan law professor said. "They are bullets." In her speech accepting the 1993 Nobel Prize for Literature in Stockholm, Sweden, the author Toni Morrison said this: "Oppressive language does more than represent violence; it is violence."

It is not violence. I am thinking back to a moment on the subway in Washington, a little thing. I was riding home late one night and a squad of noisy kids, maybe seventeen or eighteen years old, noisily piled into the car. They yelled across the car and a girl said, "Where do we get off?"

A boy said, "Farragut North."

The girl: "*Faggot* North!"

The boy: "Yeah! Faggot North!"

General hilarity.

First, before the intellect resumes control, there is a moment of fear, an animal moment. Who are they? How many of them? How dangerous? Where is the way out? All of these things are noted preverbally and assessed by the gut. Then the brain begins an assessment: they are sober, this is probably too public a place for them to do it, there are more girls than boys, they were just talking, it is probably nothing.

They didn't notice me and there was no incident. The teenage babble flowed on, leaving me to think. I became interested in my own reaction: the jump of fear out of nowhere like an alert animal, the sense for a brief time that one is naked and alone and should hide or run away. For a time, one ceases to be a human being and becomes instead a faggot.

The fear engendered by these words is real. The remedy is as clear and as imperfect as ever: protect citizens against violence. This, I grant, is something that American society has never done very well and now does quite poorly. It is no solution to define words as violence or prejudice as oppression, and then by cracking down on words or thoughts pretend that we are doing something about violence and oppression. No doubt it is easier to pass a speech code or hate-crimes law and proclaim the streets safer than actually to make the streets safer, but the one must never be confused with the other. Every cop or prosecutor chasing words is one fewer chasing criminals. In a world rife with real violence and oppression, full of Rwandas and Bosnias and eleven-year-olds spraying bullets at children in Chicago and in turn being executed by gang lords, it is odious of Toni Morrison to say that words are violence.

Indeed, equating "verbal violence" with physical violence is a treacherous, mischievous business. Not long ago a writer was charged with viciously and gratuitously wounding the feelings and dignity of millions of people. He was charged, in effect, with exhibiting flagrant prejudice against Muslims and outrageously slandering their beliefs. "What is freedom of expression?" mused Salman Rushdie a year after the ayatollahs sentenced him to death and put a price on his head. "Without the freedom to offend, it ceases to exist." I can think of nothing sadder than that minority activists, in their haste to make the world better, should be the ones to forget the lesson of Rushdie's plight: for minorities, pluralism, not purism, is the answer. The campaigns to eradicate prejudice—all of them, the speech codes and workplace restrictions and mandatory therapy for accused bigots and all the rest—should stop, now. The whole objective of eradicating prejudice, as opposed to correcting and criticizing it, should be repudiated as a fool's errand. Salman Rushdie is right, Toni Morrison wrong, and minorities belong at his side, not hers.

WRITING TASKS—JONATHAN RAUCH

1. Write a deductive essay agreeing or disagreeing with one of the following statements from Rauch's essay:

    "But the very last thing society should do is seek to utterly eradicate racism and other forms of prejudice." (Paragraph 2)

    "Where there is genuine freedom of expression, there will be racist expression." (Paragraph 3)

    "An enlightened and efficient intellectual regime lets a million prejudices bloom, including many that you or I may regard as hateful or grotesque." (Paragraph 8)

    ". . . stamping out prejudice really means forcing everyone to share the same prejudice, mamely that of whoever is in authority." (Paragraph 8)

    "It is no solution to define words as violence or prejudice as oppression, and then by cracking down on words or thoughts pretend that we are doing something about violence and oppression." (Paragraph 34)

    Before you begin, find the passage you have selected in the essay and read it again in the context of the paragraphs before and after so you understand the meaning of the quotation fully. Collect your thoughts with a thorough prewriting. Divide your potential content into subpoints before beginning your first draft.

2. In the last paragraph of his essay Rauch quotes novelist Salman Rushdie: "What is freedom of expression? Without the freedom to offend, it ceases to exist." Write an essay exploring your thoughts on this statement. Do you think freedom of expression should be restricted when it offends others? If so, at what point does the offensiveness of speech justify its restriction? Or is freedom of expression so valuable that any restrictions on it should be resisted? Take Rauch's arguments into consideration as you prepare your paper. You might also get some ideas from the other essays in this text: "Toxins in the Mother Tongue" by David James Duncan on page 300, "In Praise of Gore" by Andrew Klaven on page 336, and "Becoming Desensitized to Hate Words" by Ellen Goodman on page 324.

Anatomy of an Assault
BRUCE SHAPIRO

Alone in my home I am staring at the television screen and shouting. On the evening local news I have unexpectedly encountered video footage, several months old, of myself riding on an ambulance gurney, bright green shirt open and drenched with blood, skin pale, knee raised, trying desperately and with utter futility to find relief from pain.

On the evening of August 7, 1994, I was among seven people stabbed and seriously wounded in a coffee bar a few blocks from my house in New Haven. Any televised recollection of this incident would be upsetting. But the anger that has me shouting tonight is quite specific, and political, in origin: My picture is being shown on the news to illustrate why Connecticut's legislature plans to lock up more criminals for a longer time. A picture of my body, contorted and bleeding, has become a propaganda image in the crime war.

I had not planned to write about this assault. But for months now the politics of the nation have in large part been the politics of crime, and I am unwilling to be a silent poster child in this debate.

The physical and political truth about violence and crime lie in their specificity, so here is what happened: I had gone out for after-dinner coffee that evening with two friends, Martin and Anna. At 9:45 we arrived at a recently opened coffeehouse on Audubon Street, a block occupied by an arts high school, a few pleasant shops, and upscale condos. Entering, we said hello to another friend, a former student of Anna's named Christina, who the day before had started working behind the counter. We sat at a small table near the front of the café; about 15 people were scattered around the room. Just before 10:00, the owner announced closing time. Martin stood up and walked a few yards to the counter for a final refill.

Suddenly there was chaos—as if a mortar shell had landed. I looked up, heard Martin call Anna's name, saw his arm raised and a flash of metal and people leaping away from a thin bearded man with a ponytail. Tables and chairs toppled. Without thinking, I shouted to Anna "Get down!" and pulled her to the floor. She clung to my shirt, I to her shoulders, and, crouching, we pulled each other toward the door.

What actually happened I was only able to tentatively reconstruct many weeks later. Apparently, as Martin headed toward the counter, the thin bearded man, whose name we later learned was Daniel Silva, asked the time from a young man named Richard, who answered and turned to leave.

Without any warning, Silva pulled out a hunting knife with a six-inch blade and stabbed in the lower back a woman leaving with Richard, a medical technician named Kerstin. Then he stabbed Richard, severing an artery in his thigh. Silva was a slight man but he moved with demonic speed and force around the counter. He struck Martin in the thigh and in the arm he raised to protect his face. Our friend Christina had in a moment's time pushed out the screen in a window and helped the wounded Kerstin through it to safety. Christina was talking on the phone with the police when Silva lunged over the counter and stabbed her in the chest and abdomen. He stabbed Anna in the side as she and I pulled each other along the wall. He stabbed Emily, a graduate student who had been sitting quietly reading a book, in the abdomen as she tried to flee through the back door. All of this happened in about the time it has taken you to read this paragraph.

Meanwhile, I had made it out the door onto the brick sidewalk with Anna, neither of us realizing yet that she was wounded. Seeing Martin through the window, I returned inside and we came out together. Somehow we separated. I had gone no more than a few steps when I felt a hard punch in my back followed instantly by the unforgettable sensation of skin and muscle tissue parting. Silva had stabbed me about six inches above my waist, just beneath my rib cage. (That single deep stroke cut my diaphragm and sliced my spleen in half.) Without thinking, I clapped my left hand over the wound even before the knife was out and its blade caught my hand, leaving a slice across my palm and two fingers.

"Why are you doing this?" I cried out to Silva in the moment after feeling his knife punch in and yank out. As I fell to the street he leaned over my face; I vividly remember the knife's immense and glittering blade. He directed the point through my shirt into the flesh of my chest, beneath my left shoulder. I remember his brown beard, his clear blue-gray eyes looking directly into mine, the round globe of a street lamp like a halo above his head. Although I was just a few feet from a café full of people and although Martin and Anna were only yards away, the street, the city, the world felt utterly empty except for me and this thin bearded stranger with clear eyes and a knife. The space around us seemed literally to have expanded into a vast and dark canyon.

"You killed my mother," he answered. My own desperate response: "Please don't." Silva pulled the knife point out of my chest and disappeared. A moment later I saw him flying down the street on a battered, ungainly bicycle, back straight, vest flapping, and ponytail flying.

After my assailant had gone I lay on the sidewalk, hand still over the wound on my back, screaming. A security guard appeared across the street from me; I called out to him but he stood there frozen. (A few minutes later, he would help police chase Silva down.) I shouted to Anna, who was hiding behind a car down the street. Still in shock and unaware of her own injury, she ran for help, eventually collapsing on the stairs of a nearby brownstone where a prayer group that was meeting upstairs answered her desperate ringing of the doorbell.

Up the street I saw a police car's flashing blue lights, then another's, then I saw an officer with a concerned face and a crackling radio crouched beside me. I stayed conscious as the medics arrived and I was loaded into an ambulance—being filmed for television, as it turns out, though I have no memory of the crew's presence.

Being a victim is a hard idea to accept. The spirit rebels against the idea of oneself as fundamentally powerless. So I didn't think much for the first days about the meaning of being a victim; I saw no political dimension to my experience.

As I learned in more detail what had happened, I thought in my jumbled-up, anesthetized state about my injured friends—although everyone survived, their wounds ranged from quite serious to critical—and about my wounds and surgery. I also thought about my assailant. Until August 7 Daniel Silva was an unemployed junk dealer and a homeowner. He is white and lived with his mother and several dogs. He had no arrest record. A New Haven police detective who was hospitalized across the hall from me recalled Silva as a socially marginal neighborhood character. He was not, apparently, a drug user and had told neighbors about much violence in his family—in fact, not long before August 7 he showed one neighbor a scar on his thigh he said was from a stab wound.

A week earlier, Silva's 79-year-old mother had been hospitalized for diabetes. After a few days the hospital moved her to a new room; when Silva saw his mother's empty bed he panicked, but nurses swiftly took him to her new location. Still, something seemed to have snapped. Earlier on the day of the stabbings, police say, Silva released his beloved dogs, set fire to his house, and rode away on his bicycle as it burned.

While I lay in the hospital, the big story on CNN was a federal crime bill then being debated in Congress. The bill passed on August 21, a few days after I returned home. In early autumn I actually read the entire text of the crime bill—all 412 pages. What I found was that not a single one of those pages would have protected me or Anna or Martin or any of the others from our assailant. Not the longer prison terms, not the 60 new death-penalty offenses, not the three-strikes-you're-out requirements, not the summary deportations of criminal aliens. And the new, tougher than tough anti-crime provisions of the Republicans' Contract with America, like the proposed abolition of the Fourth Amendment's search and seizure protections, offer no more practical protection.

On the other hand, the mental-health and social-welfare safety net shredded throughout the '80s by Ronald Reagan and conservatives of both parties might have made a difference in the life of someone like my assailant—and thus in the life of someone like me. My assailant's growing distress in the days before August 7 was obvious to his neighbors. He had muttered darkly about relatives planning to burn down his house. A better-funded, more comprehensive social safety net might just have saved me and six others from untold pain and trouble.

From my perspective—the perspective of a crime victim—the Contract with America and its conservative Democratic counterparts are really blueprints for making the streets even less safe. Want to take away that social income subsidy called welfare? Fine. Connecticut governor John Rowland and the state legislature recently agreed to cut off all benefits after 21 months. So more people in New Haven and other cities will turn to the violence-breeding economy of crack, or emotionally implode from sheer desperation. Cut funding for those soft-headed social workers? Fine, let more children be beaten without the prospect of outside intervention, more Daniel Silvas carrying their own traumatic scars into violent adulthood. Get rid of the few amenities prisoners enjoy, like sports equipment, musical instruments, and the right to get college degrees, as proposed by the congressional right? Fine, we'll make sure that those inmates are released to their own neighborhoods tormented with unchanneled rage.

"Why didn't anyone try to stop him?" I can't even begin to guess the number of times I had to answer that question. Each time, I repeated that Silva moved too quickly, that it was simply too confusing. And each time, I found the question not just foolish but offensive.

"Why didn't anyone stop him?" To understand that question is to understand, in some measure, why crime is such a potent political issue. To begin with, the question carries not empathy but an implicit burden of blame; it really asks "Why didn't *you* stop him?" It is asked because people don't like to imagine themselves as victims. It's far easier to graft onto oneself the aggressive power of the attacker, to embrace the delusion of oneself as Arnold Schwarzenegger defeating a multitude singlehandedly.

The country is at present suffering from a huge version of this same delusion. This myth is buried deep in the political culture, nurtured in the historical tales of frontier violence and vigilantism and by the action-hero fantasies of film and television.

"Why didn't anyone stop him?" That question and its underlying implications see both heroes and victims as lone individuals. But on the receiving end of a violent attack, the fight-or-flight dichotomy didn't apply. Nor did that radically individualized notion of survival. At the coffeehouse that night, at the moments of greatest threat, there were no Schwarzeneggers, no stand-alone heroes. But neither were there abject victims. Instead, in the confusion and panic of life-threatening attack, *people reached out to one another.*

The political point here is that the Rambo justice system proposed by the right is rooted in that dangerous myth of the individual fighting against a hostile world.

I do understand the rage and frustration behind the crime-victim movement, and I can see how the right has harnessed it. For weeks I thought obsessively and angrily of those minutes on Audubon Street, when the security guard refused to approach me—as if I, wounded and helpless, were the dangerous one.

Near the six-month anniversary of the stabbings I called the prosecutor and learned that in December Silva's lawyer filed papers indicating that he intends to claim a "mental disease or defect" defense. If it is successful it would send him to a maximum-security hospital for the criminally insane for the equivalent of the maximum criminal penalty. In February the court was still awaiting a report from Silva's psychiatrist. "There's a backlog," I was told; the case is not likely to come to trial until the end of 1995 at the earliest. Intellectually, I understand that Silva is securely behind bars, that the court system is overburdened, that the delay makes no difference in the long-term outcome. But emotionally, viscerally, the delay is devastating.

Another of my bursts of victim consciousness involved the press. Objectively, I know that many people who took the trouble to express their sympathy to me found out only through news stories. And sensitive reporting can for the crime victim be a kind of ratification of the seriousness of an assault, a reflection of the community's concern. One reporter did produce level-headed and insightful stories about the Audubon Street attack. But most other reporting was exploitative, intrusive, and inaccurate. I was only a few hours out of surgery, barely able to speak, when the calls from television stations and papers started coming to my hospital room. Anna and Martin, sent home to recover, were ambushed by a TV crew as they emerged from their physician's office and later were rousted from their beds by reporters from another TV station ringing their doorbell.

The very same flawed judgments about "news value" contribute significantly to a public conception of crime that was as completely divorced from the facts as a Schwarzenegger movie. One study a few years ago found that reports on crime and justice constitute 22 to 28 percent of newspaper stories, "nearly three times as much attention as the presidency or the Congress or the state of the economy." And the most spectacular crimes—the stabbing of seven people in an upscale New Haven coffee bar, for instance—are likely to be the most "newsworthy" even though they are statistically the least likely to occur.

Media coverage also brings us to another crucial political moral: The "seriousness" of crime is a matter of race and real estate. This has been pointed out before, but it can't be said too often. Seven people stabbed in a relatively affluent, mostly white neighborhood near Yale University—this was big news on a slow news night.

Horrendous as it was, though, no one was killed. Four weeks later, a 15-year-old girl named Rashawnda Crenshaw was driving with two friends about a mile from Audubon Street. As the car in which she was a passenger turned a corner, she was shot through the window and killed. Apparently her assailants mistook her for someone else. Rashawnda Crenshaw was black and the shooting took place in the Hill, the New Haven neighborhood with the highest poverty rate. The local news coverage lasted just long enough for Rashawnda Crenshaw to be buried.

Anyone trying to deal with the reality of crime, as opposed to the fantasies peddled to win elections, needs to understand the complex suffering of those who are survivors of traumatic crimes, and the suffering and turmoil of their families. For weeks after leaving the hospital I awoke nightly, agitated and drenched with perspiration. For two months I was unable to write; my brain simply refused to concentrate. Into any moment of mental repose would rush images from the night of August 7; or, alternatively, my mind would simply not tune in at all.

What psychologists call post-traumatic stress disorder is, among other things, a profoundly political state in which the world has gone wrong, in which you feel isolated from the broader community by the inarticulable extremity of experience. I have spent a lot of time in the past few months thinking about what the world must look like to those who have survived repeated violent attacks—whether they are children battered in their homes or prisoners beaten or tortured behind bars—as well as about those, like rape victims, whose assaults are rarely granted public ratification.

The right owes much of its success to the anger of crime victims and the argument that government should do more for us. This appeal is epitomized by the rise of restitution laws, statutes requiring offenders to compensate their targets. On the surface it is hard to argue with the principle of reasonable restitution, particularly since it implies community recognition of the victim's suffering. But I wonder if these laws really will end up benefiting someone like me or if they are just empty vote-getting devices that exploit victims and could actually hurt our chances of getting speedy, substantive justice. H. Scott Wallace, former counsel to the Senate Judiciary Subcommittee on Juvenile Justice, writes in *Legal Times* that the much-touted Victim Restitution Act is "unlikely to put a single dollar into crime victims' pockets, would tie up the federal courts with waves of new damage actions, and would promote unconstitutional debtors' prisons."

I also worry that the rhetoric of restitution confuses—as does so much of the imprisonment-and-execution mania dominating the political landscape—the goals of justice and revenge. Revenge, after all, is just another version of the individualized, take-out-the-bad-guys myth.

What it all comes down to is this: What do survivors of violent crime really need? What does it mean to create a safe society? Do we need courts so overburdened by nonviolent drug offenders that the Daniel Silvas go untried for 18 months, the delays leaving victims and suspects alike in limbo? Do we need to throw nonviolent drug offenders into mandatory-sentence proximity with violent sociopaths and career criminals?

If the use of my picture on television unexpectedly brought me face to face with the memory of August 7, I relive some part of the attack daily as I watch the gruesome, voyeuristically reported details of the stabbing deaths of two people in California, Nicole Brown Simpson and Ronald Goldman.

But the public obsession with this trial, I am convinced, has no more to do with the real experience of crime victims than does the anti-crime posturing of politicians. I do not know what made my assailant act as he did. Nor do I think crime and violence can be reduced to simple political categories. I do know that the answers will not be found in social Darwinism and atomized individualism, in racism, in dismantling cities and increasing the destitution of the poor. To the contrary: Every fragment of my experience suggests that the best protections from crime and the best aid to victims are the very social institutions most derided by the right. As crime victim and citizen, I want the reality of a safe community—not a politician's fantasyland of restitution and revenge. That is my testimony.

WRITING TASKS—BRUCE SHAPIRO

1. Shapiro says "for months now the politics of the nation have in large part been the politics of crime" (his essay appeared in April 1995). Certainly the question of what to do about crime has been a major issue in our country for many years. Some favor longer sentences, tougher courts, less plea bargaining, and the hiring of more police. Others say that crime will not be sufficiently reduced until we do more about the problems of unemployment, poverty, and care for the mentally ill. Write an essay in which you explain the major arguments on both sides. You do not need to solve the

crime problem of the United States. Just show that there are reasonable arguments on both sides of the issue.

2. Shapiro accuses the media of being exploitative and intrusive when reporting crime. Watch a local television news program for several days, paying special attention to the way in which crimes are reported. The following days see how the same stories were covered in a local newspaper. Did the newspaper and the television program report the same stories? Did they say substantially the same things about each story? Write a paper comparing or contrasting the crime coverage in the newspaper and on the local television news program.

The War Room at Bellevue
GEORGE SIMPSON

Bellevue. The name conjures up images of an indoor war zone: the wounded and bleeding lining the halls, screaming for help while harried doctors in blood-stained smocks rush from stretcher to stretcher, fighting a losing battle against exhaustion and the crushing number of injured. "What's worse," says a long-time Bellevue nurse, "is that we have this image of being a hospital only for . . ." She pauses, then lowers her voice, "for crazy people."

Though neither battlefield nor Bedlam is a valid image, there is something extraordinary about the monstrous complex that spreads for five blocks along First Avenue in Manhattan. It is said best by the head nurse in Adult Emergency Service: "If you have any chance for survival, you have it here." Survival—that is why they come. Why do injured cops drive by a half-dozen other hospitals to be treated at Bellevue? They've seen the Bellevue emergency team in action.

9:00 P.M. It is a Friday night in the Bellevue emergency room. The after-work crush is over (those who've suffered through the day, only to come for help after the five-o'clock whistle has blown) and it is nearly silent except for the mutter of voices at the admitting desk, where administrative personnel discuss who will go for coffee. Across the spotless white-walled lobby, ten people sit quietly, passively, in pastel plastic chairs, waiting for word of relatives or to see doctors. In the past 24 hours, 300 people have come to the Bellevue Adult Emergency Service. Fewer than 10 percent were true emergencies. One man sleeps fitfully in the emergency ward while his heartbeat, respiration, and blood pressure are monitored by control consoles mounted over his bed. Each heartbeat trips a tiny bleep in the monitor, which attending nurses can hear across the ward. A half hour ago, doctors in the trauma room withdrew a six-inch stiletto blade from his back.

When he is stabilized, the patient will be moved upstairs to the twelve-bed Surgical Intensive Care Unit.

9:05 P.M. An ambulance backs into the receiving bay, its red and yellow lights flashing in and out of the lobby. A split second later, the glass doors burst open as a nurse and an attendant roll a mobile stretcher into the lobby. When the nurse screams, "Emergent!" the lobby explodes with activity as the way is cleared to the trauma room. Doctors appear from nowhere and transfer the bloodied body of a black man to the treatment table. Within seconds his clothes are stripped away, revealing a tiny stab wound in his left side. Three doctors and three nurses rush around the victim, each performing a task necessary to begin treatment. Intravenous needles are inserted into his arms and groin. A doctor draws blood for the lab, in case surgery is necessary. A nurse begins inserting a catheter into the victim's penis and continues to feed in tubing until the catheter reaches the bladder. Urine flows through the tube into a plastic bag. Doctors are glad not to see blood in the urine. Another nurse records pulse and blood pressure.

The victim is in good shape. He shivers slightly, although the trauma room is exceedingly warm. His face is bloodied, but shows no major lacerations. A third nurse, her elbow propped on the treatment table, asks the man a series of questions, trying to quickly outline his medical history. He answers abruptly. He is drunk. His left side is swabbed with yellow disinfectant and a doctor injects a local anesthetic. After a few seconds another doctor inserts his finger into the wound. It sinks in all the way to the knuckle. He begins to rotate his finger like a child trying to get a marble out of a milk bottle. The patient screams bloody murder and tries to struggle free.

Meanwhile in the lobby, a security guard is ejecting a derelict who has begun to drink from a bottle hidden in his coat pocket. "He's a regular, was in here just two days ago," says a nurse. "We checked him pretty close then, so he's probably okay now. Can you believe those were clean clothes we gave him?" The old man, blackened by filth, leaves quietly.

9:15 P.M. A young Hispanic man interrupts, saying his pregnant girl friend, sitting outside in his car, is bleeding heavily from her vagina. She is rushed into an examination room, treated behind closed doors, and rolled into the observation ward, where, much later in the night, a gynecologist will treat her in a special room—the same one used to examine rape victims. Nearby, behind curtains, the neurologist examines an old white woman to determine if her headaches are due to head injury. They are not.

9:45 P.M. The trauma room has been cleared and cleaned mercilessly. The examination rooms are three-quarters full—another overdose, two asthmatics, a young woman with abdominal pains. In the hallway, a derelict who has been sleeping it off urinates all over the stretcher. He sleeps on while attendants change his clothes. An ambulance—one of four that patrol Manhattan for Bellevue from 42nd Street to Houston, river to river—delivers a middle-aged white woman and two cops, the three of them soaking wet. The woman has escaped from the psychiatric floor of a nearby hospital and tried to drown herself in the East River. The cops fished her out. She lies on a stretcher shivering beneath white blankets. Her eyes stare at the ceiling. She speaks clearly when an administrative worker begins routine questioning. The cops are given hospital gowns and wait to receive tetanus shots and gamma globulin—a hedge against infection from the befouled river water. They will hang around the E.R. for another two hours, telling their story to as many as six other policemen who show up to hear it. The woman is rolled into an examination room, where a male nurse speaks gently: "They tell me you fell into the river." "No," says the woman, "I jumped. I have to commit suicide." "Why?" asks the nurse. "Because I'm insane and I can't help [it]. I have to die." The nurse gradually discovers the woman has a history of psychological problems. She is given dry bedclothes and placed under guard in the hallway. She lies on her side, staring at the wall.

The pace continues to increase. Several more overdose victims arrive by ambulance. One, a young black woman, had done a striptease on the street just before passing out. A second black woman is semiconscious and spends the better part of her time at Bellevue alternately cursing it and pleading with the doctors. Attendants find a plastic bottle coated with methadone in the pocket of a Hispanic O.D. The treatment is routinely the same, and sooner or later involves vomiting. Just after doctors begin to treat the O.D., he vomits great quantities of wine and methadone in all directions. "Lovely business, huh?" laments one of the doctors. A young nurse confides that if there were other true emergencies, the overdose victims would be given lower priority. "You can't help thinking they did it to themselves," she says, "while the others are accident victims."

10:30 P.M. A policeman who twisted his knee struggling with an "alleged perpetrator" is examined and released. By 10:30, the lobby is jammed with friends and relatives of patients in various stages of treatment and recovery. The attendant who also functions as a translator for Hispanic patients adds chairs to accommodate the overflow. The medical walk-in rate stays steady—between eight and ten patients waiting. A pair of derelicts, each with battered eyes, appear at the admitting desk. One has a dramatically swollen face laced with black stitches.

11:00 P.M. The husband of the attempted suicide arrives. He thanks the police for saving his wife's life, then talks at length with doctors about her condition. She continues to stare into the void and does not react when her husband approaches her stretcher.

Meanwhile, patients arrive in the lobby at a steady pace. A young G.I. on leave has lower-back pains; a Hispanic man complains of pain in his side; occasionally parents hurry through the adult E.R. carrying children into the pediatric E.R. A white woman of about 50 marches into the lobby from the walk-in entrance. Dried blood covers her right eyebrow and upper lip. She begins to perform. "I was assaulted on 28th and Lexington, I was," she says grandly, "and I don't have to take it *anymore*. I was a bride 21 years ago, and, God, I was beautiful then." She has captured the attention of all present. "I was there when the boys came home—on Memorial Day—and I don't have to take this kind of treatment."

As midnight approaches, the nurses prepare for the shift change. They must brief the incoming staff and make sure all reports are up-to-date. One young brunet says, "Christ, I'm gonna go home and take a shower—I smell like vomit."

11:50 P.M. The triage nurse is questioning an old black man about chest pains, and a Hispanic woman is having an asthma attack, when an ambulance, its sirens screaming full tilt, roars into the receiving bay. There is a split-second pause as everyone drops what he or she is doing and looks up. Then all hell breaks loose. Doctors and nurses are suddenly sprinting full-out toward the trauma room. The glass doors burst open and the occupied stretcher is literally run past me. Cops follow. It is as if a comet has whooshed by. In the trauma room it all becomes clear. A half-dozen doctors and nurses surround the lifeless form of a Hispanic man with a shotgun hole in his neck the size of your fist. Blood pours from a second gaping wound in his chest. A respirator is slammed over his face, making his chest rise and fall as if he were breathing. "No pulse," reports one doctor. A nurse jumps on a stool and, leaning over the man, begins to pump his chest with her palms. "No blood pressure," screams another nurse. The ambulance driver appears shaken. "I never thought I'd get here in time," he stutters. More doctors from the trauma team upstairs arrive. Wrappings from syringes and gauze pads fly through the air. The victim's eyes are open yet devoid of life. His body takes on a yellow tinge. A male nurse winces at the gunshot wound. "This guy really pissed off somebody," he says. This is no ordinary shooting. It is an execution. IV's are jammed into the body in the groin and arms. One doctor has been plugging in an electrocardiograph and asks everyone to stop for a second so he can get a reading. "Forget it," shouts the doctor in charge. "No time." "Take it easy, Jimmy," someone yells at the head physician. It is apparent by now that the man is dead, but the doctors keep trying injections and finally they slit open the chest and reach inside almost up to their elbows. They feel the extent of the damage and suddenly it is all over. "I told 'em he was dead," says one nurse, withdrawing. "They didn't listen." The room is very still. The doctors are momentarily disgusted, then go on about their business. The room clears quickly. Finally there is only a male nurse and the still-warm body, now waxy-yellow, with huge ribs exposed on both sides of the chest and giant holes in both sides of the neck. The nurse speculates that this is yet another murder in a Hispanic political struggle that has brought many such victims to Bellevue. He marvels at the extent of the wounds and repeats, "This guy was really blown away."

Midnight. A hysterical woman is hustled through the lobby into an examination room. It is the dead man's wife, and she is nearly delirious. "I know he's dead, I know he's dead," she screams over and over. Within moments the lobby is filled with anxious relatives of the victim, waiting for word on his condition. The police are everywhere asking questions, but most people say they saw nothing. One young woman says she heard six shots, two louder than the other four. At some point, word is passed that the man is, in fact, dead. Another woman breaks down in hysterics; everywhere young Hispanics are crying and comforting each other. Plainclothes detectives make a quick examination of the body, check on the time of pronouncement of death, and begin to ask questions, but the bereaved are too stunned to talk. The rest of the uninvolved people in the lobby stare dumbly, their injuries suddenly paling in light of a death.

12:30 A.M. A black man appears at the admission desk and says he drank poison by mistake. He is told to have a seat. The ambulance brings in a young white woman, her head wrapped in white gauze. She is wailing terribly. A girl friend stands over her, crying, and a boyfriend clutches the injured woman's hands, saying, "I'm here, don't worry, I'm here." The victim has fallen downstairs at a friend's house. Attendants park her stretcher against the wall to wait for an examination room to clear. There are eight examination rooms and only three doctors. Unless you are truly an emergency, you will wait. One doctor is stitching up the elbow of a drunk who's been punched out. The friends of the woman who fell down the stairs glance up at the doctors anxiously, wondering why their friend isn't being treated faster.

1:10 A.M. A car pulls into the bay and a young Hispanic asks if a shooting victim has been brought here. The security guard blurts out, "He's dead." The young man is stunned. He peels his tires leaving the bay.

1:20 A.M. The young woman of the stairs is getting stitches in a small gash over her left eye when the same ambulance driver who brought in the gunshot victim delivers a man who has been stabbed in the back on East 3rd Street. Once again the trauma room goes from 0 to 60 in five seconds. The patient is drunk, which helps him endure the pain of having the catheter inserted through his penis into his bladder. Still he yells, "That hurts like a bastard," then adds sheepishly, "Excuse me, ladies." But he is not prepared for what comes next. An X-ray reveals a collapsed right lung. After just a shot of local anesthetic, the doctor slices open his side and inserts a long plastic tube. Internal bleeding had kept the lung pressed down and prevented it from reinflating. The tube releases the pressure. The ambulance driver says the cops grabbed the guy who ran the eight-inch blade into the victim's back. "That's not the one," says the man. "They got the wrong guy." A nurse reports that there is not much of the victim's type blood available at the hospital. One of the doctors says that's okay, he won't need surgery. Meanwhile blood pours from the man's knife wound and the tube in his side. As the nurses work, they chat about personal matters, yet they respond immediately to orders from either doctor. "How ya doin'?" the doctor asks the patient. "Okay," he says. His blood spatters on the floor.

So it goes into the morning hours. A Valium overdose, a woman who fainted, a man who went through the windshield of his car. More overdoses. More drunks with split eyebrows and chins. The doctors and nurses work without complaint. "This is nothing, about normal, I'd say," concludes the head nurse. "No big deal."

WRITING TASKS — GEORGE SIMPSON

1. Although this essay is full of drama and tension, Simpson has only related the scene objectively—that is, he has made no effort to play on our emotions with subjective language or make judgments about the scene. This is what he saw and heard; that's all. Describe a scene in which a great deal of action takes place—a parade, an amusement park, a sports event, an elementary school at recess, a busy shopping mall, a public performance of some kind. Select objective detail to create a dominant impression without being emotional or judgmental.

2. Describe an event that has physical action, but no human presence: an electrical storm with thunder and lightning; the gradual rising of the sun over a country scene or a city scene; a fire sweeping through a brush-covered canyon; a gentle rain washing the pavement. Use details which convey sights, sounds, smells, and motion.

Black Men and Public Space
BRENT STAPLES

My first victim was a woman—white, well dressed, probably in her late twenties. I came upon her late one evening on a deserted street in Hyde Park, a relatively affluent neighborhood in an otherwise mean, impoverished section of Chicago. As I swung onto the avenue behind her, there seemed to be a discreet, uninflammatory distance between us. Not so. She cast back a worried glance. To her, the youngish black man—a broad six feet two inches with a beard and billowing hair, both hands shoved into the pockets of a bulky military jacket—seemed menacingly close. After a few more quick glimpses, she picked up her pace and was soon running in earnest. Within seconds she disappeared into a cross street.

That was more than a decade ago. I was twenty-two years old, a graduate student newly arrived at the University of Chicago. It was in the echo of that terrified woman's footfalls that I first began to know the unwieldy inheritance I'd come into—the ability to alter public space in ugly ways. It was clear that she thought herself the quarry of a mugger, a rapist, or worse. Suffering a bout of insomnia, however, I was stalking sleep, not defenseless wayfarers. As a softy who is scarcely able to take a knife to a raw chicken—let alone hold one to a person's throat—I was surprised, embarrassed, and dismayed all at once. Her flight made me feel like an accomplice in tyranny. It also made it clear that I was indistinguishable from the muggers who occasionally seeped into the area from the surrounding ghetto. That first encounter, and those that followed, signified that a vast, unnerving gulf lay between nighttime pedestrians—particularly women—and me. And I soon gathered that being perceived as dangerous is a hazard in itself. I only needed to turn a corner into a dicey situation, or crowd some frightened, armed person in a foyer somewhere, or make an errant move after being pulled over by a policeman. Where fear and weapons meet—and they often do in urban America—there is always the possibility of death.

In that first year, my first away from my hometown, I was to become thoroughly familiar with the language of fear. At dark, shadowy intersections, I could cross in front of a car stopped at a traffic light and elicit the *thunk, thunk, thunk, thunk* of the driver—black, white, male, or female—hammering down the door locks. On less traveled streets after dark, I grew accustomed to but never comfortable with people crossing to the other side of the street rather than pass me. Then there were the standard unpleasantries with policemen, doormen, bouncers, cabdrivers, and others whose business it is to screen out troublesome individuals *before* there is any nastiness.

I moved to New York nearly two years ago and I have remained an avid night walker. In central Manhattan, the near-constant crowd cover minimizes tense one-on-one street encounters. Elsewhere—in SoHo, for example, where sidewalks are narrow and tightly spaced buildings shut out the sky—things can get very taut indeed.

After dark, on the warrenlike streets of Brooklyn where I live, I often see women who fear the worst from me. They seem to have set their faces on neutral, and with their purse straps strung across their chests bandolier-style, they forge ahead as though bracing themselves against being tackled. I understand, of course, that the danger they perceive is not a hallucination. Women are particularly vulnerable to street violence, and young black males are drastically overrepresented among the perpetrators of that violence. Yet those truths are no solace against the kind of alienation that comes of being ever the suspect, a fearsome entity with whom pedestrians avoid making eye contact.

It is not altogether clear to me how I reached the ripe old age of twenty-two without being conscious of the lethality nighttime pedestrians attributed to me. Perhaps it was because in Chester, Pennsylvania, the small, angry industrial town where I came of age in the 1960s, I was scarcely noticeable against a backdrop of gang warfare, street knifings, and murders. I grew up one of the good boys, had perhaps a half-dozen fistfights. In retrospect, my shyness of combat has clear sources.

As a boy, I saw countless tough guys locked away; I have since buried several, too. They were babies, really—a teenage cousin, a brother of twenty-two, a childhood friend in his mid-twenties—all gone down in episodes of bravado played out in the streets. I came to doubt the virtues of intimidation early on. I chose, perhaps unconsciously, to remain a shadow—timid, but a survivor.

The fearsomeness mistakenly attributed to me in public places often has a perilous flavor. The most frightening of these confusions occurred in the late 1970s and early 1980s, when I worked as a journalist in Chicago. One day, rushing into the office of a magazine I was writing for with a deadline story in hand, I was mistaken for a burglar. The office manager called security and, with an ad hoc posse, pursued me through the labyrinthine halls, nearly to my editor's door. I had no way of proving who I was. I could only move briskly toward the company of someone who knew me.

Another time I was on assignment for a local paper and killing time before an interview. I entered a jewelry store on the city's affluent Near North Side. The proprietor excused herself and returned with an enormous red Doberman pinscher straining at the end of a leash. She stood, the dog extended toward me, silent to my questions, her eyes bulging nearly out of her head. I took a cursory look around, nodded, and bade her good night.

Relatively speaking, however, I never fared as badly as another black male journalist. He went to nearby Waukegan, Illinois, a couple of summers ago to work on a story about a murderer who was born there. Mistaking the reporter for the killer, police officers hauled him from his car at gunpoint and but for his press credentials would probably have tried to book him. Such episodes are not uncommon. Black men trade tales like this all the time.

Over the years, I learned to smother the rage I felt at so often being taken for a criminal. Not to do so would surely have led to madness. I now take precautions to make myself less threatening. I move about with care, particularly late in the evening. I give a wide berth to nervous people on subway platforms during the wee hours, particularly when I have exchanged business clothes for jeans. If I happen to be entering a building behind some people who appear skittish, I may walk by, letting them clear the lobby before I return, so as not to seem to be following them. I have been calm and extremely congenial on those rare occasions when I've been pulled over by the police.

And on late-evening constitutionals I employ what has proved to be an excellent tension-reducing measure: I whistle melodies from Beethoven and Vivaldi and the more popular classical composers. Even steely New Yorkers hunching toward nighttime destinations seem to relax, and occasionally they even join in the tune. Virtually everybody seems to sense that a mugger wouldn't be warbling bright, sunny selections from Vivaldi's *Four Seasons*. It is my equivalent of the cowbell that hikers wear when they know they are in bear country.

WRITING TASKS—BRENT STAPLES

1. Staples says that his mere presence in an area often changes the behavior or attitudes of those in the same area. He calls these changes "the language of fear." Go back through the essay and list the kinds of behavior changes he mentions (for example, "hurried steps" and "the locking of car doors"). From your own experience, add items to the list of things people do when they feel threatened by or uncomfortable with another's presence. Then write a deductive essay on the language of fear or the language of disgust or rejection or avoidance or whatever word you think is most appropriate for the content you have generated. Use many examples, both specific and typical.

2. If you have not already done so, read Cynthia Heimel's essay "If I Were a Black Man" on page 326. Though Heimel takes a different approach, she covers much of the same ground that Staples does. Write an essay based on the content of the two essays. Begin with a section exploring the similarities between the two authors' views and then, in the discussion section of your paper, support or deny those views. Use specific information to support your argument.

Sins of the Flesh
SALLIE TISDALE

I went to the butcher's several times a week as a child. Meat was always in my life. The butcher shop was just down the street from our house, past the old, squat Carnegie Library, the Elks Club, the Groceteria, the bakery, and the big stucco fire department with its long driveway. I loved the Meat Market best; it was orderly, with the hushed front room encased in windows. The floor was golden oak, shiny and clean, facing a horseshoe of white metal display cases curving away like the fabric of space. The air held the scent of clean skin.

I would lay my hot cheeks against the cool glass and gaze at the meat inside: flaccid steaks, roasts, and sausages in neat rows like tile or shingles laid atop one another in patterns of soft red, pink, and maroon. I knew the textures—they were my textures. I liked to examine the down on my legs, the way the irises of my eyes opened and closed when I turned the light above the bathroom mirror off and on, the intricate maze of my belly button. I pulled scabs off and chewed them, and licked the ooze that followed. The rump roast in the glass case made a delicate curve, the curve of my own pliable buttocks. Me, but not me.

On panting summer days our basement beckoned, crowded and lifeless, the air cool, musty, and dim after the glazed sunlight. No one would find me there, if anyone cared to look for me. Most of the small basement was filled with a freezer, which my mother, one in a long line of carefully organized women, kept filled as a hedge against catastrophe. (Distantly, my mother's voice at the top of the stairs: "Shut the freezer!"—trailing off into words I didn't bother to hear.) Its heavy white lid seemed to lift from the stiff latch with relief and swing up so that a waft of the freezer's queer fog blew in my face. My taut, tanned skin could breathe again in the damp. There was often a whole side of beef and more in the freezer, broken up among the TV dinners and the quarts of bean soup and ice cream. Each cut was wrapped in white freezer paper and labeled with a red wax crayon in strange abbreviations: "FLK STK 4#" and "P CHOPS – 6." The irregular, heavy packets sat in the cold trough like a haphazard pile of white rocks littered with food.

There was never a meal without meat: every afternoon the house filled with the scents of frying oil and roasting flesh. The long dining table leaned toward my father's end, anticipating the heavy cuts on the platter beside him—the pot roast, the round roast beef, the piles of rust-colored chops dripping juice. He carved. At Thanksgiving he leaned over the enormous turkey to get a good purchase, the double blades of the electric carving knife slicing in a noisy blur.

My father was a volunteer fireman, and every few weeks the town alarm would sound during dinner, and he would move so fast, so instinctively, that time seemed to stand still: the knife or fork or bite of food falls to the table, his chair scrapes back along the floor, we children scoot out of his way as he thunders past, "Goddammit!" trails him out the back door, the door slams, and seconds later his pickup roars out of the driveway.

On quiet nights we squabbled for drumsticks, thick hamburger patties, the fatty end of the roast. I always had the chicken's back with its fat, heart-shaped tail, which my grandmother called the pope's nose, and when we were done our plates were littered with the rags of bones.

Buying meat was like this every time: I am with my mother, an efficient, plain woman with the smell of academics around her. She much preferred reading to cooking, but she cooked every day. The butcher, Mr. Bryan, is my father's best friend; like all my father's friends, he is a fireman. He stands behind the counter, a tall, jolly man with a hard, round stomach covered in a white apron streaked with blood. He has saved his best meat for my mother, kept it apart for her inspection: a pot roast, a particular steak, perhaps giblets for her special dressing, the hard nubbins of chicken hearts and kidneys, the tiny livers purple-red like gems in his palm.

Now and then Mr. Bryan went to the back of the store and brought my mother something really special: a whole beef heart, balanced like a waxy pyramid on his hands, or a cow's tongue, one of my favorite things. Sometimes I would come into the kitchen in the morning and find a tongue set out waiting for the pot, an enormous apostrophe of flesh covered in pale papillae. Tongue takes forever to cook, boiling for many hours on the stove, and it filled the kitchen with a tender mist and steamed the windows gray. When it was done, my mother sliced the tongue as soft as angel cake into thin, delicious strips unlike anything else, melting, perfumed. When all the rest of the world wouldn't bend, flesh would bend.

You will think me disingenuous if I tell you now that I didn't know what meat was. I couldn't know; the shift from cow to beef is a shift so monumental and sudden that it's hard to conceive. Perhaps small children cannot know this even when they are witnesses, and I was never a witness. I have never seen an animal slaughtered for meat. And if you had leaned over me when I was four or five or six and suggested I eat an animal, I might have been shocked. I loved animals more, and more easily, than I loved my parents. I held my old dog, a dour mongrel Lab, for hours in my room sometimes, telling him what I couldn't tell anyone else; I was weak with him because he kept my secrets. I loved horses, goats, deer, and the cattle chewing stupidly by the back-road fences; in my bedroom I kept lizards, snakes, chameleons, and a rat, and that was all my mother allowed. And it was my mother who one day told me where meat came from, as though it were the most natural thing.

I was about seven when I asked, that age when one begins to see the depth of betrayal in the world, that one can't really count on things after all. And my mother answered yes, the chicken we ate for dinner was the same as the chickens down the street I would cluck at through the fence, the ones with the thick white feathers that filled the breeze. The peeled skin of the wieners Mr. Bryan gave me were loops of intestine washed clean, and their pulp a ground mash of bodies and bones. The unbelievable objects had a name, a face, a history; the sweet and salty taste was the taste of blood, the same as my blood. It came all at once, like a blow, that pickled pigs' feet was not a colorful metaphor but the very thing, that I had eaten a *pig's* foot, and much more.

I lived on bare noodles and peanut-butter sandwiches for a long time after that. I wouldn't allow my mother to spoon the sausage-flavored spaghetti sauce onto my plate. A few years later it seemed less important, the resistance too hard. Perhaps I had had other surprises; it's hard to remember whole sections of those years. I've gone years without eating meat as an adult, and years when I was too tired not to eat whatever was in front of me. And there have been times when I craved flesh, when I broiled and roasted, made scratch gravy and giblet dressing like my mother's, or sat at my long dining table with steamed clams clattering against my fork, times when I longed for the irreducible flavors of meat, to be full of meat. Yet I will even now find myself knocked flat sometimes when I see meat in front of me and realize what I'm doing. It's a heartfelt knowledge; it is visceral, gut-level, organic. I hold the steak with a fork and begin to cut a slice, and my stomach turns upside down; it feels as if I'm cutting my own flesh off and that I'll choke to death upon it, like a prisoner fed his own treacherous, boiled tongue.

One shock after another. Breasts and hips and hair; more of the pleasures and debts of flesh. I began to bleed several days a month, and when I sat to pee the smell rose up yeasty and rich. I found furtive darting touches: I found lips, saliva, tongues, sweat, fingers. My dog decayed from the inside out, and stank and stumbled and licked the mysterious lumps under his fur. I traced his ribs so near the surface the day before he died. Then my mother yellowed and thickened and wept and died, and my father's big arms hung loose and his black hair turned gray. . . . I moved out to the fleshy edges of things, and finally I grew wings like angel wings, and I flew away.

The word "butcher" comes—a long way down the years—from the word "buck." He-goat. They are set aside, butchers, into their own unions, their own neighborhoods, their own bars, set aside. I don't know if it means anything that besides Mr. Bryan, my father's closest friend was the undertaker; it may not be anything more than the limits of a small town. But I think of the Butcher's Mass, their special blessing, and the *shehitah* of the Jews. The *shochet,* the slaughterer, who must be pious and above reproach, must be as swift and painless as he can be in the killing, murmuring a benediction near the animal's ear and following with a graceful stroke across the throat, I think of Mr. Bryan's cleaver.

The Meat Market burned down on a hot day under a blank blue sky. It was apocalypse. It was a great fire. I stood at the end of the alley and watched the flames spurt out the back door in gouty bursts. I heard a shriek of metal inside and guessed the white metal cooler had turned red and ignited its own frost. The smoke billowed out the back door in a cottony black cloud, and I clapped my hands. Men in turnouts and boots rushed past and paid me no attention, and I saw my father paying out the hose from the pumper with great speed.

The meat burned; the water washed it clean. I learned later that Mr. Bryan had inherited the Meat Market from his father, and he'd secretly hated it all those years, going home at night with the stink of blood on his hands and hair. He is still jolly and thick-fingered, and he still comes by to visit my father, who is tired and gruff and without cheer. They have been retired from fires, too old to go into the heat and pull things out. For myself, I know you can't be cleansed until you know how dirty you really are. I still live far away, still seek salvation from my many sins.

WRITING TASKS—SALLIE TISDALE

1. Describe a scene from your childhood. It might be a room at home, a classroom, a garage, a corner of the yard, a vacant lot, or any other place that your present-day thoughts return to. Try to capture some of the sights, smells, sounds, textures, even tastes of that place. Review Tisdale's descriptions to see what kind of detail she includes. Then do a thorough prewriting draft to prod your memory. Before you write the paper, think about what importance this place has for you, then present your details to convey that meaning.

2. When Tisdale learns where the meat on her family table comes from, she becomes an instant vegetarian. Later, the issue seems less important and she returns to meat-eating, but her conscience still bothers her from time to time and she feels tainted. Do you have any beliefs or principles that the world you live in is constantly tempting you to relinquish? Most of us make at least some compromises, either to "get along" or because we can't resist temptation. Write a paper about one or more compromises you commonly make. Explain the situations in which you compromise and why.

Part Four
DAILY WRITING

This part includes eight week-long units of thirty-minute writing tasks. The writing you do will be free writing, a form of prewriting. Besides giving you regular practice sessions through the use of daily writing, we're trying to show you that one way to find something to write about is to write. These thirty-minute tasks take no special skill or knowledge. For instance, one week you'll spend the thirty-minute practice sessions writing about your current life. The first thirty minutes you'll describe what's taking place in your life at the moment. For the next sessions you'll write about the contents of your wallet, purse, or medicine cabinet or about interesting activities and places. During the successive weeks, you'll write about such things as past experiences, world events, people you know, even dreams and fantasies—but for no longer than thirty minutes. Besides giving you daily practice at writing, these tasks will provide raw material that you can use as a resource for the formal assignments you'll be doing.

25

Keeping a Journal

This section is going to ask you to spend some time doing a great deal of writing. If you spend thirty minutes each day writing one or two pages in a notebook, your graded work will get better. Thirty minutes! Every day?

Yes. A very simple command—sit down and write—but one that is hard to meet because many forces compete for attention.

One student journal writer describes her experience with the busy world this way:

> The outside world is so confusing. At times I feel I'm dreaming. I sense I'm in a forest—something from Grimm's fairy tales. I'm lost. It is night. All around me at unexpected moments creatures keep popping up out of the dark, whispering and screaming for my attention. I want to ignore them and find the path out, but some eerie fascination keeps drawing me deeper into the woods.

Like this writer, all of us at times feel the eerie fascination of the market-place. Its pull is hard to resist. In the thirty minutes most of us spend struggling to fill a blank page, by merely flicking a television knob we can take a fairy-tale journey across America to see the destruction left by an earthquake, tornado, or torrential rains. In an instant we can be lifted to the Middle East to see a village left in rubble from a terrorist attack. Carried to Finland we might hear a report on the efforts of the superpowers to stop the sale of nuclear weapons. We might see the World Tennis Championship or the World Series or the Academy Awards. We certainly would hear pitches for dog food, beer, cars, deodorants, or headache or hemorrhoid remedies. With all this going on, who has time to practice writing? you might ask. No doubt it would be easier to meditate in a typhoon. Still, to improve your writing you must practice. And practice. And practice.

The practice writing you will be doing is relaxed writing—some call it free writing. When you are doing free writing, your work should be unbound, snaring fleeting hunches, half-remembered experiences, and images as soon as the mind shapes them. When you are doing formal writing, your work should be more controlled. Formal writing gets reports, essays, and research projects done; free writing helps you train and prepare to write reports, essays, and research projects. When doing free writing, you need not be concerned with grammar, logic, spelling, punctuation—the niceties of writing. Instead, you will work to capture the flow of your thought—limbering the writing muscles as runners might limber their legs before a race.

Creative People and Journals

By this point you may have gotten the impression that free writing involves more than meeting a course assignment.

It may.

Without much searching in the library you would find that creative people from all fields have written regularly in diaries, journals, daybooks, and notebooks. For many, the entries not only allowed them to express themselves by keeping a history of their experiences but also fed their life works.

Leonardo da Vinci, the great Renaissance artist and scientist, kept journal entries about his observations of birds and his theories of flight; the nineteenth-century French painter Paul Gauguin kept a notebook that captured his memories, dreams, and thoughts on art; and contemporary artist Claes Oldenberg consciously set out to generate his art from his own life and psychology. He developed a "scrapbook" of a fantasy city, which became a source for his work. Oldenberg has said, "Everything I do is completely original—I made it up when I was a little kid." He began by capturing it all in a notebook.

Psychologist Carl Jung kept a notebook he called the "Black Book." It numbers five volumes and traces his personal growth in both writing and art. The deep value of keeping a personal notebook is reflected in a comment from his autobiography, *Memories, Dreams, and Reflections:* "All my works, all my creative activity, have come from fantasies and dreams which began in 1912. Everything that I accomplished in later life was already contained in them, although at first only in the form of emotions and images."

Modern photographer Edward Weston kept daybooks to chart the details of his life and the growth of his inner self and art; contemporary educator John Holt kept a log of his experiences teaching elementary school children; a young Jewish girl named Anne Frank kept a record of her life while hiding with her family from the Nazis. Writers such as Gustave

Flaubert, Henry James, F. Scott Fitzgerald, Anaïs Nin, Graham Greene, Virginia Woolf, and Albert Camus kept diaries, journals, and notebooks at different times in their lives.

Journal Styles

Often a journal entry will be brief. Something—a gesture, an idea, an observation, or a bit of conversation—will capture the journal keeper's interest and will be recorded. For instance, Graham Greene's African journal published under the title *In Search of a Character* makes several brief entries dated February 10:

> The cows with the elegant snow-white birds—pique-boeufs, not egrets—which attend them like guardian angels. The birds are so sleek and smooth that their feathers seem of porcelain. Innumerable butterflies . . .

> Names of Africans. Henry with a y, Attention, Deo Gratias . . .

> Men playing mysterious game altering the number of beans that lie in rough troughs on a home-made board . . .

> A coil of caterpillars brought home by a leper to sell or eat.

And under February 12 Greene briefly notes:

> The water at the bow of the pontoons the colour of burnt sugar.

> A first sentence perhaps: "Each day after breakfast the captain read his breviary in the deck-house." . . .

> The approach to Bakuma and the excitement of Père Henri: "my home."

> "Not your prison?"

> "No. Yonda is my prison."

In other entries Greene, whose fictional characters often face a crisis of faith, becomes more philosophical. Again from the section dated February 10:

> How often people speak of the absurdity of believing that life should exist by God's will on one minute part of the immense universe. There is a parallel absurdity which we are asked to believe, that God chose a tiny colony of a Roman empire in which to be born. Strangely enough two absurdities seem easier to believe than one.

And under March 7 he records:

> Hinduism is a tropical religion: a reaction from indiscriminate slaughter, which only happens in the tropics. For every insect one kills in Europe, one must kill a hundred at least in tropical countries. One kills without thinking—a smear on one's napkin or the pages of one's book.

Greene's fleeting details, observations, and thoughts may not have been of immediate value beyond keeping him in the habit of writing and looking hard and close at himself and life. Yet by regularly making notebook entries while on a journey through Africa, he stored away enough to draw on for a novel he titled *A Burnt-Out Case*.

Of course, not everything that goes into a notebook will find its way into a future work. Indeed, writing daily in a notebook may seem to involve a series of wasted motions. But there is one advantage. The material you collect will have a time to cool off so that later you can come back to it and begin to see how it might be used in another way.

Sometimes the entries will not be as brief as the ones from Greene but instead will be extended impressions recorded with care and in detail. Albert Camus must have made thousands of short and long entries in his notebooks. This excerpt published in *Notebooks: 1935–1942* influenced the shaping of situations and characters in his novel *The Stranger*.

> The old woman who dies in the old people's home. Her friend, the friend she has made over a period of three years, weeps "because she has nothing left." The caretaker of the little mortuary, who is a Parisian and lives at the mortuary with his wife. "Who could have told them that at seventy-four he would end up at an old people's home at Marengo?" His son has a job. They left Paris. The daughter-in-law didn't want them.

> Scenes. The old man finally "raised his hand." His son put them in an old people's home. The gravedigger who was one of the dead woman's friends. They often went to the village together in the evening. The old man who insisted on following the procession to the church and then to the cemetery. Since he is lame, he cannot keep up and walks twenty yards behind. But he knows the country and takes shortcuts that enable him to catch up with the procession several times until he falls behind again.

> The Arab nurse who nails down the coffin has a cyst on her nose and wears a permanent bandage.

> The dead woman's friends: little old people ridden with fancies. Everything was wonderful in the past. One of them to a neighbor:

"Hasn't your daughter written to you?" "No." "She might remember that she does have a mother."

The other has died—as a sign and a warning to them all.

You can see in this passage that Camus has captured an interesting situation, drawn brief portraits of the people there, suggested the setting, recorded snatches of dialogue, and responded to the entire entry by commenting on the fear that may be running through these old people: "The other has died—as a sign and a warning to them all." When he made the entry, he may not have had a hint that the "little old man" would become Perez in *The Stranger* and that the funeral would become the funeral of the central character's mother. How could he have known? This entry along with all the others are scraps from his daily experience. But by keeping them in a notebook, he had them handy when he needed them.

Of course, after an artist becomes successful, the critic can analyze his or her notebook entries. Many critics like to do that. But notebook entries are not made for analysis. They are made to sustain the creative person in work and are written without concern for what future critics or the admiring public may think. So, like a visual artist, when you work in your notebook don't write as if some critic, whether an English teacher, a parent, or a helpful friend, is peeking over your shoulder. In your notebook you have one audience—yourself. If you wish to share your entries, that's your decision, but as a working principle, keep in mind that you're writing for you.

Where to Keep Daily Writing

Perhaps the best place to keep daily writing is in a large notebook. If you use a pocket-sized pad, you will not have room to stretch out; your writing will be cramped; you will quickly fill the pages. Soon you may be toting around several tiny volumes of daily writing—an awkward situation.

You might be tempted to use a calendar book, one of those appointment books that have the days divided into neat squares. While the calendar book may be fine for keeping records of assignments and appointments, it is too limited for free writing. After all, when your thoughts start flowing, how can you contain them in a 4-by-6-inch square that represents the space for that day's entry?

Better to use a regular 10-by-11-inch three-ring binder. A ringed binder is more effective than a permanently bound book because the binder will give you more flexibility. Flexibility is what you want for your daily writing. You will often find time on your hands, perhaps while riding a bus, waiting for a class to begin, or just sitting in the cafeteria or library. You can use some of this free time to make an entry. If you have been storing your work in a binder, then there is no need to carry it with you. You can write an entry on any sheet of notebook paper. When you return home, all you have to do is snap open the rings and insert the new sheet or sheets.

A permanently bound book lacks this advantage. You must lug it with you. You may also wish to develop a section with a specific focus, adding entries over a period of time. You can do that with a ringed binder; you cannot with a bound book. It is also a good idea to have a section where you keep old papers, written tests, book reviews, and reports—all the writing you do in such classes as history, psychology, sociology, or geology. Often, just as practice writing in the form of a notebook entry becomes the spark to ignite a formal class assignment, an old paper can become the base for future work. A binder makes it easy to save papers that might be reworked. Of course, the choice of a book to work in is yours. So you should feel comfortable with the one you pick.

Guidelines for Practice

To get this practice rolling and to collect material to use in other assignments, we offer several weeks of journal exercises. After that you are on your own. Meanwhile, here are some suggestions for working:

1. Keep all your writing in a single book, preferably a three-ring binder. The binder will give you the flexibility you need in shuffling and rearranging your work into sections.
2. Date all entries so that you will have a chronological history of your free-writing progress.
3. Try to set aside a thirty-minute block of time to complete each exercise. Write at least two pages—two authentic pages—but do not bloat the size of your writing to fill the page. If you finish in less than two pages, write something else.
4. Write clearly enough so that you will be able to read the entry when you go back, and leave plenty of space between entries.
5. Always keep in mind that this is practice. Although the material can be reworked if you need it for a formal assignment, in your journal write it once. If you write a line or phrase you do not like, leave it and keep going.
6. Don't be concerned with mechanics. Don't stop to look up words. Don't stop to revise. Instead, write to capture the flow of your thought, the detail of experience.

26
First Week: Free Writing

You have your notebook. You have set aside some time. You are ready to begin. For the first exercises you will do unfocused writing. The goal here is to write nonstop for at least twenty minutes. Don't stop to think or judge or arrange your thought—just write, letting the words pepper the page.

Some beginning writers get scared when set free. They might say, "I can't get it loose. I just shut my eyes and it's all a blank. No thought—except 'What shall I write about? What shall I write about?' Beyond that there's only a void, a big zero."

The problem is not uncommon with beginning writers, and probably it is not uncommon with professional writers either. But professional writers have learned to live with it, knowing it will pass. So here is what you do: describe your "zero." If you are sitting in a quiet place, notebook open to a fresh sheet, pen ready to start recording, and nothing comes, describe the nothing.

Here is how one student started his unfocused writing:

> I can't think . . . mind's a blank. Eyes closed. See nothing but black . . . something purple, circles expanding in the black—reminds me of a lake I visited in the Cascades. A bowl. What was it? Devil's punch bowl. I tossed a rock as far toward its center as I could. The rings . . .

Though this entry continues by discussing the circles floating toward shore, it starts off describing the color black many of us might see if our eyes are pressed shut. Then some purple comes in the shape of expanding circles; finally, the writer's mind begins to free-associate—that is, to make loose, spontaneous connections. His mind is becoming less constrained. It is opening up for imaginary flight. If you give yours the same opportunity, it will fly, too.

One goal to keep in mind before you start free writing is to be honest. To be honest does not mean you have to confess or to "come clean," as a detective in a thirties cop film might say. Instead it means to write the truth, the kind of truth with a little *t*, not a big *T*. The little-*t* truth has to do with firsthand experience: the facts of your life, your imagination, your dreams. It is a personal truth, the truth of your life experience. This truth is uniquely yours because it is filtered through your eyes and your mind. In your daily writing, work to corral your unique experience. Remember, too, that you should be less interested in recording your interpretation—the whys behind your experience—and more interested in describing it—herding its details onto the page.

There is another kind of truth to keep in mind while making entries in your notebook—the truth of the words you use. Of course, no words are untruthful in themselves; their falsity depends on how accurately or inaccurately they are used to describe experience. All good writers try to use words accurately by being as concrete and specific as their subjects allow them. But for beginning writers that may be hard.

This is the age of the marketplace, and there is little doubt that marketplace language, the language of advertising, politics, talk shows, and so on, has affected our language. All of us have spent too many hours listening to the drone of disc jockeys, television commentators, politicians, and show business personalities for our language not to be tainted. It is safe to generalize that much of this language, if not downright false in the way it presents experience, is certainly misleading and almost always general and vague. They do not give buyers information; instead they try to give them feelings.

Often, the ad writer's vague language will creep into a beginning writer's prose. The beginning writer may be attempting to express a sincere feeling, but often the words smack of the ad writer's talent for saying very little.

Here is one student's first attempt at describing a trip to the beach:

> Yesterday I spent a delightful day at the beach. Whenever I feel lost or just want to be with friends I go to the cove and lie on the sand to collect my thoughts. The sky was a New England blue. Many of my friends were there. I have known some of them since elementary school. To see them makes me feel good. Some were flying kites, some were playing volleyball. Everyone was having a good time. It picks me up to go.

This writer may wish to be sincere, but this piece is general and vague. Not much is being said except that the writer feels good going to the beach whenever he feels "lost." What does "lost" mean? The writer doesn't confront the feeling, but going to the beach will cure the condition because thoughts can be collected and friends are doing it. At the beach everyone has a good time. Consequently, the beach will pick him up.

In contrast here is part of another brief entry that deals with the beach. This student has tried to capture the detail of the experience in concrete language. In itself the entry may seem unconnected to any specific point. But for notebook entries the goal is to practice and to collect raw material. This piece is fresh, unlike the first example, because the writer trusts what her eyes, ears, and nose tell her: She focuses on the actual experience, not on what she thinks about it.

> Walking across the sand. Hot. The sun eating at my back. The sand so hot I feel it burning through my sandals. Bodies scattered everywhere on towels, some lying, some sitting. All of them young. Only the young come to 39th Street. They grease themselves up, streaks of silver reflecting off the grease coating their arms and backs. The beach has the smell of cocoa butter. The smell mixes with the music from boomboxes.

This writer has packed her work with detail. Besides collecting some specifics she may use in a later piece, she has touched on a theme that could be expanded into a formal work—the contrast between the young and the old. In any case, she is collecting raw material and getting practice doing it.

WRITING TASK—FIRST WEEK: FREE WRITING

Each day for the next five days write as fast as you can without interruption for thirty minutes. Keep the writing going. Don't stop. If you draw a blank, describe the blank—the zero, the nothing, or the void, whatever you might call it. You may be like many beginning writers and hear a voice that seems to come from some mischievous gnome riding on your shoulder. This critic is never happy with anything you write. It nags at each word and carps over sentences and condemns each paragraph. This tiny creature is a pest. If you have a critical gnome that tells you to give up, don't; there is a way to beat the gnome.

The gnome is a little like a pet. When you most want to do something, it will decide to run up against your leg or screech or growl. But if you reach down and give it a couple of strokes, the chances are it will curl up in its favorite corner so you can finish your job. So the best way to deal with this pest is to give it a couple of strokes. You stroke it by recording what it says and by giving it credit for having said it. You might do it something like this:

> The grouchy gnome speaks, "You know you can't write. What are you doing it for? If I've told you once, I've told you a thousand times—YOU CAN'T WRITE! Now don't misunderstand me, I'm

not saying you're dumb. Maybe you are, maybe you aren't. Who's to judge? BUT WRITE YOU CAN'T! So stop. Go do something you do well. Take a nap!"

If you hear a voice like this and you record it, you may find some new path to your creative depths. After all, in folklore a gnome is reputed to be a creature that lives underground and guards buried gold. Once you get past it you may be free to mine the tunnels of your imagination. In fact, by writing down its chatter you may be led to answer it; then you have a dialogue. Who knows what kind of honest encounter could come from that?

So the message is to write. Write about specific experience in concrete language. Keep writing. Keep the flow going. Remember, you are not working for perfection. You are practicing.

After thirty minutes, stop. Reread the entry; if you have anything to add, add it. As a final check, see if you have dated the entry. You might also want to jot down the day and place: "Monday, September 12, 1996 Library." Now, before you begin; go back and read the guidelines on page 385.

27
Second Week: Current Life

You spent the first week's practice doing unfocused tasks to help you capture bits and pieces of experience. This week will be slightly different. We'll give you more direction. The exercises will concentrate on your current life. In the words of Henry David Thoreau, you will begin a "simple and sincere account" of your life. He writes:

> I, on my side, require of every writer, first and last, a simple and sincere account of his own life, and not merely what he has heard of other men's lives; some such account as he would send to his kindred from a distant land; for if he has lived sincerely, it must have been in a distant land to me.

The distant land Thoreau writes of is the land of the mind. Although we often work with common materials, none of us sees, smells, touches, or hears the world as anyone else does. This is what makes each mind a unique landscape.

One writer, a mother who returned to college after a five-year absence, began to chart her immediate life in this fashion:

> I'm in a place where I never seem to get anything done; the laundry, dishes, trips to the market, birthday parties, term papers. Two children with runny noses, skinned knees, and elbows—that damned skateboard—a midnight toothache. Why does it all happen at once? A cosmic question!

> The car breaks down; trip to the mechanic's: "Can't do it now, lady. Next Tuesday," he says. Why do I feel so weak around mechanics and hardware and paint salesmen? Real power.

Walk to the bus. Thirty minutes to school. Books dropping, wind, clouds. The rain comes. Cold, cold days.

Everything working against me.

Tuesday rolls around. Phone the mechanic and imagine him leaning back in a chair, puffing a cigar, his feet propped up on my gutted VW engine. He says, "Have it tomorrow morning. How's 'bout nine." He says it not like a question but like a command. He knows he has me trapped. Slam down the receiver and press down a scream—another day on the bus.

"Mommy, can I have a jelly sandwich"—it too is not a question it is a command: "GET ME A JELLY SANDWICH NOW!" Peanut butter, jelly, milk, cookie crumbs, gum balls—all smashed and ground into the floor. Need to scrape it off. Need a chisel.

Must read *Gatsby* by Friday.

Wednesday A.M. Back to the mechanic's: "That's $78.50." More than I had intended to spend. Oil, grease job—you bet, a grease job—brakes, spark plugs, points. "The points, lady, that's what's giving you trouble. That's why it won't start. Ought to have 'em changed at least once every two years." His cheeks, so smoothly shaved look like a barber with a straight razor did it; odd, always think of mechanics as grubby. A cynical smile—small sharp teeth under a lavish mustache. Teeth for chewing into my bankroll, teeth for biting into my time.

I need a vacation! Spring—a fantasy: I see myself flying over snow and landing in Bermuda, lying on some beach. White, white sand. Blue, blue sky. Blue, blue water. With my recent luck, blue, blue sharks. The sharks are in the surf, I'm swimming for the beach. Stroking toward safety. Why do I want a degree? I want leisure. I want escape. I wish I had a harpoon. The college is my white whale.

Overall this is a rough piece of writing—well, it should be. To be rough is the nature of free writing. No one was sitting on the writer's shoulder giving her commands about proper punctuation, spelling, and organization. Those commands come with formal writing, not with practice writing.

The only direction she was given was to write nonstop for thirty minutes about her current life. She does it, not by sitting down and figuring it out but by taking the first step on the exciting journey. She gets into the movement instead of analyzing whether what she writes will be correct. Potters do the same. They thrust their hands into the clay to find the shapes hidden in their imagination. Critics have another method. They stand back and analyze the result to see if it has artistic value. The one group plunges forward and gets the job done; the other sits and calculates.

Calculating is an important part of formal writing, but in free writing it can block the work.

So this writer has thrust herself into her life's flow. By groping around, she has captured the chaos and frustration that she feels by recording those fleeting thoughts and images that seem to swim just below the surface.

Often her catch is surprising. For instance, the encounter with the mechanic begins with a stereotypical image—a cigar-chomping bandit, who pridefully poses with his latest kill. The image then becomes more realistic—a meticulous man, who shaves his cheeks as carefully as a professional barber would. And finally, the image turns surrealistic—a cartoon character, perhaps a giant rabbit, who eats at her bankroll and her time as if they were hunks of lettuce.

And she uses concrete words and phrases from her daily life—not clichés as they might be gleaned from advertising, but language that comes from looking at the particulars of her world. Here are a few words and phrases taken from the lists she compiles:

laundry	jelly
dishes	milk
trips to the market	cookie crumbs
birthday parties	gum balls
term papers	oil
runny noses	grease
skinned knees and elbows	brakes
skateboards	spark plugs
midnight toothache	points
peanut butter	

Concrete words and phrases create a feeling that a work is made from more than straw and air. Snatches of dialogue help make it seem real. People talking to us are part of our daily lives. Shreds of their talk hang in our minds: If lines from a recent conversation come to you while writing nonstop, record them. This writer quotes one line from her child and several from her mechanic:

> "Can't do it now, lady. Next Tuesday. . . . Have it tomorrow morning. How's 'bout nine. . . . That's $78.50. . . . The points, lady, that's what's giving you trouble. That's why it won't start. Ought to have 'em changed at least once every two years.

And she also includes fantasy. When you are practicing writing, your mind may want to drift. If so, follow it by recording where it goes. The writer's fantasy starts in an idyllic setting—"Lying on some beach. White,

white sand. Blue, blue sky"—followed by a tug back to her real life—"Blue, blue sharks." Some of a writer's richest images may come from fantasies; be sure to record yours when they appear.

Finally, our writer has uncovered some provocative questions she may wish to explore in more direct ways. "Why do I feel so weak around mechanics and hardware and paint salesmen?" "Why do I want a degree?"

For us to overexplore a single journal entry may be a mistake if you take the entry and our comments about it as a model to emulate. If you ever feel that urge, don't give in to it. We offer the example and comments as possibilities, not as formulas. Don't, like Cinderella's stepsisters, try to cram your foot into another's shoe.

WRITING TASK—SECOND WEEK: CURRENT LIFE

What follows is a group of five tasks designed to focus your practice. Each exercise will lead you to write something about your current life. In another section you will do exercises designed to lead you into your life history, but in these exercises you are to capture some of the present—the now of your life.

As a reminder, be sure to set aside thirty minutes for uninterrupted writing. Keep the pen moving across the page for the full time, trying to fill at least two pages without worrying about punctuation, grammar, or spelling. Give yourself plenty of space so your entries will not be crowded. Write legibly enough so you will be able to reread the entry. Finally, be sure to date your entry.

One last suggestion. Before you begin, relax a moment. Close your eyes or rest your head on the desk top. Feel your breathing. Let the breathing become rhythmical. Sometimes a minute or two of relaxation will let a busy mind clear. It will then be easier to focus and begin.

FIRST DAY:

This entry is to capture where you are in your life. It might be a good idea to begin with a comment on your general situation as you sense it. For instance, in the example above, the writer begins with a broad comment: "I'm in a place where I never seem to get anything done." She then lets her mind sweep through her recent life. She records the specifics, the bits of dialogue, the frustrations, the questions, the fantasies—everything that comes to her.

You might also keep this thought in mind while you write: There is no reason to worry about whether what you record is true—true in a permanent sense. Indeed, if the woman who wrote the example had done the exercise the following week, the entry might have been completely different. Your goal is to capture the truth of the moment in as much detail as you can.

Now take a moment to relax. With your eyes closed, consider where you are in your life now. When the moment is right, begin to write your entry.

SECOND DAY:

In yesterday's entry you described where you are in your current life. Today you are going to continue the process by recording impressions of where you live.

"Where you live." If you think about the phrase, it may suggest outlandish possibilities. If you have read enough science fiction, recording impressions of where you live might lead you to the outer reaches of the solar system and back to earth. But if you have a less expansive nature, you might be content to focus on your country, state, county, city, neighborhood, or house. Or if you tend to be nomadic and wish to narrow the focus further, you might describe your van. And these are just the literal possibilities. There are metaphorical ways of looking at "where you live."

If you see yourself as a spirit temporarily housed in a body, where you live—for now—could be inside a bag of skin. But for this assignment, you can skip that kind of metaphysical chin rubbing. Try instead to keep your work simple. This exercise assumes that where you live means your immediate physical surroundings—maybe your room, house, or apartment complex, but certainly nothing larger than your neighborhood.

Keep in mind that your entry need not cover every aspect of where you live. Instead try to capture fleeting impressions and details. Let your mind loose, recording the associations it makes. Perhaps your mind will connect with other places where you have lived; work those details into your entry, but always come back to your immediate surroundings. Remember, be specific. Never let your mind linger for long in general statements such as this:

> I live in a pretty white house with a big lawn and some palm trees near the center of town. I like it here. The neighbors are . . .

Instead, get to the details and the associations they bring:

> My front lawn has gone brown from the drought, but it still has two fat palms about two stories high with drooping limbs. I used to swing on them when I was a kid: Ahhhhhh—Tarzan. People could hear my scream all over town (at least my mom said they could). Ahhhhhhh, ahhh, ahhhhhhhh! But now things are different. I've gotten older and the house . . .

Be specific. Capture the details. Now, for thirty minutes write about where you live.

THIRD DAY:

Today you can begin to take the next step in exploring your current life by making a list of the personal items in your possession. Keep in mind that a list need not be limited to naming individual items but can also include brief descriptions of the items and associations you have with them. To start the writing session you might empty the contents of your wallet or purse on the desk. Arrange the items in whatever way suits you, then begin to study them. Take them in your hand. Read the writing on the ones that have writing. Smell the ones that have smells. Read the numbers on the ones that have numbers. Then, in your own time, begin to record your list. If exploring the contents of your purse or wallet doesn't capture your interest, go to the medicine cabinet or cosmetic table. Follow the same procedure by listing the jars, bottles, tins, and toothbrushes and any associations you have with these items.

As with this week's other entries, this writing session should last for thirty minutes. Be sure to date the entry and to leave yourself plenty of space—don't crowd your entries.

FOURTH DAY:

What are some of the activities you do? You attend classes, read, write papers, take tests; you drive, walk, bike, or ride a bus or subway to school; you sleep and roll out of bed in the morning; you talk with friends, teachers, parents; you may also hold a job. Many activities you do are commonplace; many, many people do them. The fact that people do them doesn't mean they're not important; they are. But you should probably consider less routine activities that add more meaning or pleasure to your life.

For today's writing you can begin by drawing up a list of activities you do or wish you did, not because you are forced to do them by the necessities of living but because you want to. Then from the list select one or two activities to write about. Record everything that comes to you: how it feels to do it; why you like it; how long you've been doing it. Record the associations you have with it; these might include the different times and places you've done it. While recording the entry, use specific language. This student entry about jogging starts off fuzzy, a way many writers begin, then goes past the general comments to the particulars of the experience:

> I like jogging because it makes me feel good. After I finish jogging, I relax. My body is limber—limber, reminds me of lumber. That's how I start in the mornings, my legs like pieces of lumber—I lumber along. But after I run for a while, I feel limber, like

a birch tree in the wind. I like the sound of my feet slapping the asphalt and the sound of breathing deep in my chest. I like to jog on cold mornings. Once there was frost on the grass. I ran across the park. Crunch, crunch, crunch.

Keep in mind that you are still working under the thirty-minute time limit—so work fast. Try not to spend time evaluating your writing; just write. Leave yourself plenty of space between and within entries. Be sure to date the entry at the top.

FIFTH DAY:

Where you are in your life now, the place you live, the items and activities that compose your current life—all these practice entries have helped collect experience that you can begin to use in your formal work. Start looking for opportunities to use them. Now, to conclude this week's daily practice, you will write about special places in your current life.

Once again, start by sitting quietly and letting your thoughts settle. Then begin to randomly list places that come to mind. These special places need not be your favorite spots, ones you associate with pleasure; they may also be places you associate with discomfort, such as a doctor's or dentist's office. Perhaps one or two places on your list will be secret places, spots you may visit for a moment or two when the world seems to be coming down around your shoulders, such as a rock overlooking a field, a window looking out to a yard or street, or a couch in a quiet place in your home.

The list you draw up may include places that are not so special but that you recorded because you listed as many as possible. Whether each place you record is truly a special place is not the point of the listing process. The listing process is to pull out a great deal of material in a short time. For example, here is a part of one student's list of special places:

the mountains: love the cool breezes that hum through the pines
the beach: but not with people—people everywhere, an anthill
restaurants: Salernos—ummmmm! El Torito, but only on Fridays
        between four and six.
El Tapito: carnitas, jalapeños, flautas
I like: my shower
the park in early morning
sitting in the quad
my granddad's garage—cans of old paint,
rusted tools, pipes, bicycle parts, at least a dozen
alarm clocks—all waiting to be fixed.

Notice the phrases that follow some of the items on the list. They add the concrete details; often they are lists themselves. This kind of random listing helps writers cover a great deal of territory so that they can find out what might be worth exploring more completely.

Now it is time for you to begin. During this practice session, take the first ten minutes to draw up your list of special places and record some associations you might have with the spots. Then after ten minutes, select one or two to write about more completely. Be sure to practice for the full time.

28

Third Week: Past Life

Your notebook is beginning to fatten from collecting the scraps of your present life. In many ways your notebook may begin to work like an artist's sketchbook, except your practice is done with words rather than lines and curves. Artists practice figure drawing through a series of quick studies—fast sketches of arms, hands, fingers. They may sketch fingers and arms. Other parts of the body will fill other pages—stomachs, chests, shoulders, and necks. An artist may have done heads and faces from several angles. No sketch is a finished piece, yet someone who flipped through all the pages would get an impression of a whole body.

The same is true of the entries you have made thus far. If someone were to scan them, though the entries are fragmented—works in progress—he or she would go away with a feeling for the whole. Of course, in the case of your notebook, the parts are not a figure but of your life. Certainly you have not been consciously composing an autobiography, but only capturing a series of passing impressions and immediate associations that make up your life in motion—a view caught on the run. And finally, like artists working to develop their skill with form, you too have been practicing to become more limber at the writing craft.

During this week's thirty-minute writing sessions, you will practice by continuing to capture experiences from your life. This week's exercises will have a basic difference from previous ones: Instead of dealing with the present you will be dealing with the past.

If you've watched your mind during the last two weeks of notebook entries, you have seen how it hops around. You may have wanted to keep it on a straight path, but it probably acted like a rabbit erratically skipping, stopping to nibble, then dashing off down a trail. No doubt you have already captured experiences and feelings from your past by following these associations. They are embedded in your previous entries. Do you recall the example used to illustrate the exercise asking you to describe where you live? It began:

> My front lawn has gone brown from the drought, but it still has two fat palms about two stories high with drooping limbs.

After the opening, this writer's mind starts associating. He connects with the past, and for a line or two he's a kid again, swinging from vines like Tarzan.

> I used to swing [from the limbs] when I was a kid: Ahhhhhh—Tarzan. People could hear my scream all over town (at least my mom said they could). Ahhhhhhh, ahhh, ahhhhhhhh!

He records the association with the past, then he returns to his original intent—to record the details of where he lives.

The point here is that the mind naturally leaps to the past. It acts like a time traveler who is not a prisoner of calendars and clocks. If you link up with past experiences, record them. This kind of practice writing is supposed to rouse associations. Memories and images should be hooking together from all parts of your experience.

Now, in order to keep the work going, this week's exercises will give you a way of nudging your memory so you can capture more details that may be of use to your formal writing. But first, here's how not to do it. Don't sit at your desk with your fingers clutching a pen and in cold blood start hacking out an autobiography. After a few minutes you'll feel as if some half-educated surgeon has cut open your skull, taken out your brain, and put it in the freezer.

Better to begin less directly. Better to let the mind do its skipping, nibbling, and dashing away. And then better to use that natural energy to sketch those parts of your past that seem to connect to your current life.

It can be done in two phases: first, by making a list of brief entries that span your life; and second, by taking the entries separately and enlarging them.

WRITING TASK—THIRD WEEK: PAST LIFE

FIRST DAY:

Make a series of brief entries in the form of an extended list that spontaneously captures memories from your past. The key word is *spontaneously,* for the goal here is not to capture only the most important events in your life—although they may be on your list—but to let the memories and images from your past come uncalled. Their relative importance to the movement of your life is not your concern. So work to create your list spontaneously and try to record each entry in no more than two or three lines. For example, here is a list of random experiences recorded by photographer Edward Weston in one of his notebooks under the heading "Notes from N.Y., 1922":

> Near the "penny bridge," a few steps from my room (Columbia Heights).
> Morning coffee with Jo from the purple cup sister gave me.
> The Hurdy Gurdy man who played to our window.
> The lone man who wandered by playing a softly quavering flute; 30 years ago. I must have heard the same man in Chicago. "God bless you sir for the money. I surely needed it."
> Almost daily I haunted the bridges, Brooklyn or Manhattan. One Sunday I walked over Williamsburg Br. at sunset—then down among the tenements on Rivington Street—memorable night.
> Two "specials" from Tina, each with $20.00 enclosed: "knowing that I would need money, that I must see Balieff's Chauve Souris."

You may find deciphering Weston's brief entries impossible. Sure, you can pick up some references to common places, but the experiences behind the entries belong to Weston. Of course, journal keeper Weston does his work for himself without being concerned if a reader can understand the entries. He drops a bucket into his experience and may be surprised at what it holds when he hoists it up. Yet no one else, while the details are in rough form, may even appreciate his catch.

Now here is a list of entries written by a student journal keeper who has returned to college to earn a second degree in psychology. Like Weston's, these also seem fragmented—written in a personalized code:

> I remember walking to school on a cold morning. It had rained—puddles covered with thin ice. Mountains with snow. Graduating from high school. The speech seemed like hours. Fear. Thought I could never do it.
> Running on the mountain trail. A trip with dad. A cabin. Fishing. Hated the smell on my hands.
> Living in the city. Once a man stopped me on the way to school. "Got a quarter, missy? Give me your lunch money." I ran.
> My first real date. Must have taken three hours to get ready. Spilled a Coke in my lap.
> Flunked geometry—the end of the world. Thought all hell would break loose. Mom shrugged her shoulders. Dad said to take it over.

Mom and dad divorced. Took me a year before I could say the word.

Away to school. Mixed feelings. Couldn't wait to get out of the house. Yet scared.

Bobby K. shot. Remember my mom weeping. Train going across the TV screen. I was 9. Didn't mean much to me.

This writer dips deeply into her past. In fact, the list appears to stretch from early memories to more recent ones. The list also includes the ups and downs of experience. Often when making life history lists of this sort, writers tend to consciously exclude difficult times. But if the mind finds its own course, the list will include both good and bad memories. Finally, notice that the list goes beyond the personal by including a memory of Robert Kennedy's assassination. Although changes, especially traumatic events, may be beyond our control, they still affect our lives. If these kinds of memories come to you, record them. Notice also that the writer quickly ties Kennedy's death to her personal world. That's natural. We see the world from our own situation.

Now, let's go back to see what this writer has done to complete the first step in recording material from her life. Her goal was simple. She had only to sit for a few moments in quiet and let the memories come to the surface. She did it by sending her thought into the past, as far back as she could. Then by letting it move forward across years of memory to the present, she randomly recalled a handful of experiences. She continued to sit quietly for a few more moments. Finally, after the strongest memories, the ones that held her interest, presented themselves, she recorded them in a few lines. She didn't judge if they were the most important. She didn't criticize herself for having any particular memory; she merely listed them on a sheet of paper in enough detail to recall them when rereading at another time.

For the first half-hour session develop a list of memories from your past. Begin by sitting quietly and directing your thought to the past. Then record in two or three lines a half dozen to a dozen of the strongest memories that come to you. They may not be big events in your life, but for the moment they will hold your interest. Be sure to write legibly enough to reread your entries, and leave plenty of space around them. And finally, after you finish the list, reread it and write the approximate dates when the events took place.

SECOND THROUGH FIFTH DAYS:

During the rest of this week's writing sessions, you will work by expanding four entries from your list. In a way each memory you've listed is like a doorway to your past. To write a brief entry is to open the door just a crack. To expand the entry is to swing the door open wide. Behind it will be a story or heaps of detail that you may have forgotten. This recalled detail can work as material for other writing. But even if you never use it, the writing practice will aid in limbering your style. The fear of confronting the blank page—if that fear is one of your hobgoblins—will lose some of its witchery.

But before you begin, here's another example that illustrates what you are supposed to be doing. Recall the list used to illustrate the last exercise. One entry dealt with the assassination of Robert Kennedy:

> Bobby K. shot. Remember my mom weeping. Train going across the TV screen. I was 9. Didn't mean much to me.

The writer selected this entry to expand. She sat quietly for thirty minutes and recorded the thoughts that came to her while focusing on the memory.

> June 5, 1968: Bobby K. killed
> I was nine then—I didn't know what being nine meant. I didn't know that it was a good time to be alive, a time to play, and laugh, and innocently cry. Crying was something you did when you got hurt or wanted your way. But looking back I can remember sensing the sadness my mother felt when Bobby Kennedy was shot. I didn't know about politics then. I only knew it usually took the TV away from me. Politics and the news. Neither were very much fun for me then. They're not now, either. I remember getting out of bed. My mother was watching the news and she was crying. I asked her why—I was confused. It was the first time I had seen her cry and I didn't see her cry again until dad left—then they were both crying. She said that a great man had died—she didn't say "was shot"—only that he died. I put the "was shot" in later. I remember being upset at first because I knew to die wasn't good, but then because I was missing the programs I liked to watch—then I think it was Captain Kangaroo or maybe Soupy Sales. How stupid a kid is—no that's not fair, not stupid but innocent. That's the key. Maybe that was my first step out of innocence—the death of Bobby K. and my not knowing what it meant. After that my family began to break up. After that . . . there's a lot of after thats. They all seem to lead to where I am now, at college, and it seems that many, many people like Bobby K., only who are not so well known, are being murdered every day by bombs and bullets and clubs. Sometimes I wish I were nine again. Nine and just cuddled up in front of Captain K. Sometimes I wish I had never learned about Bobby K.

Did you notice how the entry begins with the focus then starts to skip and hop? It moves from the far past to the present and pauses at places in between. The writer doesn't linger with any one thought but records whatever comes to her in relation to the focus.

Each day for the rest of the week, reread the list of memory experiences. Select the one you feel most curious about. Then for thirty minutes expand it by recording whatever comes to mind.

29
Fourth Week: Daily Activities

In this week's writing sessions you will describe daily experiences from the inside or the outside. Feel free to do whichever you wish—or do both.

Though there are a couple of ways of going about it, a description of the day is an exercise close to traditional diary keeping. To do it writers sit down (usually in the evening) and describe the highlights of their experience from the time they crawled out of bed to the time they took up the pen. The danger in this kind of entry is that it can become routine and dull. A typical example might begin like this:

> John called this morning. We talked for two hours about which college he should attend. He went through the entire list—UCLA, U. of Arizona, Berkeley . . .

And so on.

If this entry were to continue in this fashion, it would give the writer practice—and that's what we want—but it would be lifeless.

Let's take the subject of lifeless writing a bit further. By this time you've probably found that writing comes more easily when your emotion gets involved. Emotion gives prose energy, and when yours comes into play, you may find it tough for the hand holding the pen to keep up with the mind generating the words. You may even feel transported, as if you had leaped into another space. If you reach that state of deep involvement, great. Stick with it. Later, if you wish to integrate a journal entry into a piece of formal writing, you bring in the intellect to prune the overgrown first effort.

The problem you'll be facing in this task is how to pump life into routine entries.

It's easy: Describe them from the inside. Get your emotion involved and expand your entries by including feelings and insights. Describe the emotional nuances, those subtle messages behind so many of your experiences, the ones you may seldom listen to. This is writing from the inside. Here is the preceding entry rewritten, after a routine beginning from the inner perspective.

> John called this morning. We talked for two hours about which college he should attend. He went through the entire list—UCLA, U. of Arizona, Berkeley . . . the list seemed endless. And he had to go through the pluses and minuses of each one. I wanted to scream, to slam down the receiver, to escape. All those thoughts were running through my mind. Then I realized he was truly confused. I listened more carefully. He said things like, "Berkeley has a great name, but that town scares me. I like the campus, but there is something wrong with the feeling there. It's the town. And I don't want to live in a dorm." As I listened, and he went through a similar routine with each school, I realized he was scared. He didn't want to leave home. Then I realized something about myself. I was feeling scared, too. Maybe that's why I wanted off the phone—his fear was tugging at mine. Then I thought, well, why shouldn't we be scared? We were both born here and neither of us has lived anyplace else.

The writer has gone beyond routine practice by recording feelings and insights—the emotional responses that connected him to the entry.

In contrast, outside entries involve describing something you saw that held your attention. To write an outside entry, take the point of view of the detached observer, someone who is not part of the event yet captures it in writing as a photographer might snap a photograph. This kind of exercise is often associated with the professional writer who collects random material for a future work. Whatever you record as a detached observer doesn't need to be earthshaking, but it should be sufficiently interesting to make you pause when you see it. One notebook keeper recorded this entry describing a boy trying to fly a kite:

> *Sitting in the park:* A little boy about six was trying to fly a kite. He was in the center of a grassy area. His father sat nearby, smoking a pipe. The boy carefully laid out about ten feet of kite string. He then lined the kite up at the end. Next, while holding the stick with the excess string wrapped around it, he ran toward the trees, the kite bumping along behind him. Finally, he stopped and flopped on the ground to rest. A minute or two later he reset the kite and ran back toward his father. Finally, after several runs, the father took the pipe from his mouth and shouted, "There's no wind." The boy was again laying out the string and the now tattered kite. He stopped, turned to his dad and said, "Dad, I run and make wind."

This entry has been done from an objective viewpoint—from the outside. Whether you choose to record daily experiences as an outsider who is merely describing an event or as an insider who includes emotional responses, you will get practice putting experience into words.

WRITING TASK—FOURTH WEEK: DAILY ACTIVITIES

For this week's thirty-minute practice sessions each day, record highlights of your day or interesting events you observed during the day.

30
Fifth Week: Dreams and Fantasies

This week will take your writing practice into another dimension. So far you've recorded unfocused entries and collected material from your current life and daily experiences. You've also collected memories. Now you'll collect dreams and fantasies.

Dreams offer excellent material for those who say, "Nothing ever happens to me. My life is so uninteresting. I have nothing to write." Well, dreams are often full of excitement. They take dreamers into landscapes and situations they might never be able to imagine while awake. One notebook keeper recorded this dream:

THE CAVE

I found myself in a strange land . . . a combination of wooded mountains and barren desert. All around me were pines, rivers, and lakes—there were even patches of snow. Yet the land was also a desert with volcanic rocks and ancient lava flows. I was walking through pine groves that seemed to be growing out of rock. It was hot, the sun like a desert sun. I came to a stream, and though I wanted to rest, I decided to move on—I felt I had an appointment, although I wasn't sure what kind. I crossed the stream, the cold water swirling around my calves. Soon I left the trees and began to walk across a wasteland, a place that looked like a moon-scape. I wanted to turn back—to go to the stream—but I couldn't. I began to climb a hill with a steep grade that ended at the face of a cliff. Rocks kept slipping under my feet. Finally, when I reached the foot of the cliff, I noticed a cave and walked to its entrance. The mouth was so black it looked as if it had been painted on the rocks with tar.

I became uneasy. I wanted to go in; after all, I had come this far—or so I thought. But I couldn't bring myself to take the step into the darkness. I woke without entering the cave.

Is a dream seen or felt as intensely as the "real" experiences we record? Though the setting seems to come from a mythic land, the writer's dream is described with all the intensity of a waking experience. She has concentrated on capturing the particulars of her dream journey, attempting to give us as full a picture as her writing skills allow.

If you are one of those people who forgets dreams, you can record fantasies. Some people call fantasizing "wool gathering" or "castle building in Spain" or "middle-distance staring" or just plain "daydreaming."

Daydreaming has the quality of "tuning out," of taking a momentary leave of absence by stepping from the realistic world of objects, people, and tasks and into an imaginary space filled with private creations or recreated combinations from daily life—pictures in the mind's eye. Daydreaming! A trip to Araby with tales of a thousand and one nights.

A child dawdling over a math problem who begins to mumble about space creatures and galactic wars, punctuating his thoughts with zooms from passing star ships; the history student who suddenly realizes she has read ten pages and can't recall doing it; the professor who falls into a profound silence while staring at the chalkboard—all are daydreaming. Albert Einstein, the scientist who described relativity, daydreamed. He once asked a friend, "Why is it I get my best ideas in the morning while I'm shaving?"

Einstein's question brings up an interesting point. People may need daydreams to relax the mind so ideas can emerge. Most of us have used expressions such as "it came from the blue," "the idea just popped into my head," or "it suddenly hit me." These experiences usually come when the intellect has dropped its guard and the intuition begins to shape itself into the images of the imagination.

Daydreams come in two varieties—brief and extended. Brief daydreams are like hunches and insights. Whenever you have one, jot it down and add it to your notebook. Extended daydreams may have recurred during our lives. These are the ones you especially want to record during this week's sessions. They offer more material for practice.

Here's an example of a recurring daydream written by a young man raised in the city:

FLY-FISHING

Ever since I saw a film about Ernest Hemingway's life I have wanted to fly-fish. Not such a big wish, but one that is totally unrelated to my life. I've never even been to the mountains, let alone waded in a stream with hip boots. Still, I have this vision of myself like the guy who played Nick Adams (Nick Adams was supposed to be Hemingway) in the early parts of the film, pulling in a trout. My daydream usually goes something like this:

The scene—early morning. The sun coming through thick pines.

The action—I crawl from my tent, stretch, and breathe deep from the fresh mountain air. The world seems great. I kick a log on the fire, which has been smoldering all night, and toss on some chips. Leaning down, I blow on a few hot embers. The flames flare up. Then I decide to catch some fresh fish for breakfast. I take up the pole that has been leaning against a tree next to my fishing vest.

Of course, the piece continues to the end of the fantasy. One technique this writer uses is to begin with a brief background statement. That's fine. If you decide to record a daydream and you know its background, include it.

WRITING TASK—FIFTH WEEK: DREAMS AND FANTASIES

During your five thirty-minute writing sessions this week, practice by recording dreams or fantasies. They need not be current—if you have dreams and fantasies that you recall from different times in your life, record them. While practicing, write as concretely as you can. Include details. Finally, be sure to keep to the task for thirty minutes. If you finish describing a dream or fantasy in less than thirty minutes, write another entry. Perhaps you will want to include your thoughts on the dream or fantasy. Also, after you have made the entry you may want to give it a title. Sometimes dream and fantasy entries have the qualities of brief narration. A title can highlight the main element.

31

Sixth Week: Portraits and Relationships

Some entries never seem finished. Dreams and fantasies may come neatly packaged with beginnings, middles, and ends, but memories are seldom as tidy as dreams and fantasies. Often, by tugging on a thread of some distant experience you may begin to unravel large parts of your personal history. You record and record and record yet seem unable to reach an end. Thirty minutes pass. Soon you've worked into the early morning—when to stop?

Well, there is no true stopping place—there is only an arbitrary one determined by the thirty-minute time limit or by the feeling that it's comfortable to step out. You see, a journal is as open-ended as life itself. We don't live a life neatly packaged like television programs. We live an organic process. When we write about it—even for writing practice—we may become involved in its intricacies.

If you're feeling uncomfortable about the open-ended nature of some of your entries, we suggest you return to them and add more detail. Or, as you already may have found to be true, the details you left unrecorded in one entry may surface in another. This week's practice will give you a chance to pick up some of the material you may have left unrecorded, for you will be writing portraits of people in your life.

To begin the portraits we suggest you develop a list of people from your past as well as your present. Keep in mind that these people should hold some significance for you. They should be people you've been emotionally connected to, not people who just casually passed through your life. It is the emotional connection that will fuel these practice entries. Now, a way to develop the list is to return to those parts of your notebook where you collected details from your current life and where you expanded entries from your memory lists. Reread those sections and make a separate list of people who appear in them. Your list should be more than a simple record of names; it should also include some brief comments to locate the people in your life.

For instance, here are three entries from an extended list developed by one student:

> Martha K: See her often. Sometimes we walk down University where the sycamores drop their leaves. No real commitment, just comfortable with her. We sometimes have lunch—introduced me to lox and cream cheese on bagels.
>
> Old Ben: Vietnam. Playing with blocks, Tinkertoys. Fishing at the jetty. Taught me about death.
>
> John C: Three years together on the football team—left and right halfbacks. Everyone called us Heckle and Jeckle. "He's Jeckle," we both once said, while pointing at each other.

Notice that this partial list includes specifics. The writer does not merely record a few general comments on the page and leave it at that. If he had, an entry might read like this:

> Martha K: A real swell person. I like to walk and have lunch with her.

But instead the writer has worked in details—"where the sycamores drop their leaves . . . introduced me to lox and cream cheese on bagels"—along with some general words that suggest the quality of the relationship—"No real commitment . . . comfortable." The use of specific detail makes writing come alive.

After developing a list of people, the next step is to select someone from the list to use for your portrait. At first glance a portrait may suggest a physical description, but yours will be much more. Besides physical and personality impressions, you'll include some background information and describe some experiences you've shared with the person. If you are writing a portrait of someone from the past and the entry leads to recent experience that connects to those early points in your life, record those details just as you did in other entries.

So this kind of portrait goes beyond a limited physical rendering; it attempts to show an evolving relationship. Here's a portrait expanded from an entry on the writer's list above:

> I can remember playing with and learning from a man I used to know as Old Ben. I'm not sure how he came to be called Old Ben, maybe because of his white, white hair that seemed to get blown every which way whenever a breeze came up. And his face was wrinkled and a deep tan from spending a lot of years in the outdoors. His laugh, though, was young. Whenever something pleased him he

would laugh at the sky. He had a way of lowering his upper lip when he laughed—I guess to cover his front teeth which were chipped and partly brown, as if rust was slowly taking them over.

When I first met him I was about seven. It was a tough time. My dad flew Navy helicopters and was on a aircraft carrier in the Persian Gulf. At that time I couldn't understand what being a pilot meant—sure, I saw films on TV and played combat with neighbor kids, but it was all a game. Because my father was gone, my grandfather used to come to stay with me when my mom had errands to run. That's how I met Old Ben—he came with my grandfather. My grandfather didn't care much for children, or at least that's what I thought then, because he would always sit in an easy chair and read. But Ben was different. He would always want to get down and play with me. He loved to build with Lincoln Logs (I had an old set that belonged to my father) and Tinkertoys. I can remember trying to keep his constructions together from one visit to the next. I would try to copy them; that's how much I liked him. Of course, I would always fail. For some reason I would end up needing a particular piece that would be in the middle of whatever he built. So when I would try to work it free, all the other pieces would cave in around my hand.

Once Old Ben and I went fishing. When I think about him now, I understand—I guess I should say appreciate—how patient he was. Last summer I watched a kid fish with his dad. The boy must have been about the age I was when Ben took me. The boy couldn't let his line stay put—reeling it in, shouting for his dad to put more bait on the hook and then to help him cast it out. His father was trying to fish also, but the demands of his son didn't give him time to do it. Finally, the father got angry. He shouted something at the boy, then reeled in the boy's line and put the pole away. The boy cried, trying to choke back the sobs. Now when Ben took me fishing, he never tried to fish himself, he just sat on a nearby rock and smoked a pipe while giving me simple advice. And once in a while when my line got tangled, he'd get up to help. Whenever I fish I think of Old Ben.

But Ben taught me more than fishing and how to build with Lincoln Logs and Tinkertoys—he taught me about death. My father was killed in a crash—that's a whole other entry and I don't want to go into it now. Everyone in the family came to our house. I remember some woman, later I found out she was a cousin, who was in her seventies, coming out of the crowd and leaning her powdered face to me—I can still smell the perfume—and saying, "It was the Lord's will. Your father is with the Lord."

Later, I asked Ben about what the woman had said. He kind of smiled, keeping the upper lip over his teeth. He said, "That probably made her feel good to believe it." Then I asked him what he thought death was. He said it was up to each person to decide. And the only way to do it was to spend some time studying death.

The idea of studying death seemed curious, but three years later I had a chance to do it: Ben gave it to me. He had a stroke and was sent to the hospital to recover. Of course he didn't—the stroke had paralyzed his right side, and he couldn't talk. He couldn't even smile because half his face was paralyzed, and his lip had a permanent lifeless droop. I used to visit him when my grandfather went. My grandfather would read aloud to Ben, never really noticing what was going on around him. While my grandfather was spending his time in books, I looked into Ben's eyes. They always seemed to be staring back at me and asking whether or not I was learning.

Notice that the entry goes back into the writer's life. It connects to some very important parts of his life—the separation from his father and the death of his father. The writer skirts these large concerns by focusing on Ben, but they lie behind most of the entry's detail. If the writer continues to keep a notebook, he will probably describe these experiences. Once you learn to trust free writing, you'll find that notebook entries often lead to the important experiences in your life. Your entries may not go directly to the target, but they get there in their own fashion, something like a boomerang tossed in one direction and coming back in another.

Notice also that in this portrait the writer gives more than a physical description and personality sketch of Ben. Certainly these descriptive facts are in the piece, but they speak beyond ordinary description by suggesting the deep relationship developing between the writer and Ben. It is easy to see that Ben becomes a surrogate father by serving as a sometime playmate, teacher, and model. He even becomes a teacher for the final lesson of life—death. The father's death took place unnaturally and at a distance. The writer could only participate in the rituals, which were probably marred by insensitive comments as suggested by the appearance of the aged cousin. Ben's death takes the writer beyond cosmetics.

Finally, notice that there is tension in this portrait—the entry is built on opposition. This is suggested by the implied contrasts between Ben and the grandfather. Although the writer does not develop the difference, in fact may not even be aware that it is developing as he writes, two conflicting views of life emerge. Ben wants to get into the boy's world: to play at building, to show him how to fish, and ultimately to teach him about death. We see the grandfather with his nose poked in a book. He seems uninterested and withdrawn. This kind of natural tension deepens the entry by helping the writer to capture a universal truth.

We may be overevaluating a notebook entry. That's not what practice in a notebook is for. Yet, if you find subjects in your daily writing that capture your interest, return to them with the idea that they can be expanded. Those interests that naturally emerge from practice are valuable to develop the emotion needed to give writing life. This portrait is still rough, as most notebook entries are. But it offers raw material for an original paper.

WRITING TASK—SIXTH WEEK: PORTRAITS AND RELATIONSHIPS

FIRST DAY:

Spend your practice time today developing a list of people to use for possible portraits. You can go about doing it in two ways. First, you might draw together a memory list by sitting quietly and allowing your mind to roam throughout your life history. As the names of important persons come to you, jot them down. Another way to draw up a list is by browsing through your previous entries to find references to others who may be important to you. Put these people on your list. Remember to add brief comments about the relationship and the experiences you've shared with them. In other words, this is to be an extended list, full of detail and observations.

SECOND DAY THROUGH FIFTH DAY:

Each day select one person from your list. Spend your practice time describing the person and the relationship you've shared with the person. Remember to include more than physical details. Include all that comes to you about the relationship.

32

Seventh Week: Social Issues

So far the bulk of your practice writing has been done by focusing on the personal aspects of your life. By concentrating on current activities, dreams, fantasies, memories, and people from your past and present, you were guaranteed subjects you knew well and had strong feelings about. These subjects acted as flywheels to keep your notebook entries moving. You will still be working with personal responses during this week's sessions, but the exercises will have a new twist. They will take you to places located beyond your personal domain.

Although we may wish to escape issues of social importance, the reality of our lives doesn't let us isolate ourselves from them. Questions about such issues as crime, poverty, abortion, ecology, energy, political corruption, industrial chicanery, and international terrorism often take up our emotional and intellectual energy. Since these and many other issues are part of the larger social fabric, we must deal with them, at least on a personal level.

Often these larger-than-our-personal-life issues—these "big issues"—are the ones beginning writers most want to confront in formal assignments. After all, the big issues are the backbone of most academic courses. They dominate sociology, psychology, history, anthropology, and literature. Their dominance may lead beginning writers to feel as if their personal experiences are not important. This attitude could be the reason many students choose to write about vague subjects, such as political corruption instead of vandalism in their own neighborhoods; the moral implications of abortion instead of the effects of abortions on women they know; or the American way of death instead of the death of a friend or relative.

Although in short formal papers the big issues are too large to cover, they can give you the opportunity for writing practice. Using them as a center for

415

daily writing gives you a chance to explore your relationship to issues beyond your immediate influence. But first you need to find out what interests you—to identify your social concerns.

The way to begin is to start your first writing session by sitting quietly and making a list of issues beyond your direct influence, the ones that occupy your thoughts or conversations. Don't formulate a position. Don't be overdetailed. Merely jot down a word or two so you'll be reminded of the concern that lies behind the issue. Here's an example of one student's concerns:

noise
abortion? not so sure!
terrorism
cigarette smokers—all smokers
language
whales—ecology
killing/battering children
not killing murderers (execution): capital punishment
trucks

No one told this writer what should be important. Her job was to sit quietly and let some concerns she has about issues beyond her control come to mind. She listed them very quickly. Then after she collected a handful, she took the exercise to the next step.

The next step is to reflect on the issues a little more. The writer returned to the list and recorded in a few phrases the thoughts she had about the entries. Here's what a few of her fleshed-out entries look like:

Noise: Portable radios blaring at the beach and pools, FM blasting in clothing shops, beauty parlors, restaurants, the cafeteria—everywhere. I can't seem to get away. Like music, all kinds, but when it's played too loudly and blares from third-rate speakers, it isn't music, it's torture. Maybe my focus here is the inconsiderate people who play music in public places.

Abortion: For some reason abortion is on my mind. Have no clear feelings about it. Just confusion. Hasn't touched my life.

Smokers: Tie in with music. Smoking in public places inconsiderate. I feel rage when around a smoker in a restaurant. They can kill themselves, but I don't want them fouling up my air. What about cars? Smog? The smog from cars is killing.

Language: Never thought about language until I took a critical thinking course. Whenever I hear a politician speak, I feel stupid—rather, I used to feel stupid—now I know better. Many of them use vague, deceptive language to fool the people—and that's me, "a people." I want to get on the politicians' cases. And TV also. Terrorism: Should have written it with an exclamation point. But what do I truly know about terrorism? Very little. But to write a notebook entry I don't have to know anything. I just need to feel something about it, and I need to write my feelings.

Remember, first draw up a brief list, then flesh out each item with your general observations.

Once the list is complete and the observations have been added, you'll select one item at a time to extend. Just as you've done in other journal-keeping tasks, you'll write everything that comes to mind during the practice time. As an illustration, here's a further expanded version of the terrorism entry. Notice how the writer lets her mind drift with the subject. She includes details from the current news, history, and films.

- A kid in a vacant lot. Several of us. Billy K. had matches and fire-crackers. Was near the 4th, hot, hot summer. Billy stuffed a fire-cracker into an anthill, lit the wick. Boom! The ants began to swarm. Lit several more. Boom! Boom! Boom! Ants going crazy. Then he lit some weeds and began to fry the swarming ants. I watched, yet knew something was wrong with doing what Billy was doing.
- Remember *Silence of the Lambs* with Jody Foster as a FBI trainee tracking a serial killer who was terrorizing young women.
- Films of Nazi Germany concentration camps (the word "concentration" seems out of place, the Nazi politicians/propagandists). The Uris novel, forget the title. Jews escaping to Israel before it was Israel.
- Highjackings, assassinations, burning buses, exploding bombs. Death. Militias, are they crazy, heroes, victims or criminals? What is all this adding up to? My thoughts are expanding but seem so confused. How do I feel about national and international terrorism? Fascinated—sickened.
- Somehow it's all mixed in with people wanting change. If change doesn't come, the terrorists attack—beat the opponent to the ground, make a midnight call—"if you value your life"—or blow up a plane, government building, school, or movie theater. Stupid. I think of the opening scenes from *The Wild Bunch*. The gang shooting up the town parade. Many slaughtered. The innocent, that's what cuts me. Children or just happy folks, everyday people, destroyed by some crazies who come out of nowhere. Boom! For no real reason.

Glancing at this example you can sense the difficulty the writer has in dealing with a large subject like terrorism. She doesn't have a great deal of information about terrorism, so once she lets her mind go, thoughts of her past come up, associations she has with terrorism from childhood. The childhood memory of terrorizing the ants echoes the sense of helplessness with which the journal entry ends.

WRITING TASK—SEVENTH WEEK: SOCIAL ISSUES

FIRST DAY:

Begin by listing the big issues in your life. Then, once the list is complete, flesh out each item by adding your general observations.

SECOND THROUGH FIFTH DAY:

Each day spend your practice period by expanding one item from your list of big issues. Let your mind roam freely. Collect the associations you make with the issue.

33
Eighth Week: Self-Reflection

You have been practicing for several weeks by exploring a subject close to you—your life. We hope you are beginning to sense the scope of self-exploration. People, places, memories, feelings, objects, events, books, films, music, dreams, even unharnessed thought—all fall into that vast, partially charted territory called your life. We also hope you have made some discoveries about yourself. One of the side benefits of pursuing daily writing is the self-examination that comes with accumulating a record of your life experiences.

If you were to ask around, you would find that educators disagree on what kinds of knowledge people need to get through life. Should they master the classics? Foreign languages? Should they be able to recite math formulas and scientific principles?

The issue becomes more confusing when you stumble across scholars and scientists who have not mastered all the important classics and who have forgotten the simple principles of geometry and physics—and are all doing just fine, thank you. But the educator reasons that these are rogues—the talented, the gifted, the intuitive—people who don't fit into the common scheme of things.

So the debate rages. You don't need to listen long to discover two views. The first supports practical education, one that stresses the nuts and bolts of living today. The second supports a more liberal education, one that points to ancient texts as keys for unlocking life's predicaments.

But there is a neutral zone where weighty thinkers can meet and proclaim in a single voice (probably because none of them can build a course around it) that one kind of knowledge is indispensable: self-knowledge, the kind that comes from self-examination. During this last week of daily writing tasks we want to lead you a few steps down the path of self-examination, or, as we prefer to call it, self-reflection.

Self-reflection has nothing to do with parading what you consider to be your hang-ups onto the page. You must have acquaintances who like to lead now-I'm-going-to-tell-you-the-truth-about-you sessions, which is usually composed of an hour's worth of slander disguised in pseudo-analytical jargon. This is not the kind of reflection we suggest. After all, if insensitive criticism and verbal harassment could lead to a deepening of our self-knowledge, the chances are we would all be perfect. We aren't. And self-slander won't help us gain insight into our lives.

Instead of making a direct assault on yourself, you'll follow a more gentle course by merely rereading your entries and recording any responses or insights you have.

Once, after considering the course of his life, P. D. Ouspensky, an esoteric philosopher, wrote:

> There exist moments in life, separated by long intervals of time, but linked together by their inner content and by a certain singular sensation peculiar to them. Several such moments always recur to my mind together, and I feel then that it is these that have determined the chief trend of my life.

"The chief trend of my life"—a very large phrase that holds some meaning for Ouspensky, but perhaps not for you. Nevertheless, the point is clear. Before he could gain this insight, Ouspensky had to collect his experience, reflect on it, and somehow come to conclusions about where he had been and where he was going. He actively reflected on his life.

Novelist Anaïs Nin, after years of keeping diaries, reflected on her recorded experiences:

> In the early diaries I speak of my feeling that I am playing many roles demanded of woman, which I have been programmed to play. But I know also that there is a part of myself that stands apart from that and wants some other kind of life, some other kinds of authenticity. R. D. Laing [a contemporary psychiatrist] describes this authenticity as a process of constantly peeling off the false selves. You can do this in many ways but you can also do it by looking at it, for there is so much that we don't want to look at.

Both Ouspensky and Nin talk about the broad insights self-reflection has brought them, the former of the intuitive threads connecting his experiences, the latter of her awareness of a self behind the social roles she plays and the difficulty in reaching that self.

Reflecting on notebook entries need not always lead to deep insights. Often a thought will come that's related to your current life. Or you may feel as if you have reexperienced what you've already described. You may then want to extend it. After rereading a dream, one student wrote:

> Returned to the cave dream. The whole experience came back to me, almost as if I were in the dream again. When I finished I felt I was still standing at the cave's mouth. Afraid, unable to move, just staring into the darkness. This is crazy, I thought, why am I scared of going in there. Then I began to imagine I went in. I told myself there was no reason to be afraid of the unknown. Unknown! The word sounded in my mind like a scream. Unknown! That's what the cave was. So I imagined I walked into the darkness. I had to put my hands in front of my face the cave was so black. I felt my way around a turn and there was a blue light ahead—a soft hazy glow. In a moment I was at the edge of an underground pond—more the size of a lake than a pond. It was beautiful. It seemed to glow. It was worth the journey through the dark. This entire imaginary journey took only a second, but I saw some truth in it. It told me that I'm often too timid when I face something I don't know or understand. Thinking the word "unknown" made me realize I'm frightened of it, but if I move ahead with some caution, it will be okay.

The sequence of this entry is simple. The writer reflects on the dream, which led her to again face the dream dilemma—to enter or not enter the cave. She suddenly realizes what the dream suggests to her—the unknown—then does in fantasy what she was unable to do while dreaming. She finally gains the insight that facing unknowns in her life needn't frighten her.

Whether or not her insight will have any lasting significance is not the point. What's important is that she's looked at a part of her life and come away with a message. She's been engaged in self-reflection.

WRITING TASK—EIGHTH WEEK: SELF-REFLECTION

During this final week of directed journal entries, spend each thirty-minute session both rereading previous entries and recording your responses to them. You may reread several entries before you have a response. That's fine. The appropriate way to do this task is the way that works best for you.

34
Continuing Work

We hope the several weeks you've spent in daily writing practice have not only perpetuated some good writing habits but also improved your writing fluency. We also hope you've accumulated a pool of material to draw from and use in more formal assignments. If you use your journal material in this fashion, you'll be in the company of many other writers who have done just that.

If Henry David Thoreau had not kept a journal, would we have the marvelous record of his life at Walden Pond? Any reader who wishes to make the effort can discover how Anaïs Nin's diaries and Albert Camus's notebooks contributed to their works. Even world statesman Winston Churchill—the man who led the British Empire through its grimmest years during World War II—claimed he was able to write his six-volume history of those years because of wartime diaries and journals.

Of course, it may be hard for you to see yourself as a Thoreau, Nin, Camus, or Churchill. But along with them and others who have kept personal records of their lives and times you may feel the satisfaction that comes with this sort of self-expression. Disclosing the self to the self, telling a private tale held in the heart, charting the soul's inner territory—these may be the deeper values of journal keeping. By this time we hope you've experienced these pleasures.

If you've become interested in this mode of self-expression, you may be just beginning your journal work. Perhaps you've also found a direction. If so, keep writing in whatever way suits you. But if you wish to continue and have no direction, we have some suggestions.

Logs

A log is similar to a diary. It is used less to explore aspects of a life, as you have been doing in this section's writing tasks, and more to record important day-to-day details. It holds one danger: Often a log can become routine and boring to keep up. To avoid a dull routine we suggest you focus your log.

Use one part to keep track of an important activity. Though you may also use the log to record interesting details along with the activity, the primary focus will be on the activity.

What is an important activity? You need to answer that question yourself. One thing is certain. Since you are a student, we assume you value your education. You may, therefore, wish to record your educational progress. Or, to be more specific, you may want to record progress in a particular subject area or course.

But more than likely education is not the only important activity you have. You may have several. Exercise, art projects, hobbies, business, a household to run, even relationships with friends and family could be important activities in your life. You must decide for yourself. Keep in mind, too, that your list of important activities also changes over time—one might last no longer than the time it takes to complete a research project, while another, such as mastering a musical instrument, might last for years.

Arnold Bennett, the early-twentieth-century novelist, used his journal to log the progress he made while writing *The Old Wives' Tale*. The following selected excerpts from Bennett's journal also include details from his life, especially details of his walking excursions into the French countryside. Study Bennett's entries along with our comments to see how he kept a log.

WEDNESDAY, OCTOBER 9TH

Yesterday I began *The Old Wives' Tale*. I wrote 350 words yesterday afternoon and 900 this morning. I felt less self-conscious than I usually do in beginning a novel. In order to find a clear 3 hours for it every morning I have had to make a timetable, getting out of bed earlier and lunching later. This morning I calculated that I could just walk to the Croix de Montmorin and back in an hour. I nearly did it this morning without trying, in heavy rain. Tomorrow I may do it. A landscape of soaked leaves and thick clouds and rain—nothing else. But I like it.

Did you notice how Bennett also includes his inner responses—"I felt less self-conscious than I usually do in beginning a novel"—and specific physical details from his walk—"A landscape of soaked leaves and thick clouds and rain"?

Read a couple more entries, watching the focus, the inner responses, and the specifics.

THURSDAY, OCTOBER 10TH

A magnificent October day, I walked 4 miles between 8:30 and 9:30, and then wrote 1,000 words of the novel. This afternoon we penetrated into the forest with our bicycles and without a map! Had to walk miles, got lost gloriously, and at last reached home after 2 hours 40 minutes of labour. Far off, in an unfrequented path, we came across 3 old women sitting in the hedge and discussing mushrooms.

WEDNESDAY, OCTOBER 16TH

I have written 7,000 words of the first chapter of the novel, and am still far from the end of it. Regarding it objectively, I do not see that it is very good, but from the pleasure I take in doing it, it must be.

Nothing but rain. I walked 4 miles in 59 minutes this morning in the rain. And this afternoon I went with Marguerite to Moret in pouring rain. A promenade on a thoroughly bad day in autumn is the next best thing to a promenade on a fine late spring morning. I enjoy it immensely. I enjoy splashing water-proof boots into deep puddles. Now it is dark, and I write this by my desk-lamp (after only 1 1/2 pages my eyes feel fatigue) and it is still raining on the window.

Again, Bennett records his inner responses—"I do not see that it [the novel] is very good, but from the pleasure I take in doing it, it must be." He also makes some observations about the weather and his walk. The closing details relate to his working conditions and add reality to his entry. By embodying inner responses, observations, and some specific details, these entries go beyond a limited log of Bennett's work activity.

He continues this practice:

MONDAY, OCTOBER 21ST

Today I finished the second chapter of my novel. I seem to be rather uneasy as to its excellence. The date of the first part worries me, as my own recollections don't begin till 10 years later than 1862. However, the effect of the novel will be a cumulative one.

Lately I have been overworking in spite of all the resolutions to the contrary. I rise at 6:30 or so, and after reading Italian, one hour's walking, etc., I begin on the novel at 9:30 and work till 12:30. Then my afternoons are often taken up with articles. I had meant to keep my afternoons quite free of composition. Nevertheless, my health, thanks to walking 4 miles in an hour each morning, is simply admirable, and I sleep well. But my eyesight is weakening.

And notice in the next selection the opening comments on nineteenth-century novelist Stendhal. Bennett has read Stendhal's journal. He momentarily regrets having taken care, unlike Stendhal, in proper sentence construction when vivid, fragmented impressions would have served him as well. He then follows with a paragraph of fragmented details that capture the rain and forest before he returns to logging the progress of his novel.

WEDNESDAY, OCTOBER 23RD

In reading Stendhal's unpublished journal in the *Mercure de France,* it seemed to me that in *my* journal I wasted a great deal of time in the proper construction of sentences. Quite unnecessary to do this in recording impressions.

Still much rain. A perfect baptism of damp this morning in the forest, though not actually raining. The forest all yellow and brown. Leaves falling continuously. Horse-chestnuts quite yellow. Sound of water occasionally dislodged from the trees by wind.

I have written over 2,000 words of the third chapter yesterday and today. I planned the chapter perfectly yesterday morning in the forest.

Finally, one last selected illustration:

SATURDAY, OCTOBER 26TH

The forest is now, for me, at nearly its most beautiful. Another fortnight and the spectacle will be complete. But it is really too close to our doors for us to appreciate it properly. If we had to walk 5 miles instead of 500 yards in order to get into one of these marvelously picturesque glades, we should think we were exceedingly lucky in being only 5 miles off and not 50. On the whole a very wet month, with, on days free from rain, heavy persistent fogs lasting till afternoon. The sound of voices is very clear in the forest in this mushroom weather. I have learnt a little about mushrooms. I have tremendously enjoyed my morning exercise in the mist or rain. But mushrooming only interests me when the sport is good.

In general, slightly too much work. 18,000 words of *Old Wives' Tale* in 2 weeks 4 days.

A work log, a collection of inner responses, observations, and specific details from his walks and the weather—all these make Bennett's entries interesting and vivid. We offer them as illustrations. They can be guides for you to follow if you choose to keep a log of your important activities. Of course, after starting your log, you will find your own way.

Extended Portraits, Imaginary Conversations, Unsent Letters

You may also keep your practice going by writing more portraits. If you've already written portraits of the people collected in your first listing, you might begin a new list and then continue the descriptive process. On the other hand, you may wish to extend the portraits you've already completed.

Since the people you've listed are emotionally important to you, you've probably found that a single portrait for each one doesn't truly capture the relationship. After all, relationships are complex, and to get at that complexity in writing may take several sessions.

We suggest you begin by rereading one of your portrait entries. Then write another descriptive entry. This time you might focus on one aspect of the relationship or on one event you and the other person shared. Keep this up for several sessions, at least until you feel the relationship has been adequately fleshed out. We suggest, as with every entry, that you date these descriptions and that you keep them together in a portrait section. Remember to continue to record memories, physical details, feelings—all the stuff that comes to you while practice writing.

After you've fully described a person and the relationship, try writing an imaginary conversation with the person. These conversations are not necessarily transcriptions of actual conversations nor are they attempts to imagine what the person might say if the person were with you. These conversations are merely you letting yourself record an inner dialogue between yourself and the other person.

Sometimes these conversations will deal with feelings that have never been expressed in the relationship—deep feelings of love or intense concern; anger or gnawing frustration; perhaps even fearful feelings. Other times they might revolve around an issue or event. You may record an imaginary conversation during which you ask for advice or give it.

To begin an imaginary conversation, review your previously written portraits and then write a brief introduction that expresses the reasons for holding the conversation—nothing formal, just a relaxed explanation to set the scene. Next, address the other person in a way that seems natural. Write down what you say and what the other person says in script form—the way a playwright might record dialogue.

What follows is an imaginary conversation between a young man and his uncle. The young man begins with a brief opening statement in order to focus the conversation, then records the dialogue that follows.

> Uncle Pete was always important to me, yet I've never told him how important. I don't know why I haven't. Maybe because I haven't had the chance or maybe because I'm just now beginning to realize how much he means to me.

Me:	Well, Pete, I'm in college now. Bet you didn't think I'd get here.
Pete:	I knew you'd get to where you wanted to go. You were the most determined toad I've ever seen.
Me:	Toad! You used to always call me toady, ever since you read me *Mr. Toad's Wild Ride,* or is that the name of the Disneyland attraction?
Pete:	I hope you're not majoring in history. You aren't one for facts. Or at least one for getting them straight.
Me:	I used to sit on your lap and you'd read. And I can remember thinking of you as my father. I knew you weren't but—
Pete:	That was when your dad was overseas. Your mother let me stay there while I got settled in Los Angeles. She is the best sister a man could have.
Me:	I still remember the stories you used to tell me about the two of you growing up in Vermont. I always wanted a younger sister after hearing them. I wanted to live in the snow, too. You made me feel so good by telling them to me. I guess I felt lonely then and you made me . . .

And so on.

If you decide to continue practice writing by recording imaginary conversations, you may find that they often circle back over the relationship as you've recorded it in the portraits. That's fine. Let them circle. Eventually, they will reach where they set out to go.

If practicing by recording imaginary conversations isn't for you, yet you would like to address a significant person in your life, we suggest you write an unsent letter. The purpose is to give yourself a chance to record what you're feeling in another format. There is no need for you to bother with including a formal salutation; just get the letter under way in a fashion with which you feel comfortable. (And don't worry about sending the letter. To send it is not the purpose.)

Here's the start of one student's unsent letter addressed to her roommate:

> Clare: I'm tired of picking up your nightgowns, shoes, stockings, sweaters, skirts, pants, books, papers, pencils, pens—everything. Tired! Tired, Tired, Tired, T-I-R-E-D! DOG TIRED! This isn't working for me, but it must be working for you. You leave messes like an unhousebroken, six-foot pigeon. And I'm not cleaning up your cage anymore. You think I'm your mother, maybe. A mother I'm not. A zookeeper I'm not. What I am is . . .

The content of unsent letters and imaginary conversations comes spontaneously. We suggest, therefore, that you give them plenty of space, recording whatever comes to mind.

Drawings and Photographs

When you first started journal keeping, we said that undirected writing—free writing—is a good way to loosen the writing process. We also said a journal is much like an artist's sketchbook, a place where writers can practice sketching fragments of their lives in words just as artists do with lines. Well, writers sometimes like to draw squiggles and curlicues, perhaps even figures from dreams or caricatures of people from their lives. They often like to decorate the margins of books and note paper.

What do these images mean? Who knows? We know only that to doodle doesn't take much artistic talent. In fact, doodling seems to grow from an urge totally separate from artistic drives. It seems to come from a need to meditate. There is a strange compulsion in some writers to let the hand follow the uncharted direction of the mind and create images in the process.

If you are a writer who finds yourself doodling, fine. Keep it going. Do it on scraps of paper or in the margins of lecture notes. Then paste the doodles into your journal. The next step is to describe them—describe all that they suggest to you. Ask yourself what the images mean. Explain where they come from. Write your responses under the doodle.

By writing about your drawings, you'll not only be practicing, but you'll also be exploring your inner nature. Here's how one writer responded to her doodles of a snake image:

> This is Mister Snake. To some people he may seem dangerous, but to me he's the source of deep wisdom. Sometimes when I catch myself drawing him I am daydreaming about some problem I face. In many ways drawing him is like talking to a wise man—someone who knows the answer I need. I guess that's a dialogue because by drawing him makes me feel as if I'm having a conversation. He doesn't always give me a straight answer, snakes are like that. They speak with forked tongue. So I have to decipher his message. It is usually very secret, for snakes are secret things. This snake, my old friend, knows many of my life's secrets. He'll never reveal them.

When this writer set out to write a response to her doodles, she didn't know what would come out; she merely started writing while focusing on her drawing.

A variation of the doodle exercise involves the use of photographs. This exercise can take a couple of forms. You might write a response to a photograph you see in a book or magazine. Or you might write a response to a photograph or photographs from your personal experience. We suggest you paste the photograph, or a photocopy of the photograph, into your journal. If that isn't possible, write brief descriptions of the photographs as part of your entries.

What follows is part of a philosophical response to a photographic slide of Salvador Dali's *Persistence of Memory:*

> This morning in art history I saw a slide of a Dali painting. A crazy thing. It was filled with melting pocket watches—pocket watches that looked more real than real watches. These watches were melting in a desert wasteland with some strange trees in the background. One watch had thousands of ants crawling out of it. Another was melting over a strange amoeba-shaped object covered with hair and with a tongue hanging out of an opening.
>
> The painting reminded me of words from an old song: "Time, time, time—what's to become of me . . ." And I began to wonder about how time worked in my life. Time is a funny thing to be thinking about, but I can't get the thought out of my mind. I wonder how time works. I know I live in time that moves forward, that is, I was born, I went to grammar school, junior high school, and high school. I know all this education has led to college, but in my mind I can be in all these places at once. Time in my mind seems to melt together.

While this writer chose to write about a photograph of a well-known painting, the following writer chose to record his responses to a series of childhood photographs. Over a period of weeks he spent thirty to forty minutes each day recording his inner responses to pictures of himself as a child and pictures of family members. His response to a photograph of himself as a baby being held by his father starts like this:

> When I look at this picture, I feel very strange. I know the man standing next to the birch tree is my father and I know the baby he holds wrapped in a blanket is me. But for some reason I can't emotionally accept the thought. My father seems so young, not any older than I am now, and I find imagining him at my age is difficult.
>
> Did he feel at 22 what I feel?
>
> At that age he had a child—me. It makes me feel he had his life under control. But here I am at 22 without an idea of what I'll be doing four years from now.
>
> My father now, compared to the picture, seems so much older. So changed. Once he was thin, athletic. Now he has a paunch and looks as if he never sees the sun. His hair, once full and wavy, is now thin. His face was smooth, now wrinkled.
>
> At this moment I wonder if somewhere there exists a photograph of him and his father. I wonder if he has ever compared him-

self to his dad's image. Where does this lead, this photographing, this photographing of fathers and sons?

Where?

Back, back, back. And forward—into the future. The never-ending future. But somehow I feel there's knowledge to be gained from studying these images.

The key to responding to images, whether drawings, paintings, or personal photographs, is to avoid trying to figure out what you are going to write before you write it, but instead to focus on the image and just write— write as an artist sketches.

Off Days

Writers have off days—days when the words don't seem to come in the right patterns. That's to be expected. Writing, like any other activity, depends on energy. On some days there are larger supplies than on others. If you have an off day, we suggest you do some simple exercises to keep yourself writing—exercises that don't require much mental effort.

One activity you might do is copy word for word a poem or a piece of professional prose you admire. The copying doesn't require much thought, since all you have to do is make sure you get the right words in the right order. But the copying will help you develop a feel for the English language. Good writers make good teachers. Use them as models.

Another activity you might pursue on an off day is writing random lists. These lists can serve as a kind of doodling with words. Be sure to center them—focus on a single aspect of your life.

To get started, here are a few ideas. List the joys and sorrows of your life and add the details you associate with each up or down experience. You might also center another list around fears—all kinds of fears: childhood fears and adult fears. Try centering on a particular period of your life and make a memory list or try centering on a relationship and make a list of its key events. You could also write a list of trips you've taken or music and books you like. No matter how you center your list, be sure to include some details, and always work in a spontaneous way.

On an off day one writer decided to write a memory list of his senior high school year. Here are the first few entries.

> Playing ball: remember the photo in the Daily Pilot. Gil pitching the ball to me, the field open all the way to the goal posts. Fumbling. Ugh!

Sally: two dates—wham. In love. Walks on the beach. Empty, empty sands. A month later, tears. Living in Denver.

John: knew John since the 6th grade. Big John—6' 49. All black hair and white teeth. A friendly bear. Joined the Marines.

Reminds me of: trip to big bear, Big Bear John—must be a connection. First time in the snow. The whole gang staying in Brenda's cabin. Took hours to clean it up. But the snow, white powder that seemed to float down, gently falling and collecting on the window ledges.

On off days this kind of practice will keep your hand moving across the page. You may also find that one entry begins to develop into a longer piece. If that happens, you're no longer having an off day.

GLOSSARY OF USAGE

The advice and information we've included in this glossary—all gleaned from current dictionaries and usage guides—represents the practice of experienced writers. The entries themselves are composed of words and phrases that frequently cause problems for inexperienced writers. The glossary, of course, serves only as a supplement to a good dictionary, perhaps the most valuable resource you can use when writing.

a, an Use *a* before a consonant sound, *an* before a vowel sound.

a university	a history	a one o'clock lunch	a C
an undertow	an hour	an orphan	an F

accept, except *Accept* means "to receive." *Except* means "but for," "other than," or "to leave out." I can accept your argument except the last point. Do not except him from the guest list.

advice, advise *Advice* is a noun that means "counsel." *Advise* is a verb that means "to give advice." I advise you to accept your attorney's advice.

affect, effect *Affect* is a verb, meaning "to influence," and *effect* is a noun, meaning "result." The treatment did not affect her illness; in fact, it had several adverse effects. Effect can also be a verb meaning "to bring about." The senator effected significant changes in her district.

aggravate *Aggravate* means "make worse." In writing you should not use it to mean "irritate" or "annoy."

ain't Nonstandard English for *am not* or *aren't*.

all ready, already *All ready* means "prepared." *Already* means "by now" or "previously." We were all ready to dance, but the band had already stopped playing.

all right   *All right* is always two words. *Alright* is a misspelling.

all together, altogether   *All together* means "in a group," "gathered in one place," or "in unison." *Altogether* means "completely" or "wholly." They went shopping all together rather than separately. They did not altogether believe his story.

allusion, illusion   An *allusion* is a reference to something. An *illusion* is a deceptive appearance. Dr. Catalano's lectures are filled with allusions from drama. After years of failure, he still believes the illusion that persistence is the secret of success.

a lot   *A lot* is always written as two words. *Alot* is a misspelling.

already   See *all ready.*

among, between   *Among* is used to refer to three or more people or things. *Between* is used with two people or things. Half the inheritance was divided between the two sisters, the other half among several charities. Sometimes *between* is used with more than two if the relationship concerns individual members of the group with each other. The nuclear treaty between the five superpowers was signed today.

amount, number   *Amount* refers to a quantity of something that cannot be counted. *Number* refers to things that can be counted. A large number of salt-water fish requires an aquarium that holds a tremendous amount of water.

an   See *a.*

and etc.   *Et cetera* (etc.) means "and so forth"; *and etc.*, therefore, is redundant.

and/or   A legalism that many people consider awkward in college writing.

anxious, eager   *Anxious* means "nervous" or "worried." *Eager* means "enthusiastically anticipating something." I am eager to begin my new job but anxious about the new responsibility.

anyone, any one   *Anyone* means "any person at all." *Any one* refers to a particular person or thing in a group. Similar definitions apply to *everyone, every one, someone, some one.* Anyone with the price of admission can come in. Any one of the membership might have started the rumor.

anyways, anywheres   Misused for *anyway* and *anywhere.*

as   Avoid using *as* for because, since, while, whether, and who. *Because* (not as) the train was late, the meeting was postponed.

as, like   See *like.*

awful   An overused word for *bad, shocking, ugly.* Also misused as a substitute for *very* or *extremely.*

bad, badly   *Bad* is an adjective and should be used in formal writing to modify nouns and as a predicate adjective after linking verbs. *Badly* should be used only as an adverb. John felt bad. The artist painted badly.

being as, being that   Do not misuse for *because.* Because (not *being as* or *being that*) life is short, grab all the gusto you can.

beside, besides   *Beside* means "next to." *Besides* means "except" and "in addition." The cowpuncher stood beside his horse. Besides one piano, the room was empty.

between   See *among.*

bring, take   Use *bring* to carry something from a farther place to a nearer one. Use *take* to carry something from a nearer place to a farther one. Take these pages to the printer and bring me yesterday's batch.

bunch   *Bunch* should not be used to refer to a crowd or group of people or things. Reserve it to refer to things that grow fastened together, such as grapes or bananas.

burst, bursted, bust, busted   The verb *burst* means "fly apart," and its principal parts are *burst, burst, burst.* The past tense *bursted* is unacceptable. *Bust* and *busted* are considered slang; therefore, they are inappropriate in college writing.

can, may   *Can* indicates ability, and *may* indicates permission. If I may use the car, I believe I can reach the store before it closes.

center around   *Center on* is more accurate than *center around.*

cite, sight, site   *Cite* means "to quote"; *sight* refers to the ability to see; and *site* refers to a place or location.

climactic, climatic   *Climactic* refers to a climax. *Climatic* refers to climate.

compare to, compare with   *Compare to* means "regard as similar." *Compare with* means "examine for similarities or differences." The boy compared his father's bald head to an egg. The investigator compared the facts of the Wellman case with the facts of the Billings incident.

complement, compliment   *Complement* means "to add to something," "to complete something." *Compliment* means "to flatter" or "to praise." The roses complemented the table decoration. John complimented Sandra for her performance. Complimentary can also mean "free." The family received complimentary airline tickets.

conscience, conscious   *Conscience* refers to a moral sense. *Conscious* is an adjective meaning "aware." A country without a conscience is a country without a heart. He is unconscious of his behavior.

continual, continuous   *Continual* means "often repeated." *Continuous* means "unceasing" or "without a break." My sleep is continually interrupted. The earth travels continuously around the sun.

convince, persuade   Careful writers use *convince* when someone changes his or her opinion. They use *persuade* when someone is moved to take action. The attorney convinced several students that capital punishment is immoral. The attorney persuaded several students to demonstrate against capital punishment.

could of   Often misused for *could have.*

couple of   Do not use *couple of* for few or several.

criteria, phenomena   *Criteria* is the plural form: the singular form *criterion* is seldom used. *Criteria* is often used as a singular noun, but careful writers use it only in the plural sense. The criteria were so ill phrased that they were hard to apply. *Phenomena* is also a plural of the same kind for the singular phenomenon. It should be treated in the same fashion. Today's unexplainable phenomena are tomorrow's scientific explanations.

data   *Data* is the plural of *datum* and means "facts" or "pieces of information." The data are irrefutable. *Data* is also used as a singular noun meaning "information." Not much reliable data is available on the existence of Unidentified Flying Objects.

deal   Misused for *bargain, transaction,* or *business transaction.*

differ from, differ with   *Differ from* means "be unlike." *Differ with* means "disagree."

different from, different than   *Different* from is widely accepted. *Different than* is acceptable when it precedes a clause. An elephant is different from a mastodon. Paris was different than I had expected.

disinterested, uninterested   *Disinterested* means "impartial." *Uninterested* means "bored" or "indifferent."

don't   *Don't* is a contraction of do not and should not be used for *does not,* whose contraction is *doesn't.*

due to Although some pedantic English professors might object to the use of *due to* in place of *because of* or *owing to,* the usage is standard and appears in a variety of writing. Jenkins became depressed due to the correction marks on his essay.

eager See *anxious.*

effect See *affect.*

enthused The preferred adjective is *enthusiastic.*

especially, specially *Especially* means "particularly" or "more than other things." *Specially* means "for a specific reason." The artist was especially pleased to receive the award. The design was specially created for her.

etc. See *and etc.*

every which way Do not use as a substitute for *in every direction* or *in disorder.*

everyone, every one See *anyone.*

everywheres Unacceptable English. Do not use for *everywhere.*

exam In college writing use *examination.*

except See *accept.*

expect Do not use to mean "suppose" or "believe." I suppose (not expect) the beach will be crowded.

explicit, implicit *Explicit* means "expressed directly or precisely." *Implicit* means "expressed indirectly or suggested." The threat was explicit—"I'll break your nose!" Although his voice was gentle, his body communicated an implicit threat.

farther, further *Farther* refers to actual distance. *Further* refers to additional time, amount, or other abstract matters. I cannot run any farther. Further encouragement is useless.

fewer, less *Fewer* refers to items that can be counted. *Less* refers to a collective quantity that cannot be counted. The marsh has fewer ducks living in it, but it also has less water to support them.

finalize Avoid using *finalize* for *complete.*

flunk Do not substitute for *fail.*

folks Do not substitute for *parents, relatives,* or *people.*

former, latter, first, last *Former* refers to the first named of two things or people. *Latter* refers to the second of two named. *First* and *last* are used to refer to items in a series of three or more. John and Bill are very successful; the former is a dentist, the latter a poet. Jogging, biking, and swimming require tremendous endurance; the last requires the most.

further   See *farther.*

get   A common verb used in a variety of common expressions: get wise to yourself, her chatter gets me, and the like. Using *get* in such ways is inappropriate in college writing.

goes   Inappropriate when used instead of *said* or *says* to introduce a quotation. It should not be used to indicate speech. He said (not *goes*), "Life is short."

good, well   *Good* is an adjective; *well* is an adverb. Burton is a good tennis player. He strokes the ball well. *Well* should be used to refer to health. You look well (not good).

had ought, hadn't ought   Often misused for *ought* and *ought not.*

herself, himself   See *myself.*

hisself   Incorrect for *himself.*

hopefully   *Hopefully* means "with hope." They prayed hopefully for the blizzard to stop. Often *hopefully* is used to mean "it is hoped" in place of *I hope;* however, *I hope* is preferred in college writing. I hope (rather than hopefully) the blizzard will stop.

illusion   See *allusion.*

implicit   See *explicit.*

imply, infer   *Imply* means "suggest." *Infer* means "conclude." Irving implied that he had studied for the quiz, but I inferred that he was unprepared.

in, into   *In* indicates a location or position. *Into* indicates movement or change. Barbara is in the study with a clairvoyant, who is in a trance. I must go into Murkwood, but I do not want to fall into danger. *Into* has also come to mean "interested in" or "involved in" something, which is an inappropriate use in college writing. My brother is interested in (not *into*) Dungeons and Dragons.

individual, party, person   *Individual* should be used to refer to a single human being when expressing that person's unique qualities. Each individual has a right to pursue his or her interests within the law. When not stressing unique qualities, use *person.* A romantic person will love the Austrian countryside. Except in legal documents, use *party* to refer to a group. Who is the missing person (not party)?

infer   See *imply.*

into See *in.*

irregardless Incorrect for *regardless.*

is because See *reason is because.*

is when, is where A common error in sentences that define. "Bandwagon" is (not *is where* or *is when*) a propaganda device by which advertisers urge consumers to become one of the millions buying their products.

kind, sort, type These are singular words and take singular modifiers and verbs. This kind of butterfly is rare in North America. When referring to more than one thing, *kind, sort,* and *type* must be made plural and then take plural modifiers and verbs. These kinds of butterflies are rare in North America.

kind of, sort of Do not use as a substitute for *somewhat* or *rather.* The course was somewhat (not *kind of* or *sort of*) dull.

lay See *lie.*

less See *fewer.*

liable See *likely.*

lie, lay These verbs are often confused. *Lie* means "to recline," and *lay* means "to place." In part, they seem to be confusing because the past tense of *lie* is the same as the present tense of *lay.*

lie ("to recline")	lay ("to place")
lie	lay
lay	laid
lain	laid
lying	laying

like, as, as if, as though *Like* is a preposition and introduces a prepositional phrase. *As, as if,* and *as though* usually function as subordinating conjunctions and introduce dependent clauses. In college writing do not use *like* as a subordinating conjunction. The sky looks as if (not *like*) the end of the world is near.

like, such as When introducing a representative series, use *such as.* To make a direct comparison with an example, use *like.* This decade has produced some playful novelists, such as Vonnegut, Coover, and Hawkes, but I still prefer to read classic writers like Hemingway.

likely, liable *Likely* is used to express probability. *Liable* is used to express responsibility or obligation. She is likely to finish first. Dr. Crane is liable for his misdiagnosis.

lots, lots of Do not substitute for *a great deal, much,* or *plenty.*

may See *can.*

may of Incorrect for *may have.*

media, medium *Media* is the plural form of *medium.* Be sure to use plural modifiers and plural verbs with *media.* The mass media—television, radio, newspapers—influence our political attitudes.

might of Incorrect for *might have.*

most Do not use for *almost.*

must of Incorrect for *must have.*

myself, herself, himself, itself, yourself These and other *-self* pronouns are reflexive or intensive—that is, they refer to or intensify a noun or another pronoun in a sentence. The family members disagree among themselves, but I myself know how the inheritance should be divided. It is inappropriate in college writing to use these pronouns in place of personal pronouns. No one except me (not *myself*) will complete the job.

no way Do not use for *no.*

nowhere near Do not substitute for *nearly.* Walters is not nearly (not *nowhere near*) as intelligent as Smith.

nowheres Do not use for *no where.*

number See *amount.*

OK, O.K., okay All are acceptable spellings.

party See *individual.*

people, persons *People* refers to a collective mass and emphasizes faceless anonymity. Either *people* or *persons* may be used to refer to individuals who make up the group and to emphasize their separate identity. People waited in lines for hours. Several people (or persons) fainted. In the latter case, standard usage favors the use of *people* over *persons,* which to our ear smacks of jargon from popular psychology.

per An English equivalent is usually preferable to the Latin *per.* The job pays $4.50 an (not *per*) hour. The raid was executed according to (not *per*) the captain's plans.

percent (per cent), percentage Both *percent* (often spelled *per cent*) and *percentage* refer to numbers and should only be used in actual references to statistics. Avoid using them to replace the word part. The part (not *percent*) of the committee that causes trouble is small. *Percent* is always preceded by a number (twenty percent, 20 percent), and *percentage* follows an adjective (a small percentage). In college writing *percent* should always be written out (not %).

person See *individual.*

persons See *people.*

persuade See *convince.*

phenomena, phenomenon See *criteria.*

plus Do not use as a substitute for *moreover.* Politics offers socially important work for young attorneys; moreover (not *plus*), it can help them get public attention.

quote, quotation *Quote* is a verb. *Quotation* is a noun. Do not use *quote* when you mean *quotation.* The *quotation* (not *quote*) is from the Bible.

raise, rise Two commonly confused verbs. *Raise (raising, raised, raised)* means "to force something to move upward." *Rise (rising, rose, risen)* means "to go up." Import quotas will raise the cost of American products. The mist rose from the swamp.

real, really *Real* is an adjective; *really* is an adverb. The race was really (not *real*) tough.

reason is because Use *that* instead of *because* in the phrase *reason is because,* or rewrite the sentence. The reason the business closed is that (not *because*) Carmen spent more money than she made.

respectfully, respectively *Respectfully* means "with respect" or "showing respect." *Respectively* means "each in the order given." They respectfully expressed their doubts. *The Sun Also Rises, As I Lay Dying,* and *Day of the Locust* were written by Hemingway, Faulkner, and West, respectively.

rise See *raise.*

said See *goes.*

says See *goes.*

sensual, sensuous *Sensual* refers to pleasures of the body, especially sexual pleasures. *Sensuous* refers to pleasures perceived by the senses. The poet's sensual desires led him to create the sensuous images readers find in his work.

set, sit Two commonly confused verbs. *Set (setting, set, set)* means "to place or to put." *Sit (sitting, sat, sat)* means "to be seated." When you mean "put something down," use a form of *set.* Beverly set her books on the table. When you refer to being seated, use a form of *sit.* Uncle Ralph would sit for hours without speaking.

should, would Use *should* when expressing a condition or obligation. Use *would* when expressing a wish or customary action. We should attend the reception. He would always read for an hour before falling asleep.

should of Incorrect for *should have.*

sight See *cite.*

sit See *set.*

site See *cite.*

someone See *anyone.*

sort See *kind.*

sort of See *kind of.*

specially See *especially.*

such as See *like, such as.*

sure Do not misuse for *surely* or *certainly.* Richard was certainly (not sure) correct by refusing to support Kraft.

sure and, sure to, try and, try to *Sure to* and *try to* are the preferred forms. Try to (not *try and*) attend.

than, then *Than* functions as a conjunction used in comparisons. *Then* is an adverb indicating time. I would rather be dancing than (not *then*) studying.

theirselves Incorrect for *themselves.*

then See *than.*

try and, try to See *sure and.*

uninterested See *disinterested.*

use to, suppose to Sometimes carelessly written for *used to* and *supposed to.*

wait for, wait on *Wait for* means "await." *Wait on* means "to serve."

ways Use *way* when referring to distance. The park is a mile away (not *ways*).

well See *good.*

which, who Never use *which* to refer to people. Use *who* or *that* to refer to people and *which* or *that* to refer to things.

would See *should.*

yourself See *myself.*

APPENDIX A
POINT OF VIEW

By point of view we mean the perspective from which you present your material. In the broadest sense you can do it from either a personal or an impersonal perspective. A personal point of view places you in the experience and leads you to use first-person pronouns (*I, me, my, we, us, our*). Or it may lead you to address your readers directly by using second-person pronouns (*you, your*). An impersonal point of view positions you out of the experience. It places you in an objective stance. When writing impersonally, you'll seldom directly address the reader or use first person pronouns. One is the point of view of personal experience and observation; the other, of reports and research.

The material will usually dictate which stance to assume. You wouldn't take a journal entry that deals with childhood experience and rework it in an impersonal way; nor would you write historical, social, or scientific research in a personal way. So when selecting a point of view ask yourself where your material came from. From research? From reports of others? From personal experience? The point of view will follow naturally from the answer to the question.

The following sections offer a number of examples of writing from different points of view—impersonal, personal, and what we call common experience, which can be either personal or impersonal, as well as examples in which the writer deliberately shifts from one point of view to another.

IMPERSONAL POINT OF VIEW

In the following paragraph, Jan Harold Brunvand uses an impersonal point of view in presenting information on folk riddles in *The Study of American Folklore*.

Folk riddles are traditional questions with unexpected answers—verbal puzzles that circulate, mostly by word of mouth, to demonstrate the cleverness of the questioner and challenge the wit of his audience. The practice of riddling can be traced to the dawn of literary expression; it is referred to in the most ancient Oriental and Sanskrit writings, in the Bible, in classical legends and myths, in European folktales and ballads, and in some of the earliest manuscripts of Medieval literature. Compilations of riddles were among the first printed books in the Middle Ages, and books of literary riddles remained a popular diversion well into the Renaissance. Since the beginning of professional interest in folklore in the nineteenth century, massive collections of folk riddles have been published in most European countries and in many countries outside Europe. Riddles have been found in the native cultures of all peoples, even the American Indians, who until recently were thought to possess only a few that had been borrowed from Europeans.

The passage is cleansed of personal pronouns; it doesn't address the reader. Brunvand is giving us the results of research. He's not giving life experiences.

Many secondhand reports are written from the impersonal stance—by writers presenting the experience of others. Since they weren't part of it, they report as outsiders. Here's an example from *Alive* by Piers Paul Read. He reports the experiences of people who survived a plane crash in the Andes. This paragraph captures the moment of the impact.

Several passengers started to pray. Others braced themselves against the seats in front of them, waiting for the impact of the crash. There was a roar of engines and the plane vibrated as the Fairchild tried to climb again; it rose a little but then there came a deafening crash as the right wing hit the side of the mountain. Immediately it broke off, somersaulted over the fuselage, and cut off the tail. Out into the icy air fell the steward, the navigator, and their pack of cards, followed by three of the boys still strapped to their seats. A moment later the left wing broke away and a blade of the propeller ripped into the fuselage before falling to the ground.

Read keeps his distance: He reports the facts objectively and lets them carry the suspense.

COMMON EXPERIENCE

Sometimes when deciding which stance to take—personal or impersonal—you'll reach a crossroads. Your material hasn't come from research or from other people's reports. It may fall more into the area of personal experience, yet not be exclusively your experience; others may have had it as well. Let's call it common experience—experience that comes from your general background and knowledge.

Common experience goes beyond our individual lives. It tilts toward the communal. It comes from our participation in society. At this moment you probably have sufficient background to write intelligently about limited aspects of television, politics, education, racism, sexism, parenting, sports, music, books, films, art, advertising, death, and catastrophes. You could write about them by generalizing from the information you've collected over the years. Your readers could follow what you're saying because they have shared these experiences. You may not be an expert in any of these areas, but to write about them is not to pretend to be an expert. You do have opinions along with enough information to develop them.

So what point of view do you use when writing from common experience? You can use either impersonal or personal. Either way, though, the writing will tend to sound more impersonal than personal—more authoritative.

Robert Paul Dye draws on common experience from radio to start "The Death of Silence." No doubt he's heard these programs and assumes his reader has also heard them or knows of them. His intent is to draw some general conclusions from them, not to reminisce about a mindless childhood spent sprawled in front of a Philco radio. He selects, therefore, an impersonal point of view.

> Radio's funniest moment occurred on the "Jack Benny Program" when a thief demanded from the great tightwad, "Your money or your life." The long silence that followed was more violently hysterical than any of the quick retorts that are the stock in trade of most comedians. Benny's use of silence, his great sense of timing, made him one of the most popular comics of this century. Benny, of course, was not the only radio artist who recognized that silence could be more effective than sound: silence followed the crash of Fibber McGee's closet, preceded McCarthy's responses to Bergen. The chillers became more chilling when there were moments of silence. Silence was used to make the romances erotic and the quiz shows suspenseful.

Contemporary poet Adrienne Rich in "When the Dead Awaken: Writing as Re-Vision" also generalizes about common experience. She expresses the problems women writers face in confronting images of women developed throughout literary history. She writes with authority. The passage seems impersonal. However, Rich begins one sentence with *I think* to clearly indicate her perspective.

A lot is being said today about the influence that the myths and images of women have on all of us who are products of culture. I think it has been a peculiar confusion to the girl or woman who tries to write, because she is peculiarly susceptible to language. She goes to poetry or fiction looking for her way of being in the world, since she too has been putting words and images together; she is looking eagerly for guides, maps, possibilities; and over and over in the "words' masculine persuasive force" of literature she comes up against something that negates everything she is about: she meets the image of Woman in books written by men. She finds a terror and a dream, she finds a beautiful pale face, she finds La Belle Dame Sans Merci, she finds Juliet or Tess or Salome, but precisely what she does not find is that absorbed, drudging, puzzled, sometimes inspired creature, herself, who sits at a desk trying to put words together.

PERSONAL POINT OF VIEW

The following anecdote comes from the *Autobiography of Malcolm X*. Malcolm X talks about his childhood veneration of leading jazzmen during the 1940s. It's his private experience. No one else went through it. It calls for a first-person point of view.

> Some of the bandsmen would come up to the men's room at about eight o'clock and get shoeshines before they went to work. Duke Ellington, Count Basie, Lionel Hampton, Coote Williams, Jimmie Lunceford were just a few of those who sat in my chair. I would really make my shine rag sound like someone had set off Chinese firecrackers. Duke's great alto saxman, Jonny Hodges—he was Shorty's idol—still owes me for a shoeshine I gave him. He was in the chair one night, having a friendly argument with the drummer, Sonny Greer, who was standing there, when I tapped the bottom of his shoes to signal that I was finished. Hodges stepped down, reaching his hand in his pocket to pay me, but then snatched his hand out to gesture, and just forgot me, and walked away. I wouldn't have dared to bother the man who could do what he did with "Daydream" by asking him for fifteen cents.

The first-person point of view is right. Notice how the writer avoids dropping the *I* on the reader's mind the way a medieval jailer might drip water on a victim's head in unrelenting cadences. When you use the first-person singular, suppress the *I*, *my*, and *me* by putting them only where you need to. In this passage Malcolm X uses *I* five times, *my* once, and *me* twice. No drip, drip, drip of personal pronouns that might drive a reader daffy.

WE

The first-person plural point of view involves the use of *we*. Never use the "editorial *we*."

> Yesterday we went to class and found we had been given a "C" on our midterm.

Nor should you use *we* to avoid personal responsibility.

> We do not like the way this class is run. Our midterms, we find, were graded in too strict a manner.

This would be appropriate if the writer were speaking for the entire class, but the chances are that the writer is speaking from personal feeling and using the we point of view as a shield.

Do use *we* when you are talking for yourself and others, but try to make the general identity of the others clear.

> Six other class members and I got together and agreed that our midterms had been graded too strictly.

Now the *we* (*our*) fits.

The *we* point of view is often used to address a common group that includes the author. But the material sometimes has less to do with concrete personal experience and more to do with a general condition. Gerald Holton closes an essay titled "Constructing a Theory: Einstein's Model" with this point of view.

> As limited human beings confronting the seemingly endless parts and interlocking puzzles of the universe, we can nevertheless hope to play, as in Newton's metaphor, with pebbles at the shore of a vast ocean. If we do it well, that play can yield the most highly desirable kind of knowledge: a survey or overview of the world of nature that grants us the perception of an order guiding the phenomena in their infinite, individual variety and in their inexhaustible interactions with one another.

That's a mouthful, isn't it? But notice that Holton clearly establishes the members of the *we* group—all "limited human beings" who are "confronting the . . . puzzles of the universe." It's a glob of people, but a somewhat limited glob. When you confront the universe and have some others who are going to join you, talk to them from a *we* perspective.

YOU

The use of *you* is right in any passage that directly addresses readers, particularly when it encourages or directs them to do something. If, for instance, you are sending readers on a journey or explaining a process, the use of *you* is natural.

Paul Roberts uses it in "How to Say Nothing in Five Hundred Words," an essay that explains how to go about writing college compositions.

> Say the assignment is college football. Say that you've decided to be against it. Begin by putting down the arguments that come to your mind: it is too commercial, it takes the students' minds off their studies, it is hard on the players, it makes the university a kind of circus instead of an intellectual center, for most schools it is financially ruinous. Can you think of any more arguments, just offhand? All right. Now when you write your paper, make sure that you don't use any of the material on this list. If these are the points that leap to your mind, they will leap to everyone else's too, and whether you get a "C" or a "D" may depend on whether the instructor reads your paper early when he is fresh and tolerant or late, when the sentence "In my opinion, college football has become too commercial," inexorably repeated, has brought him to the brink of lunacy.

Beginning writers seldom have problems addressing "you the reader" but sometimes stumble when using the indefinite *you*, which means "anyone."

> When you travel east along the southern route to Tucson, you'll enjoy stopping at Ajo Drug for a thick malt and hamburger.

The problem here is that the writer has failed to suggest that the reader has any intention of doing what the writer proposes. The writer is talking to an indefinite *you*. The sentence could have been written more effectively with *anyone*.

> Anyone who likes hamburgers and malts and is traveling east along the southern route to Tucson should stop at Ajo Drug for lunch or dinner.

But perhaps the writer wanted to use *you*. It does have a certain intimacy. The writer could have done it by using an *if* clause to identify the reader.

> If you're traveling to Tucson along the southern route and you like hamburgers and malts, then stop at Ajo Drug.

Although it works in a situation like this, we suggest you avoid using the indefinite *you*. It often causes trouble.

SHIFTS IN POINT OF VIEW

Usually, once you decide whether your point of view will be personal or impersonal, you should stick to it. Keep in mind, though, that you can shift back and forth within a personal point of view. You may move from first-person singular to first-person plural and even to second person. But the shift must be well thought out. It must be done skillfully.

Sometimes writers shift to the *you* once a passage is under way in order to draw readers in, to make them feel like participants. In the following passage the shift is smooth. As a result, the experience is one that readers can identify with:

> Last week I walked up to Kings Point and saw a spectacular sight. If you ever get up there at dusk, you'll see the desert stretching toward a deep blue sky mopped with red clouds. You'll see . . .

In contrast, shifts to *you* that are made awkwardly are jarring:

> The physical threat to a quarterback passing from the "pocket" is intolerable. To stand there to the last millisecond, waiting for your receiver to reach the place the ball is supposed to go while you are being rushed by mammoth defensive linemen, takes sheer courage.

If directed toward potential quarterbacks, this passage would work. It wasn't, however. Writer Arnold J. Mandell directed it toward a general reader. Our guess is that not many general readers can identify with the experience. The shift is clumsy. Mandell would have written a more effective passage by avoiding the indefinite *you*, perhaps writing it like this:

> The physical threat to a quarterback passing from the "pocket" is intolerable. To stand there to the last millisecond, waiting for a receiver to reach the place the ball is supposed to go while being rushed by mammoth defensive linemen, takes sheer courage.

Now the point of view is impersonal. Don't you feel safer with a little more distance between you and the charging linemen?

Sometimes beginning writers really muddle a passage by shifting to *you*. Often the shift takes a form similar to this:

> At first, students may find enrolling in college confusing, but if they follow the orderly process established by Admissions, it will be easy. First, before your appointment, fill out and return the preregistration forms. Then you must be sure to keep your counseling . . .

Did you catch the awkward shift from *students* to *you*? Don't make these kinds of shifts. If you know your audience, you probably won't. For instance, if this writer had intended his directions for students themselves, he might have written it like this:

> At first, you may find enrolling in college confusing, but if you follow the orderly process established by Admissions, it will be easy. First, before your . . .

Or if the directions were for a more general audience—parents, teachers, clerks, and school administrators—he might have written it in this fashion:

At first, students may find enrolling in college confusing, but if they follow the orderly process established by Admissions, it will be easy. First, before their appointments, they should fill out and return the preregistration forms. Then they must be sure to keep their counseling . . .

There is a way this should not be written—with the deadly *one.*

At first, one may find enrolling in college confusing, but if one follows the orderly process established by Admissions, it will be easy. First, before one's appointment, one should fill out and return the preregistration forms. Then one must be sure to keep one's counseling . . .

Our recommendation is that one should avoid the use of one when one writes. Its use adds sand to a fluid process.

We close this section on shifts in point of view with a long passage from Jules Henry's *Culture Against Man.* Henry begins with *I,* swings to *we* ("our language," "urge us," "our culture," "we must search"), shifts to *you,* then returns to *we.* Notice that he uses the *you* to separate various members of his *we* group: "If you are propelled by drives," and "if you are moved mostly by values." Henry has a strong grip on his point of view. It does not slip away.

Fundamentally, values are different from what I call drives, and it is only a semantic characteristic of our language that keeps the two sets of feelings together. To call both competitiveness and gentleness "values" is as confusing as to call them both "drives." Drives are what urge us blindly into getting bigger, into going further into outer space and into destructive competition; values are the sentiments that work in the opposite direction. Drives belong to the occupational world; values to the world of the family and friendly intimacy. Drives animate the hurly-burly of business, the armed forces, and all those parts of our culture where getting ahead, rising in the social scale, outstripping others, and merely surviving in the struggle are the absorbing functions of life. When values appear in those areas, they act largely as brakes on drivenness. Though the occupational world is, on the whole, antagonistic to values in this sense, it would nevertheless be unable to function without them, and it may use them as veils to conceal its underlying motivations.

In our own culture the outstanding characteristic of promotable executives is drive. It is no problem at all to locate jobs requiring an orientation toward achievement, competition, profit, and mobility, or even toward a higher standard of living. But it is difficult to find one requiring outstanding capacity for love, kindness, quietness, contentment, fun, frankness, and simplicity. If you are propelled by drives, the culture offers innumerable opportunities for you; but if you are moved mostly by values, you really have to search, and if you do find a job in which you can live by values, the pay and prestige are usually low. Thus, the institutional supports—the organizations that help the expression of drives—are everywhere around us, while we must search hard to find institutions other than the family which are dedicated to values.

APPENDIX B
TONE

TONE

> "I love your new coat," Bill said, touching the fabric. "It's soft. Where did you find it?"

Obviously, someone is paying someone else a compliment. The statements are straightforward, honest. But with some slight changes, we can get a new meaning from the dialogue.

> Raising his eyebrows, wrinkling his nose, and elevating his voice to a falsetto, Bill said, "I *love* your new coat. It's so . . . soft. Where *did* you *find* it?"

By making these changes in the descriptive detail, but without altering the dialogue, we've created a different tone. Do you hear the deception behind the words? For *soft*, interpret *floppy* or *shapeless*. And after the question "Where *did* you *find* it?" add the line "In a trash heap?" The speaker is no longer offering appreciation, but snide criticism.

If you overheard these comments, the meaning would be carried in the tone the speaker used to say the words. You'd hear it. Most people convey tone in speech without much thought. If they feel pleasant, they sound pleasant. If they feel snotty, they sound snotty. But to achieve tone in writing you have to make more conscious choices.

To keep it simple we want to start off by talking about tone in general terms. First, tone has something to do with the kinds of English you use, and there are many kinds. Should you write in the kind of English a college president might use in reporting the state of the school? The kind a television news reporter might use to write copy? The kind your favorite thriller or romance writers might use? Or maybe the kind you might use to write letters to friends?

There is no single kind of English to use for all circumstances. If you're writing a report for educators, then the circumstances might require that you write in the English of the college president. If you're writing for a universal audience, then the English the television reporter uses might be appropriate. And, obviously, if you're writing to a friend, then you'll use the kind of English closest to the way you talk. What you always need to keep in mind are the situation and the audience.

TONE IN SPOKEN ENGLISH

Let's consider the way we speak to people. Although writing isn't recorded speech—far from it—it may help to understand how we use different kinds of English when speaking in different situations. Different situations force you to adjust your English and the way you use it.

For example, if you were talking to a toddler you might say something like "See the kitty. Pretty kitty. Fuzzy kitty. Touch kitty. Isn't it nice?"—and you'd be smiling a big I-love-you-baby smile. If, however, you were called on in a college class, say a psychology class, you wouldn't talk as if speaking to a child: "Freud was a great man. He studied dreams. He also thought a lot." You'd address the group in more formal English: "Freud was the father of psychoanalysis, who thought through the concept of the unconscious."

After class with friends, your English would become more relaxed, full of slang, and more than likely stuffed with "ya knows" and "what'd you thinks." Talking with an employer or a professor or anyone who might have the power to evaluate your performance, you would probably avoid the casual street English you'd use with friends; your English, like a military recruit facing an officer, might come to attention. English, then, can be looked at as formal and informal. The informal kind is reflected in the everyday way we talk to family and friends; the formal kind in the way we talk to our loan officers, bankers, college deans, and so on. Of course, there are various levels of formal and informal English, but for your immediate uses, these two will serve as touchstones.

TONE IN WRITTEN ENGLISH

In a broad sense, written tone, like spoken tone, can be looked at as formal or informal. It just depends on what kind of English you're writing in at the moment. Now, since most of us have little trouble adjusting our speech to meet the circumstances of a face-to-face situation, we suggest that you consciously evaluate the writing situation as you automatically do the speaking one.

For instance, imagine you are going to write a report for a course in consumer economics. Your job is to write objectively—to present the information in an unbiased way by reporting facts, not your opinions. Your topic is truth in labeling. You decide to focus on the cosmetics industry and zero in on hair-dye manufacturers. Since you've been asked to write an objective report, you would write it in a formal tone, perhaps like this paragraph from *Consumer Reports*:

> "Warning: Contains an ingredient that can penetrate your skin and has been determined to cause cancer in laboratory animals."
>
> In January 1978, the U.S. Food and Drug Administration proposed a regulation that would require a warning label with those words to appear on all hair dyes containing a widely used chemical. But none of the estimated 33 million American women—and the unknown number of men—who dye their hair will ever see the warning. For obvious reasons hair-dye companies don't want it on their products. Some companies have therefore "reformulated" their hair dyes so that the cancer-causing chemical is no longer included.

This is no way to write home from summer camp. Much too formal. Much too objective. But this would serve for any unbiased report.

If, however, the situation changed, and you were to use the information to put forth your attitudes about the industry's attempts to avoid accurate labeling, the tone might shift from formal to informal. You might write a paragraph something like this one:

> About ten years ago, the Food and Drug people were on their toes. They forced hair-dye makers using a chemical called for short 4-MMPD to warn buyers that it might cause cancer. Cancer! The industry went into shock. Not because of the threat its product posed for 33 million women and an undetermined number of men who use the stuff. But because the hazardous labeling might cut into profits. Many companies, therefore, "reformulated" their dyes. They excluded 4-MMPD. Good, you might be thinking, a blow for truth and better health. Wrong! These companies haven't stopped using dangerous chemicals. They've merely switched to ones that have yet to be tested by the Feds.

In this example the sentences are simpler and shorter, the words are less complex, the details less ponderous, and the whole paragraph moves readers forward without giving them much time to stop and think. The tone, then, is more casual than the first example, less formal, a little more souped up. Word choice, sentence structure, the way details are used, even the imagery help create the tone.

From these last examples, you've probably come to suspect that there is more to tone than the use of formal and informal English. Besides formal or informal, readers often declare a writer's tone to be ironic, snide, wry, scholarly, pompous, dry, sardonic, witty, scathing, gentle, tongue-in-cheek—the labels are endless. Moreover, a writer's tone often implies, but never directly states, an attitude toward a subject.

For example, consider the tone of this opening paragraph from a piece titled "The Ultimate White Sale" published in *Mother Jones*. What do you think the writer's attitude is toward the Ku Klux Klan? How would you label the tone?

> The New Klan came riding in this decade right on the coat tails of the New South. Dry-look Grand Wizard David Duke has been making the talk-show rounds, promoting his Knights of the Ku Klux Klan. Its new face is cool, Madison Avenue, and cleaned up; it no longer claims to murder blacks—although Duke has been known to occasionally dust off his swastika.

The attitude? It would be safe to bet the writer doesn't like Duke's new Klan. And the tone? Well, naming a tone isn't as important as the impression it leaves with the reader. But clearly the tone suggests cynicism, a cynicism over the chances that the Klan would change its ways and perhaps even a wider cynicism over the way people and ideas are merchandised.

Notice, for instance, how the writer uses the title, "The Ultimate White Sale." Although we may not know it at first, by the end of the paragraph we can see that the title is used cuttingly. The idea of a department store's semi-annual sheet and pillow case sale (keeping in mind that both pillow cases and sheets are part of the Klan's costume) links with Duke's attempts to sell white supremacy. The idea of cynical merchandising also connects with words and phrases such as *dry-look, promoting, Madison Avenue,* and *claims.* The writer wants us to see that his packaging offers nothing more than a new wrapper for the same old garbage—that the Klan's "new face" still fronts the old policies of terror and suppression: "Duke has been known to occasionally dust off his swastika." And Duke, like so many other hucksters, makes the "talk-show rounds."

A writer's tone isn't always as distinguishable as the tone in the above example. Sometimes a writer will deliberately write in a flat style while using humorous details and images. The result is deadpan humor—a kind of humor that results from a comedian delivering jokes while maintaining an absolutely expressionless face. Samuel L. Clemens, who wrote under the name Mark Twain, uses this technique in the following paragraph from Mark Twain's *Autobiography,* in which he describes the church in his birthplace, Florida, Missouri.

Most of the houses were of logs—all of them, indeed, except three or four; these latter were frame ones. There were none of brick, and none of stone. There was a log church, with a puncheon floor and slab benches. A puncheon floor is made of logs whose upper surfaces have been chipped flat with the adz. The cracks between the logs were not filled; there was no carpet; consequently, if you dropped anything smaller than a peach, it was likely to go through. The church was perched upon short sections of logs, which elevated it two or three feet from the ground. Hogs slept under there, and whenever the dogs got after them during services, the minister had to wait till the disturbance was over. In winter there was always a refreshing breeze up through the puncheon floor; in summer there were fleas enough for all.

The humor is here. Imagine a church floor with cracks so large a peach could almost drop through. Imagine a congregation sitting through Sunday service munching peaches, for that matter. But the incongruity of eating peaches in church with dogs and hogs battling below is humorous. Clemens tells it in a deadpan tone. The tone also reveals an unflappable attitude; Clemens doesn't judge the experience. Snorting hogs and barking dogs chewing on each other was merely a "disturbance." A winter breeze coming up through the floor was "refreshing." And the fleas? Well, at least everyone got a share.

In contrast to Clemens's understated tone, Richard Selzer, writer and surgeon, launches this passage with an exaggerated praise: "I sing of skin, layered fine as baklava, whose colors shame the dawn. . . ." *Awe* seems to be the most accurate word to describe Selzer's attitude toward skin.

I sing of skin, layered fine as baklava, whose colors shame the dawn, at once the scabbard upon which is writ our only signature, and the instrument by which we are thrilled, protected, and kept constant in our natural place. Here is each man bagged and trussed in perfect amiability. See how it upholsters the bone and muscle underneath, now accenting the point of an elbow, now rolling over the pectorals to hollow the grotto of an armpit. Nippled and umbilicated, and perforated by the most diverse and marvelous openings, each with its singular rim and curtain. Thus the carven helix of the ear, the rigid nostrils, the puckered continence of the anus, the moist and sensitive lips of mouth and vagina.

What is it, then, this seamless body-stocking, some two yards square, this our casing, our facade, that flushes, pales, perspires, glistens, glows, furrows, tingles, crawls, itches, pleasures, and pains us all our days, at once keeper of the organs within, and sensitive probe, adventurer into the world outside?

Enough! We could spend a great deal of time giving you examples of various tones. But our mission is more practical. We want to make you aware of tone in your own work. Ask yourself, "What's the appropriate tone for my piece?" "Formal or informal?" "Should it express an attitude?" "What attitude?" And so on.

Let's face it. Tone conveys involvement. How can a writer express an attitude without feeling connected to the subject? Sure, there are scholarly pieces that at first glance seem toneless. But they're rare, and the chances are that a close look will reveal a tone, perhaps a reserved one, the voice of the meticulous explorer.

There are segments of the writing community, however, that attempt to scour away tone. Your college admissions office, for instance:

> We are pleased to inform you of your acceptance to Fairview College. In the upper right-hand corner of this page, you will find a number. This is your identification number. Please use it in any further communication you have with us in the future.
>
> Good luck in the pursuit of your education.
>
> Office of Admissions

And good luck to you, buddy!

This kind of tone is dangerous. When enough people who don't know any better read it throughout their lives, it becomes a standard in their minds for good writing. Don't make that mistake. Unless you are putting someone on—maybe an admissions officer—don't write in this official tone. It's deadly. In fact, it's so deadly we suggest that the admissions office would serve you better by writing something like this instead:

> You're in!
>
> Now, because we have so many people with the same last names and because we are swamped with letters, whenever you write to us use the number we've printed in the upper right-hand corner.
>
> Welcome to our campus, #92139.

At least it would be more honest.

One more thought on tone. In Getting Started we suggested you keep your tone consistent. Certainly writers shift their tone now and then, but as a practical practice, you should try to stay consistent. Whatever you do, avoid awkward shifts from an informal tone into a formal one—like this:

> My grandmother used to avoid black cats, ladders, and activity on Friday the thirteenth. Once I saw her stop in a crosswalk and hold up traffic while she bent over to pick up a penny with her arthritic fingers. What did she do with it? What else. She dropped it into her shoe for good luck. I guess she came from the old school of simple cause and effect, the school of superstition.
>
> Superstitions are often thought of as naive, popular beliefs that are logically or scientifically untenable. Hence, the alternative term *folk belief* is often employed, carrying with it the connotations of unsophistication and ignorance that the word *folk* has in popular usage. Well, my grandmother may have been unscientific but she was not illogical. She operated with an ironbound logic . . .

This kind of fractured tone is unacceptable. It usually comes from confusion. In this case the writer has become confused in writing about personal experience while trying to sprinkle in bits and pieces of official information. This kind of effort needs to be rewritten. The writer needs to integrate the formally written information with an informal tone.

APPENDIX C
COHERENCE

One problem you need to avoid is the sense that your sentences seem disconnected—that they are running on watered fuel, spurting and coughing into action. When this happens, coherence has broken down: your sentences aren't working together. Sometimes the flow is broken because you have tacked an irrelevant sentence into your prose; this is a unity problem and can be corrected by simply cutting the offending statement. A coherence problem runs deeper; the parts belong but have not been properly joined.

As is usually the case in writing instruction, the problem is much easier to show than to explain. Take a look, therefore, at his example to see what we mean.

> Nowhere can I relax more than at my favorite lake. I like a lake with clear skies and fresh water. At the beach, salt water always makes me itch and the smog is often terrible. There's privacy at my lake with no more than a handful of campers scattered throughout the pines and meadows. The beach is usually packed, and I go away feeling more like an egg in a carton than a human being. I like fishing for trout, cooking the trout for breakfast, hiking the trails, cooking trout for lunch, napping in the shade, reading, cooking even more trout for dinner, and sleeping under the stars. Sometimes I go to Harry's, a beer bar that serves down-home meals and country sounds. After about ten days at my lake and Harry's, I'm ready for another semester.

Do you feel the disconnections, the spaces between the sentences? Reading it is almost like being led on a tour by a guide who has your nose between his fingers. Who yanks your head from side to side while rapidly declaring, "Look at this—Now this—And this!" Who makes no connections. Who doesn't show the relationships between sites. Who just yanks and announces. That's pretty much what this writer does to us. He hasn't smoothed our way. He hasn't connected his sentences. To write coherently a writer has to learn to blend sentences together. Often this means supplying more information for the reader so that the relationships are clear.

Now read the rewritten draft of the sample paragraph. The writer has supplied the connections and filled in the empty spaces.

> Nowhere can I relax more than at a lake I visit each August outside of Cedar City, Utah. I like the lake with its clear skies and fresh water more than the beach near my house with its smog and salty sea that leaves my skin itchy. My lake offers privacy with usually only a handful of campers scattered throughout the pines and meadows; the beach is usually packed, and I go away feeling more like an egg in a carton than a human being. My days at the lake move in nice circles: fishing for trout at dawn, cooking trout for breakfast, hiking the trails, cooking trout for lunch, reading and napping in the shade, cooking trout for dinner, fishing for trout at dusk, and sleeping under the stars. Two or three evenings during my vacation I break the circle by going to Harry's, a beer bar that serves downhome meals and lots of country sounds. After about ten days of my lake and a few evenings at Harry's, I'm ready for home and another semester.

We can follow the writer's thought; the sentences connect. He has successfully rewritten the paragraph to make it coherent. One way he has achieved coherence is by filling in some empty spaces with more information. We as readers now know where the lake is located, why it's so important to him, and how he sees the time he spends there moving in circles. Since we haven't the power to mind-gaze, we need this kind of information to follow his point.

He has also achieved coherence by combining sentences, using subordinate clauses and phrases and punctuation techniques to tie them together. For instance, in the first draft he wrote

> I like a lake with clear skies and fresh water. At the beach, salt water always makes me itch and the smog is often terrible.

After examining the ideas in these two sentences, he sees clearly that they relate through contrast. He decides to make them cohere by combining the ideas around "more than" to clearly show the contrasting relationship. He also uses a *that* clause to pack more information into the new sentence.

I like the lake with its clear skies and fresh water more than the beach near my house with its smog and salty sea that leaves my skin itchy.

Later he uses a semicolon to show another contrast. First he wrote

There's privacy at my lake with only a handful of campers scattered throughout the pines and meadows. The beach is usually packed, and I go away feeling more like an egg in a carton than a human being.

In the revision he ties these thoughts together:

My lake offers privacy with usually only a handful of campers scattered throughout the pines and meadows; the beach is usually packed, and I go away feeling more like an egg in a carton than a human being.

We've offered these opening examples and comments to awaken you to the importance of writing coherently. Guiding a reader through your writing is not a matter of catch-as-catch-can. It takes careful thought. You must anticipate the reader. But once you begin to think through what you're saying and develop a sense of a reader peering over your shoulder, you'll keep your writing coherent without too much effort.

TRANSITIONAL DEVICES

Transitions are some mechanical tactics writers use to keep their work coherent. As we said in Getting Started, transitions serve as guideposts to direct the readers' attention. Let's study some of the standard transitional techniques. They will help you guide your readers.

Transitional Words and Phrases. When you give directions, develop illustrations, pack your writing with difficult information, or shift into a new pattern, you'll need to take some care in drawing your readers along. At these times we suggest you use obvious transitions. Plain ones. Ones that give a clear signal. You can select from a stock of standard ones. Here are a few, listed by how they function.

Similarity	likewise, similarly
Difference	but, however, still, yet, nevertheless, on the other hand, on the contrary, in contrast, at the same time
Addition	moreover, and, in addition, equally important, next, first, second, third, in the first place, in the second place,

	again, also, too, besides, furthermore
Illustration	for example, for instance, to illustrate
Time	soon, in the meantime, afterward, later, meanwhile, earlier, simultaneously, finally
Direction	here, there, over there, beyond, nearby, opposite, under, above, to the left, to the right, in the distance
End	in conclusion, to summarize, finally, on the whole
Restatement	in short, in other words, in brief, to put it differently
Result	therefore, then, as a result, consequently, accordingly, thus

Author, educator, and former U.S. senator from California, S. I. Hayakawa uses a few overt transitions to keep his reader awake while reading this paragraph.

> *To cite another example*, students trying to express themselves in writing may write poorly. In order to improve their writing, says the English teacher, I must teach them the fundamentals of grammar, spelling, and punctuation. *By thus* placing excessive emphasis on grammar and mechanics while ignoring the students' ideas, the teacher quickly destroys student interest in writing. That interest destroyed, the students write even more poorly. *Thereupon* the teacher redoubles his dose of grammar and mechanics. The students become increasingly bored and rebellious. Such students fill the ranks of "remedial English" classes in high school and college.

Hayakawa is sparing in the use of overt transitions. But because they offer an easy way to link sentences, beginning writers tend to overuse them. We suggest you guard against this mistake. Too many *on the other hand*'s, *moreover*'s, *furthermore*'s, and *in contrast to*'s have about the same effect on a reader that an out-of-tune piano has on a listener.

Also be sure you use the transition with a proper sense to connect your thoughts.

> We could go to the mountains; on the other hand, we could go to the desert.

Why *on the other hand*? The phrase announces a contrast—usually an extended one. Since no real contrast exists, the writer should have written

> We could go to the mountains or the desert.

Repetition of Key Words and Phrases. Repeating key words and phrases—much more subtle than using mechanical transitions—will also help keep your writing coherent. One of the simplest tactics is to interweave pronouns along with the subject. This kind of repetition keeps the readers' attention focused. Conservationist Cleveland Amory uses this technique in discussing coyote survival behavior:

> In such situations, the *coyote's* only hope lies in *his* cleverness. And stories of *coyotes* outwitting hunters are legion. *Coyotes* will work in teams, alternately resting and running to escape dogs set upon them. *They* have even been known to jump on automobiles and flat cars to escape dogs. And *they* have also successfully resisted bombing. Lewis Nordyke reports that once when a favorite *coyote* haunt in Texas became a practice range for bombing, the *coyotes* left—temporarily. Soon *they* were back to investigate and found that the bombing kept people out. *They* decided to stay. Meanwhile, they learned the bombing schedule and avoided bombs.

In "The Death of Marilyn Monroe" Diana Trilling repeats personal pronouns to maintain coherence in a paragraph that compares Ernest Hemingway with the actress:

> Of Ernest Hemingway, for example, I feel, much as I do of Marilyn Monroe, that *he* was unable to marshal any adequate defense against the painful events of *his* childhood, and this despite his famous toughness and the courage *he* could call upon in war, in hunting, in all the dangerous enterprises that seduced *him*. *He* was an innocent man, not a naive man, though not always intelligent. Marilyn Monroe offers us a similar paradox. Even while *she* symbolized an extreme of experience, of sexual knowingness, *she* took each new circumstance of life, as it came to *her* or as *she* sought it, like a newborn babe. And yet this was not what made *her* luminous—*her* innocence. The glow was not rubbed off *her* by *her* experience of the ugliness of life because finally, in some vital depth, *she* had been untouched by it.

Any repeated key word or phrase—not just pronouns—or any synonyms that carry the meaning of a key word or phrase can serve a transitional function. But remember, the word or phrase must be key—one that carries the meaning of the passage.

Poet Erica Jong uses this technique in a paragraph from "The Artist as Housewife." She says a major difficulty the female poet faces is "to raise a voice." She then links the idea to authenticity, a word she repeats throughout the passage.

The main problem of a poet is to *raise a voice*. We can suffer all kinds of kinks and flaws in a poet's work except lack of *authenticity*. *Authenticity* is a difficult thing to define, but roughly it has to do with our sense of the poet as a mensch, a human being, an author (with the accent on authority). Poets arrive at *authenticity* in very different ways. Each poet finds her own road by walking it—sometimes backward, sometimes at a trot. To achieve *authenticity* you have to know who you are and approximately why. You have to know yourself not only as defined by the roles you play but also as a creature with an inner life, a creature built around an inner darkness. Because women are always encouraged to see themselves as role players and helpers ("helpmate" as a synonym for "wife" is illuminating here), rather than as separate beings, they find it hard to grasp this *authentic sense of self.* They have too many easy cop-outs.

Transitional Sentences. Besides obvious mechanical and repetitive transitional techniques, writers sometimes use transitional sentences to maintain coherence. Sometimes these sentences serve as resting points for readers by gathering up what has been said and pointing to what will be said. Jessica Mitford in a paragraph from *The American Way of Death* uses this technique.

The next step is to have at Mr. Jones with a thing called a trocar. This is a long, hollow needle attached to a tube. It is jabbed into the abdomen, poked around the entrails and chest cavity, the contents of which are pumped out and replaced with "cavity fluid." This done, and the hole in the abdomen sewed up, Mr. Jones's face is heavily creamed (to protect the skin from burns which may be caused by leakage of the chemicals), and he is covered with a sheet and left unmolested for a while. *But not for long—there is more, much more, in store for him.* He has been embalmed, but not yet restored, and the best time to start the restorative work is eight to ten hours after embalming, when the tissues have become firm and dry.

Parallel Structure. Writers also use parallel structure—structures that repeat word patterns—to generate cohesiveness in their writing. The movement of parallel structures creates a rhythm that builds expectations in the reader. Lionel Casson in a passage from Ancient Egypt uses simple parallel structure to stress how far back Egyptian history goes. Casson opens with a brief topic sentence, then writes three sentences that repeat a pattern: *It was, It flourished,* and *It was viewed.*

Egypt was ancient even to the ancients. It was a great nation a thousand years before the Minoans of Crete built their palace at Knossos, about 900 years before the Israelites followed Moses out of bondage. It flourished when tribesmen still dwelt in huts about the

Tiber. It was viewed by Greeks and Romans of 2,000 years ago in somewhat the same way the ruins of Greece and Rome are viewed by modern man.

In more sophisticated hands parallel structure can penetrate the psyche by going beyond a mere technique for organizing information and shaping an emotional cohesiveness for the reader. Joan Didion reaches for this impact in the opening paragraph of *The White Album*.

> *We tell* ourselves stories in order to live. The princess is caged in the consulate. The man with the candy will lead the children into the sea. The naked woman on the ledge outside the window on the sixteenth floor is a victim of accidie, or the naked woman is an exhibitionist, and it would be "interesting" to know which. *We tell* ourselves that it makes some difference whether the naked woman is about to commit a mortal sin or is about to register a political protest or is about to be, the Aristophanic view, snatched back to the human condition by the fireman in priest's clothing just visible in the window behind her, the one smiling at the telephoto lens. *We look* for the sermon in the suicide, for the social or moral lesson in the murder of five. *We interpret* what we see, select the most workable of the multiple choices. *We live* entirely, especially if we are writers, by the imposition of a narrative line upon disparate images, by the "ideas" with which we have learned to freeze the shifting phantasmagoria which is our actual experience.

Transitions Connecting Paragraphs.   So far we've illustrated transition as a way of maintaining coherence within paragraphs. But we want to point out the importance of connecting paragraphs. The standard tactic is to use a transitional word or phrase to make the connection. You've probably noticed that several paragraphs we've used as illustrations obviously connect with paragraphs that came before them. Hayakawa's begins "To cite another example"; Trilling's "Of Ernest Hemingway, for example"; Amory's, "In such situations." All are using obvious transition as they glide from paragraph to paragraph. Sometimes writers will close one paragraph with a sentence or phrase that sets up the paragraph that follows. X. J. Kennedy uses this technique in an essay titled "Who Killed King Kong?"

> Why does the American public refuse to let King Kong rest in peace? It is true, I'll admit, that Kong outdid every monster movie before or since in sheer carnage. Producers Cooper and Schoedsack crammed into it dinosaurs, headhunters, riots, aerial battles, bullets, bombs, bloodletting. Heroine Fay Wray, whose function is mainly to scream, shuts her mouth for hardly one uninterrupted minute

from first reel to last. It is also true that Kong is larded with good
healthy sadism, for those whose joy it is to see the frantic girl dangled from cliffs and harried by pterodactyls. *But it seems to me that
the abiding appeal of the giant ape rests on other foundations.*

Kong has, *first of all*, the attraction of being manlike. His simian
nature gives one huge advantage over giant ants and walking vegeta-
bles in that an audience may conceivably identify with him. Kong's
appeal has the quality . . .

Combining Transitional Devices. We don't want to leave you with the
impression that writers select one method of transition and use it exclusively.
If you glance back at Kennedy's piece, you'll see that he uses repetition and
parallel structure as well as an overt transitional phrase. Most writing is
webbed with transitional techniques. The following illustration is an excerpt
from "Prediction as a Side Effect" by Isaac Asimov. Words and phrases that
provide coherence have been underlined and keyed as follows:

P = pronoun
R = repetition
S = synonym
T = transition
* = pronouns not marked because there is no previous noun to which
    they refer

In the 1650s, the French duellist, poet, and science-fiction writer

Cyrano de Bergerac (yes, he really lived, nose and all) wrote a tale of a trip to
                            P
the Moon. In it, his hero thought of various ways of reaching the Moon,
         P   P   R
each logical after a fashion. One way, for instance, was to strap vials of dew
P   T
about his waist. The dew rose, when the day grew warm and turned it to va-
     P   R   P
por. Might it not draw the man up as well, once it rose? (The idea was
         P   S   P R   S
wrong, but it had the germ of the balloon in it.)
         P   P
    Another of Cyrano's notions was that his hero might stand on an iron
         T   R   S   R
plate and throw a magnet up into the air. The magnet would draw the
                                                R

iron plate upward, together with the man upon it. When the iron plate
  R   R P   R

reached the magnet, both would tend to fall down again, but before that
         R   P   P

could happen, the voyager would quickly seize the magnet and throw it up
                        S   R   R P

again, drawing the plate still higher and so on. (Quite impossible of course,
        R   R

but it sounds so plausible.)
    P

And a third idea was to use rockets.
               R

It* so happens that now, three centuries after the time of Cyrano, we* do
                                          R

use rockets to reach the Moon. It is the only method by which we can reach
                         P   S   R   R

the Moon, at least so far and for the foreseeable future.
    R

The first man to show that this was so in the scientific sense was Isaac
                       P

Newton, in the 1680s, and we still use his equations to guide our astronauts
                         R   P   P

in their flights. However, as it* turns out, the first to consider the use of
  P   T

rockets was not Newton, but the science-fiction writer Cyrano, thirty years
  R   R   R   R

before Newton.
    R

APPENDIX D
INTRODUCTIONS

When you write an introduction, you must clearly state or strongly imply the central point, and you must shape the beginning so that it leads naturally into the discussion. At the outset of a draft, you will be wise to write an introduction that flatly states, no matter how awkwardly, the central point. Later, once the entire draft is written, you can rework the beginning or throw it out and create a more vigorous one.

Also, since an introduction must lead readers into the discussion, don't back up too far to get a running start. For instance, if your subject is neighborhood vandalism, you would be unwise to start with a history of the Mafia.

Your introduction should also be appropriate and interesting. The kind you write will depend on the kind of essay and reader you envision. An essay written for an academic course would have a more formal introduction than one written for a student magazine. Here's a never rule: Never write an introduction that reports the rigors you underwent writing the essay.

To write an interesting introduction is almost always to write in concrete language and specific detail. If your prose limps along, the readers' interest will wane. Avoid general, imprecise language, like this:

> What do you buy when you buy an airline ticket? If you are going to fly in an airplane, it is important to know what you are guaranteed. If you read the fine print on the ticket, you will see you are not guaranteed much.

This introduction does little but present the subject and allow the writer to get twenty-eight extra words into the paper. He would show more consideration for the reader if he would merely start with the last sentence and toss out the first two. There are any number of effective ways to try to hook the readers' interest. All of them would use concrete language and specific detail.

> What do you buy when you buy an airline ticket? What does it entitle you to, and what are the airline's legal obligations to you? What's their responsibility if they cause you to miss a connection or blow a hotel reservation? Next time you're sitting in an airport, waiting for your delayed flight to get off the ground, you can pass the time and cool off your indignation by reading the fine print on your ticket. A page headed "Conditions of Contract" could serve as a syllabus for a course in travel education.

Phrases such as "miss a connection," "blow a hotel reservation," "sitting in an airport," "waiting for your delayed flight," and so on add specifics most readers can relate to.

The writer of the paragraph above uses a common introductory technique: He begins by asking questions that the discussion will answer. Many other approaches are possible. A writer may begin an essay in any one of a variety of ways as long as the opening is appropriate, arouses some interest, and leads the reader into the discussion. Following are examples of some often-used techniques. There are more, many more, possibilities. Remember that no single method is suitable for all occasions, and none will work on any occasion if used awkwardly or mechanically.

USE FACTS AND STATISTICS

Sometimes a writer will begin by cleverly using facts and statistics. Or, to put it another way, by dramatizing facts or statistics related to the central point. We want to stress the word dramatize. For most readers, wading through murky lists of facts and statistics is dull going. A good writer will dramatize the information so that readers will want to plunge into the rest of the essay.

Consider how Harry Stein dramatizes statistics in the opening paragraph of "How to Make It in the Water."

> First the bad part. It appears that swimming is here to stay. All signs point in that direction. Drop by a public pool on a ninety-five-degree afternoon and see for yourself; there they'll be, by the hundreds, churning through the water like a herd of water bugs. Then there are the statistics. A. C. Nielsen, the television ratings guy, reports that 103,000,000 Americans swim regularly. Which makes swimming by far the nation's most popular leisure activity, ahead of bicycling (with a mere 75,000,000), fishing (63,900,000), camping (58,100,000), bowling (44,400,000), and tennis (29,000,000).

In the following paragraph Eric Lax in "Quick, Make a Mussel!" dramatizes facts to hook the reader.

> This is about Mussels, not muscles. Consider: compared with an equal weight of T-bone steak, 3.5 ounces of mussels have the same amount of protein, one quarter the calories, one eighteenth the fat, eleven times the calcium and twice the phosphorus; mussels also pump fifty percent more iron into your body.

OFFER A DEFINITION

Often writers will begin by offering definitions. Good writers won't fall back on the dictionary to supply them with ready-made quotes and leave it at that. Instead they will generate some interest that goes beyond the limits of a dictionary definition by casting descriptions in their own language and drawn from their own understanding.

In beginning a section on lions in *The Bestiary*, T. H. White opens by defining *beasts*.

> Leo the Lion, mightiest of beasts, will stand up to anybody. The word "beasts" should properly be used about lions, leopards, tigers, wolves, foxes, dogs, monkeys and others which range about with tooth and claw—with the exception of snakes. They are called beasts because of the violence with which they rage, and are known as "wild" because they are accustomed to freedom by nature and are governed by their own wishes. They wander hither and thither, fancy free, and they go wherever they want to go.

Leo Rosten in *The Joys of Yiddish* begins a description of a *shlimozl* with a definition.

> Pronounced shli-MOZ-zl, to rhyme with "thin nozzle." A chronically unlucky person; someone for whom nothing seems to go right or turn out well; a born "loser." Let me illustrate by combining four folk sayings: "When a shlimozl winds a clock, it stops; when he kills a chicken, it walks; when he sells umbrellas, the sun comes out; when he manufactures shrouds, people stop dying."

Often an introductory definition will be less formally structured than these just quoted and will seem to be closer to description (of course, definition is a form of description). For instance, in the opening paragraph of a short piece on packing in the Adirondacks, Anna La Bastille defines *lean-to*, a type of shelter available for public use on the trails.

> The lean-to is part of the history and tradition of the Adirondacks. A three-sided open shelter, it was originally designed as tem-

porary quarters for hunters and fishermen in the 1800s but soon evolved into a more permanent structure, often used as a base camp by turn-of-the-century vacationers. There are some 200 lean-tos in the Adirondacks.

USE A DRAMATIC NARRATIVE

A writer may use a dramatic narrative to plunge the reader into the midst of an incident and then may follow with an exposition of the central point. Peter Eastman begins "Thermal Injury," an article on burns, with this technique.

> Robert, 27 years old, a graduate student; his wife, Anne; Frank, just graduated from Torrance High School; and Sue, Frank's best girl, are breaking an overnight camp on the west bank of Jenny Lake in the Sequoia National Forest.
>
> Morning mists move slowly off the little lake. Pine needles scent the air. Packs are ready to be hoisted.
>
> Robert pulls a cartridge from his tiny backpacker's stove. The shut-off valve sticks. Butane hisses for a moment, explodes loudly, and suddenly he is on fire. Knocked to the ground and shocked by the blasts, he sits numbly watching his blazing clothes.

George Orwell begins an essay on poverty in Marrakech with this narrative.

> As the corpse went past the flies left the restaurant table in a cloud and rushed after it, but they came back a few minutes later.
>
> The little crowd of mourners—all men and boys, no women— threaded their way across the marketplace between the piles of pomegranates and the taxis and the camels, wailing a short chant over and over again. What really appeals to the flies is that the corpses here are never put into coffins, they are merely wrapped in a piece of rag and carried on a rough wooden bier on the shoulders of four friends. When the friends get to the burying-ground they hack an oblong hole a foot or two deep, dump the body in it and fling over it a little of the dried-up, lumpy earth, which is like broken brick.

USE REVERSAL

Another effective introductory technique for essays is to reverse the train of thought that the opening sentences establish. Joseph Morgenstern in a review of the film *Easy Rider* uses the reversal. It comes in the last sentence.

Time and again I wanted to reach out and shake Peter Fonda and Dennis Hopper, the two motorcyclist heroes of *Easy Rider*, until they stopped their damn-fool pompous poeticizing on the subject of doing your own thing and being your own man. I dislike Fonda as an actor; he lacks humor, affects insufferable sensitivity, and always seems to be fulfilling a solemn mission instead of playing a part. I didn't believe in these Honda hoboes as intuitive balladeers of the interstate highways, and I had no intention of accepting them as protagonists in a modern myth about the destruction of innocence. To my astonishment, then, the movie reached out and profoundly shook me.

One kind of reversal is the straw man device. A writer sets up someone else's view in the introduction and knocks it down in the discussion. This technique usually begins with a direct quotation or summary that represents the position opposing the writer's. William Murray uses this method in the following quotation.

A recent issue of the "Calendar" section in the *Los Angeles Times* listed twelve theater openings, sixteen ongoing major productions, 56 small-theater shows and 46 presentations in community play-houses. We would seem to be in the middle of a theatrical renaissance of unparalleled dimensions. Compared to what's available in L.A. and the immediate surrounding area, London is a backwater and New York a wasteland. Why isn't more being written about this phenomenon? Has L.A. become an Athens in a Periclean golden age of drama? Of course not.

Note that using any reversal technique requires a deft touch to make sure the writer's real position is clear.

OPPOSE A COMMONLY HELD OPINION

A writer may begin by opposing a commonly held opinion about a subject. In the introduction to "The Joy of Maps," William Hjortsberg tries to shock the reader by challenging the general conception that maps are untrustworthy.

"All maps are bad!" This draconian dictum survives from a math course I took as an undergraduate more years ago than I like to remember. The course, Math 1, known as Math for Idiots, covered such everyday matters as maps and calendars, seemingly simple items that grew increasingly complex as their mysteries were revealed.

Richard Reeves in "Equal Credit for Ghosts" attempts to hook the reader by shaking his belief that celebrities write their own books.

In Jeb Magruder's Watergate book, one line of the acknowledgements reads: "I would also like to thank Patrick Anderson for his invaluable advice and assistance on this book." That was one of the three sentences in the book that Magruder wrote himself.

John Dean, on the other hand, actually did write a manuscript. It wasn't, however, *Blind Ambition*—that was written by Taylor Branch. What Dean wrote was a pile of pages, unpublishable according to some sources, incoherent according to others. When last seen, Dean was on the book promotion trail, telling talk show hosts about the lonely agonies he endured as a writer.

This is not about Watergate; it is about ghostwriting.

APPENDIX E
CONCLUSIONS

Like introductions, conclusions come in variety; no single one serves all purposes. Your only obligation is to design one that naturally follows from the entire paper and clearly ends it. Avoid writing a conclusion that seems tacked on, and never—never, never, never—write one that raises a new question or apologizes for not covering the subject.

The samples that follow are just a few of the many ways writers end essays. Notice how methods tend to overlap. One has a quotation, but the quotation is a definition. Another holds an anecdote, but the anecdote includes a quotation. Several use questions. The label placed on a method isn't important. What is important is to write a conclusion that echoes the entire essay.

OFFER A BRIEF SUMMARY

In college writing, the most common practice is to restate the central point and then summarize the subpoints to reinforce what has come before. Too often the summary method seems mechanical, but it can be effective if the writer handles it in an interesting way. A summary conclusion does have one strong advantage—it clearly links with the rest of the essay. The following paragraphs from a student paper that deals with investing in the stock market illustrate the summary method. Although we've left the discussion out, you can easily see what it covered.

The introduction:

If you have any cash stuffed in jars or mattresses or just lying around in some passbook account, lazily accruing 5 1/4 percent interest, you would be wiser to fling it on a crap table. A crap game would give better odds at coming out ahead, for, as sure as a mouse with enough time will eat a pound of cheese, double-digit inflation will nibble your money away. At least on the crap table, although you would be bucking tremendous odds against winning, you would have a sporting chance. And there is always the payoff and the high you would get from watching the dice skip and jump over the green felt. But if you are too conservative for the Vegas thrill, then you might want to try the stock market. Even though the market is at an all-time low, it has some advantages for the cautious investor. First, you get paid for playing in the forms of dividends. Second, you get tax breaks. And third, there's better than fifty/fifty odds the market will rise.

Now the concluding summary:

> Is the market a good risk? It's clearly better than rat-holing your money or even stashing it in a savings account. Moreover, you get paid for playing, taxes work to your advantage, and the market, like an angry drunk pushed to the floor, will rise.

DRAW AN INFERENCE

A writer may use the conclusion to deepen the dimension of an essay. One student ended a paper on being robbed and threatened at pistol point by shifting from the external details of the experience to an implicit psychological fact. Notice the following writer's use of questions to put the reader in a reflective mood.

> And what does it mean when somebody holds you up? Just the loss of a few dollars? Or just the loss of a wallet and some mementos—a few peeling photographs, worn identification cards, tattered ticket stubs? Yes, it means that. And it means more. It means you have become part of that chosen group that no longer feels safe after dark to walk the neighborhood streets.

Although the writer draws a fresh inference from the whole paper, she does not raise a new issue. She has, instead, highlighted an implicit aspect that ran beneath the surface of the entire essay.

USE AN ANECDOTE

A writer may also conclude an essay with an anecdote—a brief story — that puts the central idea in clear perspective. Nora Gallagher closes with this method in an article that deals with homosexual rights.

A group of citizens tried to remove a gay group's name from a Bicentennial plaque. They met with resistance from City Councilman Leon Mezzetti, who said, "I wouldn't necessarily want the gays teaching my children, but the rules were that for 50 bucks you got your name on the plaque. And the gay people, God bless 'em, are following the rules . . .

"This is America. You can't change the rules after the fact, or you may as well tear the plaque down."

LINK THE SUBJECT TO THE READER

A writer may conclude by drawing a lesson that links the subject to the readers' condition. Tom Wicker in "Kennedy Without End, Amen" explores the significance of John Kennedy's brief term as president. Wicker adds a new dimension to his essay by linking the lessons Kennedy learned to the readers' learning process.

In his life, I wrote those many years ago, "he had had his dreams and realized them," but he learned also the hard lessons of power and its limitations. After his death, the rest of us began to learn those lessons, too. The shots ringing out in Dealey Plaza marked the beginning of the end of innocence.

USE A QUOTATION

A writer may conclude with a quotation that deepens the meaning of an essay. One student who wrote a description of her creative process used a quotation from Joseph Campbell to knot the threads of her thought.

At best my artistic process seems haphazard, a kind of inner blindman's bluff that finds its expression in chaotic collages. My groping and stumbling used to bother me until I came across a passage in Joseph Campbell's "The Inspiration of Oriental Art." He writes, "There is an important Chinese term, *wu wei, not doing*, the meaning of which is not *doing nothing*, but *not forcing*. Things will open up of themselves, according to their nature."

A writer may find that a quote is especially effective to end an interview or profile. Michelle Arnot concludes an article on the pleasures of massage that highlights the methods of New York masseuse Joan Witkowski.

If you're not getting rubbed the wrong way, you may well become addicted. Joan finds that her vacations cause panic among her clients. "I have to sneak away," she reports. "But it's always nice to come back. It's great to feel needed."

Or kneaded.

A CONCLUDING NOTE ON CONCLUSIONS

By the way—and we save this by the way for last to burn it into your mind—never, absolutely never, write "The End" after an essay's conclusion.

APPENDIX F
MANUSCRIPT FORMAT

Following standard manuscript form is a courtesy to the reader who expects things to be done properly. Manuscript form is merely a convention that defies logical explanation, but to ignore proper form is to risk annoying a reader—one who might be grading a college essay you have submitted.

MATERIALS

For handwritten papers use 8 1/2-by-11-inch lined white paper with neat edges, not paper torn from a spiral notebook. Use black or blue ink and write on one side only. Skip every other line to make reading and correcting your composition easier.

For typewritten papers use 8 1/2-by-11-inch white typing paper but not flimsy onionskin. Double-space between lines and use one side only. Be sure that you have a good ribbon in the typewriter and that the keys are clean. If you are using a word processor or personal computer to prepare your paper, print the final version in letter-quality mode. If your printer uses a ribbon, make sure the ribbon is fresh.

Unless otherwise directed, use a paper clip to hold pages together. Many instructors do not like pages stapled together, and no instructor likes the upper left-hand corner dogeared and torn to hold the pages in place.

MARGINS

Leave about an inch and a half margin at the left and top of the paper and an inch at the right and bottom to avoid a crowded appearance. On notebook paper the ruled vertical line indicates a proper left margin.

478

INDENTIONS

Indent the first line of every paragraph uniformly—one inch in a handwritten manuscript, five spaces in a typewritten one.

PAGING

Place the proper Arabic numeral (2, not II), without a period or parentheses, in the upper right-hand corner of each page following your last name.

TITLE

The title will be the first words your readers confront, so it deserves some attention. Often you'll write the exact title after the paper is polished because it will be only then that you will have a full view of the content of your paper. But we suggest you always begin with a working title, one that fences in the subject's range.

Whatever you do, don't write tricky titles designed to shock an audience into reading your essay: Gentlewomen Prefer Blondes, Plummeting Grades Suggest Brainrot, Thinking Can Land You in Jail, and such. In some eyes they may be cute, but to the steady gaze they are worthless. And never write empty titles: My Summer Vacation, Memories of Youth, A Work in Progress. Useless things seem to announce several paragraphs of boredom and tend to send readers into depression. The best policy is to use the title to let your readers know what's coming as accurately as you can.

When you write a title at the top of the first page, don't put it in quotation marks. It's your title; you're not quoting someone else's. If by chance your title happens to include a quotation, then put marks around that part. And never underline your own title. Words underlined in handwritten papers indicate that if they were printed, they would be put in italics.

In handwritten papers place the title in the center of the first line of notebook paper and begin the first sentence two lines below it. In typed papers place the title two spaces below the identification information and begin the first sentence two spaces below it. Capitalize the first and last words of the title, any word that follows a colon, and all other words except articles, conjunctions, and prepositions of fewer than five letters. Underline titles of books, periodicals, newspapers, pamphlets, plays and films, long poems, and long musical compositions. Use quotation marks for titles of articles, short stories, short poems, songs, chapter titles and other subdivisions of books or periodicals, and episodes of radio and television programs.

IDENTIFICATION

See examples of how to provide identification for papers with and papers without title pages in Chapter 21, "Research Paper."

CREDITS

INDEX